Lecture Notes in Computer Science   4322

Commenced Publication in 1973
Founding and Former Series Editors:
Gerhard Goos, Juris Hartmanis, and Jan van Leeuwen

T0223269

Fabrice Kordon   Janos Sztipanovits (Eds.)

Reliable Systems on Unreliable Networked Platforms

12th Monterey Workshop 2005
Laguna Beach, CA, USA, September 22-24, 2005
Revised Selected Papers

 Springer

Volume Editors

Fabrice Kordon
Université Pierre et Marie Curie
Laboratoire d'Informatique de Paris 6
104 Avenue du Président Kennedy, 75016 Paris, France
E-mail: Fabrice.Kordon@lip6.fr

Janos Sztipanovits
Vanderbilt University
School of Engineering
Nashville, TN 37235-6306, USA
E-mail: janos.sztipanovits@vanderbilt.edu

Library of Congress Control Number: 2007921535

CR Subject Classification (1998): D.1.3, D.2-3, D.4.5, F.3, C.2.1, C.2-4

LNCS Sublibrary: SL 2 – Programming and Software Engineering

ISSN   0302-9743
ISBN-10   3-540-71155-4 Springer Berlin Heidelberg New York
ISBN-13   978-3-540-71155-1 Springer Berlin Heidelberg New York

Springer is a part of Springer Science+Business Media

springer.com

© Springer-Verlag Berlin Heidelberg 2007
Printed in Germany

Typesetting: Camera-ready by author, data conversion by Scientific Publishing Services, Chennai, India
Printed on acid-free paper   SPIN: 12026487   06/3142   5 4 3 2 1 0

Preface

Networked Systems: Realization of Reliable Systems on Unreliable Networked Platforms

The Monterey Workshops series was initiated in 1993 by David Hislop with the purpose of exploring the critical problems associated with cost-effective development of high-quality software systems. During its 12-year history, the Monterey Workshops have brought together scientists that share a common interest in software development research serving practical advances in next-generation software-intensive systems. Each year is dedicated to a given topic such as "Software Engineering Tools: Compatibility and Integration" (Vienna in 2004), "Engineering for Embedded Systems: From Requirements to Implementation" (Chicago in 2003), "Radical Innovations of Software and Systems Engineering in the Future" (Venice in 2002), "Engineering Automation for Software Intensive System Integration" (Monterey in 2001), etc.

This 12th Monterey Workshop was held in Laguna Beach, CA during September 22–24, 2005.

Context of the 12th Workshop

Networked computing is increasingly becoming the universal integrator for large-scale systems. In addition, new generations of wireless networked embedded systems rapidly create new technological environments that imply complex interdependencies amongst all layers of societal-scale critical infrastructure, such as transportation, energy distribution and telecommunication. This trend makes reliability and safety of networked computing a crucial issue and a technical precondition for building software-intensive systems that are robust, fault tolerant, and highly available.

The 12th Monterey Workshop on "Networked Systems: Realization of Reliable Systems on Unreliable Networked Platforms" focused on new, promising directions in achieving high software and system reliability in networked systems.

All presentations at the workshop were by invitation upon the advice of the Program Committee.

Invited Speakers

Myla Archer	Naval Research Lab, USA
Barrett Bryant	University of Alabama, Birmingham, USA
David Corman	Boeing, St Louis, USA
Nick Dutt	UCI, USA
Holger Giese	University of Paderborn, Germany
Chris Gill	Washington University at St Louis, USA
Helen Gill	NSF, USA
Klaus Havelund	NASA, USA

David Hislop	Army Research Office, USA
Liviu Iftode	Rutgers, USA
Vana Kalogeraki	UC Riverside, USA
Gabor Karsai	Vanderbilt University, USA
Kane Kim	University of California at Irvine, USA
Moon-Hae Kim	Konkuk University, Korea
Raymond Klefstad	UCI, USA
Hermann Kopetz	Vienna University of Technology, Austria
Fabrice Kordon	University of Pierre & Marie Curie, Paris, France
Ingolf Krueger	UCSD, USA
Akos Ledeczi	Vanderbilt University, USA
Edward Lee	UC Berkeley (Keynote Presentation), USA
Chenyang Lu	Washington University, USA
Luqi	Naval Postgraduate School, USA
Zohar Manna	Stanford University, USA
Oliver Marin	University of Pierre & Marie Curie, Paris, France
Nenad Medvidovic	USC, USA
Laurent Pautet	Télécom Paris, France
Raj Rajkumar	Carnegie Mellon University, USA
Martin Rinard,	MIT, USA
Man-tak Shing	Naval Postgraduate School, USA
Janos Sztipanovits	Vanderbilt University, USA
Wei-Tek Tsai	Arizona State University, USA
Andre Van der Hoek	UCI, USA
Nalini Venkatasubramanian	UCI, USA
Ben Watson	Lockheed Martin, USA
Albert Wavering	NIST, USA
Victor Winter	University of Nebraska at Omaha, USA
Feng Zhao	Microsoft Research (Keynote Presentation), USA

Papers included in this volume were selected among the submissions from the workshop's discussions.

Workshop Topics

Software is the new infrastructure of the information age. It is fundamental to economic success, scientific and technical research and national security. Our current ability to construct the large and complex software systems demanded for continued economic progress is inadequate.

The workshop discussed a range of challenges in networked systems that require further major advances in software and systems technology:

– **System Integration and Dynamic Adaptation.** A new challenge in networked systems is that stable application performance needs to be maintained in spite of the dynamically changing communication and computing platforms. Consequently, the run-time architecture must include active control mechanisms for adapting the system/software components to changing conditions. Global system characteristics need to be achieved by increased run-time use of reflection (systems that utilize their own models), advanced interface modeling, self-adaptation, and self-optimization.

- **Effects of Dynamic Structure.** The structure of networked systems is complex and highly dynamic. Because systems are formed by ad hoc networks of nodes and connections, they lack fine-grain determinism for end-to-end behaviors that span subsystem and network boundaries. In addition, there are end-to-end system qualities such as timeliness and security that can only be evaluated in this dynamically integrated context.
- **Effects of Faults.** Faults and disruptions in the underlying communication and computing infrastructure are the normal events. Since well-understood techniques for fault-tolerant computing, such as n-modular redundancy, are not applicable in the dynamically changing networked architecture, new technology is required for building safe and reliable applications on dynamic, distributed platforms.
- **Design for Reliability.** Although there are varieties of metrics and established practices for characterizing the expected failure behavior of a system after it is fielded and there are established practices for specifying the desired reliability of a system, the evaluation of system or software reliability prior to fielding is a significant problem.
- **System Certification.** The process for certifying that a system meets specified reliability goals under the range of conditions expected in actual use currently involves exhaustive analysis of a system, including its development history and extensive testing. Current methods do not give systems engineers the confidence they would like to have in concluding that a system will have particular reliability characteristics.
- **Effects of Scale.** Another risk that overlays all proposed solutions is scale. Scale also addresses both run-time and design-time concerns. Typically, demonstrations are the convincing drivers to technology adoption. Demonstrations of new technologies however are usually small-scale, focused efforts. It is an open problem how to scale up a demonstration that addresses the number of nodes and connections, and the number of software developers, analysts, and integrators to provide enough proof to justify technology transition.

These challenges are exaggerated in networked-embedded software systems, where computation and communication are tightly integrated with physical process.

Approaches

There have been important new developments during the past five years that improve our chance to meet the new challenges listed above. Contributions at the workshop identified and discussed research approaches that have direct and immediate relevance to the new challenges. Listed below are the major themes that came up in many forms in the presentations and captured in the contributions of these proceedings.

Model-based software development of network-centric system-of-systems. Model-based design is rapidly becoming one of the prominent software/system development paradigms. Models with precisely defined syntax and semantics capture system/software invariants that can be formally analyzed and used for predicting/ verifying system behavior and for generating code. A new challenge in network-centric system-of-systems is that design invariants need to be maintained actively during run-time due to the dynamically changing communication and computing platforms. Consequently, the relationship between design-time modeling and model analysis and run-time behavior needs to be fundamentally different: emphasis needs to be shifted toward correct-by-construction approaches that can guarantee selected behavioral properties without the need for system-level verification, and the run-time architecture must include active control for adapting the system/software to changing conditions. Global system characteristics need to be achieved by increased run-time use of reflection (systems that utilize their own models), advanced interface modeling, self-adaptation, and self-optimization.

Foundations of future design and programming abstractions. Programming abstractions have a crucial role in the design of highly concurrent, dynamic, and time-critical networked systems. Today's abstractions have been developed for programs with static structure, closed architectures, and stable computing platforms that are not scalable, understandable, and analyzable in complex, networked, real-time systems. We need abstractions that go beyond a narrow view of programming languages to integrate modeling, design, and analysis. They must satisfy the need for blending solid formal foundations with domain-specific expressions and must yield behavior that is predictable and understandable to system designers, even in the face of uncertain or dynamic system structure. To accomplish this, they must serve both the modeling role and the design role, leveraging generators, visual notations, formal semantics, probabilistic modeling, and yet-to-be-developed techniques for gaining an effective multiplicity of views into a design. And they must effectively express concurrency, quality-of-service constraints, and heterogeneity.

Active fault management in network-centric systems. It is important to recognize that software will never be perfect large-scale, networked systems-of-systems. Software and platform components may fail at any time. The notion of active fault management accepts this as a fact and instead of attempting to mask the faults, it focuses on their containment, mitigation, and management. Active fault management is a novel technique that is gaining acceptance in complex engineering systems (e.g., aerospace vehicles) and promises reliability through detecting, isolating and recovering from faults using algorithmic techniques for contingency management. The software engineering community took notice of these engineering techniques and applies them to software artifacts. The resulting fault management architectures are layered, as different methods may be needed on different levels of abstractions in systems and, preferably, they have to be proactive, so that they detect early precursors to larger problems (e.g., memory leak in dynamically allocated memory, or memory fragmentation) such that the system will have sufficient time to take preventive action.

Intelligent, robust middleware. Complexity of large-scale networked systems requires careful consideration on reusability of code. Middleware technologies offer architectural solutions for separating application code from highly reusable components or layers in software stacks. We need to develop and validate a new generation of intelligent middleware technologies that can adapt dependably in response to dynamically changing conditions for the purpose of always utilizing the available computer and network infrastructure to the highest degree possible in support of system needs. Emerging architectures, such as service-oriented architecture (SOA), provide focus for this new generation of middleware research that will ultimately enable software whose functional and QoS-related properties can be modified either statically, (e.g., to reduce footprint, leverage capabilities that exist in specific platforms, enable functional subsetting, and minimize hardware/software infrastructure dependencies) or dynamically (e.g., to optimize system responses to changing environments or requirements, such as changing component interconnections, power-levels, CPU/network bandwidth, latency/jitter, and dependability needs).

Model-based development of certifiable systems. Systems that are safety certified are arguably some of the most costly to develop. As a result, software architectures for such systems are typically very deterministic in order to enable provable mitigation of safety hazards. The limitations of these approaches are quickly becoming unacceptable due to the advent of ad-hoc mobile networks requiring a much more dynamic structure and expected unavailability of certain resources for these safety critical systems. Model-based development approaches must be applied to enable the development of these systems within reasonable cost. These approaches should include the development of modeling syntax and semantics to express safety-critical aspects and perhaps constrain dynamism, the provision of design-time and run-time analysis that leverages this model and addresses the concerns of the safety community in the context of a network-centric system of systems, the automatic generation of artifacts that are proven by analysis to be safe, and the establishment of trust in such tools and techniques by the safety community as a whole.

Acknowledgement

We are grateful to the Steering Committee, the Local Organizing Committee and the invited speakers for making the workshop a success. We gratefully acknowledge sponsorship from the Army Research Office (David Hislop) and from the National Science Foundation (Helen Gill).

January 2007   Fabrice Kordon
                                                               Janos Sztipanovits

Organization

Executive Committee

Conference Chair:	Kane Kim (University of California, Irvine, USA)
Program Chairs:	Fabrice Kordon (Université Pierre & Marie Curie, France)
	Janos Sztipanovits (Vanderbilt University, USA)

Technical Program Committee

Carlos Delgado Kloos	University Carlos III of Madrid, Spain
Bertil Folliot	University of Pierre & Marie Curie, Paris, France
Tom Henzinger	Ecole Polytechnique Federale de Lausanne, Switzerland
Kane Kim	University of California at Irvine, USA
Insup Lee	University of Pennsylvania, USA
Chenyang Lu	Washington University, USA
Tom Maibaum	King's College, London, UK
Ugo Montanari	University of Pisa, Italy
Laurent Pautet	Télécom Paris, France
Wolfgang Pree	University of Salzburg, Austria
Doug Schmidt	Vanderbilt University - ISIS, USA

Table of Contents

Reinventing Computing for Real Time

Edward A. Lee and Yang Zhao

University of California, Berkeley
{eal,ellen_zh}@eecs.berkeley.edu

Abstract. This paper studies models of computation, software techniques, and analytical models for distributed timed systems. By "timed systems" we mean those where timeliness is an essential part of the behavior. By "distributed systems" we mean computational systems that are interconnected on a network. Applications of timed distributed systems include industrial automation, distributed immersive environments, advanced instrumentation systems, networked control systems, and many modern embedded software systems that integrate networking. The introduction of network time protocols such as NTP (at a coarse granularity) and IEEE 1588 (at a fine granularity) makes possible time coherence that has not traditionally been part of the computational models in networked systems. The main question we address in this paper is: Given time synchronization with some known precision, how does this change how distributed applications are designed and developed? A second question we address is: How can time synchronization help with realizing coordinated real-time events.

1 Introduction

Despite considerable progress in software and hardware techniques, when embedded computing systems absolutely must meet tight timing constraints, many of the advances in computing become part of the problem, not part of the solution. Although synchronous digital logic delivers precise timing determinacy, advances in computer architecture and software have made it difficult or impossible to estimate or predict the execution time of software. Moreover, networking techniques introduce variability and stochastic behavior, and operating systems rely on best effort techniques. Worse, programming languages lack time in their semantics, so timing requirements are only specified indirectly. This paper studies methods for programming ensembles of networked real-time, embedded computers where time and concurrency are first-class properties of the program.

This contrasts with established software techniques, where time and concurrency are afterthoughts. The prevailing view of real-time appears to have been established well before embedded computing was common. Wirth reduces real-time programming to threads with bounds on execution time, arguing that "it is prudent to extend the conceptual framework of sequential programming as little as possible and, in particular, to avoid the notion of execution time" [30]. In this sequential framework, "computation" is accomplished by a terminating sequence of state transformations. This core abstraction underlies the design of nearly all

F. Kordon and J. Sztipanovits (Eds.): Monterey Workshop 2005, LNCS 4322, pp. 1–25, 2007.
© Springer-Verlag Berlin Heidelberg 2007

computers, programming languages, and operating systems in use today. But unfortunately, this core abstraction does not fit embedded software very well.

This core abstraction fits reasonably well if embedded software is simply "software on small computers." In this view, embedded software differs from other software only in its resource limitations (small memory, small data word sizes, and relatively slow clocks). In this view, the "embedded software problem" is an optimization problem. Solutions emphasize efficiency; engineers write software at a very low level (in assembly code or C), avoid operating systems with a rich suite of services, and use specialized computer architectures such as programmable DSPs and network processors that provide hardware support for common operations. These solutions have defined the practice of embedded software design and development for the last 25 years or so. In an analysis that remains as valid today as 18 years ago, Stankovic laments the resulting misconceptions that real-time computing "is equivalent to fast computing" or "is performance engineering" [29].

Of course, thanks to the semiconductor industry's ability to follow Moore's law, the resource limitations of 25 years ago should have almost entirely evaporated today. Why then has embedded software design and development changed so little? It may be that extreme competitive pressure in products based on embedded software, such as consumer electronics, rewards only the most efficient solutions. This argument is questionable, however. There are many examples where functionality has proven more important than efficiency. It is arguable that resource limitations are not the only defining factor for embedded software, and may not even be the principal factor.

Stankovic argues that "the time dimension must be elevated to a central principle of the system. Time requirements and properties cannot be an afterthought" [29]. But in mainstream computing, this has not happened. The "time dimension," of course, is inextricably linked to concurrency, and prevailing models of concurrency (threads and message passing) are in fact obstacles to elevating time to a central principle.

In embedded software, several recent innovations provide unconventional ways of programming concurrent and/or timed systems. We point to six cases that define concurrency models, component architectures, and management of time-critical operations in ways significantly different from prevailing software engineering techniques. The first is nesC with TinyOS [8], which was developed for programming very small programmable sensor nodes called "motes." The second is Click [16], which was created to support the design of software-based network routers. These first two have an imperative flavor, and components interact principally through procedure calls. The third is Simulink with Real-Time Workshop (from The MathWorks), which was created for embedded control software and is widely used in the automotive industry. The fourth is SCADE (from Esterel Technologies, see [2], which was created for safety-critical embedded software and is used in avionics. These two have a more declarative flavor, where components interact principally through messages rather than procedure calls. The fifth is the family of hardware description languages, including Verilog, VHDL, and

SystemC, which express vast amounts of concurrency, principally using discrete-event semantics. The sixth example is LabVIEW, from National Instruments, a dataflow programming environment with a visual syntax designed for embedded instrumentation applications. The amount and variety of experimentation with alternative models of computation for embedded systems is yet a further indication that the prevailing software abstractions are inadequate.

The approach in this paper leverages the concept of actor-oriented design [20], borrowing ideas from Simulink and from Giotto [12], an experimental real-time programming language. However, it addresses a number of limitations in Simulink and Giotto by building similar multitasking implementations from specifications that combine dataflow modeling and distributed discrete-event modeling. In discrete-event models, components interact with one another via events that are placed on a time line. Some level of agreement about time across distributed components is necessary for this model to have a coherent semantics. While distribution of discrete-event models has long been used to exploit parallel computing to accelerate execution [31], we are not concerned here with accelerating execution. The focus is instead on using a model of time as a binding coordination agent. This steers us away from conservative techniques (like Chandy and Misra [3]) and optimistic techniques (like Time Warp [15]). One interesting possibility is based on distributed consensus (as in Croquet [28]). In this paper, we focus on techniques based on distributing discrete-event models, with functionality specified by dataflow models. Our technique allows out of order execution without sacrificing determinacy and without requiring backtracking. The use of dataflow formalisms [26] supports mixing untimed and event-triggered computation with timed and periodic computation.

2   Embedded Software

There are clues that embedded software differs from other software in quite fundamental ways. If we examine carefully why engineers write embedded software in assembly code or C, we discover that efficiency is not the only concern, and may not even be the main concern. The reasons may include, for example, the need to count cycles in a critical inner loop, not to make it fast, but rather to make it predictable. No widely used programming language integrates a way to specify timing requirements or constraints. Instead, the abstractions they offer are about scalability (inheritance, dynamic binding, polymorphism, memory management), and if anything further obscure timing (consider the impact of garbage collection on timing). Counting cycles, of course, becomes extremely difficult on modern processor architectures, where memory hierarchy (caches), dynamic dispatch, and speculative execution make it nearly impossible to tell how long it will take to execute a particular piece of code. Embedded software designers may choose alternative processor architectures such as programmable DSPs not only for efficiency reasons, but also for predictability of timing.

Another reason engineers stick to low-level programming is that embedded software has to interact with hardware that is specialized to the application.

In conventional software, interaction with hardware is the domain of the operating system. Device drivers are not typically part of an application program, and are not typically created by application designers. But in the embedded software context, generic hardware interfaces are rarer. The fact is that creating interfaces to hardware is not something that higher level languages support. For example, although concurrency is not uncommon in modern programming languages (consider threads in Java), no widely used programming language includes in its semantics the notion of interrupts. Yet the concept is not difficult, and it can be built into programming languages (consider for example nesC [8] and TinyOS [13], which are widely used for programming sensor networks).

It becomes apparent that the avoidance of so many recent improvements in computation is not due to ignorance of those improvements. It is due to a mismatch of the core abstractions and the technologies built on those core abstractions. In embedded software, time matters. In the 20th century abstractions of computing, time is irrelevant. In embedded software, concurrency and interaction with hardware are intrinsic, since embedded software engages the physical world in non-trivial ways (more than keyboards and screens). The most influential 20th century computing abstractions speak only weakly about concurrency, if at all. Even the core 20th century notion of "computable" excludes all interesting embedded software, since to be "computable" you must terminate. In embedded software, termination is failure.

Embedded systems are integrations of software and hardware where the software reacts to sensor data and issues commands to actuators. The physical system is an integral part of the design and the software must be conceptualized to operate in concert with that physical system. Physical systems are intrinsically concurrent and temporal. Actions and reactions happen simultaneously and over time, and the metric properties of time are an essential part of the behavior of the system. Prevailing software methods abstract away time, replacing it with ordering. In imperative languages such as C, C++, and Java, the order of actions is defined by the program, but not their timing. This prevailing imperative abstraction is overlaid with another, that of threads or processes, typically provided by the operating system, but occasionally by the language (as in Java).

The lack of timing in the core abstraction is a flaw, from the perspective of embedded software, and threads as a concurrency model are a poor match for embedded systems. They are mainly focused on providing an illusion of parallelism in fundamentally sequential models, and they work well only for modest levels of concurrency or for highly decoupled systems that are sharing resources, where best-effort scheduling policies are sufficient. Indeed, none of the six examples given above include threads or processes in the programmer's model.

Embedded software systems are generally held to a much higher reliability standard than general purpose software. Often, failures in the software can be life threatening (e.g., in avionics and military systems). The prevailing concurrency model in general-purpose software that is based on threads does not achieve adequate reliability [19]. In this prevailing model, interaction between threads is extremely difficult for humans to understand. The basic techniques for controlling this interaction use semaphores and mutual exclusion locks, methods that date back to the 1960s [5] and 1970s [14]. These techniques often lead to deadlock or livelock. In general-purpose computing, this is inconvenient, and typically forces a restart of the program (or even a reboot of the operating system). However, in embedded software, such errors can be far more than inconvenient. Moreover, software is often written without sufficient use of these interlock mechanisms, resulting in race conditions that yield nondeterministic program behavior. In practice, errors due to misuse (or no use) of semaphores and mutual exclusion locks are extremely difficult to detect by testing. Code can be exercised for years before a design flaw appears. Static analysis techniques can help (e.g. Sun Microsystems' LockLint), but these methods are often thwarted by conservative approximations and/or false positives, and they are not widely used in practice.

It can be argued that the unreliability of multithreaded programs is due at least in part to inadequate software engineering processes. For example, better code reviews, better specifications, better compliance testing, and better planning of the development process can help solve the problems. It is certainly true that these techniques can help. However, programs that use threads can be extremely difficult for programmers to understand. If a program is incomprehensible, then no amount of process improvement will make it reliable. Formal methods can help detect flaws in threaded programs, and in the process can improve the understanding that a designer has of the behavior of a complex program. But if the basic mechanisms fundamentally lead to programs that are difficult to understand, then these improvements will fall short of delivering reliable software. Incomprehensible software will always be unreliable software.

Prevailing practice in embedded software relies on bench testing for concurrency and timing properties. This has worked reasonably well, because programs are small, and because software gets encased in a box with no outside connectivity that can alter the behavior. However, applications today demand that embedded systems be feature-rich and networked, so bench testing and encasing become inadequate. In a networked environment, it becomes impossible to test the software under all possible conditions. Moreover, general-purpose networking techniques themselves make program behavior much more unpredictable.

What would it take to achieve concurrent and networked embedded software that was absolutely positively on time, to the resolution and reliability of digital logic? Unfortunately, everything would have to change. The core abstractions of computing need to be modified to embrace time. Computer architectures need change to deliver precisely timed behaviors. Networking techniques need to change to provide time concurrence. Programming languages have to change to embrace time and concurrency in their core semantics. Operating systems have to change to rely less on priorities to (indirectly) specify timing requirements. The separation of operating systems from languages has to be rethought. Software engineering methods need to change to specify and analyze the temporal dynamics of software. What is needed is nearly a reinvention of computer science.

No individual project, obviously, could possibly take all of this on. Fortunately, there is quite a bit of prior work to draw on. To name a few examples, architecture techniques such as software-managed caches promise to deliver much of the benefit of memory hierarchy without the timing unpredictability [1,6]. Operating systems such as TinyOS [13] provide simple ways to create thin wrappers around hardware. Programming languages such as Lustre/SCADE [2,11] provide understandable and analyzable concurrency. Embedded software languages such as Simulink provide time in their semantics. Our own prior work shows how to generate hard-real time code from dataflow graphs [27].

In this paper, we focus on programming languages, pursuing abstractions that include time and concurrency as first-class properties, creating mechanisms for programming ensembles of networked embedded computers, rather than just programming individual computers, and creating mechanisms for tightly integrating hardware behavior into programs. We focus on applications in instrumentation and in distributed gaming; the first of these requires more precise timing synchronization, so we will leverage the new IEEE 1588 standard, which provides time synchronization across ethernet networks at resolutions down to tens of nanoseconds. The second requires time synchronization at more human scales, large fractions of a second, and may be able to effectively use time synchronization protocols such as NTP (network time protocol).

3   Concurrency and Time

We will focus on ways of giving programs where concurrency and time are essential aspects of a design, and most particularly on ways of compiling such programs to produce deployable real-time code. Time is a relatively simple issue, conceptually, although delivering temporal semantics in software can be challenging. Time is about the ordering of events. Event x happens before event y, for example. But in embedded software, time also has a metric. That is, there is an amount of time between events x and y, and the amount of time may be an important part of the correctness of a system.

In software, it is straightforward to talk about the order of events, although in concurrent systems it can be difficult to control the order. For example, achieving a specified total ordering of events across concurrent threads implies interactions across those threads that can be extremely difficult to implement correctly. Research in distributed discrete-event simulation, for example, underscores the subtleties that can arise (see for example [15]).

It is less straightforward to talk about the metric nature of time. Typically, embedded processors have access to external devices (timers) that can be used to measure the passage of time. Programs can poll for the current time, and they can set timers to trigger an interrupt at some time in the future. Using timers in this way implies immediately having to deal with concurrency issues. Interrupt service routines typically preempt currently executing software, and hence conceptually execute concurrently.

Concurrency in software is a challenging issue because the basic software abstraction is not concurrent. The basic abstraction in imperative languages is that the memory of the computer represents the current state of the system, and instructions transform that state. A program is a sequence of such transformations. The problem with concurrency is that from the perspective of a particular program, the state may change on its own at any time. For example, we could have a sequence of statements:

```
x = 5;
print x;
```

that results in printing the number "6" instead of "5". This could occur, for example, if after execution of the first statement an interrupt occurred, and the interrupt service routine modified the memory location where x was stored. Or it could occur if the computer is also executing a sequence of statements:

```
x = 6;
print x;
```

and a multitasking scheduler happens to interleave the executions of the instructions of the two sequences. Two such sequences of statements are said to be nondeterminate because, by themselves, these two sequences of statements do not specify a single behavior. There is more than one behavior that is consistent with the specification.

Nondeterminism can be desirable in embedded software. Consider for example an embedded system that receives information at random times from two distinct sensors. Suppose that it is the job of the embedded software to fuse the data from these sensors so that their observations are both taken into account. The system as a whole will be nondeterminate since its results will depend on the order in which information from the sensors is processed. Consider the following program fragment:

```
y = getSensorData();    // Block for data
x = 0.9 * x + 0.1 * y;  // Discounted average
print x;                // Display the result
```

This fragment reads data from a sensor and calculates a running average using a discounting strategy, where older data has less effect on the average than newer data.

Suppose that our embedded system uses two threads, one for each sensor, where each thread executes the above sequence of statements repeatedly. The result of the execution will depend on the order in which data arrives from the sensors, so the program is nondeterminate. However, it is also nondeterminate in another way that was probably not intended. Suppose that the multitasking scheduler happens to execute the instructions from the two threads in interleaved order, as shown here:

```
y = getSensorData();    // From thread 1
y = getSensorData();    // From thread 2
x = 0.9 * x + 0.1 * y;  // From thread 1
x = 0.9 * x + 0.1 * y;  // From thread 2
print x;                // From thread 1
print x;                // From thread 2
```

The result is clearly not right. The sensor data read by thread 1 is ignored. The discounting is applied twice. The sensor data from thread 2 is counted twice. And the same (erroneous) result is printed twice.

A key capability for preventing such concurrency problems is atomicity. A sequence of instructions is atomic if during the execution of the sequence, no portion of the state that is visible to these instructions changes unless it is changed by the instructions themselves.

Atomicity can be provided by programming languages and/or operating systems through mutual exclusion mechanisms. These mechanisms depend on low-level support for an indivisible test and set. Consider the following modification:

```
acquireLock();          // Block until acquired
y = getSensorData();    // Block for data
x = 0.9 * x + 0.1 * y;  // Discount old value
print x;                // Display the result
releaseLock();          // Release the lock
```

The first statement calls an operating system primitive that tests a shared, boolean-valued variable, and if it is false, sets it to true and returns. If it is true, then it blocks, waiting until it becomes false. It is essential that between the time this primitive tests the variable and the time it sets it to true, that no other instruction in the system can access that variable. That is, the test and set occur as one operation, not as two. The last statement sets the variable to false.

Suppose we now build a system with two threads that each execute this sequence repeatedly to read from two sensors. The resulting system will not exhibit the problem above because the multitasking scheduler cannot interleave the executions of the statements. However, the program is still not correct. For example, it might occur that only one of the two threads ever acquires the lock, and so only one sensor is read. In this case, the program is not fair. Suppose that the multitasking scheduler is forced to be fair, say by requiring it to yield to the other thread each time releaseLock() is called. The program is still not correct, because while one thread is waiting for sensor data, the other thread is blocked by the lock and will fail to notice new data on its sensor. This seemingly trivial problem has become difficult. Rather than trying to fix it within the threading model of computation, we will show that alternative models of computation make this problem easy.

Suppose the program is given by the diagram in figure 1. Suppose that the semantics are those of Kahn process networks (see [21]) augmented with a nondeterministic merge, as done in the YAPI model of computation [4]. In that figure, the components (blocks) are called actors. They have ports (shown by small triangles), with input ports pointing into the blocks and output ports pointing out. Each actor encapsulates functionality that reads input values and produces output values.

In PN semantics, each actor executes continually in its own thread of control. The Sensor1 and Sensor2 actors will produce an output whenever the corresponding sensors have data (this could be done directly by the interrupt service routine,

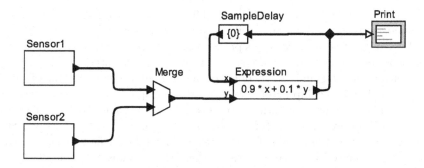

Fig. 1. Process network realization of the sensor fusion example

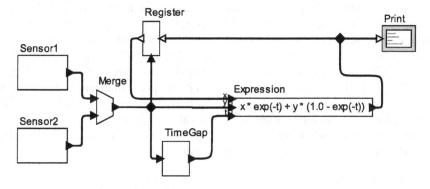

Fig. 2. Discrete event realization of an improved sensor fusion example

for example). The connections between actors represent sequences of data values. The Merge actor will nondeterministically interleave the two sequences at its input ports, preserving the order within each sequence, but yielding arbitrary ordering of data values across sequences. Suppose it is "fair" in the sense that if a data value appears at one of the inputs, then it will "eventually" appear at the output [25]. The remaining actors simply calculate the discounted average and display it. The SampleDelay actor provides an initial "previous average" to work with (which prevents this program from deadlocking for lack of data at the input to the Expression actor). This program exhibits none of the difficulties encountered above with threads, and is both easy to write and easy to understand.

We can now focus on improving its functionality. Notice that the discounting average is not ideal because it does not take into account how old the old data are. That is, there is no time metric. Old data is simply the data previously observed, and there is no measure of how long ago it was read. Suppose that instead of Kahn process networks semantics, we use discrete-event (DE) semantics [18]. A modified diagram is shown in figure 2. In that diagram, the meaning of a connection between actors is slightly different from the meaning of connections in figure 1. In particular, the connection carries a sequence of data values as before, but each value has a time stamp. The time stamps on any given sequence are nondecreasing. A data value with a time stamp is called an event.

The Sensor1 and Sensor2 actors produce output events stamped with the time at which their respective interrupt service routines are executed. The Merge actor is no longer nondeterministic. Its output is a chronological merge of the two input sequences. The TimeGap actor produces on its output an event with the same time stamp as the input but whose value is the elapsed time between the current event and the previous event (or between the start of execution and the current event if this is the first event). The expression shown in the next actor calculates a better discounted average, one that takes into account the time elapsed. It implements an exponential forgetting function.

The Register actor in figure 2 has somewhat interesting semantics. Its output is produced when it receives a trigger input on the bottom port. The value of the output is that of a previously observed input (or a specified initial value if no input was previously observed). In particular, at any given time stamp, the value of the output does not depend on the value of the input, so this actor breaks what would otherwise be an unresolvable causality loop.

Even with such a simple problem, threaded concurrency is clearly inferior. PN offers a better concurrency model in that the program is easier to construct and to understand. The DE model is even better because it takes into account metric properties of time, which matter in this problem.

In real systems, the contrasts between these approaches is even more dramatic. Consider the following two program fragments:

```
acquireLockA();
acquireLockB();
x = 5;
print x;
releaseLockB();
releaseLockA();
```

and

```
acquireLockB();
acquireLockA();
x = 5;
print x;
releaseLockA();
releaseLockB();
```

If these two programs are executed concurrently in two threads, they could deadlock. Suppose the multitasking scheduler executes the first statement from the first program followed by the first statement from the second program. At this point, the second statement of both programs will block! There is no way out of this. The programs have to be aborted and restarted.

Programmers who use threads have tantalizing simple rules to avoid this problem. For example, "always acquire locks in the same order" [17]. However, this rule is almost impossible to apply in practice because of the way programs are modularized. Any given program fragment is likely to call methods or procedures that are defined elsewhere, and those methods or procedures may acquire locks. Unless we examine the source code of every procedure we call, we cannot be sure that we have applied this rule.

Deadlock can, of course, occur in PN and DE programs. If in figure 1 we had omitted the SampleDelay actor, or in figure 2 we had omitted the Register actor, the programs would not be able to execute. In both cases, the Expression actor requires new data at all of its input ports in order to execute, and that data would not be able to be provided without executing the Expression actor.

The rules for preventing deadlocks in PN and DE programs are much easier to apply than the rule for threads. For certain models of computation, whether deadlock occurs can be checked through static analysis of the program. This is true of the DE model used above for the improved sensor fusion problem, for example. So, not only was the model of computation more expressive in practice (that is, it more readily expressed the behavior we wanted), but it also had stronger formal properties that enabled static checks that prove the absence of certain flaws (deadlock, in this case).

We will next examine a few of the models of computation that have been used for embedded systems and that form the basis for the work described here.

4   Imperative Concurrent Models

TinyOS has an imperative flavor. What this means is that when one component interacts with another, it gives a command, "do this." The command is implemented as a procedure call. Since this model of computation is also concurrent, we call it an imperative concurrent models of computation.

In contrast, when components in Simulink and SCADE interact, they simply offer data values, "here is some data." It is irrelevant to the component when (or even whether) the destination component reacts to the message. These models of computation have a declarative flavor, since instead of issuing commands, they declare relationships between components that share data. We call such models of computation declarative concurrent models of computation.

TinyOS is a specialized, small-footprint operating system for use on extremely resource-constrained computers, such as 8 bit microcontrollers with small amounts of memory [8]. It is typically used with nesC, a programming language that describes "configurations," which are assemblies of TinyOS components.

A visual rendition of a two-component configuration is shown in figure 3, where the visual notation is that used in [8]. The components are grey boxes with names. Each component has some number of interfaces, some of which it uses and some of which it provides. The interfaces it provides are put on top of the box and the interfaces it uses are put on the bottom. Each interface consists of a number of methods, shown as triangles. The filled triangles represent methods that are called commands and the unfilled triangles represent event handlers. Commands propagate downwards, whereas events propagate upwards.

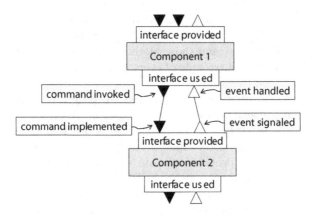

Fig. 3. A representation of a nesC/TinyOS configuration

After initialization, computation typically begins with events. In figure 3, Component 2 might be a thin wrapper for hardware, and the interrupt service routine associated with that hardware would call a procedure in Component 1 that would "signal an event." What it means to signal an event is that a procedure call is made upwards in the diagram via the connections between the unfilled triangles. Component 1 provides an event handler procedure. The event handler can signal an event to another component, passing the event up in the diagram. It can also call a command, downwards in the diagram. A component that provides an interface provides a procedure to implement a command.

Execution of an event handler triggered by an interrupt (and execution of any commands or other event handlers that it calls) may be preempted by another interrupt. This is the principle source of concurrency in the model. It is potentially problematic because event handler procedures may be in the middle of being executed when an interrupt occurs that causes them to begin execution again to handle a new event. Problems are averted through judicious use of the atomic keyword in nesC. Code that is enclosed in an atomic block cannot be interrupted (this is implemented very efficiently by disabling interrupts in the hardware).

Clearly, however, in a real-time system, interrupts should not be disabled for extensive periods of time. In fact, nesC prohibits calling commands or signaling events from within an atomic block. Moreover, no mechanism is provided for an atomic test-and-set, so there is no mechanism besides the atomic keyword for implementing mutual exclusion. The system is a bit like a multithreaded system but with only one mutual exclusion lock. This makes it impossible for the mutual exclusion mechanism to cause deadlock.

Of course, this limited expressiveness means that event handlers cannot perform non-trivial concurrent computation. To regain expressiveness, TinyOS has tasks. An event handler may "post a task." Posted tasks are executed when the machine is idle (no interrupt service routines are being executed). A task may call commands through the interfaces it uses. It is not expected to signal events, however. Once task execution starts, it completes before any other task

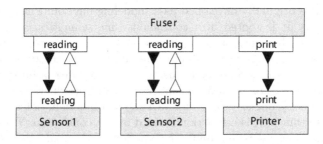

Fig. 4. A sketch of the sensor fusion problem as a nesC/TinyOS configuration

execution is started. That is, task execution is atomic with respect to other tasks. This greatly simplifies the concurrency model, because now variables or resources that are shared across tasks do not require mutual exclusion protocols to protect their accesses. Tasks may be preempted by event handlers, however, so some care must be exercised when shared data is accessed here to avoid race conditions. Interestingly, it is relatively easy to statically analyze a program for potential race conditions [8].

Consider the sensor fusion example from above. A configuration for this is sketched in figure 4. The two sensors have interfaces called "reading" that accept a command a signal an event. The command is used to configure the sensors. The event is signaled when an interrupt from the sensor hardware is handled. Each time such an event is signaled, the Fuser component records the sensor reading and posts a task to update the discounted average. The task will then invoke the command in the print interface of the Printer component to display the result. Because tasks execute atomically with respect to one another, in the order in which they are posted, the only tricky part of this implementation is in recording the sensor data. However, tasks in TinyOS can be passed arguments on the stack, so the sensor data can be recorded there. The management of concurrency becomes extremely simple in this example.

In effect, in nesC/TinyOS, concurrency is much more disciplined than with threads. There is no arbitrary interleaving of code execution, there are no blocking operations to cause deadlock, and there is a very simple mechanism for managing the one nondeterministic preemption that can be caused by interrupts. The price paid for this, however, is that applications must be divided into small, quickly executing procedures to maintain reactivity. Since tasks run to completion, a long-running task will starve all other tasks.

5 Declarative Concurrent Models

Simulink, SCADE, LabVIEW and hardware description languages all have a declarative flavor. The interactions between components are not imperative in that one component does not "tell the other what to do." Instead, a "program" is a declaration of the relationships among components.

Simulink was originally developed as a modeling environment, primarily for control systems. It is rooted in a continuous-time semantics, something that is intrinsically challenging for any software system to emulate. Software is intrinsically discrete, so an execution of a Simulink "program" often amounts to approximating the specified behavior using numerical integration techniques.

A Simulink "program" is an interconnection of blocks where the connections are the "variables," but the value of a variable is a function, not a single value. To complicate things, it is a function defined over a continuum. The Integrator block, for example, takes as input any function of the reals and produces as output the integral of that function. In general, any numerical representation in software of such a function and its integral is an approximation, where the value is represented at discrete points in the continuum. The Simulink execution engine (which is called a "solver") chooses those discrete points using sometimes quite sophisticated methods.

Although initially Simulink focused on simulating continuous dynamics and providing excellent numerical integration, more recently it acquired a discrete capability. Semantically, discrete signals are piecewise-constant continuous-time signals. A piecewise constant signal changes value only at discrete points on the time line. Such signals are intrinsically easier for software, and more precise approximations are possible.

In addition to discrete signals, Simulink has discrete blocks. These have a sampleTime parameter, which specifies the period of a periodic execution. Any output of a discrete block is a piecewise constant signal. Inputs are sampled at multiples of the sampleTime.

Certain arrangements of discrete blocks turn out to be particularly easy to execute. An interconnection of discrete blocks that all have the same sampleTime value, for example, can be efficiently compiled into embedded software. But even blocks with different sampleTime parameters can yield efficient models, when the sampleTime values are related by simple integer multiples.

Fortunately, in the design of control systems (and many other signal processing systems), there is a common design pattern where discrete blocks with harmonically related sampleTime values are commonly used to specify the software of embedded control systems.

Figure 5 shows schematically a typical Simulink model of a control system. There is a portion of the model that is a model of the physical dynamics of the system to be controlled. There is no need, usually, to compile that specification into embedded software. There is another portion of the model that represents a discrete controller. In this example, we have shown a controller that involves multiple values of the sampleTime parameter, shown as numbers below the discrete blocks. This controller is a specification for a program that we wish to execute in an embedded system.

Real-Time Workshop is a product from The MathWorks associated with Simulink. It takes models like that in figure 5 and generates code. Although it will generate code for any model, it is intended principally to be used only on the discrete controller, and indeed, this is where its strengths come through.

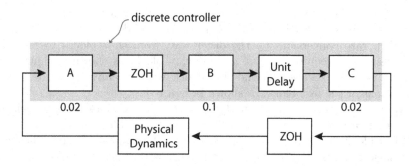

Fig. 5. A representation of a Simulink program

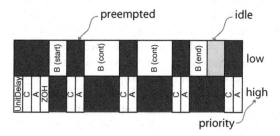

Fig. 6. A simplified representation of a Simulink schedule

The discrete controller shown in figure 5 has fast running components (with sampleTime values of 0.02, or 20 ms) and slow running components (with sampleTime values of 0.1, or 1/10 of a second). In such situations, it is not unusual for the slow running components to involve much heavier computational loads than the fast running components. It would not do to schedule these computations to execute atomically, as is done in TinyOS and Click (and SCADE). This would permit the slow running component to interfere with the responsivity (and time correctness) of the fast running components.

Simulink with Real-Time Workshop uses a clever technique to circumvent this problem. The technique exploits an underlying multitasking operating system with preemptive priority-driven multitasking. The slow running blocks are executed in a separate thread from the fast running blocks, as shown in figure 6. The thread for the fast running blocks is given higher priority than that for the slow running blocks, ensuring that the slow running code cannot block the fast running code. So far, this just follows the principles of rate-monotonic scheduling [23]. But the situation is a bit more subtle than this, because data flows across the rate boundaries. Recall that Simulink signals have continuous-time semantics, and that discrete signals are piecewise constant. The slow running blocks should "see" at their input a piecewise constant signal that changes values at the slow rate.To guarantee that, the model builder is required to put a zero-order hold (ZOH) block at the point of the rate conversion. Failure to do so will trigger an error message. Cleverly, the code for the ZOH runs at the rate of the slow block but at the priority of the fast block. This makes it completely unnecessary to do semaphore synchronization when exchanging data across these threads.

When rate conversions go the other way, from slow blocks to fast blocks, the designer is required to put a UnitDelay block, as shown in figure 5. This is because the execution of the slow block will typically stretch over several executions of the fast block, as shown in figure 6.

To ensure determinacy, the updated output of the block must be delayed by the worst case, which will occur if the execution stretches over all executions of the fast block in one period of the slow block. The unit delay gives the software the slack it needs in order to be able to permit the execution of the slow block to stretch over several executions of the fast one. The UnitDelay executes at the rate of the slow block but at the priority of the fast block.

This same principle has been exploited in Giotto [12], which constrains the program to always obey this multirate semantics and provides (implicitly) a unit delay on every connection. In exchange for these constraints, Giotto achieves strong formal structure, which results in, among other things, an ability to perform schedulability analysis (the determination of whether the specified real-time behavior can be achieved by the software).

The Simulink model has weaknesses, however. The sensor fusion problem that we posed earlier does not match its discrete multitasking model very well. While it would be straightforward to construct a discrete multitasking model that polls the sensors at regular (harmonic) rates, reacting to stimulus from the sensors at random times does not fit the semantics very well. The merge shown in figure 2 would be challenging to accomplish in Simulink, and it would not benefit much from the clever code generation techniques of Real-Time Workshop.

In figure 2, we give a discrete-event model of an improved sensor fusion algorithm with an exponential forgetting function. Discrete-event modeling is widely used in electronic circuit design (VHDL and Verilog are discrete-event languages), computer network modeling and simulation (OPNET Modeler and Ns-2, for example), and many other disciplines. In discrete-event models, the components interact via signals that consist of events, which typically carry both a data payload and a time stamp. A straightforward execution of these models uses a centralized event queue, where events are sorted by time stamp, and a runtime scheduler dispatches events to be processed in time order. Compared to the Simulink/RTW model, there is much more flexibility in DE because discrete execution does not need to be periodic. This feature is exploited in the model of figure 2, where the Merge block has no simple counterpart in Simulink.

A great deal of work has been done on efficient and distributed execution of such models, much of this work originating in either the so-called "conservative" technique of Chandy and Misra [3] or the speculative execution methods of Jefferson [15]. More interesting is the work in the Croquet Project, which focuses on optimistic techniques in the face of unreliable components. Croquet has principally been applied to three-D shared immersion environments on the internet, similar to the ones that might be used in interactive networked gaming. Much less work has been done in adapting these models as an execution platform for embedded software, but there is some early work that bears a strong semantic resemblance to DE modeling techniques [24][9]. A significant challenge is to achieve the timed semantics efficiently while building on software abstractions that have abstracted away time.

6   Discrete-Event Runtime Framework

The ability of TinyOS and nesC to create thin wrappers around hardware provides a simple and understandable mechanism for creating event-triggered, fine-grained, atomic reactions to external events. When these external events trigger significant computations, nesC programs will "post tasks" that are executed later. These tasks, however, all execute atomically with respect to one another, and hence a long-running task will block other tasks. This can create unacceptable latencies, and often forces software designers to manually divide long-running tasks into more fine-grain ones.

Simulink and Giotto, by contrast, freely mix long-running tasks with hard-real-time fine-grained tasks by exploiting the properties of an underlying priority-driven multitasking real-time operating system. They do this without requiring programmers to specify priorities or use mutexes or semaphores. However, these tasks are required to be periodic, and their latencies are strongly related to their periods, so they lack the event-triggered, reactive nature of nesC programs.

These two ideas can be combined within a dataflow framework with elements borrowed from discrete-event models to specify timing properties. Dependencies within the dataflow model can be statically analyzed, and with a carefully chosen variant of dataflow called heterochronous dataflow (HDF) [10], schedulability becomes decidable and synthesis of efficient embedded software becomes possible. We believe that the resulting language will prove expressive, efficient, understandable, and analyzable.

We are building a prototype of this combination of HDF and DE using the Ptolemy II framework [7]. This prototype can synthesize multitasking C code for execution on embedded processors or general-purpose processors. That is, the target language for the compiler will be C. The source language will be graphical, exploiting the graphical syntaxes supported by Ptolemy II. We will specifically target instrumentation applications, and, at coarser temporal granularity, distributed games. We leverage a C code generator for Ptolemy II that supports HDF [10], built by Jackie Mankit Leung and Gang Zhou, for code generation.

The overall architecture of an application is a distributed discrete-event model of interactions of concurrent real-time components (which we call actors). The components themselves have functionality that can be specified either by dataflow models, combinations of dataflow and state machines (heterochronous dataflow), or conventional programming languages (C or Java, in this case).

Discrete-event semantics is typically used for modeling physical systems where atomic events occur on a time line. For example, hardware description languages for digital logic design, such as Verilog and VHDL, are discrete-event languages.

So are many network modeling languages, such as OPNET Modeler[1] and Ns-2[2]. Our approach is not to model physical phenomena, but rather to specify coordinated real-time events to be realized in software. Execution of the software will first obey discrete-event semantics, just as done in DE simulators, but it will do so with specified real-time constraints on certain actions. Our technique is properly viewed as providing a semantic notion of model time together with a relation between the model time of certain events and their physical time.

Our premise is that since DE models are natural for modeling real-time systems, they should be equally natural for specifying real-time systems. Moreover, we can exploit their formal properties to ensure determinism in ways that evades many real-time software techniques. Network time synchronization makes it possible for discrete-event models to have a coherent semantics across distributed nodes. Just as with distributed DE simulation, it will be neither practical nor efficient to use a centralized event queue to sort events in time order. Our goal will be to compile DE models for efficient and predictable distributed execution.

We emphasize that while distributed execution of DE models has long been used to exploit parallel computation to accelerate simulation [31], we are not interested in accelerated simulation. Instead, we are interested in systems that are intrinsically distributed. Consider factory automation, for example, where sensors and actuators are spread out physically over hundreds of meters. Multiple controllers must coordinate their actions over networks. This is not about speed of execution but rather about timing precision. We use the global notion of time that is intrinsic in DE models as a binding coordination agent.

For accelerated simulation, there is a rich history of techniques. So-called "conservative" techniques advance model time to t only when each node can be assured that they have seen all events time stamped t or earlier. For example, in the well-known Chandy and Misra technique [3], extra messages are used for one execution node to notify another that there are no such earlier events. For our purposes, this technique binds the execution at the nodes too tightly, making it very difficult to meet realistic real-time constraints.

So-called "optimistic" techniques perform speculative execution and backtrack when the speculation is incorrect [15]. Such optimistic techniques will also not work in our context, since backtracking physical interactions is not possible.

Our method is called PTIDES, Programming Temporally Integrated Distributed Embedded Systems [32]. It is conservative, in the sense that events are processed only when we are sure it is safe to do so. But we achieve significantly looser coupling than Chandy and Misra using a new method that we call *relevant dependency analysis*. We leverage the concept of causality interfaces introduced in [22], adapting these interfaces to distributed discrete-event models. We have developed the concept of "relevant dependency" to formally capture the ordering constraints of temporally ordered events that have a dependency relationship. This formal structure provides an algebra within which we can perform schedulability analysis of distributed discrete-event models.

---

[1] http://opnet.com/products/modeler/home.html
[2] http://www.isi.edu/nsnam/ns

Our emphasis is on efficient distributed real-time execution. Our framework uses model time to define execution semantics, and constraints that bind certain model time events to physical time. A correct execution will simply obey the ordering constraints implied by model time and meet the constraints on events that are bound to physical time.

6.1   Motivating Example

We motivate our programming model by considering a simple distributed real-time application. Suppose that at two distinct machines A and B we need to generate precisely timed physical events under the control of software. Moreover, the devices that generate these physical events respond after generating the event with some data, for example sensor data. We model this functionality with an actor that has one input port and one output port, depicted graphically as follows:

This actor is a software component that wraps interactions with device drivers. We assume that it does not communicate with any other software component except via its ports. At its input port, it receives a potentially infinite sequence of time-stamped values, called events, in chronological order. The sequence of events is called a signal. The output port produces a time-stamped value for each input event, where the time stamp is strictly greater than that of the input event. The time stamps are values of model time. This software component binds model time to physical time by producing some physical action at the real-time corresponding to the model time of each input event. Thus, the key real-time constraint is that input events must be made available for this software component to process them at a physical time strictly earlier than the time stamp. Otherwise, the component would not be able to produce the physical action at the designated time.

Figure 7 shows a distributed DE model to be executed on a two-machine, time-synchronized platform. The dashed boxes divide the model into two parts, one to be executed on each machine. The parts communicate via signal s_1. We assume that events in this signal are sent over a standard network as time-stamped values.

The Clock actors in the figure produce time-stamped outputs where the time stamp is some integer multiple of a period p (the period can be different for each clock). Upon receiving an input with time stamp t, the clock actor will produce an output with time stamp np where n is the smallest integer so that $np \geq t$. There are no real-time constraints on the inputs or outputs of these actors.

The Merge actor has two input ports. It merges the signals on the two input ports in chronological order (perhaps giving priority to one port if input events

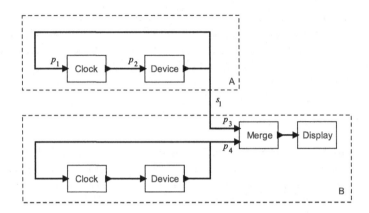

Fig. 7. A simple distributed instrumentation example

have identical time stamps). A conservative implementation of this Merge requires that no output with time stamp t be produced until we are sure we have seen all inputs with time stamps less than or equal to t. There are no real-time constraints on the input or output events of the Merge actor.

The Display actor receives input events in chronological (time-stamped) order and displays them. It also has no real-time constraints.

A brute-force implementation of a conservative distributed DE execution of this model would stall execution in platform B at some time stamp t until an event with time stamp t or larger has been seen on signal s_1. Were we to use the Chandy and Misra approach, we would insert null events into s_1 to minimize the real-time delay of these stalls. However, we have real-time constraints at the Device actors that will not be met if we use this brute-force technique. Moreover, it is intuitively obvious that such a conservative technique is not necessary. Since the actors communicate only through their ports, there is no risk in processing events in the upper Clock-Device loop ahead of time stamps received on s_1. Our PTIDES technique formalizes this observation using causality analysis.

To make this example more concrete, we have in our lab prototype systems provided by Agilent that implement IEEE 1588. These platforms include a Linux host and simple timing-precise I/O hardware. Specifically, they include a device driver API where the software can request that the hardware generate a digital clock edge (a voltage level change) at a specified time. After generating this level change, the hardware interrupts the processor, which resets the level to its original value. Our implementation of the Device actor takes input events as specification of when to produce these level changes. That is, it produces a rising edge at physical time equal to the model time of an input event. After receiving an input, it outputs an event with time stamp equal to the physical time at which the level is restored to its original value. Thus, its input time stamps must precede physical time, and its output events are guaranteed to follow physical time. This physical setup makes it easy to measure precisely the real-time behavior of the system (oscilloscope probes on the digital I/O connectors tell it all).

The feedback loops around the two Clock and Device actors ensure that the Device does not get overwhelmed with requests for future level changes. It may not be able to buffer those requests, or it may have a finite buffer. Without the feedback loop, since the ports of the Clock actor have no real-time constraints, there would be nothing to keep it from producing output events much faster than real time.

This model is an abstraction of many realistic applications. For example, consider two networked computers controlling cameras pointing at the same scene from different angles. Precise time synchronization allows them to take sequences of pictures simultaneously. Merging two synchronous pictures creates a 4D view for the scene (three physical dimensions and one time).

PTIDES programs are discrete-event models constructed as networks of actors, as in the example above. For each actor, we specify a physical host to execute the actor. We also designate a subset of the input ports to be *real-time ports*. Time-stamped events must be delivered to these ports before physical-time exceeds the time stamp. Each real-time port can optionally also specify a *setup time* τ, in which case it requires that each input event with time stamp t be received before physical time reaches $t - \tau$. A model is said to be *deployable* if these constraints can be met for all real-time ports. Causality analysis can reveal whether a model is deployable.

The key idea is that events only need to be processed in time-stamp order when they are causally related. We defined formal interfaces to actors that tells us when such causal relationships exist.

6.2   Summary of Relevant Dependency Analysis

A formal framework for analyzing causality relationships to determine the minimal ordering constraints on processing events is given in [32]. We give a summary of the key results here. The technique is based on causality interfaces [22], which provide a mechanism that allows us to analyze delay relationships among actors. The interface of actors contains ports on which actors receive or produce events. Each port is associated with a signal. A *causality interface* declares the dependency that output events have on input events.

A program is given as a composition of actors, by which we mean a set of actors and connectors linking their ports. Given a composition and the causality interface of each actor, we can determine the dependencies between any two ports in the composition. However, these dependencies between ports do not tell the whole story. Consider the Merge actor in figure 7. It has two input ports, and the dependency analysis tells that there is no path between these ports. However, these ports have an important relationship, noted above. In particular, the Merge actor cannot react to an event at one port with time stamp t until it is sure it has seen all events at the other port with time stamp less than or equal to t. This fact is not captured in the dependencies. To capture it, we use *relevant dependencies*. Based on the causality interface of actors, the *relevant dependency* on any pair (p_1, p_2) of input ports specifies whether an event at p_1 will affect an output signal that may also depend on an event at p_2. Given the

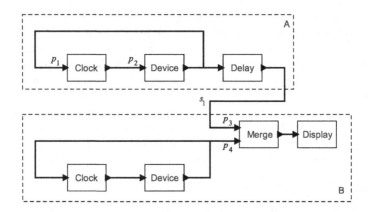

Fig. 8. The motivating example with a delay actor

relevant dependency interfaces for all actors in a composition, we can establish the relevant dependency between any two input ports in the composition.

When the relevant dependency from input port p_1 to p_2 is r, $r \in \mathbb{R}_0$, this means that any event with time stamp t_2 at p_2 can be processed when all events at p_1 are known up to time stamp $t_2 - r$. When the relevant dependency from p_1 to p_2 is ∞, this means that events at p_2 can be processed without knowing anything about events at p_1.

What we gain from the dependency analysis is that we can specify which events can be processed out of order, and which events have to be processed in order. Recall that p_2 is designated as a real-time port. Relevant dependency analysis tells us that events at p_2 can be processed without knowing anything about events at p_3 or p_4. This is the first result we were after. It means that the arrival events over the network into p_3 need not interfere with meeting real-time constraints at p_2. This would not be achieved with a Chandy and Misra policy. And unlike optimistic policies, there will never be any need to backtrack.

If we modify the model in figure 7 by adding a Delay actor with a delay parameter d, we get a new model as shown in figure 8. Relevant dependency analysis now tells us that an event with time stamp t at p_4 can be processed if all events with time stamps smaller than or equal to $t - d$ at p_3 have been processed. With the same assumptions as discussed in section 6.1 (an event with model time t is produced at physical time t by the Device process, and the network delay is bounded by C), at physical time $t - d + C$ we are sure that we have seen all events with time stamps smaller than $t - d$ at p_3. Hence, an event e at p_4 with time stamp t can be processed at physical time $t - d + C$ or later. Note that although the Delay actor has no real-time properties at all (it simply manipulates model time), its presence loosens the constraints on the execution.

In [32] we show that relevant dependencies induce a partial order (called the *relevant order*) on events. We use notation $<_r$ for the relevant order. We interpret $e_1 <_r e_2$ to mean that e_1 must be processed before e_2. Two events e_1 and e_2 are not comparable, denoted as $e_1 \|_r e_2$, if neither $e_1 <_r e_2$, nor $e_2 <_r e_1$. If $e_1 \|_r e_2$, then e_1, e_2 can be processed in any order. What we mean by "processed" is that the actor that is the destination of the event is *fired*, meaning that it is executed and allowed to react to the event. It is then straightforward to show that any execution that respects the relevant order correctly implements discrete-event semantics.

We further show in [32] that this technique can be adapted to distributed execution if we are given bounds on the communication latency and on the timing synchronization order.

7   Conclusion

Existing methods for addressing real-time computation typically deal with a portion of the problem of constructing and executing real-time programs. Real-time operating systems (RTOSs) provide mechanisms for prioritizing tasks and triggering computations in response to timer interrupts. Time-triggered networking techniques such as the Time Triggered Architecture (TTA) provide deterministic sharing of networking resources and insulation from faults. Network time synchronization protocols such as NTP and IEEE 1588 provide a common time base across computers on a network. All of these technologies, however, are used with relatively conventional concurrency models (threads and processes) and conventional programming languages. This paper elevates timing and distribution to the level of the programmers model, so that applications are built by directly expressing timing and distribution properties. The objective is a framework for designing deployable timed distributed systems. Our technique adapts discrete-event semantics, traditionally used for modeling and simulation, for use as a programmers' model for distributed real-time software.

Acknowledgements

This paper describes work that is part of the Ptolemy project, which is supported by the National Science Foundation (NSF award number CCR-00225610), and Chess (the Center for Hybrid and Embedded Software Systems), which receives support from NSF, the State of California Micro Program, and the following companies: Agilent, DGIST, General Motors, Hewlett Packard, Infineon, Microsoft, and Toyota.

References

1. O. Avissar, R. Barua, and D. Stewart. An optimal memory allocation scheme for scratch-pad-based embedded systems. *Trans. on Embedded Computing Sys.*, 1(1):6–26, 2002.
2. G. Berry. The effectiveness of synchronous languages for the development of safety-critical systems. White paper, Esterel Technologies, 2003.
3. K. M. Chandy and J. Misra. Distributed simulation: A case study in design and verification of distributed programs. *IEEE Trans. on Software Engineering*, 5(5), 1979.

4. E. A. de Kock, G. Essink, W. J. M. Smits, P. van der Wolf, J.-Y. Brunel, W. Kruijtzer, P. Lieverse, and K. A. Vissers. YAPI: Application modeling for signal processing systems. In *37th Design Automation Conference (DAC'00)*, pages 402–405, Los Angeles, CA, 2000.

5. E. Dijkstra. Cooperating sequential processes. In E. F. Genuys, editor, *Programming Languages*. Academic Press, 1968.

6. A. Dominguez, S. Udayakumaran, and R. Barua. Heap data allocation to scratch-pad memory in embedded systems. *Journal of Embedded Computing*, 1(4), 2005.

7. J. Eker, J. W. Janneck, E. A. Lee, J. Liu, X. Liu, J. Ludvig, S. Neuendorffer, S. Sachs, and Y. Xiong. Taming heterogeneity—the Ptolemy approach. *Proceedings of the IEEE*, 91(2):127–144, 2003.

8. D. Gay, P. Levis, R. v. Behren, M. Welsh, E. Brewer, and D. Culler. The nesc language: A holistic approach to networked embedded systems. In *Programming Language Design and Implementation (PLDI)*, 2003.

9. A. Ghosal, T. A. Henzinger, C. M. Kirsch, and M. A. Sanvido. Event-driven programming with logical execution times. In *Seventh International Workshop on Hybrid Systems: Computation and Control (HSCC)*, volume Lecture Notes in Computer Science 2993, pages 357–371. Springer-Verlag, 2004.

10. A. Girault, B. Lee, and E. A. Lee. Hierarchical finite state machines with multiple concurrency models. *IEEE Transactions On Computer-aided Design Of Integrated Circuits And Systems*, 18(6):742–760, 1999.

11. N. Halbwachs, P. Caspi, P. Raymond, and D. Pilaud. The synchronous data flow programming language LUSTRE. *Proceedings of the IEEE*, 79(9):1305–1319, 1991.

12. T. A. Henzinger, B. Horowitz, and C. M. Kirsch. Giotto: A time-triggered language for embedded programming. In *EMSOFT 2001*, volume LNCS 2211, Tahoe City, CA, 2001. Springer-Verlag.

13. J. Hill, R. Szewcyk, A. Woo, D. Culler, S. Hollar, and K. Pister. System architecture directions for networked sensors. In *9th International Conference on Architectural Support for Programming Languages and Operating Systems (ASPLOS)*, pages 93–104, 2000.

14. C. A. R. Hoare. Monitors: An operating system structuring concept. *Communications of the ACM*, 17(10):549–557, 1974.

15. D. Jefferson. Virtual time. *ACM Trans. Programming Languages and Systems*, 7(3):404–425, 1985.

16. E. Kohler, R. Morris, B. Chen, J. Jannotti, and M. F. Kaashoek. The click modular router. *ACM Transactions on Computer Systems*, 18(3):263–297, 2000.

17. D. Lea. *Concurrent Programming in Java: Design Principles and Patterns*. Addison-Wesley, Reading MA, 1997.

18. E. A. Lee. Modeling concurrent real-time processes using discrete events. *Annals of Software Engineering*, 7:25–45, 1999.

19. E. A. Lee. The problem with threads. *Computer*, 39(5):33–42, 2006.

20. E. A. Lee, S. Neuendorffer, and M. J. Wirthlin. Actor-oriented design of embedded hardware and software systems. *Journal of Circuits, Systems, and Computers*, 12(3):231–260, 2003.

21. E. A. Lee and T. M. Parks. Dataflow process networks. *Proceedings of the IEEE*, 83(5):773–801, 1995.

22. E. A. Lee, H. Zheng, and Y. Zhou. Causality interfaces and compositional causality analysis. In *Foundations of Interface Technologies (FIT), Satellite to CONCUR*, San Francisco, CA, 2005.

23. C. L. Liu and J. W. Leyland. Scheduling algorithms for multiprogramming in a hard real time environment. *Journal of the ACM*, 20(1):46–61, 1973.

24. J. Liu and E. A. Lee. Timed multitasking for real-time embedded software. *IEEE Control Systems Magazine*, pages 65–75, 2003.

25. P. Panangaden and V. Shanbhogue. The expressive power of indeterminate dataflow primitives. *Information and Computation*, 98(1):99–131, 1992.

26. T. M. Parks. A comparison of MPI and process networks. In *International Parallel and Distributed Processing Symposium, Workshop on Java for Parallel and Distributed Computing*, Denver, CO, 2005.

27. J. L. Pino, S. Ha, E. A. Lee, and J. T. Buck. Software synthesis for dsp using Ptolemy. *Journal on VLSI Signal Processing*, 9(1):7–21, 1995.

28. D. A. Smith, A. Kay, A. Raab, and D. P. Reed. Croquet: A collaboration system architecture. White paper, 2003.

29. J. A. Stankovic. Misconceptions about real-time computing: a serious problem for next-generation systems. *Computer*, 21(10):10–19, 1988.

30. N. Wirth. Toward a discipline of real-time programming. *Communications of the ACM*, 20(8):577–583, 1977.

31. B. P. Zeigler, H. Praehofer, and T. G. Kim. *Theory of Modeling and Simulation*. Academic Press, 2nd edition, 2000.

32. Y. Zhao, E. A. Lee, and J. Liu. Programming temporally integrated distributed embedded systems. Technical Report UCB/EECS-2006-82, EECS Department, University of California, Berkeley, May 28 2006.

Applying Service-Oriented Development to Complex Systems: BART Case Study

Ingolf H. Krüger[1], Michael Meisinger[2], and Massimiliano Menarini[1]

[1] Computer Science and Engineering Department
University of California, San Diego
La Jolla, CA 92093-0404, USA
{ikrueger,mmenarin}@cs.ucsd.edu
[2] Institut für Informatik
Technische Universität München
Boltzmannstr. 3, 85748 Garching, Germany
meisinge@in.tum.de

Abstract. Complex distributed systems with control parts are difficult to develop and maintain. One reason of the complexity is the high degree of interaction and parallelism in these systems. Systematic, architecture-centric approaches are required to model, implement and verify such systems. To manage complexity, we apply a service-oriented development process, yielding manageable and flexible architecture specifications. We specify interaction patterns defining services using an extended Message Sequence Chart notation. We model a portion of the BART system as a case study, demonstrating the applicability of our methodology to this domain of complex, distributed, reactive systems. Our approach allows us to separate the problem of orchestrating the interactions between distributed components and developing the control algorithms for the various control tasks. We provide a brief overview of service-oriented development and service-oriented architectures, as well as a detailed description of our results for the BART case study.

1 Introduction

Distributed, reactive systems are notoriously difficult to develop – especially when they are interaction- *and* control-intensive. The Bay Area Rapid Transit (BART) system with its Advanced Automatic Train Control (AATC) as controlling software is a telling example; another such area, which is increasingly recognized across academia and industry as a challenging application area for advanced software technologies is the automotive domain with its mix of safety-critical and comfort functions. The shift from monolithic to highly networked, heterogeneous, interactive systems, occurring across application domains, has led to a dramatic increase in both development and system complexity. At the same time the demands for safety, reliability, and other quality attributes have increased.

The major challenge in developing such systems is to manage the complexity induced by the distribution and interaction of the corresponding components.

F. Kordon and J. Sztipanovits (Eds.): Monterey Workshop 2005, LNCS 4322, pp. 26–46, 2007.

Model-based development techniques and notations have emerged as an approach to dealing with this complexity, in particular during the analysis, specification and design phases of the development process; popular examples are UML, SysML, ROOM and SDL. Each of these examples proposes managing the complexity of software development by separating the two major modeling concerns: system structure and system behavior.

In application domains such as process control, automotive, avionics, telecommunications and networking, the logical and physical component distribution has introduced the additional challenge of modeling, analysis and handling of cross-cutting concerns such as security and Quality-of-Service. Because system functions are scattered across modeling and implementation entities, the cross-cutting concerns in the system are increasingly difficult to trace and to ensure during all steps of the development process.

Service-Oriented Development (SOD) and Architectures (SOA) have been suggested as an approach to system development and architecture that helps address both system complexity *and* cross-cutting concerns, including the mentioned quality properties. Because services typically emerge from the interplay of multiple system components, SOD places particular focus on the interaction between components and system-wide functions.

1.1   Service-Oriented Architectures and Development

The center of concern in model-based design has so far mostly been individual components rather than their interplay. In contrast, service-oriented design emphasizes the interaction among components by using the notion of service to decouple abstract behavior from implementation architectures supporting it. The term "service" is used in multiple different meanings and on multiple different levels of abstraction throughout the Software and Systems Engineering community. Web Services currently receive a lot of attention from both academia and industry. Figure 1 shows a typical "layout" of applications composed as a set of (web) services. Often such systems consist of at least two distinct layers: a domain layer and a service layer. The domain layer houses all domain objects and their associated logic. The service layer acts as a façade to the underlying domain objects - in effect, offering an interface that shields the domain objects from client software. Typically, services in this sense coordinate workflows among the domain objects; they may also call, and thus depend on, other services. Some of the services, say Service 1 and Service 2 in our example, may reside on the same physical machine, whereas others, such as Service n may be accessible remotely via the Internet.

The layout shown in Figure 1 is prototypical not only of the typical situation we find for applications structured in terms of web services, but also for other domains where complex, often distributed applications are expected to offer externally accessible interfaces. Abstracting from the domain-specific details we observe that services often encapsulate the coordination of sets of domain objects to implement "use cases". We focus on the coordination aspect of each use case and define services as *partial* interaction specifications.

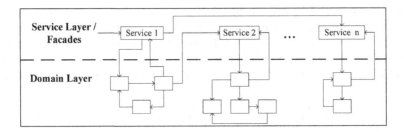

Fig. 1. Service-Oriented Architectures

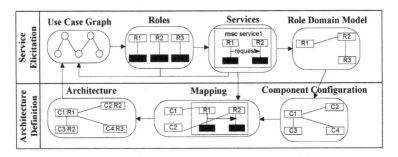

Fig. 2. Service-Oriented Development Process

Our approach to service-oriented development rests on the observation that services orchestrate a set of entities, each of which makes a *partial* contribution to the execution of the service. Whereas in traditional, component-oriented development approaches, component interplay is often treated as an afterthought, we place the orchestration aspect of services in the center of the development process from the outset. We have developed a two-phase, iterative development process as shown in Figure 2[15,13]. In the following, we first give a brief overview of this process as we have applied it, among others, to the development of service-oriented automotive software; then we describe the extensions we introduce in this paper to deal with complex, control-intensive systems.

Phase (1), Service Elicitation, consists of defining the set of services of interest - we call this set the service repository. Phase (2), Architecture Definition, consists of mapping the services to component configurations to define deployments of the architecture.

In phase (1) we identify the relevant use cases and their relationships in the form of a use case graph. This gives us a relatively high-level, scenario-based view on the system. From the use cases we derive sets of roles and services as interaction patterns among roles. Roles describe the contribution of an entity to a particular service independently of what concrete implementation component will deliver this contribution. An object or component of the implementation may play multiple roles at the same time. The relationships between the roles, including aggregations and multiplicities, develop into a role domain model. Together with a data domain model, indicating the types of data being manipulated by the system under consideration, the role domain model and the service specification are the foundation for the abstract core of the service-oriented architecture.

In phase (2) the role domain model is refined into a component configuration, onto which the set of services is mapped to yield an architectural configuration. These architectural configurations can be readily implemented and evaluated as target architectures for the system under consideration.

This process is iterative both within the two phases, and across: Role and service elicitation feeds back into the definition of the use case graph; architectures can be refined and refactored to yield new architectural configurations, which may lead to further refinement of the use cases.

The process of transferring house-ownership between two parties (also known as the *escrow* process) is a good example to better illustrate the utility of roles, services and components. Typically, the escrow process involves a number of players, including the seller, the buyer, a mortgage company, multiple real-estate agents, notary-publics, house inspectors, insurance agents and an escrow and title company. The process itself is precisely defined; the various actions of negotiating the price, signing an offer document, provisioning the money, providing proof of insurance, etc. are partially ordered, culminating in the transfer of title if all actions are performed within the required time and ordering – the process can be described properly without mentioning of any *concrete* players, such as a specific buyer, seller or bank. Instead, we can define the *escrow service* as the proper interplay among the set of players (which we call roles). An instance of the service emerges by mapping the roles to concrete players (which we call components). The service captures the deployment-independent aspects of the system under consideration; a concrete deployment (mapping of roles to components) defines an architecture configuration.

Following the process presented above allows us to specify system-wide services separately and map them subsequently to a given deployment architecture. Integration-complexity is addressed early in the development process by focusing on component interactions as the defining element of services. In the following section we show how we can also address control complexity in our apporach.

1.2   Contribution

To be successful in applying SOD and SOA to complex distributed systems with control challenges, software engineers need a thorough understanding of how to identify services and a corresponding architecture systematically, how to specify the services and architecture, how to implement, validate and verify the resulting specifications, and how to address the control requirements. In this paper, we present our approach to SOD/SOA based on a clear understanding of services as partial interaction patterns, combined with a systematic, flexible, iterative development process for services and service-oriented architectures. Using the BART case study, we explain the benefits of our notations and process, as well as the tool-chain we have developed.

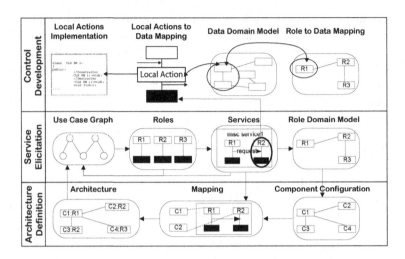

Fig. 3. Service-Oriented Development Process with Control

The main contribution of this paper is to show the applicability and efficacy of service-oriented development for complex distributed systems with control parts. We show how service-oriented development helps to develop effective architectures for complex distributed systems and how control algorithms can be independently developed and integrated into this approach. This helps us to manage the integration complexity that is caused by the high degree of distribution and thus parallelism of the system. Figure 3 depicts the development process and how we deal with control. The control problem is reduced to a set of local actions, the algorithms are developed and implemented independently from the service-oriented architecture and are called from the various roles in their local actions.

2   Complex Systems with Reactive and Control Parts

The systems we are addressing with our service-oriented approach are complex distributed systems. The complexity we refer to here stems from the need to integrate multiple different parts whose interplay is difficult to grasp with traditional techniques. Rather than treating component interplay as an afterthought, addressed only during late stages of deployment and integration, we focus on *services*, defined as the interaction patterns among roles, throughout the development process.

Complex reactive systems are often used in control applications. In this field, often the control is applied to actuators and sensors that interact with the physical world. Some of the complexity arises then from the fact that part of the domain (the physical world to be controlled) is best modeled using continuous data types and behavior, wheres the remainder of the domain can best be characterized using discrete data types and behavior. This system class is known as *hybrid* systems [2]. Particularly challenging are complex hybrid systems where the complexity of the distributed communication is increased by real time requirements of control algorithms. For instance, control algorithms can impose tight constraints on the latency and jitter of the communication infrastructure. Furthermore, if an algorithm has to deal with continuous measures the task of sampling and discretizing the control can transform a simple set of differential equations into a storm of messages that needs to be exchanged between components.

Distributed control systems, if developed in an ad-hoc fashion, result in tight coupling between modules and complex, inflexible data exchange to establish and maintain global state. To alleviate these problems, various software infrastructures and middlewares [24,7] have been developed. The complexity of developing new control application from scratch time and again has led to the introduction of reusable standard platforms [17]. For instance, in industrial control the use of Function Blocks (IEC 61499) allows isolation of the control algorithms from the distributed interaction.

Because of what Leveson defines as the "curse of complexity" [16] it is, however, difficult and error-prone to separate the control blocks from the distributed communication infrastructure. The real challenge is to keep a system-level view while breaking down the problem into subproblems of a manageable size. To this end, our service-oriented approach permits breaking down the system into services capturing the interaction patterns among roles. Role states and their transitions capture the partial state-based behavior of any component that participates in the execution of this service.

Our way of integrating the hybrid aspects into a system specification is to associate the control parts with local activities of the roles. These activities are invoked as the corresponding service is executed.

In the remainder of this paper we focus on the analysis of the interactions between system entities. The control algorithms can be modeled and developed using well-established techniques and be called via local activities upon the reception of some message by a role.

2.1 The BART Case Study

The BART case study [25] describes parts of the Advanced Automatic Train Control (AATC) system of the Bay Area Rapid Transit (BART) system. BART is the San Francisco area, heavy commuter rail train system. The case study describes the part of the train system that controls spreed and acceleration of the trains. Certain other parts such as communication error recovery and train routing have been left out for the purposes of the case study. The part of the AATC system described here is suitable as a case study, because it provides a relevant level of detail and shows the complexity and interdependencies of the entire system, yet still remains of manageable size. BART was previously used as a case study in the area of distributed systems and for the application of formal methods [9].

The BART system automatically controls over 50 trains on a large track network with several different lines. Manual operation of the train control is limited mostly to safety issues and to cases of emergency or malfunction. Tracks are unidirectional. Certain sections of the track network are shared by trains of different lines. The system needs to operate switches and gates to ensure correct traffic flow. Tracks are separated into track segments, which may be protected by gates. Gates operate similar to traffic lights and establish the right-of-way where tracks join or merge at switches.

The AATC system controls the train movement – switch and gate handling will transparently be provided by another system. One important AATC requirement is to optimize train speeds and the spacing between the trains to increase the throughput on the congested parts of the network, while constantly ensuring train safety. The AATC system operates computers at the train stations which each control a local part of the track network. A station is responsible for controlling all trains in its area. Stations communicate with the trains via a radio network and with neighboring stations using land-based network links. Each train has two AATC controllers on board with one being the master. Trains receive acceleration and brake commands from the station computers via the radio communication network and feed back information about train speed and other engine status values. The radio network has the capability to track the trains' positions.

The case study concentrates on the parts of the AATC system that controls the trains' acceleration and braking. Controlling the trains must occur efficiently with a high throughput of trains, while ensuring certain safety regulations and conditions. The specification strictly defines certain safety conditions that must never be violated, such as a train must never enter a segment closed by a gate, or, the distance between trains must always exceed the safe stopping distance of the following train under any circumstances.

The system operates in 1/2 second cycles. In each cycle the station control computers receive train information, compute commands for all trains under their control and forward these commands to the trains. All information and commands are time-stamped. Commands to trains become invalid after 2 seconds. If a train does not receive a valid command within 2 seconds, it goes into emergency braking. The control algorithm needs to take this delay, track information and train status into account to compute new commands that never violate the safety conditions. To ensure this, each station computer is attached to an independent safety control computer (VSC) that validates all computed commands for conformance with the safety conditions.

Computing the trains' commands is a complex control problem. Inputs to the corresponding algorithm include the train position estimates, train speeds and accelerations, static track data (track grades, maximum speeds), switch and gate information from the interlocking system, information from the neighboring stations, interceptions from the safety control computer. The control algorithm needs to balance and optimize train throughput, adherence to the schedule, passenger comfort (not too strong braking and acceleration changes), engine wear and most importantly safety. In normal operations, the station computer computes the train commands in fixed time cycles. However, in case of a detected emergency condition, the system needs to react immediately and take appropriate measures to ensure maximum safety of passengers and equipment.

We focus on modeling the reactive behavior of a station computer and the trains, the safety control computer and the interlocking system as well as certain other external interfaces, as described, in detail, below. We apply our service-oriented development approach to distinguish the different services of the system and to specify a service model than will help us to design a service-oriented architecture. This architecture needs to be effective in supporting the requirements that are listed in the case study. We show how we can abstract from the actual control problems and integrate the necessary computation results and trigger conditions into our reactive model.

Our approach enables rapid architecture design for the AATC; this results in a high level design model that can systematically be refined into an implementable system. We can ensure the correctness of the reactive behavior and integrate the required control parts that trigger the reactive behavior.

3 Applying Service-Oriented Development to the BART Case Study

We have applied our previously introduced service-oriented development approach to the cross-cutting interaction aspects of the BART case study [25]. We have followed the process described above to elicit use cases and an initial role domain model and subsequently have identified and specified the basic services of the system. It is interesting to notice that in the BART case study the set of requirements include very specific information about the prescribed deployment of the system. We used the requirements, which are part of the architecture definition, as part of the input to our service elicitation phase as suggested by our iterative development process. This allowed us to refine our model for a suitable target architecture and to generate prototypic executable code to test the system under development.

In the following, we will explain the steps of the process we have followed in more detail.

3.1 Use Case Elicitation

From the requirements that are present in form of the BART case study document, we came up with a list of use cases:

1. A *train* determines its current status from different sensors in a *consist* (group of cars in a train).
2. A *train* communicates its current status (position, speed, acceleration value) to the responsible *control station*
3. A *control station* receives status messages from all trains in the controlled area in regular time intervals

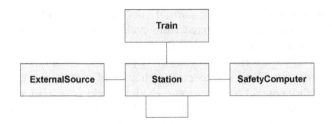

Fig. 4. High Level BART Role Domain Model

4. A *control station* receives external input for the controlled area from the *interlocking system* (gate&switch) control and manual speed limit settings
5. A *control station* computes speed and acceleration commands for each *train* in the controlled area
6. A *control station* forwards all commands of an interval cycle to the *VSC* for a reliable safety check
7. The *VSC* relays all safe commands via the comlink to the *trains* in the area
8. A *train* receives a command from its responsible *control station*, and checks the command validity (timestamp). It applies the command to all actuators in the consist.

Each use case, of course, can be broken down into more detailed steps, leading to a comprehensive use case view of the BART system. Analyzing these use cases leads to a first list of basic actors, or *roles*, which we depict in form of a structure diagram. From the use cases, we identify Train, Control Station, the Safety Computer (VSC) and an External Data Source as actors. This leads us to an initial role domain model where we depict the connections between the different actors. Fig. 4 shows the initial role model.

3.2   Modeling Services and Roles

We model roles and services together. We start with the initial role domain model of Fig. 4. We systematically go though the list of use cases and identify interaction patterns defining services. In a sense, the services we identify are a refinement of the elicited use cases. In the process of identifying interaction patterns, we may identify further actors; we add these as roles to the role domain model. Finally, after modeling all services the resulting role domain model looks as depicted in Fig. 5.

For specifying the services, we use the extended MSC notation of [10,15]. This notation is based on the Message Sequence Chart [8] standard and provides an intuitive graphical language for specifying interaction patterns and is well-accepted among engineers. Extensions to the standard notation were cautiously made based on a formal semantics to provide increased expressiveness and more

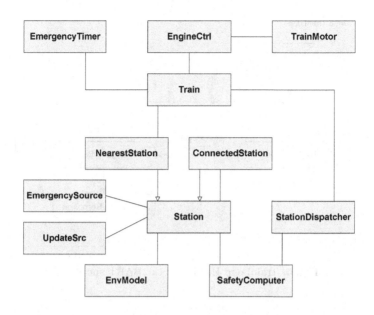

Fig. 5. BART Role Domain Model

powerful operators suitable for modeling service-oriented systems. To model the services, we can make use of our tool-chain introduced in [12].

In our service model, we capture the interactions between the station computer (and its subcomponents) with a train (and its subcomponents). Other entities, such as external data sources, are part of the interactions as well. In modeling the interactions, we concentrate on specific use cases and abstract from any concrete deployment architectures. In particular, we do not yet take any multiplicities of the entities into account. We specify the interactions between a train and the station computer, for instance, no matter of how often this specific interaction happens subsequently or in parallel.

Good design principles suggest a hierarchic design of the service model. The requirements imply a continuous, cyclic operation of a station computer unless an emergency happens. The High Level MSC (HMSC) in Fig. 6 specifies this concept. Intuitively, an HMSC is a graph depicting a *roadmap*, or *flow*, through a set of services. The HMSC in Fig. 6 shows an infinite flow of activities of normal train operation, preempted by exceptional behavior in case of an emergency situation, which needs to be solved after which the situation returns to normal operations. This MSC shows how we model infinite flows of behavior, hierarchic MSCs and preemptive behavior; we introduce each of these aspects now in more detail. Our notation allows us to specify preemptive behavior based on the occurrence of a preemptive message (indicated on the dashed arrow) in an interaction. In this case the interaction at the tail end of the dashed arrow is preempted and continues with the interaction referred to at the tip of the dashed arrow; this can be seen as a preemption handler.

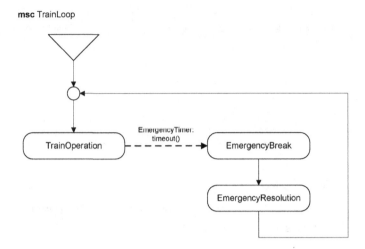

Fig. 6. TrainLoop HMSC for the BART specification

Fig. 7. TrainOperation HMSC for the BART specification

The MSC in Fig. 6 does not yet specify any detailed interaction behavior. MSC references, depicted by the labeled rounded boxes, indicate that more detailed specifications of parts of the behavior are to be found in further MSCs. The functionality for "TrainOperation", referenced in Fig. 6, for instance, is specified in the MSC shown in Fig. 7. This HMSC shows a composition of four services by means of the "join"-Operator, depicted as $\otimes$. The semantics attached to the join of two services is the interleaving of the two behavior specifications, synchronized on common messages.

The *join* operator is a powerful means to combine and synchronize *overlapping* services – this ability to disentangle service specifications is central in our approach. We call services overlapping if they share at least two roles and at least one message between shared roles. *join* synchronizes its operands on shared messages, while imposing no ordering on all others; in other words, a join is the parallel composition of its operands, with the restriction that the operands synchronize on shared messages. Interactions that are shared in both services will occur only once in the resulting service. This means that all interactions causally before a shared interaction within *both* services must have occurred before the shared interaction can itself happen. The *join* operator does not change the order of interactions in any of the operands. It only restricts the occurrence of shared messages. For a formal definition of the join semantics, see [10,14].

In general, the operators available in HMSCs are as follows:

– **Sequence**, by connecting two MSC references with an arrow. This operator expresses that the behaviorat the tail end of the arrow precedes the behavior at the tip of the arrow.
– **Non-deterministic choice** is indicated by means of multiple paths leading out of a reference (or a small circle, used for graphical convenience). At execution time the path to follow is chosen nondeterministically.
– **Join***, represented by $\otimes$, which joins two or more services as described above.
– **Parallel**, which represents the interleaving of its operands.
– **Preemption***; the preemptive message (or set of messages) is indicated as a label to the dashed arrow. The service at the tail of the arrow is preempted if and when the preemptive message occurs; in that event, the execution of the service at the tip of the arrow commences.

Operators marked by * are extensions of the MSC standard. All operators have a precisely defined semantics, which is given in detail in [10]. HMSCs can be transformed into Basic MSCs by applying the algorithm given in [10]. This algorithm transforms an HMSC into a finite state automaton. Subsequently, using the well-known algorithm for translating finite state machines into regular expressions, this automaton is transformed into an expression using only basic interactions (message exchanges) and operators for Basic MSCs. Therefore, in our methodology we do not distinguish between HMSCs and Basic MSCs.

Fig. 8 shows the specification of the functionality of a train sending current status values to the nearest station, processing this information. This specification uses the syntax of an extended Basic MSC, which shows an interaction among roles. Messages are depicted as horizontal arrows between two roles (represented as vertical axes labeled with the name of the role). Messages can have parameters to indicate transmission of data values. The roles visible in this diagram are a subset of the roles of the entire system. Furthermore, some of the

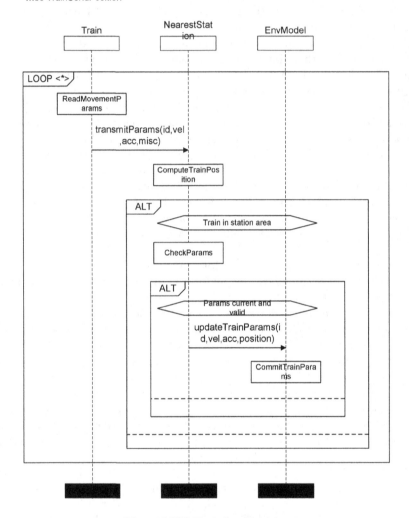

Fig. 8. MSC TrainSendPosition

roles are specializations of previously introduced roles. The role *NearestStation*, for instance, is a specialization of the *Station* role, which represents the external interface of a station computer for interactions. *NearestStation* represents the station computer of the station, in whose area of responsibility the train currently is. How this distinction is implemented, is irrelevant at this level of abstraction. The *EnvModel* role in this MSC represents an entity responsible for managing all data related to conditions in the environment of a station. Fig. 5 shows the dependencies of roles in the role domain model.

We make use of MSC operators, depicted as labeled boxes, to express repetition and choice in the interaction flow. The $LOOP< * >$ box around all the interactions in the MSC expresses repetitive behavior. In our case we are interested in specifying an infinite loop of interactions for activities required to submit a train's position to the responsible station. The *ALT* boxes indicate alternative or optional behavior. Different alternatives are separated by horizontal dashed lines through the box. To indicate optional behavior, we leave one of the alternatives empty. By means of state markers at the top of each compartment we indicate the conditions determining which alternative is chosen. In Fig. 8, a station only processes a train's information if the train is in the station's area of responsibility.

In general, we use the following operators in Basic MSCs:

- **ALT** to express choice, guarded by conditions. If conditions are omitted, the choice between the alternatives is non-deterministic.
- **LOOP** to express repetitive behavior. Loops can be limited to a certain number of repetitions, can be infinite or or can be guarded by a loop condition. If the loop condition is true, the interaction behavior in the box will occur.
- **PAR** to express interleaving. The interactions in both compartments occur independently of one another.
- **JOIN*** to express interleaved composition synchronized on common messages. Common messages are equally named messages between the same two roles.
- **PREEMPT*** to express preemptive behavior. The behavior in the upper compartment is preempted if the specified preemptive message occurs. In this case, the behavior resumes as specification in the lower compartment.
- **TRIGGER*** to express liveness conditions. Whenever the behavior in the upper compartment occurs, it is followed, eventually, by the behavior specified by the lower compartment.

Similar to HMSC operators, all Basic MSC operators marked by * are extensions of the MSC standard. All operators have a precisley defined semantics explained in [10].

We integrate control aspects into reactive interaction specifications by means of *local actions*. Local actions are depicted as labeled boxes on role axes. The meaning of this syntax is that a role performs an activity based on the information available until this point in time. Information can be local variables, data previously received via messages and the role state. The local activity may have a duration, but does not include any communication with other roles while it executes. Activities may change local variables and the role state, which can be used in further interactions or to determine alternative branches of behavior. For instance, the local action *CheckParams* is executed by the role *NearestStation*. The local action can be engineered and implemented independently, given its interface (such as the variables it accesses and controls) is well defined.

ProvideNewCommands (Fig. 9(a)), *SafetyCheckCommands* (Fig. 9(c)) and *ReceiveTrainCommand* (Fig. 9(b)) show other examples of services specified in the BART case study. The *ProvideNewCommands* MSC, for instance, contains the *ComputeTrainCommand* local action. It implements a complex control

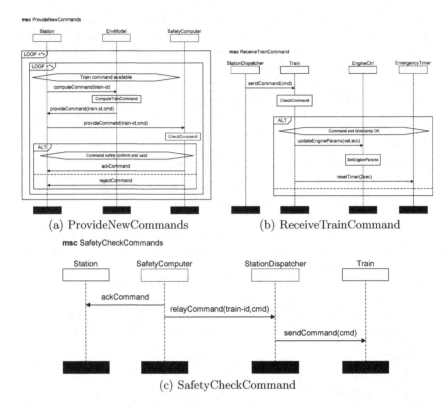

(a) ProvideNewCommands   (b) ReceiveTrainCommand

(c) SafetyCheckCommand

Fig. 9. Some of the BART specification MSCs

algorithm that is based on the position and state of all trains, knowledge of the physical constraints the train is subject to and other requirements, such as the maximization of travelers' comfort. The *TrainSendPosition* MSC guarantees that the data required will be delivered to the *EnvModel* role, and the *Commit-TrainsParams* action persists the data to the role-local state, to be available to the *ComputeTrainCommand* action.

3.3 Mapping the Service Model to Components

The first step in transitioning from a service model with roles and interactions to an implementable architecture is to define the *component types* of the architecture. Component types are blueprints of *component instances* in the architecture. We have to define component types, their communication interfaces to other component types and the services they implement.

It is required that the component model is a refinement of the structural role model introduced above. Fig. 1 shows an example role-to-component mapping for the BART case study.

Table 1. BART Role Mapping

Component Type	Role	Description
FastCPU	Station EnvModel StationDispatcher	A fast CPU computer for operative station control
SlowCPU	SafetyComputer	A slow CPU computer with high reliability (MTBF) used for checking safety conditions
Train	Train TrainMotor EmergenyTimer EngineCtrl	Train computing unit on board of a train
InterlockingSystem	UpdateSrc TrainMotor	The interlocking system, which controls switches and gates

The behavior of the component types can be derived from the service specifications with the following procedure (described in detail in [18]):

1. For each role that a component implements, project the interaction behavior into a state machine. This state machine will be enabled for all incoming messages that the role will receive as part of the interaction, and it will produce all messages that the role is sending. Furthermore, it will implement the local actions and control the role's local variable and control state.
2. Compose all particular role state machines for that component type into a single product state machine. Perform minimization and optimization steps to produce a result with a manageable number of states.

Repeating these two steps for all component types results in state machine specifications for each of the component types. Each component type combines the behaviors of all the services it is involved in according to the role-to-component mapping. These state machine specifications fulfill the reactive behavior specified by the services and perform the required local actions. A concrete algorithm efficiently implementing these steps in the component synthesis algorithm is described in [10,11].

3.4 Defining a Component Architecture

Fig. 10 shows a simple sample architecture, which can implement the service model that we have specified above.

The component architecture shows the structure of the system's components and their connections. Components are instances of a certain component type

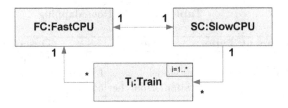

Fig. 10. BART Components Architecture

and can be present multiple times in a system configuration. Each instance has a defined name and a specific type.

3.5   Designing an Efficient Component Architecture Using Services

Our process distinguishes between roles and components, and provides methodological steps to map a set of roles to a component type. An interesting question is how to design the underlying architecture. The process is iterative in nature. This means that the system modeler can start with a high level, simple view of the system through all steps of the development process and later iteratively refine the respective models.

It is important to structure the service model and similarly the component architecture so that they can be extended and modified efficiently, and are also intuitive to understand and communicate. These are basic principles of architecture design. For component architectures we know several structuring patterns and best practices, described, for instance, in [5,3,4,22]. Layered architectures and pipes-and-filters architectures are well-known examples.

For service-oriented architectures, the question of how to structure a service model and its roles arises. In our approach, we basically follow the same proven principles for designing component architectures with extensions required for handling our more powerful model of roles. Roles capture structural dependencies (decomposed subroles, communication links to other roles); in addition, they can also assume a certain state or condition (such as the *NearestStation* or *ConnectedStation* vs. the *Station* roles). One heuristic we apply in modeling roles is to let the structural decomposition be the guiding principle. The arrangement of roles then follows the classic rules of architecture design. Within the structural framework, we allow for a further refinement of roles with guard conditions and the states roles assume. This heuristic works particularly well, in deployment contexts that are component- rather than service-oriented. If the deployment platform supports service implementations, as exemplified by the web services platform, then the structural decomposition need not be the guiding principle – rather, services *are* the components in such platforms; the roles the can be chosen to represent the external interface of the service, i.e. the behavior of the environment in which the service operates.

Another use for roles relating to the specification of complex control systems is to let them represent *operational modes* of components – in the BART example, for instance, we have used this to describe interactions with the "nearest station". These operational roles represent predicates on the state space of the component implementing the respective role in a service execution.

4   Evaluation and Discussion

The service-oriented methodology introduced in this paper enables us to separate system structure and behavior, as well as interaction behavior and control aspects. We model the computations that need to be carried out to fulfill certain environmental constraints (such as the Worst Case Stopping Profile mentioned in the BART requirements specification) as local activities of system entities that produce output conditions and data – provided that sufficient hardware is in place and all required input data is present. Thereby, we abstract from the actual computations while still being able to react to the pertinent system states. This allows us to separate the development of the communication infrastructure, the system level orchestration of components and the development of control algorithms for the various parts of the system.

For instance, in case the system identifies a hazardous condition requiring immediate attention, it transitions into an emergency state that immediately triggers appropriate reactions. All affected trains get immediately notified of the emergency situation and are commanded to perform emergency braking; all surrounding control stations get notified as well. This behavior preempts the regular operation of cyclically computing the appropriate train movement commands and communicating them to the trains.

In presenting this case study, we have shown how to model the recurrent (cyclic), reactive and continuous behavior of the AATC part of the BART system. We have shown how to interface computational results and interaction and state-based behavior of the system. We ave demonstrated how the service-oriented development process can be applied for complex systems that are precisely specified and where extensive safety, convenience and interface constraints need to be met to ensure the reliable, correct operation of the system.

The experience we had in working on the BART case study and on other complex systems, such as in the automotive domain, helped us in refining the service-oriented technique we are developing. To cope with problems where there is a complex control component we developed a way to isolate the control part in local actions of roles. We then just need to guarantee that enough information is available in the role state to enable independent development of the corresponding control algorithms. We found that decomposing the problem using services allows us to focus on the various scenarios separately and address control issues independently by most of the high level system integration effort. Of course, the application of a new service-oriented approach to control problems has the usual drawback of any new methodology: there is a learning curve involved in adopting it. However, we believe that the benefits in tackling complexity that the use of SOA grants is well worth the effort.

The work we have presented in this paper has connections with the work on monitoring end-to-end deadlines we presented in [1] and on the exploration of service-oriented architectures using aspects [13]. In fact, in [1] we used a template-based code generation technique to create code that monitors the deadlines in an implementation of a distributed system starting from a service-oriented specification. The code generator inserts ad-hoc calls to procedures implemented independently by the specific system to verify message deadline expirations. A similar approach can cater to our control problem by calling procedures explicitly named in local actions. The aspect-oriented approach described in [13] converts services to aspects (using AspectJ), defines a component architecture using classes and weaves the aspects into an executable that can be used to evaluate different architectures. This aspect-oriented approach can be used to weave implementations for the control parts into the interaction-oriented framework derived from the service specifications as illustrated in this paper.

5   Related Work

Our approach is related to the Model-Driven Architecture (MDA) [19] and architecture-centric software development (ACD) [23]; similar to MDA and ACD we also separate the software architecture into abstract and concrete models. In contrast to MDA and ACD, however, we consider services and their defining interaction patterns as first-class modeling elements of *both* the abstract and the concrete models. Furthermore, we do not apply a transformation from abstract to concrete models. Our work is related to the work of Batory et al [20]; we also identify collaborations as important elements of system design and reuse. Our approach, in particular, makes use of MSCs as the notation for interaction patterns and is independent from any programming language constructs.

Often, the notion of service-oriented architectures is identified with technical infrastructures for *implementing* services, including the popular web-services infrastructure [21]. Our work, in contrast, supports *finding* the services that can later be exposed either as web-services, or implemented as "internal" services of the system under consideration. Because our entire approach is interaction-based it is perfectly general with respect to the types of architectures we can model.

In contrast to [6], we associate the hybrid behavior with local actions rather than with local states of the roles; this enables us to reuse the automaton synthesis algorithms we have developed in [11] almost verbatim – we just have to introduce transition annotations to represent the calls to the evaluation functions for the control functions.

6   Summary and Outlook

We have applied a service-oriented development process and corresponding notations to a portion of the BART system as a case study, demonstrating the applicability of our methodology to this domain area as well as the power of our approach to manage the complexity of this distributed, reactive system. In the paper we have addressed the problem of creating a service-oriented architecture using a suitable specification language, to describe systems where distributed control is required. Using our interaction-oriented service notion we were able to disentangle the concerns of describing the interactions between entities in the system and the development of control strategies for the various entities. We found our technique to be successful in tackling the complexity of the system class we have explored.

As future work mention updating the existing tools to support a complete and automated development approach for service-oriented systems with substantial control parts, following the process outlined in this paper.

Acknowledgments

Our work was partially supported by the UC Discovery Grant and the Industry-University Cooperative Research Program, as well as by funds from the California Institute for Telecommunications and Information Technology (Calit2). Further funds were provided by the Deutsche Forschungsgemeinschaft (DFG) within the project *InServe*. We are grateful to Roshni Malani for her comments on an earlier version of our case study.

References

1. J. Ahluwalia, I. Krüger, M. Meisinger, and W. Phillips. Model-Based Run-Time Monitoring of End-to-End Deadlines. In *Proceedings of the Conference on Embedded Systems Software (EMSOFT)*, 2005.
2. M. S. Branicky. Introduction to hybrid systems. *Handbook of Networked and Embedded Control Systems*, pages 91–116, 2005.
3. F. Buschmann, R. Meunier, H. Rohnert, P. Sommerlad, and M. Stal. *A System of Patterns. Pattern-Oriented Software Architecture*. Wiley, 1996.
4. M. Fowler. *Patterns of Enterprise Application Architecture*. Addison-Wesley, 2002.
5. E. Gamma, R. Helm, R. Johnson, and J. Vlissides. *Design Patterns. Elements of Reusable Object-Oriented Software*. Addison-Wesley, 1995.
6. R. Grosu, I. Krüger, and T. Stauner. Hybrid Sequence Charts. In *In Proceedings of the 3rd IEEE International Symposium on Object-Oriented Real-Time Distributed Computing (ISORC 2000)*. IEEE, 2000.
7. B. Heck, L. Wills, and G. Vachtsevanos. Software technology for implementing reusable, distributed control systems. *IEEE Control Systems Magazine*, 23(1):21–35, February 2003.
8. ITU-TS. Recommendation Z.120 : Message Sequence Chart (MSC). Geneva, 1996.
9. F. Kordon and L. Michel, editors. *Formal Methods for Embedded Distributed Systems*. Springer, 2004.
10. I. Krüger. *Distributed System Design with Message Sequence Charts*. PhD thesis, Technische Universität München, 2000.
11. I. Krüger, R. Grosu, P. Scholz, and M. Broy. From MSCs to Statecharts. In F. J. Rammig, editor, *Distributed and Parallel Embedded Systems*, pages 61–71. Kluwer Academic Publishers, 1999.

12. I. Krüger, R. Mathew, and M. Meisinger. From Scenarios to Aspects: Exploring Product Lines. In *Proceedings of the ICSE 2005 Workshop on Scenarios and State Machines (SCESM)*, 2005.

13. I. Krüger, R. Mathew, and M. Meisinger. Efficient Exploration of Service-Oriented Architectures using Aspects. In *Proceedings of the 28th International Conference on Software Engineering (ICSE)*, 2006.

14. I. H. Krüger. Capturing Overlapping, Triggered, and Preemptive Collaborations Using MSCs. In M. Pezzè, editor, *FASE 2003*, volume 2621 of *LNCS*, pages 387–402. Springer Verlag, 2003.

15. I. H. Krüger and R. Mathew. Systematic Development and Exploration of Service-Oriented Software Architectures. In *Proceedings of the 4th Working IEEE/IFIP Conference on Software Architecture (WICSA)*, pages 177–187. IEEE, 2004.

16. N. G. Leveson. System safety in computer-controlled automotive systems. In *SAE Congress*, March 2000.

17. R. Lim and R. Qu. Control and communication mechanisms in distributed control application platform. In *IEEE International Conference on Industrial Informatics, 2003*, pages 102–106. IEEE, August 2003.

18. R. Mathew and I. H. Krüger. Component synthesis from service specifications. In S. Leue and T. J. Syst, editors, *Scenarios: Models, Transformations and Tools International Workshop, Dagstuhl Castle, Germany, September 7-12, 2003, Revised Selected Papers, Lecture Notes in Computer Science*, volume 3466. Springer, 2005.

19. OMG Model Driven Architecture. http://www.omg.org/mda.

20. Y. Smaragdakis and D. Batory. Implementing Layered Designs with Mixin Layers. In *Proceedings of ECOOP 1998*, volume 1445 of *LNCS*, pages 550–570. Springer Verlag, 1998.

21. J. Snell, D. Tidwell, and P. Kulchenko. *Programming Web Services with SOAP*. O'Reilly, 2002.

22. D. Trowbridge, U. Roxburgh, G. Hohpe, D. Manolescu, and E. Nadhan. *Integration Patterns. Patterns & Practices*. Microsoft Press, 2004.

23. UML 2.0. http://www.omg.org/uml.

24. L. Wills, S. Kannan, B. Heck, G. Vachtsevanos, C. Restrepo, S. Sander, D. Schrage, J.V.R., and J. Prasad. An open software infrastructure for reconfigurable control systems. In *Proceedings of the 2000 American Control Conference. Vol4*, pages 2799–2803, 2000.

25. V. Winter, F. Kordon, and L. Michel. The BART Case Study. In F. Kordon and L. Michel, editors, *Formal Methods for Embedded Distributed Systems*, pages 3–22. Springer, 2004.

Towards Dynamic Partitioning of Reactive System Behavior: A Train Controller Case Study

Victor Winter[1] and Deepak Kapur[2]

[1] Department of Computer Science, University of Nebraska at Omaha
[2] Department of Computer Science, University of New Mexico

Abstract. Based on our investigations of a case study of controllers for train systems [6,7,13,14], we present a model of reactive systems which emphasizes *dynamic* partitioning of system behavior into *normal* and *abnormal*. The class of reactive systems considered are non-strict in the sense that their behavior is not entirely governed by past events; instead, future events must also be considered in the design of controllers for such systems.

1 Overview

Motivated by the increasing complexity and oftentimes critical nature of software-based controllers for reactive systems we have been studying the problem of developing reactive system models and accompanying domain-specific languages suitable for certain classes of reactive systems [6]. Our goal is to develop a framework that facilitates the specification, verification, and transformation-based development of software-based control functions for these reactive systems [13][14]. Towards this end, we have been using the BART Case Study [11] to provide concrete details of a reactive system indicative of the class of reactive systems in which we are interested.

In general, a reactive system can be modelled in terms of a vector of *monitored variables* quantified over a set $\mathcal{M}$ and a vector of *controlled variables* quantified over a set $\mathcal{C}$ [5,10]. The state space of a reactive system can then be defined as the cartesian product of the values of the monitored and controlled variables.

$$State = \{(\vec{m}, \vec{c}) \mid \vec{m} \in \mathcal{M} \land \vec{c} \in \mathcal{C}\} \tag{1}$$

A *transition function* on states is defined capturing how the system state changes in response to changing values of one or more controlled variables and environmental factors. In this context, the *control problem* entails the discovery of a sequence of allowable assignments to the controlled variables such that the resulting system behavior *satisfies* a set of primary requirements, often couched in terms of a safety policy and *optimizes*, to the extent possible, an additional set of secondary requirements such as throughput. Central to the notion of primary and secondary requirements is the notion of conflict. In particular, situations can arise where primary and secondary requirements cannot be satisfied simultaneously. In such situations, primary requirements take precedence over secondary

F. Kordon and J. Sztipanovits (Eds.): Monterey Workshop 2005, LNCS 4322, pp. 47–69, 2007.

requirements. There are two important assumptions that we make in the context of the control problem.

1. The values that can be assigned to controlled variables are capable of realizing a wide range of behaviors, including behaviors that are prohibited from the perspective of secondary requirements. For example, a train may engage its emergency brake when needed to satisfy a primary (safety) requirement (e.g., to avoid a collision). However, a train should never use the emergency brake as a means for satisfying secondary requirements.
2. Environmental events can force the control function to make unexpected changes to the values of one or more controlled variables in order to satisfy a particular set of system requirements (e.g., safety requirements).

Our key observation is that system behaviors should not be treated alike (e.g., a train engaging its emergency brake to avoid a collision vs. a train coming to a gradual halt at a station). Instead, the behaviors should be partitioned into two sets *normal* and *abnormal*. Furthermore, this partitioning should be based on some criterion related to the *expected* behavior of a given reactive system.

The static partitioning of system states is not new and has been used in the design of a variety of systems [12]. However, the contribution of this paper is a definition of partitioning that is (1) behavior-centric rather than state-centric, and (2) is dynamic in nature in the sense that the partition can vary over time.

The rationale for dynamic partitioning is based on the belief that adopting a strictly reactive classification scheme may be too rigid for systems in which nondeterministic events leading to abnormal states are extremely rare and/or the normal behavioral capabilities of the system are significantly restricted. It may be worthwhile instead to consider a dynamic classification scheme (driven by expected system behavior) that enables a greater number of behaviors and thus gives the control function more flexibility in how it can go about satisfying its requirements. In turn, this flexibility may make it possible for the control function to more satisfactorily address competing sets of secondary requirements.

The remainder of the paper is as follows: Section 2 describes a basic domain-specific reactive system model suitable for modelling train systems and defines the notion of feasible train behavior in this setting. Section 3 states the control problem we want to solve and discusses how dynamic partitioning of system behavior impacts the solution to this problem. Section 4 extends the basic system model described in Section 2 so that the control problem must take into account the transmission of messages over an unreliable medium. Section 5 discussed how *message-buffers* may be effectively used to mask the effects of unreliable message transmission. Section 6 discusses the relationship between message-buffers and other nondeterministic events (e.g., an automobile stalled on the track). Section 7 discusses some related work in the area of train acceleration control, and Section 8 concludes.

2   A Basic Domain-Specific Reactive System Model

We are interested in developing reactive system models, of the kind described in the previous section, for train systems having characteristics similar to the BART system [11]. These systems contain a variety of components including a track, switches, signals and stations, and trains.

The train systems under consideration must satisfy a variety of constraints. A primary set of constraints concern themselves with system safety. A secondary set of constraints concern themselves with issues like passenger comfort, minimization of wear and tear on mechanical components, optimization of throughput, and so on. Figure 1 gives an example of the kinds of constraints that influence the behavior of trains within such systems.

Primary Constraints (Safety):

- A train should never get so close to its leading train that if the leading train stops abruptly (e.g., derails) a collision becomes unavoidable.
- A train should stop at signals when told to do so.
- A train should not exceed the speed limit of the track segment on which it is travelling.

Secondary Constraints:

- System throughput should be optimized.
- Large and frequent changes in speed and acceleration should be avoided.
- Changing from acceleration to braking (or vice versa) should be avoided.

Fig. 1. An example of system constraints

2.1   A Description of System Components

A *track* is modelled as a connected acyclic graph having labelled directed edges and whose overall structure has the characteristics of a tree (the in-degree of every node is less-than 2). In this graph, edges correspond to *track segments* and can vary in length, where the length of a track segment is given in some unit of measure (e.g., feet). The nodes and edges in the graph form a relation $\mathcal{R}$ where $(n, e) \in \mathcal{R}$ implies that the node n is the beginning (i.e., the source node) of the directed edge e. Each track segment also has an associated speed denoting the maximum speed a train may travel on the track segment. If a train exceeds the maximum speed of a track segment, its risk of derailment becomes unacceptably high.

For a given track, the directed path taken by a train is determined by *switches*. Switches are the mechanism used to route trains to particular destinations. In the model, every node may have a corresponding switch. A switch can be in a number of distinct states, and the state of a switch can vary over time. The purpose of the switch is to select, from the set of directed edges associated with the node, that edge which belongs to the directed path the train should follow.

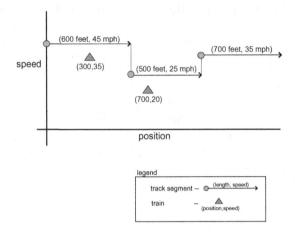

Fig. 2. A projection of trains and route onto a 2-dimensional coordinate system

A *signal* is a mechanism for controlling the flow of trains within a track. For example, if a node on a route has a switch that is in an inappropriate state, a signal can be used to stop a train from passing over this node until the switch is in the proper state. Conceptually speaking, a signal plays a role similar to a traffic light. A signal may be associated with any node in the system whose in-degree is equal-to 1. In the framework presented, a *station* can essentially be modelled as a signal. In reality, stations represent points on the track where a train may stop for the purpose of taking on or letting off passengers.

A *train* is modelled as a point mass (having no length) that travels along the edges of the track. The path followed by a train is called its *route*. In order for a route to be well-formed, it must form a directed path with respect to the layout of the track. For a given route, points along the route are uniquely defined in terms of an absolute 1-dimensional coordinate system (e.g., the x-axis). This enables the position of a train to be unambiguously expressed using a single variable quantified over this coordinate system.

The control problem that we are considering assumes that switches and signals are set by the environment. Because of this assumption we can, without loss of generality, view the track as consisting of a single route. For such a route, a *train state* is modelled by a triple of the form *(position,speed,acceleration)*. The diagram in Figure 2 is a projection of two train states, onto a 2-dimensional coordinate system. The x-axis represents position and the y-axis represents speed (acceleration information is not present in the projection). We would like to point out that in Figure 2, the speed attribute of track segments is displayed as a (discontinuous) step function. In order to remain is a safe state, the speed of a train must be below this step function.

A *train system* consisting of n trains can now be defined as a tuple of the form:

$$System = (track, train_1, train_2, ..., train_n, signals, stations, switches) \quad (2)$$

In the train systems considered, the relationship between an *object train* and its corresponding *lead train* is of central importance. Specifically, an *object train*, which we denote by OT, is a train whose behavior we are (currently) considering. A *lead train*, which we denote LT, is the train immediately in front of the object train. In general, the behavior of OT can be significantly effected by the behavior of LT. For example, if LT derails then OT may need to take drastic actions to avoid a collision with LT.

2.2   Feasible Train Behavior

In this framework, a train *behavior* is function from time to train states over a given time interval. In the physical world, time is a continuous quantity. However, if one is willing to accept certain behaviorial approximations, time can be modelled in discrete terms. Specifically, one unit of time corresponds to the interval between between two temporally adjacent sense-react steps in the system. For proper values of n, a time interval $t_{1..n}$ can be modelled as a discrete sequence $t_1, t_2, ..., t_n$ where each t_i corresponds to a sense-react step. Given this model of time, a train behavior over a period $t_1, ..., t_n$ can be modelled as a discrete sequence of train states $\langle st_{t_1}, st_{t_2}, ..., st_{t_n} \rangle$. In this model, train state sequences have an implicit notion of time associated with them. In such a sequence, moving from a train state at time t_i to the train state at time t_{i+1} is referred to as a state *transition*. Figure 3 shows the behavior of a train (not to scale) over a period of 8 consecutive sense-react steps.

While it is true that train state sequences can be used to adequately model the salient behavioral characteristics of train, not all such sequences constitute an actual train behavior. For a given physical train system (irrespective of system requirements such as safety, etc.) only a subset of train state sequences are actually *feasible*. In this context, feasibility is determined by a number of factors. These factors can be broadly categorized as (1) basic laws of physics, (2) operational capabilities of the train system, and (3) environmental factors. In order for a train state sequence to be feasible it must be consistent with the aforementioned items. Given a set of system requirements, consistency with respect to these various items can be defined in a conservative manner. For example, the derailment of a train might be modelled as a behavior in which a train comes to

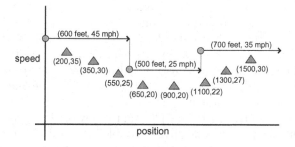

Fig. 3. The behavior of a train (not to scale) over a period of 8 sense-react steps

Basic Laws of Physics

Behavioral Element	Condition	Feasibility	Comment
$(p_1, s_1, a_1), (p_2, s_2, -)$	$p_2 \approx p_1 + s_1 \Delta t + \frac{1}{2} a_1 \Delta t^2$	Feasible	Laws of physics.
$(p_1, s_1, a_1), (p_2, s_2, -)$	$s_1 > 0 \wedge p_1 > p_2$	Infeasible	Train should be moving forward.

Operational Capabilities

Behavioral Element	Condition	Feasibility	Comment
(p, s, a)	$0 < s < MAX\_SPEED$	Feasible	Train motor can cause the train to travel within a certain speed range.
$(p_1, s_1, a_1), (p_2, 0, a_2)$	$a_1 * a_2 < 0$	Infeasible	The acceleration cannot change sign (i.e., mode) without first passing through an acceleration value of zero.

Environmental Factors

$(p_1, s_1, a_1), (p_2, 0, -)$	$p_1 = p_2 \wedge s_1 = 40\ mph$	Feasible	A derailed train can instantly halt.
(p, s, a)	$s < 0$	Infeasible	Environmental factors cannot cause a train to move backwards.

Fig. 4. Examples of feasible and infeasible behaviors

an instantaneous halt – a behavioral approximation with respect to the laws of physics that is driven by safety requirements.

While a completely formal characterization of feasible behavior lies beyond the scope of this paper we nevertheless would like to give the reader a semi-formal understanding of what constitutes feasible behavior. Figure 4 gives some examples of feasible and infeasible behaviors. (Recall that a train state is modelled as a position, speed, acceleration triple (p, s, a).)

When viewed at the system-level, there are a number of additional constraints restricting feasible behavior. For example, the trains travelling along a given route must form a total order, and (during normal behavior) this ordering must be preserved over time. The total ordering constraint implies that an object train cannot move from a position behind its lead train to a position in front of its lead train. The total ordering constraint also implies that trains may not move past a train that has derailed. Thus, all trains enroute behind a derailed train must eventually come to a halt.

We now describe the set of feasible train behaviors in a semi-formal fashion. Let $\mathcal{M}$ denote the position and speed variables of a train state and let $\mathcal{C}$ denote the acceleration variable. In the context of a given train system, a transition function $next : \mathcal{M} \times \mathcal{C} \rightarrow \mathcal{M}$ for an individual is defined that models how a train state changes, under ideal circumstances, from one sense-react step to the next. The function *next* accounts for all train behaviors that respect the laws of physics as well as the operational capabilities of the train. However, *next* does not account for behaviors resulting from environmental factors – a deficiency that will be addressed shortly.

Let (p_1, s_1, a_0) denote the initial state of a train and let $\langle a_1, a_2, \ldots, a_k \rangle$ denote a sequence of acceleration values. With the help of the function *next*, we can successively combine train states and acceleration values to generate the following behavioral model:

$$\langle (p_1, s_1, a_1), (p_2, s_2, a_2), \ldots, (p_k, s_k, a_k) \rangle$$

(3)

$$\text{where } \forall i : 0 < i < k \rightarrow next(p_i, s_i, a_i) = (p_{i+1}, s_{i+1})$$

In an ideal setting, the behavior of a train model will be identical to the actual behavior of the corresponding physical train. However, due to a number of environmental factors (e.g., the derailment of a train) the behavior of a model, operating without the benefit of sensor updates, will over time diverge from the behavior of its corresponding physical system. Within the context of our modelling framework, sensor updates can be seen as functions that modify the set of feasible behaviors in a manner that reflects environmental factors. Our definition of the set of feasible behaviors should include this new class of behaviors.

To account for environmental impact on train behavior, we will model environmental factors as a finite set of nondeterministic events: $\Omega = \{e_1, e_2, ..., e_n\}$. The elements of Ω denote explicit kinds of events that we believe the environment is capable of producing (e.g., derailment, positional drift, unexpected blockage of the track, and so on). Each of these events can alter the state of a train in a particular way. Furthermore, combinations of events can take place simultaneously. Thus, a given environmental state $\mathcal{E}nv$ is modelled as a subset of Ω. Environmental states can be given a formal semantics by defining them in terms of a function on train states. Given these assumptions, the set of all possible non-empty environmental conditions can now modelled as $\mathcal{P}(\Omega) - \{\emptyset\}$.

The generation of feasible train behaviors via *next* can now be modified to account for environmental factors as follows:

$$\langle (p_1, s_1, a_1), (p_2, s_2, a_2), \ldots, (p_k, s_k, a_k) \rangle$$

where $\forall i : 0 < i < k \rightarrow \mathcal{E}nv^i(next((p_i, s_i, a_i))) = (p_{i+1}, s_{i+1})$
and where $\mathcal{E}nv^i$ denotes the environmental conditions in effect during the transition from state i to state $i + 1$.

(4)

We can now define the notion of state transition at the system level for a system of n trains as the composition of the state transitions of each individual train.

2.3   Predictive Behavior

In a traditional approach, a train acceleration control function is developed whose goal at every sense-react step is to calculate the acceleration value needed for one (i.e., the very next) state transition. However, under certain circumstances, it is worth considering the consequences of generalizing the acceleration control function so that it calculates and stores the next k state transitions $\langle a_1, a_2, \ldots, a_k \rangle$. In this approach, the control function of an object train can factor in to its control algorithm the sequence of accelerations $\langle a_1, a_2, \ldots, a_k \rangle$ that has been calculated for its lead train. We say that control functions that make use of such future expected behavior are *non-strict* from a strictly reactive viewpoint.

In this section, we are considering a basic system model in which train control functions assign a single value to the acceleration variable of their respective trains during each sense-react step. In Section 4, we consider a variation of the basic train model in which acceleration values must be transmitted to the train over an unreliable medium.

A fundamental question now arises whether such calculations are useful. For trains whose operational capabilities are unrestricted by behavioral requirements (e.g., the emergency brake may be used at any time), the number k of unsupervised steps that a train can make while still preserving safety properties can be increased by simply slowing trains down. Though this comes at the expense of optimizing secondary requirements (e.g., a stopped object train will never collide with its lead train though such a behavior will not satisfy important secondary requirements such as throughput). However, for trains whose operational capabilities are restricted by behavioral requirements (e.g., the emergency brake may only be used under *abnormal* conditions) the impact of pre-computing k state transitions on the optimization of secondary requirements becomes more interesting.

3   The Train Acceleration Control Problem

We are interested in developing software controllers capable of controlling the behavior of trains in systems having the characteristics of the kind described in the previous section. Specifically, we are interested in systems whose properties include:

1. The system contains multiple trains.
2. The state of an individual train can be modelled by a triple of the form (p, s, a) where p, s, and a are variables that respectively denote the position, speed, and acceleration of the train.
3. For a given train, the value of the position and speed variables are provided via sensors and are periodically updated.
4. The acceleration is the only variable that the control function can set.
5. The acceleration variable may only be assigned to a new value in a periodic fashion.
6. At all times, train behavior must satisfy a set of primary requirements (i.e., a safety policy).
7. Train behavior should strive to optimize a set of secondary requirements.

The *train acceleration control problem* described above is a classic example of a reactive control problem. In this problem, the position and speed variables of a train state are the *monitored variables*, and the acceleration variable is the *controlled variable* or *actuator*. The value of a monitored variable is periodically updated using information obtained from sensors, and the value of a controlled variable is periodically updated with values computed by a control function. All updates occur during a cyclic process known as a *sense-react step*. A sense-react step can be decomposed into two parts: a sense step and a react step. During the sense step, monitored variables are updated using information obtained from various sensors, and during the react step, controlled variables are updated with values resulting from various computations.

In Figure 5, an interaction diagram is given, in the UML, showing the flow of information between a train, its corresponding control function, and the rest of the system (e.g., other trains). In our model, we assume each train has a corresponding control function which accepts as input a relevant description of the system state, performs some calculations, and then transmits a message to its corresponding train. The content of these messages control the behavior of the train.

In most reactive systems, it is tacitly assumed that the delay between the sense-step and the react-step is negligible and that a sense-react step can therefore be treated as a single point in time. In our framework, we also make this assumption.

The train acceleration control problem assumes that switches and signals are a benign part of the environment. Specifically, it is assumed that the environment sets switches and signals in a manner that does not prohibit a train from satisfying a given set of objectives (e.g., a train should travel on a particular route and satisfy a variety of safety properties).

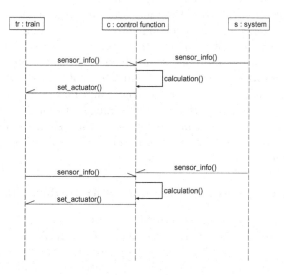

Fig. 5. An interaction diagram showing the flow of information between a train, its corresponding control function, and the rest of the system

Given the above assumptions and by making use of the function $\mathcal{E}nv^i \circ next$, introduced in Section 2.2, the acceleration control problem for a single train can be reduced to a search problem whose goal is to find a sequence of acceleration values $\langle a_1, a_2, \ldots, a_k \rangle$ realizing a feasible train behavior over a given time interval that satisfies a given set of properties under the set of environmental conditions $\mathcal{P}(\Omega)$.

3.1 A State-Centric Partitioning of Train Behavior

In the BART system, maximum braking is achieved using *open-loop* braking and non-maximum braking is achieved using *closed-loop* braking [11]. Influenced by this paradigm, we are interested in solving the train acceleration control problem for trains having two braking capabilities – the first braking capability is to be used under normal conditions and the second braking capability is to be used (exclusively) in emergency situations and then only when absolutely necessary. As a result, we assume the following assumption and constraint holds for the class of train system we considering.

Assumption 1. *The distance it takes a train to come to a full stop is significantly shorter when using the train's maximum braking capabilities than it is when using the train's normal braking capabilities.*

Constraint 1. *Use of a train's maximum braking capabilities should be avoided and should be reserved only for emergency situations.*

The constraint above results in a fundamental shift in how one views train states and train behavior. In particular, it suggests that train behaviors should be partitioned into two sets, which we will call *normal* and *abnormal*. Maximum braking may not be employed in the context of *normal* behaviors. Thus, all train states having acceleration values belonging to the set of maximum braking values may only be an element of an *abnormal* behavior. We refer to this state-based determination of normal and abnormal behavior as being *state-centric*.

A system of trains is considered to be in a normal behavior if all of its trains are exhibiting normal behavior. Under what conditions then can a train system transition from a normal behavior to an abnormal behavior? We believe that it is only in response to a nondeterministic event that a system should be permitted to (as a last resort) transition to an abnormal behavior – a behavioral context in which maximum braking is permitted.

3.2 A Behavior-Centric Partitioning of Train Behavior

The basic partitioning scheme described in Section 3.1 is static in nature: maximum braking indicates an abnormal behavioral context. According to the safety constraint given in Section 3.1, a transition from a normal system behavior to an abnormal system behavior may only be initiated by a nondeterministic event (e.g., an object train engages its emergency brake in response to the derailment of its lead train).

In this paper we propose using a dynamic partitioning scheme to define the conditions under which a system is permitted to transition from a normal behavior to an abnormal behavior. The main objective of a dynamic partitioning scheme is to create a model in which there is more flexibility with respect to the normal/abnormal transition. In practice, there are a number of reasons why it may be beneficial to take a more refined view of the partitioning of train accelerations and their implied behaviors. For example, in a train system where trains have a wide range of diverse acceleration capabilities it may be possible to exercise a more optimal control over train behavior using a dynamic partitioning scheme. Such a heterogeneous system of trains is implicitly suggested in [3]. Similar conclusions may also be drawn for systems in which train behavior is dependent upon an unreliable transmission medium – an issue which is discussed in detail in Section 4.

In a dynamic partitioning scheme, abnormal conditions can be inferred from certain train behaviors, that would otherwise be considered normal. As a result, this type of partitioning can be viewed as being *behavior-centric*. The intuition behind this perspective is that, in a dynamic partitioning scheme, trains advertise a portion of their intended future behavior. The control function of one train (an object train) can then factor the advertised behavior of another train (a lead train) into its behaviorial calculations. Deviations from an advertised behavior should only be permitted in response to a forcing nondeterministic event which, in turn, provide the justification for the allowing system to transition into an abnormal state.

We propose a control framework where *message-buffers* are used to implement sequences of acceleration commands. Specifically, the contents of a message-buffer contains acceleration commands that a train is expected to carry out in the future. A more detailed discussion of message-buffers is given in Section 5.

The behavioral dependency of one train on the message-buffer of another raises a question as to the assumptions underlying message-buffer changes. In particular, how can message-buffer contents be changed in such a way that safety properties are not violated? In Section 5.1 a message-buffer change policy is described that is based on the notion of refinement. This policy defines conditions that are necessary for message-buffer changes to satisfy our safety policy.

4   System Architecture

In this paper, we consider a system architecture where the computational resources of the system are centrally located. In particular, control functions do not reside on the trains themselves. As a result, sensor information and actuator commands must be transmitted respectively from the train and the system to the control function and from the control function to the train. It is worth mentioning that from the perspective of the control function, the decoupling of a train from its controller only needs to be modelled only if, in the physical system, the transmission of messages is not reliable (e.g., message transmissions are missed from time to time).

4.1   An Analysis of the Effects of Unreliable Transmission

In a reactive system, there is a limit to the number of transitions that a system can make without receiving new sensor information. (If such a limit did not exist, the system would not be reactive.) We use the term *predictive_capability* to refer to this limit. In practice, this limit is determined by the ability of the system to satisfy a set of constraints. For example, a train may need to stop at a particular signal. A train should not exceed the speed limit of the track segment on which it is travelling, and so on. By definition then, the predictive capability of a state in a reactive system is the number of unsupervised transitions that may be made from this state while still guaranteeing that a given set of constraints are satisfied. We are interested in a control function that yields train behaviors in which each state in the behavior has a predictive capability that equals or exceeds a globally defined predictive_capability value.

Figure 6 shows the behavior of a train (not to scale) as it moves from a track segment having a maximum speed of 45 mph to a track segment having a

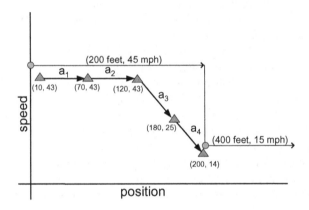

Fig. 6. Optimal deceleration (not to scale) under error-free transmission

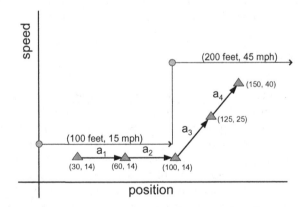

Fig. 7. Optimal acceleration (not to scale) under error-free transmission

maximum speed of 15 mph. In this figure, the transmission of actuator commands is assumed to be error-free. As a result, the control function is able issue the actuator commands a_1, a_2, a_3, and a_4 respectively during the sense-react steps occurring at times t_1, t_2, t_3, and t_4. Thus, the train slows down "just in time" as it enters the track segment whose maximum speed limit is 15 mph. Figure 7 is similar to Figure 6 and shows an optimal acceleration as a train enters a new track segment whose maximum speed limit is greater than the maximum speed limit of the track segment on which the train is currently travelling.

For systems in which a control function must transmit a message to the entity it controls (e.g., a train), the loss of a message due to transmission noise results in a situation where the entity is forced to make an unsupervised transition. Similarly, the loss of a second message would force the entity to make a second unsupervised transition. The impact of an environment, in which transmission is unreliable, on a traditional control function is that it constrains the behavioral space of the entity. In other words, one way for a control function to compensate for transmission noise is to compute behaviors that are more conservative.

In the case where the entity is a train, the control function needs to command the train to slow down earlier than would be the case if the transmission was error-free. However, simply computing such anticipatory behaviors is not sufficient to address the effects of unreliable transmission. A decision must be made as to the value of an actuator during an unsupervised transition. A superficial analysis may suggest that the value of an actuator during an unsupervised transition should simply be a repetition of the most recent value that had been assigned to the actuator. However, further analysis shows that such an approach (even if physically possible) leads to behaviors that are extremely conservative. Furthermore, if control messages are frequently lost, such a model can also lead to erratic train behavior.

A second possibility is to set the value of an actuator to some "neutral" value during unsupervised transitions. The determination of what value is neutral is highly dependent on the set of properties (e.g., safety properties) that the system should satisfy. For example, in the context of the train acceleration control problem, an acceleration value of 0 that might arguably be considered neutral. However, this neutral value leads to extremely conservative behavior. Suppose one is considering a train system where 1 in n messages is guaranteed to arrive. Furthermore, let us assume that one message may be sent during each sense-react step. Under such an assumption, a worst-case analysis shows that it will take control function n sense-react steps to achieve what would otherwise be achieved in a single-sense react step. In general then, this approach will yield train behaviors that are "stretched" by a factor of n.

A third possibility is to modify the content of the message sent by the control function. One possibility is to have the control function send messages of the form (*next_acceleration,final_speed*) where *next_acceleration* is the value to which the actuator should be set and *final_speed* is the final speed the train should reach. After reaching the *final_speed* the train should then make adjustments to its acceleration, independently from the control function in order to maintain this speed.

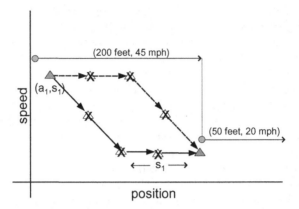

Fig. 8. A scenario (not to scale) where anticipatory messages are used to mitigate unreliable transmission

It is worth noting that complex messages like (*next_acceleration,final_speed*) require that the train itself be given some control intelligence. It is this intelligence then that allows the train to undertake unsupervised transitions.

While messages of the form (*next_acceleration,final_speed*) represent a significant improvement over the previously mentioned alternatives, they nevertheless still result in behaviors that are overly conservative. For example, suppose we have system where it is guaranteed that at least 1 in 4 messages will arrive (i.e., if a message is sent during the course of four consecutive transmissions, we assume it has arrived). To simplify the discussion, let us further assume that the transmission of sensor information to the control function is error-free. Thus, in this setting the notion of transmission noise only applies to messages sent by the control function. Figure 8, shows a scenario (not to scale) that highlights the nature of the conservative behaviorial approximation. To mitigate the effects of unreliable transmission the control function anticipates reductions in track speed limits and sends messages early. If the message is received after its first transmission the train reduces in speed resulting in a behavior whose throughput is not optimal.

4.2 The Relationship Between Predictive_Capability and Transmission Reliability

The model that best captures transmission reliability is dependent on a number of domain-specific assumptions. Reasonable models might include binomial or poisson distributions. An important factor that must be considered is the number of message transmissions that an acceleration command is dependent upon. For example, a control function for a given train OT will need information about (1) the state of OT, and (2) the state of the train LT that is immediately in front of OT. A control function may also be dependent on other information such as the current state of various signals in the system.

Let us assume that the type of information mentioned in the previous paragraph is transmitted in several distinct messages. It is worth mentioning that if any of these messages fails to arrive, the acceleration control function will be unable to compute the next acceleration command. The point here is that the relationship between transmission reliability and predictive_capability (as defined in Section 4.1) is nontrivial. In contrast, the decision on how a train should respond to missed message is a binary one. That is, in response to a missed message, a train either believes that it has enough information to make a given unsupervised transition under normal conditions or it believes that the missed message has transitioned the train into an abnormal state, in which case the train engages its emergency brake.

A detailed analysis of the issues mentioned in the previous paragraphs lies beyond the scope of this paper. For our purposes, it suffices to assume that the abstraction provided by the predictive_capability captures all of the issues mentioned.

5 Using Message Buffers to Mask the Effects of Unreliable Transmission

We present a solution to the train acceleration control problem for a system of the kind described in Section 4 where the transmission of messages, both to and from the control function, is not reliable, and where reliability is indirectly captured by the value of *predictive_capability* for the system. The solution presented here extends a solution we have developed for a similar system in which transmission was assumed to be 100% reliable [14]. The extension makes use of a *message buffer* that resides on a train and stores expected future actuator commands. Messages are computed by the control function after the proper sensor information has been received. A computed message consists of a sequence of actuator commands that the train should carry out over a given time interval. For example, if the current time is t_{i+1}, then a message would contain acceleration commands for the times $t_{i+1}, ..., t_{i+k}$ where k is the predictive_capability of the system.

In the general case, during each sense-react step a train consumes the next actuator command from its message buffer and carries out the command. An exceptional condition is reached when an attempt is made to consume an actuator command from an empty message buffer. This condition transitions the system into an abnormal state and the train initiates an emergency stop sequence.

Messages are transmitted during every sense-react step in which a control function has received sufficient sensor information to compute a message. In the expected case, this usually means that a message will be transmitted and received every sense-react step. Note that there is a significant amount of redundancy that exists between a message m_i sent at time t_i and a message m_{i+1} sent at time t_{i+1}. It is this redundancy that is the mechanism used to mask the effects of unreliable transmission. The basic principle here is that if one can assume that under normal conditions 1 in n messages will arrive, then if one sends an acceleration command n times then, under normal conditions, it will arrive.

Message buffers are overwritten with the contents of newly arriving messages. However, it is important that such overwriting yield a new buffer whose contents *refines* the previous buffer contents; otherwise safety violations can result.

An important property of our solution is that it is able to handle a message arrival model that is *non-uniform*. By this we mean that, during a message broadcast associated with a given sense-react step, some trains may receive messages while messages to other trains may be lost.

5.1   Message Refinement

In our framework, a control function can be abstractly viewed as a function that computes a sequence of messages $m_1, m_2, m_3, ..., m_n$. Given a non-uniform message arrival model, the message sequence computed by the control function must satisfy certain properties in order to assure that safety properties are satisfied. In particular, let b_i denote the contents of a train's message buffer at time t_i and let m_i denote a message that has been sent to the train at time t_i. In our model, the contents of the train's message buffer will be overwritten by m_i. We will show that $b_i \sqsubseteq m_i$ (for the definition of $\sqsubseteq$ given below) is necessary to assure that safety properties are satisfied.

In the discussion that follows, we write $\langle a_{i+1}, a_{i+2}, ..., a_{i+n} \rangle$ to denote a sequence of acceleration commands to be carried out at times $t_{i+1}, t_{i+2}..., t_{i+n}$. Sequences of acceleration commands are used to model both messages sent from control functions to trains as well as the contents of a train's message buffer. In this context, we use the symbol E to denote the emergency stop sequence. We also use Greek symbols, such as α and β, to denote sequences consisting of 0 or more acceleration commands. We now define refinement as follows:

Definition 1. $\forall \alpha, \beta : \alpha \sqsubseteq \alpha\beta$

Definition 2. $\forall \alpha, \beta : \alpha\beta \sqsubseteq \alpha E$

Definition 1 states that extending sequences of acceleration commands constitutes a refinement. Definition 2 states that the truncated form of a message extended with the emergency stop sequence also constitutes a refinement.

In this setting, we will show that if one permits messages to overwrite the contents of message buffers in a manner that is not consistent with $\sqsubseteq$, then it becomes possible to reach system states where safety properties are violated. An example of such a state is one where there exists a train that cannot avoid a collision with its lead train should the lead train derail.

Let $eval : train\_state * sequence \rightarrow behavior$ denote a function that takes a train state and a sequence of acceleration commands as input and returns a sequence of train states as its output. Let st^1 and st^2 denote the states of two distinct trains, and let seq_1 and seq_2 denote two sequences of acceleration commands. We write $safe(eval(st^1, seq_1), eval(st^2, seq_2))$ to denote that the behavior $eval(st^1, seq_1)$ is safe with respect to the behavior $eval(st^2, seq_2)$. If we assume that the train behaviors that are compared by the *safe* predicate begin with initial states that are safe (e.g., a lead train is in front of its object train), then without loss of generality the arguments to *safe* may be commuted. That is, $safe(A, B) = safe(B, A)$.

As as aside, we would like the reader to note that, due to the effects of unreliable transmission, it is possible for a situation to arise where every move in a message buffer is completed (i.e., the message buffer becomes empty) before a new message arrives. Along similar lines, a non-uniform message arrival model will give rise to situations where the message buffer of one train is overwritten by a sequence of acceleration commands from a newly arriving message while another train must carry out acceleration commands belonging to an older message that was received sometime in the past. It is precisely because of these issues that unsafe conditions can arise if messages do not refine the contents of message buffers.

Theorem 1. *Let st_i^X, b_i^X, and m_i^X respectively denote the state, non-empty message buffer, and current message (computed by the control function) for train X. Our refinement theorem can then be stated as follows:*

$$\forall\ st_i^X, b_i^X, \exists\ m_i^X, st_i^Y, b_i^Y, m_i^Y\ :$$

$$b_i^X \not\sqsubseteq m_i^X \wedge$$
$$safe(eval(st_i^X, b_i^X), eval(st_i^Y, b_i^Y)) \wedge$$
$$safe(eval(st_i^X, m_i^X), eval(st_i^Y, m_i^Y)) \wedge$$
$$\neg safe(eval(st_i^X, m_i^X), eval(st_i^Y, b_i^Y))$$

Proof

1. **Case 1:** m_i^X implies a behavior that is faster than that implied by b_i^X.
   (a) In this case, let X denote the object train and Y denote its lead train.
   (b) Choose st_i^Y and b_i^Y in such a manner that the behavior implied by b_i^X is optimal (from the perspective of speed) with respect to the behavior implied by b_i^Y. From this it follows that $\neg safe(eval(st_i^X, m_i^X), eval(st_i^Y, b_i^Y))$.
   (c) Now choose m_i^Y in such a manner that $safe(eval(st_i^X, m_i^X), eval(st_i^Y, m_i^Y))$ holds.
   (d) Suppose conditions exist such that the control functions for X and Y respectively compute the messages m_i^X and m_i^Y.
   (e) Further suppose, that X receives the message m_i^X but Y does not receive its corresponding message m_i^Y. Q.E.D.
2. **Case 2:** m_i^X implies a behavior that is slower than that implied by b_i^X.
   (a) In this case, let Y denote the object train and X denote the lead train.
   (b) Choose st_i^Y and b_i^Y in such a manner that the behavior of b_i^Y is optimal (from the perspective of speed) with respect to the behavior implied by b_i^X. From this it follows that $\neg safe(eval(st_i^X, m_i^X), eval(st_i^Y, b_i^Y))$.
   (c) Now choose m_i^Y in such a manner that $safe(eval(st_i^X, m_i^X), eval(st_i^Y, m_i^Y))$ holds.
   (d) Suppose conditions exist such that the control functions for X and Y respectively compute the messages m_i^X and m_i^Y.

(e) Further suppose, that X receives the message m_i^X but Y does not receive its corresponding message m_i^Y. Q.E.D.

Corollary 1. $\forall\, b_i, m_i, m_{i+1} : b_i \sqsubseteq m_i \rightarrow m_i \sqsubseteq m_{i+1}$

6   Message Buffers and "other" Nondeterministic Events

Section 5 discussed how message buffers can be used to mask the effects of unreliable transmission – a source of nondeterminism. In this section we take a look at the interaction between message buffers and other sources of nondeterminism in the system. The major issue that we are concerned with here is a situation where there is a forced reduction in the speed of a lead train. Such a reduction in speed can be abrupt in the case of a derailment, or somewhat abrupt in the case of an emergency brake, or may simply represent a deviation from the behavior implied by the acceleration commands belonging to a previous message buffer (e.g., an automobile is stalled on the track and the operator of the lead train brings the train to a gradual halt). In all cases a forced reduction in speed has, as its root cause, a nondeterministic event. Thus, the system is transitioned into an abnormal state where the message buffer of the object train can be refined by emergency brake commands if need be.

Figure 9 highlights the properties that a message buffer-based behavior of an object train OT must satisfy in order to assure that safety properties are met. Specifically, it must be the case that after carrying out all the acceleration commands in the message buffer the object train will be in a state where an emergency brake brings it to a halt at a position that is behind the last known position of the lead train LT. Recall that the unreliable nature of the message transmission implies that situations can arise where every acceleration command in the message buffer of the object train is carried out before a new message

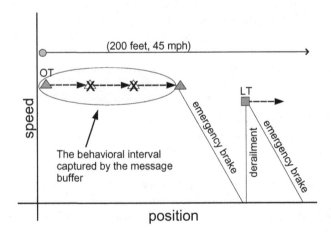

Fig. 9. The relationship between a message buffer, the emergency brake, and nondeterministic events

arrives. If, at this time, a new message does not arrive the object train initiates an emergency brake. On the other hand it is possible, under abnormal conditions, for the newly arriving message to itself contain an emergency brake command. In either case, a collision with the lead train will be avoided and the transition to an abnormal system state was the result of a nondeterministic event.

7   Related Work

Over the years, a variety of techniques and methodologies have been applied to the BART case study. The objective of these investigations is to demonstrate how a given technique, combination of techniques, or methodology might be effectively used to address one or more of the challenges faced during the development of BART's train acceleration control function. In such a "proof of concept", it is reasonable to expect that certain simplifications may be made to the BART system requirements. These simplifications typically consist of making modifications to the basic system model or relaxing various constraints. For example, the behavioral model of a train may be simplified or various assumptions about the system (e.g., noisy transmission of messages) may be relaxed or removed.

In [6,7,13,14], we developed a domain-specific language in which it is possible to formally specify train acceleration control functions. In these specifications it is possible to directly express, using specification language primitives, a variety of safety properties that a train behavior must satisfy. This is made possible by modelling various portions of the system in unifying framework called a *profile*. In particular, train behaviors are modelled as profiles, track routes are modelled as profiles, and signals (and stations) are modelled as profiles. The specification language provides an overloaded relational operator $\ll$ on profiles. Using this primitive operator, safety properties can be expressed in terms of boolean expressions involving relational comparisons between profiles. For example, if *pf* denotes the profile of a train and *track* denotes the profile of a track route, then the expression $pf \ll track$ denotes that the speed of the train should never exceed the speed limit of the track segment on which it is travelling.

By providing a concrete semantics for various domain-specific language constructs in ML a framework is created where rewrite rules, whose application is properly controlled, can be used to transform a specification into an executable ML program. In this translation process, a number of transformations can be added for the purpose of optimizing the resultant ML program. These optimizing transformation result in an executable program that is significantly more efficient than its unoptimized counterpart.

To facilitate experimentation we developed a simulator in which the behavior of various train acceleration control functions can be studied. Within the simulator, it is possible to generate a variety of track and signal configurations. A train acceleration control function can be placed within a generated system model and run for a given number of sense-react steps. During the course of simulation, each system state is checked for safety violations against a set of static properties. For example, a train may not exceed the speed limit of the track segment on which it is travelling and an object train may not be in front of its lead train.

In [4], the SCR (Software Cost Reduction) tabular notation is used to formally specify a train acceleration control function. In SCR, a system is modelled in terms of a collection of monitored and controlled variables. Historical system information is modelled through auxiliary variables called *mode classes* and *terms*. In SCR, requirements are organized and managed with the help of dictionaries and tables. Dictionaries describe the various static elements of the system such as: (1) system constants, (2) variable types, (3) variable attributes, and (4) system properties. Tables, on the other hand, are used to describe dependencies between variables. These dependencies are typically in first-order logic. The SCR* Toolset, developed by the NRL, provides a variety of tools that can be used to analyze SCR artifacts.

In [1], techniques based on relational programming are used to develop a train acceleration control function for the BART system. The system is decomposed in an incremental fashion into four major subcomponents: (1) Safety-Stop, (2) Safety-Speed, (3) Smoothness, and (4) Time-Optimization. In contrast to a functional paradigm, the relational nature of the decomposition results in set of system components whose composition can be easily reasoned about.

In [8], a train control function is developed in ADA using the Hierarchical Object-Oriented Design (HOOD) technique. The semantics of the relevant subset of ADA is then developed in a denotational fashion and implemented in Prolog. The result is an ADA interpreter that is capable of executing the train control function. Within the logic framework provided by Prolog, a precondition/postcondition approach to verification is taken to verify that a minimum safe distance between trains is maintained and that the track speed limit is never exceed. Partial evaluation is used to improve the ability of the Prolog system to complete the verification.

In [9], a methodology called the *Evolutionary Methodology* is used to develop a trusted System Requirements Document (SRD) for a train acceleration control function. The methodology consists of an initial specification of the system in UML followed a translation of this specification into Z. Along the way, a variety of V & V activities are performed. The reason for moving from UML to Z is that Z has a formal semantics and there are a variety of tools available for analyzing the consistency and completeness of Z specifications. The Object Constraint Language (OCL) was also considered as a translational target, but at the time of writing, the authors choose Z due to the maturity of its analytical tool set.

In [2], a model-based development language called **L***f***P** (language for prototyping) is used to specify a train control function and verify certain safety properties. **L***f***P** is a graphical Architecture Description Language focusing on embedded distributed systems. Two primary goals of this language are to (1) provide a framework in which software artifacts can be formally verified, and (2) to support automated program generation. Within **L***f***P**, a primary approach to verification is to translate an **L***f***P** specification into a corresponding Data

Decision Diagram (DDD). (DDD's are an extension of Binary Decision Diagrams (BDD) in which non-boolean values can be considered.) Within the framework of DDD's, the set of reachable states can now be explored. Safety properties like *"trains should not collide with one another"* can now be formally verified for a given DDD model. Simplifying assumptions about the train model include a limited set of possible accelerations, and reliable transmission of messages.

In [3], a train system is considered whose system architecture is significantly different from the BART system architecture. In particular, a train system is viewed as a collection of trains which operate in an autonomous fashion. The computational resources needed to control a train are located on the train itself and the track's switching system is made passive (i.e., though steering alone a train can determine which route it will follow). The acceleration control function for the train is dependent on a variety of sensor information which it receives via radio transmission. The proposed train system also has the property that train cars can be connected and disconnected from one another while the train cars are in motion. Thus, trains can have different lengths at different times. Furthermore, in such a model the notion of a train being "too close" to another train is no longer a concern.

8 Conclusion

In this paper we presented a reactive system paradigm where a dynamic state classification scheme is used to identify system states as being either normal or abnormal. This classification of states is driven by the assumption that the range of capabilities permitted when the system is in a normal state is more restricted than when it is in an abnormal state. It is further assumed that system requirements are such that the system should avoid abnormal states.

The dynamic component of our state classification scheme is based on the behavioral context of the system. Specifically, the current state of the system together with the expected future behavior of the system. In this framework, it is assumed that a control function may not transition the system from a normal state to an abnormal state in an unrestricted manner. In particular, control functions must be constructed in such a fashion that departures from expected behavior may only take place when forced to do so by nondeterministic events. Furthermore, the behavior of the system must be such that when a departure from expected behavior occurs, safety properties are nevertheless still maintained.

We demonstrated the ideas of dynamic partitioning by applying them to a train system having characteristics similar to the BART system. A key characteristic of the kind system architecture we considered is that a train acceleration control function exercises control over its train via messages sent over an unreliable medium. The unreliable transmission of messages gives rise to situations where a train is forced to perform state transitions in an unsupervised fashion. In this setting, the primary nondeterministic events responsible for triggering a transition from a normal state to an abnormal state are: (1) a train exceeds its threshold of unsupervised transitions, and (2) a forced reduction in speed (e.g., the response of an object train to the derailment of its lead train).

In this system, message redundancy is used to mitigate the impact of an unreliable medium. Specifically, a message buffer is employed to store the sequence of actuator commands that one would expect the acceleration control function to issue in the future. In this paradigm, safety properties are maintained by assuring that message buffers are only modified in a manner that constitutes a refinement. The definition of refinement is dependent upon what assumptions one is willing to make regarding the transmission medium. In particular, the definition of refinement that we developed assumes that message arrival is non-uniform. That is, during any given sense-react step, some trains may receive their message while message to other trains may be lost.

References

1. F. B. Bastani, V. Reddy, P. Srigiriraju, and I.-L. Yen. Validation of a Relational Program. In V. Winter and S. Bhattacharya, editors, *High Integrity Software*, pages 243–264. Kluwer Academic Publishing, 2001.
2. F. Breant, J.-M. Couvreur, F. Gilliers, F. Kordon, I. Mounier, E. Paviot-Adet, D. Poitrenaud, D. Regep, and G. Sutre. Modeling and verifying behavioral aspects. In F. Kordon and M. Lemoine, editors, *Formal methods for embedded distributed systems : how to master the complexity*. Kluwer Academic Publishing, 2004.
3. J. Gausemeier, J. Berssenbrgge, and V. Binger. Future Potentials of Rail-Based Cargo Transportation for the Courier, Express and Parcel-Market. In *World Congress on Railway Research*, 2001.
4. C. Heitmeyer. Using SCR to Specify the BART Requirements. In V. Winter and S. Bhattacharya, editors, *High Integrity Software*, pages 137–168. Kluwer Academic Publishing, 2001.
5. R. Janicki, D. L. Parnas, and J. Zucker. Tabular representations in relational documents. In *Relational methods in computer science*, pages 184–196, New York, NY, USA, 1997. Springer-Verlag New York, Inc.
6. D. Kapur and V. L. Winter. On the Construction of a Domain Language for a Class of Reactive Systems. In V. Winter and S. Bhattacharya, editors, *High Integrity Software*, pages 169–196. Kluwer Academic Publishing, 2001.
7. D. Kapur, V. L. Winter, and R. S. Berg. Designing a Controller for a Multi-Train Multi-Track System. In C. Zaroliagis, editor, *Electronic Notes in Theoretical Computer Science (ENTCS)*, volume 50:1. Elsevier Science Publishers, 2001.
8. L. King, G. Gupta, and E. Pontelli. Verification of a Controller for BART. In V. Winter and S. Bhattacharya, editors, *High Integrity Software*, pages 137–168. Kluwer Academic Publishing, 2001.
9. M. Lemoine and G. Gaudiere. From UML to Z. In F. Kordon and M. Lemoine, editors, *Formal methods for embedded distributed systems : how to master the complexity*. Kluwer Academic Publishing, 2004.
10. D. L. Parnas and J. Madey. Functional Documentation for Computer Systems Engineering. In *Science of Computer Programming*, volume 25:1. Elsevier, October 1995.

11. V. Winter, F. Kordon, and M. Lemoine. The BART Case Study. In F. Kordon and M. Lemoine, editors, *Formal Methods for Embedded Distributed Systems: How to master the complexity*, pages 3–22. Kluwer Academic Publishing, 2004.

12. V. L. Winter, J. M. Covan, and L. J. Dalton. Assuring Passive Safety in High Consequence Systems. *IEEE Computer*, 31(4):35–36, April 1998.

13. V. L. Winter, D. Kapur, and R. S. Berg. A Refinement-based Approach for Developing Software Controllers for Train Systems. In V. Winter and S. Bhattacharya, editors, *High Integrity Software*, pages 197–240. Kluwer Academic Publishing, 2001.

14. V. L. Winter, D. Kapur, and G. Fuehrer. Formal Specification and Refinement of a Safe Train Control Function. In F. Kordon and M. Lemoine, editors, *Formal methods for embedded distributed systems : how to master the complexity*. Kluwer Academic Publishing, 2004.

The GridLite DREAM: Bringing the Grid to Your Pocket

Chris A. Mattmann[1,2] and Nenad Medvidovic[1]

[1] University of Southern California
Los Angeles, CA 90089, USA
{mattmann, neno}@usc.edu
[2] Jet Propulsion Laboratory, 4800 Oak Grove Drive, M/S 171-264
Pasadena, CA 91109, USA
mattmann@jpl.nasa.gov

Abstract. The emergence of small, mobile, inexpensive computing platforms has made computation possible virtually anywhere, and has opened up countless opportunities for distributed and decentralized collaboration and information sharing among a wide range of actors. The software-intensive systems of today are increasingly shaped by their decentralized, resource-constrained, embedded, autonomic, and mobile (DREAM) computing environments. In this paper we present GridLite, a software architecture-based grid platform suitable for deployment in DREAM environments. Our prototype implementation of GridLite represents an effective and highly efficient marriage of our OODT data grid and Prism-MW architectural middleware solutions. The ultimate goal of GridLite is to extend the reach of the grid all the way to people's "pockets". Our initial experience suggests that this goal is achievable and worthy of further active pursuit.

1   Introduction

The emergence of small, mobile, embedded, inexpensive computing platforms (e.g., PDAs, cell phones, GPS receivers) has made computation possible virtually anywhere. In turn, this has opened up countless possibilities for distributed and decentralized collaboration and information sharing among a wide range of individuals and organizations, including engineers, scientists, health and humanitarian workers, emergency response teams, law enforcement agencies, and average citizens. Fleets of mobile devices are, or will soon be, employed in complex scenarios such as land and sea exploration, environment monitoring, traffic management, fire fighting, and damage surveys in times of natural disaster. The software-intensive systems of today are increasingly shaped by their *decentralized, resource-constrained, embedded, autonomic,* and *mobile* (*DREAM*) computing environments.

In parallel with this development, another exciting and promising direction in modern computing has emerged *the grid.* Grid computing connects dynamic collections of individuals, institutions, and resources to create virtual organizations, which support sharing, discovery, transformation, and distribution of data

F. Kordon and J. Sztipanovits (Eds.): Monterey Workshop 2005, LNCS 4322, pp. 70–87, 2007.

and computational resources. Distributed workflow, massive parallel computation, and knowledge discovery are only some of the applications of the grid. Grid applications involve large numbers of distributed devices executing large numbers of computational and data components. As such, they require techniques and tools for supporting their design, implementation, and dynamic evolution.

The grid has revolutionized the manner in which both computation-intensive and data-intensive software systems are constructed and deployed. The grid paradigm, however, makes a number of limiting assumptions that curtail its adoption, utility, and deployment in the emerging DREAM computing environments. These assumptions include availability of powerful processors, large amounts of memory, capacious and reliable network links, and stability of software systems deployed on the grid. Two independently conducted studies [13,20] to date have indicated that existing grid technologies suffer from several recurring shortcomings, which are particularly magnified in the context of the emerging DREAM environments. We will highlight several of the shortcomings for illustration. First, existing grid solutions are implemented using technologies (e.g., CORBA, Web services) that are unsuitable for DREAM environments. Second, grid protocols (e.g., Grid Resource Allocation Management, GridFTP, Meta Directory Service) require heavy-weight processing and memory resources to poll and monitor nodes in a grid-based system. Third, the grid solutions assume stable network connectivity and bandwidth. Fourth, the topology of a deployed grid-based system is essentially static, and any modification to an existing deployment may require a (manual) restart of the entire system. Finally, the existing grid technologies provide no system design, implementation, deployment, and evolution guidance to their users; instead, they implicitly assume that the users will somehow "figure it out". This is particularly problematic when one considers that the systems deployed on the grid may be highly complex, and that the typical users of the grid (e.g., scientists, health workers) may have no formal training in software development.

While most of the above difficulties may be overcome by engineering more efficient underlying infrastructure, the lack of development guidance for grid-based software systems also requires enriching grid computing with an appropriate body of software development concepts, constructs, principles, and techniques. We believe that the area of *software architecture* [25] provides such a body of knowledge. Software architectures are high-level abstractions for modeling the structure, behavior, and key properties of software systems. These abstractions involve descriptions of elements from which systems are built, interactions among the elements, patterns that guide their composition, and constraints on those patterns. In general, a system is defined as a set of *components* (elements that encapsulate computations and state in a system), *connectors* (elements that embody interactions), and a *configuration* (overall organization of components and connectors). Furthermore, software architectural *styles* are key design idioms that embody best practices in the design of systems in specific domains (e.g., DREAM).

Software architecture plays an important role in our proposed research agenda, as we illustrate throughout the rest of this paper. We will argue for an architecture-based approach to use grid computing as a means of constructing software systems in the DREAM environments. Our position is that, in order to address the afore-mentioned limitations of the grid paradigm, a new type of software solution must be constructed. To that end we propose, and have implemented an early prototype of, *GridLite*, a software architecture-based grid platform suitable for deployment in DREAM environments[19]. GridLite is heavily influenced by, and its early design and implementation directly rely on, our OODT data grid[18] and Prism-MW architectural middleware[17] platforms. The ultimate goal of GridLite is to extend the reach of the grid all the way to people's "pockets".

The remainder of the paper is organized as follows. Section 2 provides the background and related work in the areas of grid computing, software architecture, and the relationship of each to DREAM environments. Section 3 lays out the architecture of GridLite, including its objectives and architectural principles. Section 4 describes and evaluates the current status of the GridLite research and the prototype implementation and infrastructure of GridLite that we have constructed called GLIDE. Section 5 rounds out the paper with our conclusions and an overview of future work.

2   Background and Related Work

Our work on GridLite has been inspired by a set of related projects and draws upon three fundamental areas of research: *computational and data grid computing, light-weight middleware and protocols*, and *implementation support for software architectures*. We discuss GridLite and its relationship to each area below. We then describe representative approaches to large-scale data sharing, with a specific focus on OODT, the grid technology in whose development we have participated and which is used by NASA and the National Cancer Institute. Finally, we summarize Prism-MW, our light-weight middleware platform that explicitly focuses on implementation-level support for software architectures in DREAM environments; we also overview a cross-section of representative light-weight middleware platforms.

2.1   Computational Grid Technologies

The *Globus Toolkit* [7,8] is an open-source, research-off-the-shelf middleware framework for constructing and deploying grid-based software systems. It combines a middleware transport layer (reified in the form of the Simple Object Access Protocol (SOAP)[9]), a suite of Grid-services and protocols (e.g. Grid Resource Allocation Management or GRAM [7], GridFTP[7], and so on) and a web services-based implementation infrastructure for constructing and deploying grid-based software systems using various programming languages, including Java, C++, and Perl.

The adoption of Globus has to date primarily been at the level of scientific and research institutions, although commercial adoption of Globus is currently occurring at IBM, Sun, and Microsoft[4]. In the large, Globus realizes the basic goal of grid systems: the establishment of *virtual organizations* (VOs) sharing computing, data, metadata, and security resources. In the small, however, Globus lacks many of the salient features that would ease its adoption and use across a more widespread family of software systems and environments. These salient features include (1) the marriage of architecture-based software development (which has been shown to facilitate and improve large-scale, distributed software construction), with the great promise and potential provided by the grid and (2) the decoupling of Globus protocols and services, such as GridFTP and GRAM, from their heavyweight origins, File Transfer Protocol (FTP) and Lightweight Directory Access Protocol (LDAP) respectively.

In addition to Globus, several other grid technologies have emerged recently. Alchemi[1] is based on the Microsoft .NET platform and allows developers to aggregate the processing power of many computers into virtual computers. Alchemi is designed for deployment on personal computers: computation cycles are only shared when the computer is idle. JXTA[16] is a framework for developing distributed applications based on a peer-to-peer topology. Its layered architecture provides abstractions of low-level protocols along with services such as host discovery, data sharing, and security.

2.2 Data Grid Technologies

GridLite is directly motivated by our own work in the area of data-grids, specifically on the Object Oriented Data Technology (OODT) system[18]. We have adopted an architecture-centric approach in OODT, in pursuit of supporting distribution, processing, query, discovery, and integration of heterogeneous data located in distributed data sources. Additionally, OODT provides methods for resource description and discovery[14] based on the ISO-11179 data model standard[15], along with the Dublin Core standard for the specification and standardization of data elements[5].

There are several other technologies for large-scale data sharing. Grid Data Farm[10] project is a parallel file system created for researchers in the field of high energy acceleration. Its goal is to federate extremely large numbers of file systems on local PCs and, at the same time, to manage the file replication across those systems, thus creating a single global file system. Similar to OODT, the SDSC Storage Resource Broker[6] is a middleware that provides access to large numbers of heterogeneous data sources. Its query services attempt to retrieve files based on logical information rather than file name or location, in much the same way that OODT maintains profile data.

2.3 Prism-MW

Prism-MW[17] is a middleware platform that provides explicit implementation-level support for software architectures. The key software architectural constructs are *components* (units of computation within a software system), *connectors* (interaction facilities between components such as local or remote method calls, shared variables, message multicast, and so on), and *configurations* (rules governing the arrangements of components and connectors)[22,25]. Prism-MW's core object model consists of several canonical classes allowing for the expression of complex architectures using a well-defined set of architectural primitives. *Brick* is an abstract class that encapsulates common features of its subclasses (*Architecture*, *Component*, and *Connector*). The *Architecture* class records the configuration of its components and connectors, and provides facilities for their addition, removal, and reconnection, possibly at system runtime. A distributed application is implemented as a set of interacting *Architecture* objects, communicating via *DistributionConnectors* across process or machine boundaries. *Components* in an architecture communicate by exchanging *Events*, which are routed by *Connectors*. Finally, Prism-MW associates the *IScaffold* interface with every *Brick*. Scaffolds are used to schedule and dispatch events using a pool of threads in a decoupled manner. *IScaffold* also directly aids architectural self-awareness by allowing the runtime probing of a *Brick*'s behavior.

Prism-MW enables several desired features of software development in DREAM domains. First, it provides the needed low-level middleware services, including decentralization, concurrency, distribution, programming language abstraction, and data marshalling and unmarshalling. Second, unlike the support in current grid-based middleware systems (including OODT), Prism-MW enables the definition and (re)use of architectural styles, thereby providing design guidelines and facilitating reuse of designs across families of DREAM systems. Third, Prism-DE[23], an architecture-based (re-)deployment environment that utilizes Prism-MW, can be extended to aid users in constructing, deploying, and evolving grid-based DREAM systems.

A number of additional middleware technologies exist that support either architectural design or mobile and resource constrained computation, but rarely both [18]. An example of the former is Enterprise Java Beans, a popular commercial technology for creating distributed Java applications. An example of the latter is XMIDDLE[11], an XML-based data sharing framework targeted at mobile environments.

3   The GridLite Architecture

In order to address the above-stated shortcomings of existing grid technologies and bring the grid "to your pocket", a new type of grid must be developed, which we dub "GridLite". GridLite is an adaptable, light-weight grid platform that is equipped with the appropriate support for application design, implementation, deployment, and evolution. To realize GridLite, we have drawn upon our experience in the areas of distributed computing[17], software architecture and in particular its role in DREAM environments[21], and distributed data management[19]. In this section, we describe the architecture of GridLite, including the three key objectives that motivated its separation into three distinct layers. GridLite is a layered solution comprising facilities for software architecture-based application development that leverage a set of core grid services, both of which are

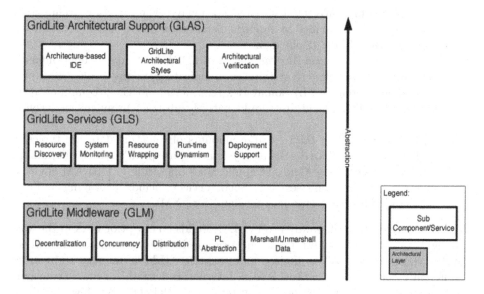

Fig. 1. The GridLite Architecture

implemented on top of a light-weight middleware platform, as depicted in Fig. 1. In the subsequent sections, we will explain each of GridLite's layers (and each layer's relationship to the objectives) in detail.

3.1 Middleware Layer (GLM)

GridLite's architectural objectives were directly inspired by the need to address the aforementioned shortcomings of the grid. To attack the first shortcoming (the current grid technologies' heavy-weight nature), we arrive at the first objective of the GridLite architecture:

Objective 1. (Light-weight) Middleware Support – Create an efficient and adaptable middleware platform to support implementation, deployment, and runtime monitoring and evolution of GridLite systems.

The middleware support in GridLite requires several features including:

1. *Decentralization* – since fleets of mobile devices are highly dynamic and distributed, and since network links are inherently unreliable in DREAM environments, the GridLite architecture should include middleware that directly aids a system's loose-coupling and decentralization.
2. *Concurrency* – grid systems typically involve massive amounts of parallel computation and data distribution. As such, any middleware support for the GridLite architecture needs the ability to support concurrency that takes advantage of the large amounts of hosts and services available.
3. *Distribution* – DREAM environments are characterized by highly mobile, dynamic, and distributed applications, unlike the existing grid environments

which are comparatively stable and stationary. The GridLite architecture needs to have the ability to support distribution at the architectural level, including distributed deployment.

4. *Programming Language Abstraction* – Both DREAM and grid environments typically involve software systems communicating via protocols across programming language (PL) boundaries (e.g., Java and C++ communicating via SOAP). Thus, GridLite should natively abstract away the underlying PL.

5. *(Un-)Marshalling of Data* – Large amounts of scientific data are typically exchanged in grid-based software systems. Consequently, the large amount of data transferred by GridLite applications operating in DREAM environments needs first-class services. Such services include packaging and unpackaging data using standard formats (e.g., XML).

To summarize, the middleware layer (GLM) builds on our prior work in the area of light-weight middleware[17], and encapsulates low-level communication on devices whose connectivity is limited and unstable. GLM is intended to abstract different communication protocols (e.g., Internet, Bluetooth) to enable transparent connections; different operating systems (e.g., PalmOS, WindowsCE, Symbian) to ensure platform portability; and different programming languages (e.g., J2ME, EVC++, Brew) to foster development flexibility and interoperability. GLM should also leverage light-weight software components (e.g., "tiny" XML parsers) to provide application extensibility, resource discovery, and data conversion. Ultimately the GLM layer should provide compatibility with existing grids, extending the reach of grid computing to pocket-sized devices. Design, implementation, and evaluation of GLM have been the early focus of our work on GridLite.

3.2   Services Layer (GLS)

We needed a means of empowering GridLite systems with native, light-weight grid services for use in DREAM environments. From this need was born our second major objective for the GridLite architecture:

Objective 2. Grid Service Development – Support development of an extensible set of grid services (e.g. resource discovery, system monitoring, and so forth).

GridLite requires several key grid services that are provided by the GLS layer. We briefly summarize each of them below:

1. *Resource Discovery* – this service enables GridLite to discover resources in its given deployment environment. A *resource* is defined as a unit of computation (e.g., an object or component), data, metadata, data-producing software, or is a computation-providing system. Resource discovery should support peer-to-peer (see [12]) or client-server based resource discovery.

2. *System Monitoring* – this service will provide the capability of monitoring data and metadata within a GridLite system. Such data has the ability to

shape the way in which a system is configured. We have recently shown[17] that monitoring data can affect a mobile software system's dependability given a particular deployment of its components. The system monitoring service uses both the data and metadata it collects to affect a GridLite software system's deployment providing maximum quality of service.

3. *Resource Wrapping* – this service allows structured retrieval of data from semi-structured resources (e.g., resources that do not necessarily adhere to a single data model and software interface) via the well-known technique of *software wrapping*[26]. In the information integration community this service is offered at the level of returning XML-formatted data from heterogeneous web sites [24].

4. *Run-time Dynamism* – this service is responsible for accepting requests and understanding how to dynamically change a running GridLite software application given its modeled architecture. The service provides an interface for the addition, removal, replacement, and redeployment of running application-level components exported by the GLAS layer above it. Its task includes ensuring component "quiescence" before disconnection, logging requests intended for components that are temporarily unavailable, updating a reinserted component's state before allowing it to engage in interactions with other components in the system, rolling back (i.e., "undoing") changes that cannot be completed because of new system events, and ensuring system integrity throughout this process.

5. *Deployment Support* – this service is responsible for physically distributing both GridLite components (e.g., different GLS components, including the deployment service itself) as well as application components to GridLite-enabled hosts. This service is a consumer of deployment commands from GridLite's GLAS architectural layer.

In summary, the services layer (GLS) encapsulates the lower-level interfaces of GLM into a set of basic GridLite services. The services include discovering resources on the grid (such as data or computation provision), monitoring grid and grid node performance, wrapping structured resources to enable access in a heterogeneous setting, dynamically "morphing" deployed system architectures, and deploying uniform grid software components in the face of different execution platforms. Experience in resource and metadata description[19] and software architectures[17] is necessary to enable GLS to utilize GLM effectively and efficiently.

3.3   Software Architectural Support Layer (GLAS)

The final, and what we would argue to be the most important, limitation of existing grid systems is the lack of any (native) support for architectural abstractions and their relationship to a grid-based software system's implementation. This issue has been identified by two independently conducted studies [13,20], and has directly motivated our third objective with the GridLite architecture:

Objective 3. Software Architectural Support – Formulate a set of software architectural principles for constructing GridLite-based applications.

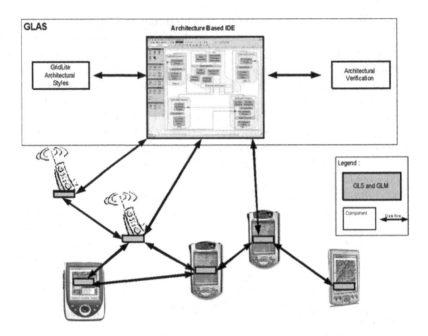

Fig. 2. The GridLite Architectural Support Layer

The software architectural support layer (shown in detail in Fig. 2) of GridLite
is reified in the form of three critical services:

1. *Architecture-based Integrated Development Environment (IDE)* – the IDE
   provides a visual interface for system design of GridLite software applications
   using the systematic primitive services detailed in the preceding sections. The
   IDE also provides facilities for (partially) automated system implementation
   from an architectural description.
2. *Architectural Styles* – in order to provide support to application developers
   for effective architectural compositions, GLAS must be able to model, ensure
   adherence to, and implement appropriate architectural styles for DREAM
   environments. An architectural style is a set of design heuristics and guidelines for composing and constructing a family of software systems [25,22].
   Our discussion thus far may have implied that peer-to-peer (P2P) is the ideal
   style for DREAM systems. However, P2P does not enforce topological constraints on applications and may result in "component soup" architectures.
   We postulate that there may be (a number of) other architectural styles that
   are well suited to DREAM environments, and it is the primary responsibility
   of the architectural styles service to provide support for designing GridLite
   software systems with a multitude of different architectural styles.
3. *Architectural Verification* – analysis of architectural models allows engineers
   to discover or verify critical system properties early in the development
   life cycle. GridLite leverages an *architecture-description language* (ADL)[22]

as the basis for architectural analysis of GridLite systems. Analysis should be conducted both in the traditional manner, at architecture specification-time[22], and by leveraging (meta-level) architectural model events, at system run-time.

In summary, the top-most (GLAS) layer of GridLite provides software architectural support. We believe that a software architecture-based approach is essential in deploying successful applications onto hundreds or thousands of DREAM nodes. GLAS should enable the expression of application architectures using a number of systematic primitives (e.g., component, connector, port, communication event, data stream) that are directly implemented in the GLM. From these primitives, complex architectures could be shaped and then dynamically reshaped based on environment events, changing requirements, dynamically discovered resources, and so on.

4   Current Status

4.1   GLIDE – A Reference Implementation of GridLite

Our reference implementation of the GridLite architecture is called "GLIDE", which stands for a *g*rid-based, *l*ightweight, *i*nfrastructure for *d*ata-intensive *e*nvironments. GLIDE is a hybrid grid middleware which combines the key architectural facilities of Prism-MW and core data grid services provided by OODT. The implementation-level class diagram of GLIDE is shown in Figure 3. At first blush, it appears that this design does not correspond directly to the GridLite architecture from Fig 1. However, that is only a by-product of our intent to reuse the facilities provided by Prism-MW and OODT to the greatest intent possible. In fact, the OODT components, placed along the periphery of the diagram, provide the GLS-level grid services (recall Section 3.2), while the Prism-MWCore section provides both the GLM-level infrastructure support and, due to Prism-MW's native support for architectural constructs, part of the GLAS-level architectural support (other aspects of the GLAS layer within GLIDE are discussed in Section 4.3).

We specialized Prism-MW to implement the core components of GLIDE shown in Fig. 3. Our intent was to retain the key properties and services of Prism-MW and provide basic grid services (recall the GLS layer described in Section 3.2) across dynamic and mobile virtual organizations. Additionally, we desired GLIDE to support architecture-based design, implementation, deployment, and evolution of data-intensive grid applications in DREAM environments. Finally, we desired that GLIDE at least partially interoperate with a heavy-weight grid counterpart: because of our prior experience with the OODT data grid platform, it seemed the most appropriate choice; indeed, OODT directly influenced our design of the key grid services provided by GLIDE. Below we describe GLIDE's realization in light of these goals and the description of the GridLite architecture from Section 3.

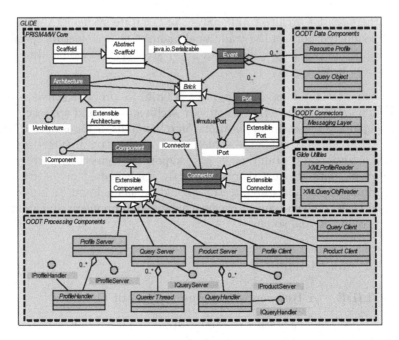

Fig. 3. GLIDE's design

Inspired by OODT's architecture, GLIDE's *Data Components* include the *Resource Profile*, a data structure which describes the location and classification of a resource available within a grid-based software system. Resources include data granules (such as a File), data-producing software systems (including the below described profile servers, product servers, query servers, and so on), computation-providing software systems, and resource profiles themselves. Resource profiles may contain additional resource-describing metadata [14]. Resource profiles directly address the GridLite *grid service development objective*, including *resource discovery* (recall Section 3.2). The *Query Object* is a data structure which contains a query expression. A query expression assigns values to a predefined set of data elements that describe resources of interest to the user and a collection of obtained results.

Again, inspired by OODT's architecture, GLIDE's *Processing Components* include *Product Servers*, which are responsible for abstracting heterogeneous software interfaces to data sources (such as an SQL interface to a database, a File System interface to a set of images, an HTTP interface to a set of web pages, and so on) into a single interface that supports querying for retrieval of data and computational resources. Users query product servers using the query object data structure. *Product Clients* connect and send queries (via a query object) to product servers. Product clients and servers are implementation-level artefacts of *grid service deployment*, including *resource wrapping*. A query results in either data retrieval or use of a remote computational resource. *Profile Servers* generate and deliver metadata[14] in the form of resource profile data structures, which are used for making informed decisions regarding the type and location of resources that satisfy given criteria. *Profile Clients* connect and send queries to profile servers. After sending a query, a profile client waits for the profile server to send back any resource profiles that satisfy the query. *Query Servers* accept query objects, and then use profile servers to determine the available data or computational resources that satisfy the user's query. Once all the resources have been collected, and processing has occurred, the data and processing results are returned (in the form of the result list of a query object) to the originating user. *Query Clients* connect to query servers, issue queries, and retrieve query objects with populated data results.

GLIDE contains one key *software connector* type. The *Messaging Layer* connector is a data bus which marshals resource profiles and query objects between GLIDE client and server components.

Each GLIDE processing component was implemented by subclassing Prism-MW's *ExtensibleComponent* class, using the asynchronous mode of operation. Asynchronous interaction directly resulted in lower coupling among GLIDE's processing components. For example, the dependency relationships between GLIDE's *Client* and *Server* processing components, which existed in OODT, was thereby removed. GLIDE's components use Prism-MW's *Events* to exchange messages. GLIDE data components are sent between processing components by encapsulating them as parameters in Prism-MW *Events*, directly addressing the GridLite *(light-weight) middleware support objective*, including *(un-)marshalling of data*. Leveraging Prism-MW's *Events* to send and receive different types of data enables homogenous interaction among the possibly heterogeneous processing components.

We found OODT's connectors not to be suitable for DREAM environments because of their heavy-weight (they are implemented using middleware such as RMI and CORBA). Furthermore, they only support synchronous interaction, which is difficult to effect in highly decentralized and mobile systems characterized by unreliable network links. To this end, we have leveraged Prism-MW's asynchronous connectors to implement the messaging layer class in GLIDE. GLIDE's connector leverages Prism-MW's port objects that allow easy addition or removal of TCP/IP connections. This allows the system's topology to be adapted at runtime, directly addressing objectives 1 and 2 of the GridLite architecture (*(light-weight) middleware services* and *run-time dynamism*, respectively). GLIDE's connector also implements event filtering such that only the requesting client receives responses from the server.

Lack of ability to easily adapt a system's software architecture is a key limitation of current grid systems, including OODT. If present, such a facility could be leveraged to improve a system's functionality, scalability, availability, latency, and so on. For example, our recent studies[17] have shown that the availability and latency of software systems in DREAM environments can be improved significantly via dynamic adaptation.

Finally, to support interoperability of GLIDE with OODT, we provide two additional utility classes: *XMLProfileReader* and *XMLQueryObjReader* parse

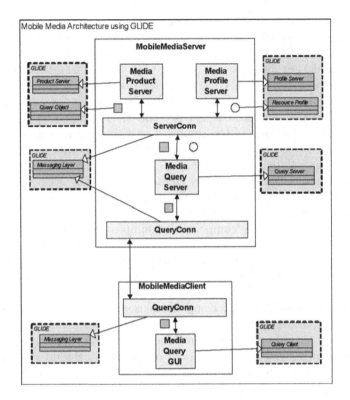

Fig. 4. Mobile Media Application Architecture

an XML representation of a resource profile and query object data structure, respectively. For brevity, we do not provide a detailed example of the XML Profile structure here, but its full treatment can be found in [14]. Each string is parsed into a GLIDE data object. Similarly, resource profiles and query objects can be serialized into XML. Thus, the level of interoperability with OODT is at the level of resource description and retrieval, and currently resource profiles and data can be exchanged between GLIDE and OODT. As part of our current work, we are investigating the Web Services Resource Framework (WS-RF) as a means of enabling interoperability between GLIDE and Globus, which uses WS-RF in its latest release (GTK 4.0).

4.2   Sample Application Using GLIDE

In order to evaluate the feasibility of GLIDE, we designed and implemented several representative applications. Here we discuss a prototype *Mobile Media Sharing* application (MMS), shown in Fig. 4. MMS allows a user to query, search, locate, and retrieve MP3 resources across a set of mobile, distributed, resource-constrained devices. Users query mobile media servers for MP3 files by specifying values for genre and quality of the MP3 (described below), and if found, the MP3s are streamed asynchronously to the requesting mobile media client.

Fig. 4 shows the overall distributed architecture of the MMS application. A mobile device can act as a server, a client, or both. *MobileMediaServer* and *MobileMediaClient* correspond to the parts of the application that are running on the server and the client devices.

MobileMediaClient contains a single component called *MediaQueryGUI*, which provides a GUI for creating MP3 queries. MP3 queries use two query parameters, *MP3.Genre* (e.g., rock) and *MP3.Quality* (e.g., 192 kb/s, 128 kb/s). *MediaQueryGUI* is attached to a *QueryConn*, which is an instance of GLIDE's messaging layer connector that forwards the queries to remote servers and responses back to the clients.

MobileMediaServer is composed of three component types: *MediaQueryServer*, *MediaProductServer*, and *MediaProfileServer*. *MediaQueryServer* parses the query received from the client, retrieves the resource profiles that match the query from *MediaProfileServer*, retrieves the mp3 file(s) in which the user was interested from the *MediaProductServer*, and sends the MP3 file(s) back to the client.

The MMS application helps to illustrate different aspects of GLIDE: it has been designed and implemented by leveraging most of GLIDE's processing and data components and its messaging layer connector, and has been deployed on DREAM devices. In the next section we evaluate GLIDE using MMS as an example.

4.3   Architecture-Based Development and Deployment Support in GLIDE

GLIDE inherits architecture-based development and deployment capabilities, including style awareness, from Prism-MW and deployment support, from PRISM-DE. Unlike most existing grid middleware solutions (e.g. OODT), which provide

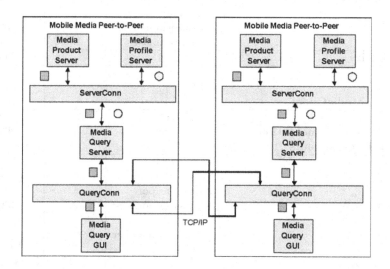

Fig. 5. Peer-to-Peer variation of the Mobile Media Application

support for either peer-to-peer or client-server styles, GLIDE does not impose any particular (possibly ill-suited) architectural style on the developers of a grid-based application. As a proof of concept, we have implemented several variations of the MMS application in different architectural styles including client-server, layered client-server, peer-to-peer, and C2 [27]. The variations of MMS leveraged existing support for these styles and were created with minimal effort. For example, changing MMS from client-server to peer-to-peer required addition of three components and a connector on the server side, and one component and one connector on the client side. Fig. 5 shows the peer-to-peer variant of MMS.

Table 1. Memory Footprint of Mobilemedia Server and Mobilemedia Client in GLIDE

MobileMediaServer	Java Packages	#Live Objects	Total Size (bytes)
Java	java.lang	36	2016
GLIDEs Implementation of OODT components	glide.product	1	24
	glide.profile	1	24
	glide.query	1	32
	glide.queryparser	1	160
	glide.structs	8	232
Application	mobilemedia.product.handlers	1	32
	mobilemedia.profile.handlers	1	8
Prism-MW	glide.prism.core	26	1744
	prism.extensions.port	1	40
	extensions.port.distribution	4	216
	glide.prism.handler	2	32
	glide.prism.util	18	1200
Total size			**5760**
MobileMediaClient			
Java	java.lang	28	1568
GLIDEs implementation of OODT components	glide.structs	7	208
Application	mobilemedia	2	384
Prism-MW	glide.prism.core	18	1304
	extensions.port	1	40
	extensions.port.distribution	3	136
	glide.prism.handler	1	16
	glide.prism.util	7	480
Total size			**4136**

4.4 DREAM Support

Resource scarcity poses the greatest challenge to any grid solution for DREAM environments. We have leveraged Prism-MW's efficient implementation of architectural constructs [17] along with the following techniques to improve GLIDE's performance and minimize the effect of the computing environment's heterogeneity: (1) MinML[3], a lightweight XML parser, to parse the resource profiles and query object data structures; (2) W3C's Jigsaw Web Server Base64 Encoding Library[2] to compress (at the product server end) and uncompress (at the product client end) the exchanged data; (3) Filtering inside the Messaging Layer to ensure event delivery only to the interested parties, thus minimizing propagation of events with large data loads (e.g., MP3 files). Specifically, GLIDE tags outgoing request events from a client with a unique ID, which is later used to route the replies appropriately; and (4) Incremental data exchange via numbered data segments for cases when the reliability of connectivity and network bandwidth prevent atomic exchange of large amounts of data.

As an illustration of GLIDE's efficiency, Table 1 shows the memory footprint of *MobileMediaServer*'s and *MobileMediaClient*'s implementation in GLIDE. The total size of the *MobileMediaServer* was 5.7KB and *MobileMediaClient* was 4.1KB, which is two orders of magnitude smaller than their implementation in OODT (707KB and 280KB, respectively). The memory overhead introduced by GLIDE on the client and server devices was under 4KB.

5 Conclusion

The GridLite architecture that we describe in this paper has the potential to shape the role and utility of existing mobile computing platforms such as PDAs, cell phones, and laptops used in everyday life. As networked computing systems must operate in DREAM environments, several avenues of research must be significantly advanced. In this paper, we have argued that grid computing provides a promising approach for engineering some classes of networked computing systems, but several limitations of the grid must be addressed before its widespread deployment and use as a computing platform for future networked environments.

In addition to proposing the architecture for GridLite, we described a reference implementation of GridLite, called GLIDE that addresses many of the described limitations of the grid using the proposed objectives of the GridLite architecture as a guide. We summarized the current status of GLIDE, and identified further avenues of research that must be explored in order to ultimately "bring the grid to one's pocket". These future avenues include assessing GLIDE's suitability, as well as possible shortcomings, as *the* reference implementation for GridLite; studying the limits of the envisaged GridLite architecture's adaptability, scalability, and efficiency; and, finally, expanding this work to other domains, such as computational grids, high-performance computing, and ubiquitous and embedded systems.

Acknowledgements. This material is based upon work supported by the National Science Foundation under Grant Numbers CCR-9985441 and ITR-0312780. Effort also supported by the Jet Propulsion Laboratory, managed by the California Institute of Technology. The authors are especially thankful to Daniel Crichton and Steve Hughes for their contributions to the OODT grid platform, as well as to Sam Malek, Marija Mikic-Rakic, and Chiyoung Seo for their work on the Prism-MW middleware platform. The authors are especially grateful to Dave Woollard for his help on formatting the paper.

References

1. Alchemi .net grid computing framework. web site, 2004.
2. Jigsaw overview, http://www.w3.org/jigsaw/. web site, 2004.
3. Minml a minimal xml parser, http://www.wilson.co.uk/xml/minml.htm. web site, 2004.
4. The globus alliance, http://www.globus.org, 2005.
5. DCMI. Dublin core metadata element set. Metadata Standard 1.1, DCMI, 1999.
6. A. Rajasekar et al. Mysrb and srb - components of a data grid. In *HPDC*, pages 301–310, July 2002.
7. C. Kesselman et al. The anatomy of the grid: Enabling scalable virtual organizations. *Intl' Journal of Supercomputing Applications*, pages 1–25, 2001.
8. I. Foster et al. The physiology of the grid: An open grid services architecture for distributed systems integration. Work in progress, Globus Research, 2002.
9. M. Gudgin et al. Simple object access protocol version 1.2. W3c reccomendation, W3C, 2003.
10. O Tatebe et al. The second trans-pacific grid datafarm testbed and experiments for sc2003. In *Intl' Symposium on Applications and the Internet*, pages 602–607, January 2004.
11. S. Zachariadis et al. Xmiddle: Information sharing middleware for a mobile environment. In *ICSE*, pages 712–721, May 2002.
12. R. Fielding. *Architectural Styles and the Design of Network-based Software Architectures*. PhD thesis, University of California, Irvine, 2000.
13. A. Finkelstein, C. Gryce, and J. Lewis-Bowen. Relating requirements and architectures: A study of data-grids. *J. Grid Computing*, 2:207–222, September 2004.
14. J. S. Hughes, D. Crichton, S. Kelly, C. Mattmann, J. Crichton, and T. Tran. Intelligent resource discovery using ontology-based resource profiles. *Data Science Journal*, 4:171–188, December 2005.
15. ISO/IEC. Framework for the specification and standardization of data elements. Standards Document 11179, ISO, 1999.
16. N. Maibaum and T. Mundt. Jxta: A technology facilitating mobile peer-to-peer networks. In *MobiWac02*, pages 7–13, 2002.
17. S. Malek, M. Mikic-Rakic, and N. Medvidovic. A style-aware architectural middleware for resource-constrained, distributed systems. *IEEE TSE*, 31(3):256–272, March 2005.
18. C. Mattmann, D. Crichton, N. Medvidovic, and J. S. Hughes. A software architecture-based framework for highly distributed and data-intensive scientific applications. In *ICSE*, pages 721–730, May 2006.

19. C. Mattmann, S. Malek, N. Beckman, M. Mikic-Rakic, N. Medvidovic, and D. Crichton. Glide: A grid-based light-weight infrastructure for data-intensive environments. In *European Grid Conference*, pages 68–77, February 2005.
20. C. Mattmann, N. Medvidovic, P. Ramirez, and V. Jakobac. Unlocking the grid. In *CBSE*, pages 322–336, May 2005.
21. N. Medvidovic, M. Mikic-Rakic, N. Mehta, and S. Malek. Software architectural support for handheld computing. *IEEE Computer*, 36(9):66–73, 2003.
22. N. Medvidovic and R. N. Taylor. A classification and comparison framework for software architecture description languages. *IEEE TSE*, 26(1):70–93, 2000.
23. M. Mikic-Rakic and N. Medvidovic. Adaptable architectural middleware for programming-in-the-small-and-many. In *Middleware*, pages 162–181, 2003.
24. I. Muslea, S. Minton, and C. A. Knoblock. Hierarchical wrapper induction for semistructured information sources. *Autonomous Agents and Multi-Agent Systems*, 4(1/2):93–114, 2001.
25. M. Shaw and D. Garlan. *Software Architecture: Perspectives on an Emerging Discipline*. Prentice Hall, 1996.
26. H. M. Sneed. The rationale for software wrapping. In *ICSM*, page 303, 1997.
27. R. N. Taylor, N. Medvidovic, K. M. Anderson, E. James Whitehead Jr., J. E. Robbins, K. A. Nies, P. Oreizy, and D. L. Dubrow. A component- and message-based architectural style for gui software. *IEEE TSE*, 22(6):390–406, 1996.

DARX - A Self-healing Framework for Agents

Olivier Marin[1,2], Marin Bertier[3], Pierre Sens[1,2], Zahia Guessoum[1,2],
and Jean-Pierre Briot[1]

[1] Laboratoire d'Informatique de Paris 6
University Paris 6 - CNRS
4 place Jussieu
75252 Paris Cedex 05, France
[2] INRIA - Rocquencourt
Domaine de Voluceau - BP 15
78153 Rocquencourt, France
[3] Unité de recherche INRIA Rennes - IRISA
Campus universitaire de Beaulieu
35042 Rennes Cedex, France

Abstract. This paper presents DARX, our framework for building failure-resilient applications through adaptive fault tolerance. It relies on the fact that multi-agent platforms constitute a very strong basis for decentralized software that is both flexible and scalable, and makes the assumption that the relative importance of each agent varies during the course of the computation. DARX regroups solutions which facilitate the creation of multi-agent applications in a large-scale context. Its most important feature is adaptive replication: replication strategies are applied on a per-agent basis with respect to transient environment characteristics such as the importance of the agent for the computation, the network load or the mean time between failures.

Firstly, the interwoven concerns of multi-agent systems and fault-tolerant solutions are put forward. An overview of the DARX architecture follows, as well as an evaluation of its performances. We conclude, after outlining the promising outcomes, by presenting prospective work.

1 Introduction

Nowadays it barely seems necessary to emphasize the tremendous potential of decentralized software solutions. Their main advantage lies in the distributed nature of information, resources and action. One software engineering technique for building such software has lately emerged in the artificial intelligence research field, and appears to be both promising and elegant: distributed agent systems [BDC00] [MCM99] [NS00].

Intuitively, multi-agent systems appear to represent a strong basis for the construction of distributed applications. The general outline of distributed agent software consists in autonomous computational entities which interact with one another towards a common goal that is beyond their individual capabilities.

F. Kordon and J. Sztipanovits (Eds.): Monterey Workshop 2005, LNCS 4322, pp. 88–105, 2007.

In addition, the multi-agent paradigm bears two attractive notions: flexibility and scalability. By definition, agents have the ability to adapt in order to meet new context requirements. A software consisting of multiple agents can therefore be dynamically modified: objectives of specific agents may be altered, new agents can be brought in to collaborate towards a computation, agents that have become partly useless for the application can be adapted or set aside, and so on... Moreover, multi-agent systems are based on communicating, autonomous entities; it ensues that there is no theoretical limit to the number of agents involved, nor is there any bound on the number of hosting machines. Distributing such systems over large scale networks may therefore tremendously increase their efficiency as well as their capacity.

However, large-scale distribution also brings forward the crucial necessity of applying dependability protocols. For instance, the greater the number of agents and hosts, the higher the probability that one of them will be subjected to failure. Multi-agent applications rely on collaboration amongst agents, hence the failure of one of the involved agents might bring the whole computation to a dead end. Therefore it appears that fault tolerance is a necessary paradigm for the design of such applications. In particular, software replication techniques provide for a range of recovery guarantees and delays [GS97]. However, replicating every agent in systems comprising up to millions of agents may not be affordable given the important time and resources consumption implied. Also, several replication strategies exist and the efficiency of each strategy depends heavily upon both the application context and the computing environment. One solution might be to design and implement mechanisms for (1) the analysis of both the context and the environment in order to single out the agents which are vital for the system, and (2) the application and the dynamic adaptation of replication schemes with respect to context and environment variations.

In this paper, we depict DARX, our architecture for fault-tolerant agent computing [MSBG01]. DARX uses the flexibility of multi-agent systems in order to offer adaptive fault tolerance by means of dynamic replication mechanisms: software elements can be replicated and unreplicated on the spot and it is possible to change the ongoing replication strategies on the fly. We have developed a solution to interconnect this architecture with two existing multi-agent platforms, namely MadKit[GF00] and DIMA [GB99], and in the long term to other platforms. The originality of our approach lies in two major orientations. Firstly, the choice of the fault tolerance protocol – which computational entities are to be made fault-tolerant, to which degree, and at what point of the execution – is not entirely incumbent upon the application developer; DARX offers automated observation and control functionalities to address these issues. And secondly, the overall architecture is conceived with a view to being scalable.

The paper is organized as follows. In section 2, the main existing approaches towards solving the fault tolerance problems in the multi-agent systems context are presented. Section 3 depicts the general design of our framework dedicated to bringing adaptive fault tolerance to multi-agent systems through selective replication. Section 4 reports on the issues raised by the implementation of DARX-compliant applications, and section 5 evaluates the performances of the resulting software. Finally, the conclusion and perspectives are drawn in section 6.

2 Related Work

Research on fault tolerance in multi-agent systems mainly focuses on the ability to guarantee the continuity of every agent computation. This approach includes the resolution of consistency problems amongst agent replicas. Other related solutions address the complex problems of maintaining agent cooperation [KCL00], providing reliable migration for independent mobile agents and ensuring the exactly-once property of mobile agent executions [PS01].

Several solutions use specific entities to protect the computational elements of multi-agent systems [H96] [KIBW99] [KCL00]. The principal contribution of these approaches is in separating the control of the agents from the functionalities of the multi-agent system.

In [H96], sentinels represent the control structure of the multi-agent system. Each sentinel is specific to a functionality, handles the different agents which interact to provide the corresponding service, and monitors communications in order to react to agent failures. Adding sentinels to a multi-agent system seems to be a good approach, however the sentinels themselves represent bottle-necks as well as failure points for the system.

A similar architecture is that of the Chameleon project [KIBW99]. Chameleon is an adaptive fault tolerance system using reliable mobile agents. The methods and techniques are embodied in a set of specialized agents supported by a fault tolerance manager (FTM) and host daemons for handshaking with the FTM via the agents. Adaptive fault tolerance refers to the ability to dynamically adapt to the evolving fault tolerance requirements of an application. This is achieved by making the Chameleon infrastructure reconfigurable. Static reconfiguration guarantees that the components can be reused for assembling different fault tolerance strategies. Dynamic reconfiguration allows component functionalities to be extended or modified at runtime by changing component composition, and components to be added to or removed from the system without taking down other active components. Unfortunately, through its centralized FTM, this architecture suffers from the same objections as the previous approach.

[KCL00] presents a fault tolerant multi-agent architecture that regroups agents and brokers. Similarly to [H96], the agents represent the functionality of the multi-agent system and the brokers maintain links between the agents. [KCL00] proposes to organize the brokers in hierarchical teams and to allow them to exchange information and assist each other in maintaining the communications between agents. The brokerage layer thus appears to be both fault-tolerant and scalable. However, the implied overhead is tremendous and increases with the size of the system. Besides, this approach does not address the recovery of basic agent failures.

In order to solve the overhead problem, [FD02] proposes to use proxies. This approach tries to make transparent the use of agent replication; that is, computational entities are all represented in the same way, disregarding whether they are a single application agent or a group of replicas. The role of a proxy is to act as an interface between the replicas in a replicate group and the rest of the multi-agent system. It handles the control of the execution and manages the state of the replicas. To do so, all the external and internal communications of the group are redirected to the proxy. A proxy failure isn't crippling for the application as long as the replicas are still present: a new proxy can be generated. However, if the problem of the single point of failure is solved, this solution still positions the proxy as a bottle-neck in case replication is used with a view to increasing the availability of agents. To address this problem, the authors propose to build a hierarchy of proxies for each group of replicas. They also point out the specific problems which remain to be addressed: read/write consistency and resource locking, which are discussed in [SBS00] as well.

3   The Architecture of the DARX Framework

This section presents DARX, our Dynamic Agent Replication eXtension, and depicts its features.

3.1   System Model and Failure Model

A distributed system is assumed, in which processes/agents communicate through messages. Communication channels are considered to be quasi-reliable. Our model follows that of partial synchrony, proposed by Chandra and Toueg in their generalization of failure detectors [CT96]. This model stipulates that, for every execution, there are bounds on process speeds and on message transmission times. However, these bounds are not known and in our model they hold only after some unknown time: the global stabilization time.

Processes are assumed to be fail/silent. Once a specific process is considered as having crashed, it cannot participate to the global computation anymore. Byzantine behaviours might be resolved with DARX, but are not yet integrated in the failure model.

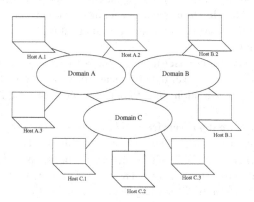

Fig. 1. A hierarchic topology aimed at scalability

Finally, for scalability issues, a hierarchic structure is imposed for the logical network topology. As shown in Figure 1, sets of hosts are organized in groups. Broadly connected machines are regrouped in *domains*, and a higher inter-domains level called the *nexus* is constructed. Within each *domain*, a single host is elected so as to participate to the higher level.

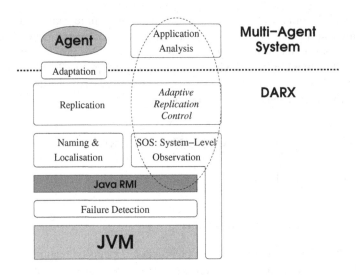

Fig. 2. DARX service-oriented architecture

3.2   Overview

Figure 2 gives a service-oriented overview of the logical architecture of DARX.

- A **failure detection service** [BMS02][BMS03] maintains dynamic lists of all the running hosts as well as of the valid software elements which participate to the supported application, and notifies the latter of suspected failure occurrences.
- A **naming and localisation service** generates a unique identifier for every agent in the system, and returns the addresses for all agent replicas in response to an agent localisation request.
- A **system observation service** monitors the behaviour of the underlying distributed system: it collects low-level data by means of OS-compliant probes and diffuses processed trace information so as to make it available for the adaptive replication control process.
- An **application analysis service** builds a global representation of the supported agent application in terms of fault tolerance requirements.
- A **replication service** brings all the necessary mechanisms for replicating agents, maintaining the consistency between replicas of a same agent, and automating replication scheme adaptation for every agent according to the data gathered through system monitoring and application analysis.
- An **interfacing service** offers wrapper-making solutions for agents, thus rendering the DARX middleware usable by various multi-agent systems and even making it possible to introduce interoperability amongst different systems.

The following describes how DARX services interact in order to supply adaptive fault tolerance to agent applications. The fault tolerance features are brought to agents from various platforms through their corresponding adaptor by an instance of a DARX server running on every location[1]. Each DARX server implements the required replication services, backed by a common global naming/location service enhanced with failure detection (see 3.3). Concurrently, a scalable observation service (see 3.4) is in charge of monitoring the system behaviour at every level of the hierarchic topology – local, *domain, nexus*. The information gathered through both means is used thereafter to adapt the fault tolerance schemes on the fly: an event-driven decision module combines system-level information and application-level information to determine the *criticity*[2] of each agent, and to apply the most suitable replication scheme.

DARX includes transparent replication management. While the supported application deals with agents, DARX handles replication groups. Each of these groups consists of software entities – replicas – which represent the same agent. Thus in the event of failures, if at least one replica is still up, then the corresponding agent isn't lost to the application. A more detailed explanation of a replication group, of its internal design and of its utilization in DARX can be found in 3.5.

For portability and compatibility issues, DARX is Java-based. Indeed, the Java language and more specifically the JVM provide – relative – hardware independence, an invaluable feature for large-scale distributed systems. Moreover, a great number of the existing multi-agent platforms are implemented in Java. In addition to all this, the remote method invocation (RMI) facility offers many useful high-level abstractions for the elaboration of distributed solutions.

3.3 Failure Detection and Naming Service

As part of the means to supply adequate support for large-scale agent applications, the DARX platform includes a hierarchical, fault-tolerant naming service. This distributed service is deployed over a failure detection service based on an adaptable implementation of the unreliable failure detector [BMS02][BMS03].

The failure detection and naming layer serves a major goal: to maintain dynamic lists of the valid sites and of the valid agents, as well as their casual replicas, participating to the application. Specific agents can thus be localized through this service. Failure detectors exchange heartbeats and maintain a list of the processes which are suspected of having crashed. Therefore, in an asynchronous context, failures can be recovered more efficiently. For instance, the failure of a process can be detected before the impossibility to establish contact arises within the course of the supported computation.

The service aims at detecting both hardware and software failures. Each DARX server integrates an independent thread which acts as failure detector/name server. Software failure is detected by monitoring the running processes on each server. Hardware failures are suspected by exchanging heartbeats among groups of servers. For

---

[1] A location is an abstraction of a physical location. It hosts resources and processes, and possesses its own unique identifier. DARX uses a URL and a port number to identify each location that hosts a DARX server.

[2] The *criticity* of a process defines its importance with respect to the rest of the application. Obviously, its value is subjective and evolves over time. For example, towards the end of a distributed computation, a single agent in charge of federating the results should have a very high *criticity*; whereas at the application launch, the *criticity* of that same agent may have a much lower value.

large-scale integration purposes, this structure maps the hierarchic topology presented in 3.1, which comprises two levels: a local one – *domains* – and a global one – the *nexus*. The logical topology ought to reflect the physical topology as much as possible: every *domain* is mapped onto a highly-connected cluster of workstations, or constituted inside it. Local groups bind themselves together by electing exactly one representative which will participate to the nexus. At this global level, each representative name server maintains a list of the known agents within the application – the replication group leaders (see 3.5) in the DARX context. This information is shared and kept up-to-date through a consensus algorithm implying all the representative name servers. When a new agent is created, it is registered locally as well as by the representative name server; likewise in the case of an unregistration. At the local level, the name servers maintain the list of all the replicas supported in their local group, disregarding whether these are leaders or not.

In this architecture, the ability to provide different qualities of service to the local and the global detectors is a major asset of our implementation. Thus on the global level, failure suspicion can be loosened with respect to the local level. This distinction is important, since a failure does not have the same interpretation in the local context as in the global one. A local failure corresponds to the crash of an agent or of a host, whereas in the global context a failure represents the crash of an entire *domain*.

Figure 3 shows how the naming service makes use of the failure detection to convey its communications. The information is exchanged between name servers via piggy-backing on the failure detection heartbeats. The local lists of replicas which are suspected to be faulty are directly reused to maintain the global view of the application. With respect to DARX, this means that the list of running agents is systematically updated. When a DARX server is considered as having crashed, all the agents it hosted are removed from the list and replaced by replicas located on other hosts. The election of a new leader within an agent replication group is initiated by a failure notification from the naming service.

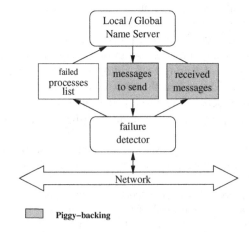

Fig. 3. Usage of the failure detector by the name server

3.4 Observation Service

DARX aims at providing decision-making support so as to fine-tune the fault tolerance for each agent with respect to its evolution and that of its context. Decisions of this type may only be reached through a fairly good knowledge of the dynamic characteristics of the application and of the environment. In order to obtain such knowledge, a scalable observation service has been designed and implemented, yet remains to be integrated in DARX.

Similarly to the naming service, the observation service piggybacks its communications on the existing flow created by the regular heartbeat emissions of the failure detection service. Moreover, it is also hierarchic; it distinguishes local and global levels.

The data collected at the local level consists in transient information such as the current memory load of a host, the overall execution time of an agent since it was created, the number of messages exchanged between two agents, ... This type of data is shared within local groups; broadcasting it or enabling subscription to it on a large scale does not appear worthwhile. Indeed, the validity of such information over a long period of time is highly questionable. Besides, its diffusion on a great number of distant locations bears a heavy cost, even though it would be diluted in the failure detection flow. Nonetheless, it may be needed to gain instantaneous information on a specific machine outside the local *domain*. For example, it may be necessary to determine the feasibility of creating a new replica in a remote *domain*. The observation service therefore allows for point-to-point subscription to data collection on distant hosts.

Statistical information, however, possesses a longer lifespan in the DARX context. Such material encompasses all the data derived by processing the local information: the average CPU load of a host over a long period of time, the failure rate of a host or of a local group, their average network load, their meantime between failures, ... It is shared at the global level. Every local group elects a member responsible for the aggregation of the statistical information, as well as for its diffusion at the global level. Statistical information about other groups can thus be retrieved at the elected local workstation.

Each local DARX server integrates an observation module. It comprises three elements: a data collection module (DCM), a data processing module (DPM) and a data exchange module (DEM). The DCM extracts the information available from the operating system, such as the CPU load or the swap activity, therefore it is chosen to be host-compliant. The DPM is Java-based and gathers application-level information; the state of an agent, for example. The DPM also interfaces with the DCM to recover system-level data, and renders it into a directly usable format for the DARX platform. On a periodic basis, the DEM broadcasts the accumulated instantaneous information to the DPMs of its local group, and contributes to the diffusion of the statistical information at the global level if it belongs to a leading observation module.

3.5 Replication Management

DARX provides fault tolerance through software replication. It is designed in order to adapt the applied replication strategy on a per-agent basis. This derives from the fundamental assumption that the *criticity* of an agent evolves over time; therefore, at any given moment of the computation, all agents do not have the same requirements in terms of fault tolerance. On every server, some agents need to be replicated with pessimistic strategies, others with optimistic ones, while some others do not necessitate any replication at all. The benefit of this scheme is double. Firstly the global cost of deploying fault tolerance mechanisms is reduced since they are only applied to a subset of the elements which constitute the distributed application. Secondly the chosen replication strategies ought to be consistent with the computation requirements and the environment characteristics, as the choice of every strategy depends on the execution context of the agent to which it is applied. If the subset of agents which are to be replicated is small enough then the overhead implied by the strategy selection and switching process may be of low significance.

In DARX, agent-dependent fault tolerance is enabled by the notion of replication group (RG): the set of all the replicas which correspond to a same agent. At its creation every replica is given a unique identifier provided by the naming service and built from the original name of the corresponding agent in the application context. An RG contains at least one active replica so as to ensure that messages destined to a specific agent will indeed be processed. Starting from this point, any replication strategy can be enforced within the RG. To allow for this, several replication strategies are made available by the DARX framework. The strategies offered can be classified in two main types: (1) **active**, where all replicas process the input messages concurrently, and (2) **passive**, in which only one replica – a primary – is in charge of the computation while periodically transmitting its state to the other replicas – its standbies. A practical example of a DARX off-the-shelf implementation is the semi-active strategy where a single leading replica forwards the received messages to its followers.

One of the noticeable aspects of DARX is that several strategies may coexist inside the same RG. As long as one of the replicas is active, meaning that it executes the associated agent code and participates in the application communications, there is no restriction on the activity of the other replicas. These replicas may either be standbies or followers of an active replica, or even equally active replicas. Furthermore, it is possible to switch from a strategy to another with respect to a replica: a follower may become a standby, a new leader with its followers may be selected amongst active replicas, and so on . . .

Throughout the computation, a particular variable is evaluated continuously for every replica: its degree of consistency (DOC). The strategy applied in order to keep a replica consistent is the main parameter in the calculation of this variable; the more pessimistic the strategy, the higher the DOC of the corresponding replica. The other parameters emanate from the observation service; they include the load of the host, the date of creation of the replica, the latency in the communications with the other replicas of the group, . . . The DOC has a deep impact on failure recovery; among the remaining replicas after a failure has occured, the one with the highest DOC is the most likely to be able of taking over the abandoned tasks of the crashed replicas.

The following information is necessary to describe a replication group:

- the *criticity* of its associated agent,
- its replication degree – the number of replicas it contains –,
- the list of these replicas, ordered by DOC,
- the list of the replication strategies applied inside the group,
- the mapping between replicas and strategies.

The sum of these pieces of information constitutes the replication policy of an RG. A replication policy must be reevaluated in three cases:

1. when a failure inside the RG occurs,
2. when the *criticity* value of the associated agent changes,
3. and when the environment characteristics vary considerably, for example when CPU and network overloads induce a prohibitive cost for consistency maintenance inside the RG.

Since the replication policy may be reassessed frequently, it appears reasonable to centralize this decision process. A leader is elected among the replicas of the RG for this purpose. Its objective is to adapt the replication policy to the *criticity* of the associated agent as a function of the characteristics of its context – the information obtained through the observation service. As mentioned earlier, DARX allows for dynamic modifications of the replication policy. Replicas and strategies can be added to or removed from a group during the course of the computation, and it is possible to switch from a strategy to another on the fly. For example if a standby crashes, a new replica can be added to maintain the level of reliability within the group; or if the *criticity* of the associated agent decreases, it is possible either to suppress a replica or to switch the strategy attached to a replica from an active form to a passive one. The policy is known to all the replicas inside the RG. When policy modifications occur, the leader diffuses them within its RG. Except when the modification results from the failure of the leader: a new election is then initiated by the naming service through a failure notification to the remaining replicas.

Figure 4 depicts the composition of a replica. In order to benefit from fault tolerance abilities, each agent gets to inherit the functionalities of a `DarxTask` object,

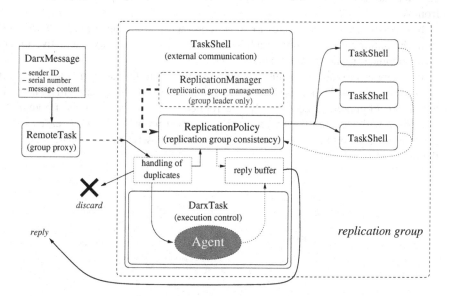

Fig. 4. Replication management scheme

enabling DARX to control the agent execution. Each task is itself wrapped into a `TaskShell`, which handles the agent inputs/outputs. Hence DARX can act as an intermediary for the agent, committed to deciding when an agent replica should really be started, stopped, suspended or resumed, and exactly when and which message receptions should take effect. Leaders are wrapped in enhanced shells, comprising an additional `ReplicationManager`. This manager exchanges information with the observation module (see 3.4) and performs the periodical reassessment of the replication policy. It also maintains the group consistency by sending the relevant information to the other replicas, following the policy requirements. Implementation-wise, there is an independent thread for every `DarxTask` as well as for every `ReplicationManager`.

Since replication must be transparent to the application, the DARX middleware is in charge of handling all communications between agents. To allow this, every replication group binds itself to proxies which channel incoming messages. These proxies implement the `RemoteTask` interface, thus referencing replication groups; it is the naming service which keeps track of every replica to be referenced, and provides the corresponding `RemoteTask`.The latter contains the addresses of all the replicas inside the associated RG, with a specific tag for the currently active replicas. A `RemoteTask` is obtained by a lookup request on the naming service using the application-relevant agent identifier as parameter.

Figure 5 shows a tiny agent application as seen in the DARX context. An emitter, agent B, sends messages to be processed by a receiver, agent A. At the moment of the represented snapshot, the value of the *criticity* of agent B is minimal; therefore the RG which represents it contains a single active replica only. The momentary value of the *criticity* of agent A, however, is higher. The corresponding RG comprises three replicas: (1) an active replica A elected as the leader, (2) a follower A' to which incoming messages are forwarded, and (3) a standby A" which receives periodical state updates from A.

In order to transmit messages to A, B requested the relevant `RemoteTask` RTA from the naming service. Since replication group A contains only one active replica, RTA references replica A and no other.

If A happens to fail, the failure detection service will ultimately monitor this event and notify A' and A" by means of the localization service. Both replicas will then modify their replication policies accordingly. The replica associated to the highest potential of leadership will become the new group leader – most probably A' in this case as semi-active replication provides stronger consistency than passive replication –, thus ending the recovery process.

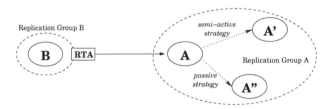

Fig. 5. A simple agent application example

4   Application Building with DARX

This section describes how a multi-agent application may be built over DARX, and hence benefit from its fault tolerance features.

At this point of our research, the application developer must respect a few guidelines and constraints which are given in this section in order for applications to benefit from DARX services. We feel it is important to point out that this constraint can easily be bypassed. Notwithstanding the possibility of generating the agent application code through model-driven architectures, an automated analysis of the original agent source code might provide the required information to enable DARX support without further modifications of the original program; the latter corresponds to undergoing research started out in [BGCAMS02].

In the meantime, our solution comprises facilities designed to make application building as painless as possible. As a Java framework, DARX includes several generic classes which assist the developer through the process of implementing a reliable multi-agent application. The choice of those generic classes comes from the study of the OMG MASIF [MASIF98] specifications, as well as that of the most recurrent aspects of various multi-agent systems, therefore DARX-compliant application building is very close to most agent developing environments.

Every agent class must extend a `DarxTask` for several reasons.

Firstly because, although it is not the only factor, the role of an agent [BGCAMS02] is essential in determining its *criticity*. For every agent, the roles it may assume must be explicitly listed by the developer. Any number of roles can be defined for an agent; each of these roles ought to be mapped to a corresponding *static criticity* in the code of the `ReplicationManager`. A *static criticity* is the importance of an agent taken out of its computation context. At runtime, a *dynamic criticity* will be evaluated in conjunction with the characteristics of the environment. Consequently, the role of the agent is part of the variables present in the `DarxTask`.

Secondly, the `DarxTask` provides a boolean for differentiating whether the agent is deterministic or not. This arises from the fundamental definition of agentry: it comprises the notion of proactivity, which is closely related to non-determinism. It follows that some agents may present non-deterministic behaviours such as unpredictable internal state changes. This complicates consistency maintenance inside RGs: for example it becomes indispensable to propagate the state changes of a leader to its followers if they do not depend entirely on the incoming messages. The provided boolean enables developers to specify the behaviour of a non-deterministic replica with respect to its role inside the RG. In the continuity of the semi-active strategy example, a leader may take stochastically funded decisions whereas its followers cannot.

Finally, the `DarxTask` is the point where DARX handles the execution of an agent: application-specific control methods to start, stop, suspend and resume the agent have to be defined for this purpose. Such methods would be very hard to implement in a general context, where the application developer would not have to intervene, without modifying the JVM: the resulting efficiency loss would be considerable. It ought to be pointed that, technically, it is the serialized `DarxTask` of the RG leader which is sent to the `TaskShell` of the passive replicas in order to perform state updates.

Since DARX overrides the localization and naming services of the agent platforms it supports, it has to take on the responsibility of channelling communications between agents. In order to emit messages, agents must declare themselves to the framework by instantiating a `DarxCommunicationInterface`; messages to other agents are emitted through this interface, built around the `RemoteTask` reference of the destinations. Messages sent to a group by means of a `RemoteTask` are thus rerouted to the group leaders, where duplicates are discarded and ordering is guaranteed. Additionally, this scheme allows tracking of the message flows by the observation service.

Also, fault tolerance protocols that are specific to the application can be developed. DARX provides a generic `ReplicationStrategy` class which may be extended to fulfill the needs of the programmer. Basic methods allow to define the consistency information within the group, as well as the way this information ought to be propagated in different cases, such as synchronous or asynchronous messages for example. A few common strategies, such as the passive and the semi-active one, are already built in DARX; others are undergoing research, like quorum-based strategies for instance.

5   Performances

This section presents performance evaluations established with DARX. Measures were obtained using JRE 1.4.1 on the Distributed ASCI Supercomputer 2 (DAS-2). DAS-2 is a wide-area distributed computer of 200 Dual Pentium-III nodes. The machine is built out of clusters of workstations, which are interconnected by SurfNet, the Dutch university Internet backbone for wide-area communication, whereas Myrinet, a popular multi-Gigabit LAN, is used for local communication.

5.1   Agent-Oriented Dining Philosophers Example

A first experiment aims at checking that there is indeed something to be gained out of adaptive fault tolerance. For this purpose, an agent-oriented version of the classic dining philosophers problem [H85] has been implemented over DARX.

In this application, the table as well as the philosophers are agents; the corresponding classes inherit from `DarxTask`. The table agent is unique and runs on a specific machine, whereas the philosopher agents are launched on several distinct hosts. Figure 6 represents the different states in which philosopher agents can be found. The

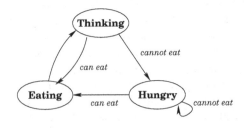

Fig. 6. Dining philosophers over DARX: state diagram

agent states in this implementation aim at representing typical situations which occur in distributed agent systems:

- **Thinking:** the agent processes data which isn't relevant to the rest of the application,
- **Hungry:** the agent has notified the rest of the application that it requires resources, and is waiting for their availability in order to resume its computation,
- **Eating:** data which will be useful for the application is being treated and the agent monopolizes global resources – the chop-sticks.

In order to switch states, a philosopher sends a request to the table. The table, in charge of the global resources, processes the requests concurrently in order to send a reply. Depending on the reply it receives, a philosopher may or may not switch states; the content of the reply as well as the current state determine which state will be next. It is arguable that this architecture may be problematic in a distributed context. For a great number of philosophers, the table will become a bottleneck and the application performances will degrade consequently. Nevertheless, the goal of this experimentation is to compare the benefits of adaptive fault tolerance with respect to fixed strategies. It seems unlikely that this comparison would suffer from such a design. Besides, the experimentation protocol was built with these considerations in mind.

Table 1. Dining philosophers over DARX: replication policies

Agent state	RD^3	Replication policy
Thinking	1	Single active leader
Hungry	2	Active leader replicated passively
Eating	2	Active leader replicated semi-actively

Since the table is the most important element of the application, the associated RG policy is pessimistic – a leader and a semi-active follower – and remains constant throughout the computation. The RGs corresponding to philosophers, however, have adaptive policies which depend on their states. Table 1 shows the mapping between the state of a philosopher agent and the replication policy in use within the corresponding RG. RD is used as an abbreviation for replication degree: the total number of RG members, leader included. The choices for the replication policies in this example are arbitrary. They correspond to the minimal fault tolerance scheme required in order to bring the computation to its end should scarce failures occur. A *thinking* philosopher may be restarted from scratch without any loss for the application, whereas a the disappearance of either a *hungry* philosopher or an *eating* philosopher might interfere with or even block the execution of the application.

5.2 Results Analysis

The experimentation protocol is the following. Eight of the DAS-2 nodes have been reserved, with one DARX server hosted on every node. The leading table replica and

---

^{3} RD: Replication Degree.

its follower each run on their own server. In order to determine where each philosopher leader is launched, a round robin strategy is used on the six remaining servers. The measure can start once all the philosophers have been launched and registered at the table.

Two values are being measured. The first is the total execution time: the time it takes to consume a fixed number of meals (100) over all the application. The second is the total processing time: the time spent processing data by all the active replicas of the application. Although the number of meals is fixed, the number of philosophers isn't: it varies from two to fifty. Also, the adaptive – "switch" – fault tolerance protocol is compared to two others. In the first one the philosophers are not replicated at all, whereas in the second one the philosophers are replicated semi-actively with a replication degree of two – one leader and one follower in every RG.

Every experiment with the same parameter values is run six times in a row. Executions where failures have occurred are discarded since the application will not necessarily terminate in the case where philosophers are not replicated. The results shown here are the averages of the measures obtained.

Figure 7 shows the total execution times obtained. At first glance it demonstrates that adaptive fault tolerance may be of benefit to distributed agent applications in terms of performance. Indeed the results are quite close to those obtained with no fault tolerance involved, and are globally much better than those of the semi-active version. In the experiments with two philosophers only, the cost of adapting the replication policy is prohibitive indeed. But this expense becomes minor when the number of philosophers – and hence the distribution of the application – increases. Distribution may also justify the notch in the plot for the experiments with the unreplicated version of the application: with six philosophers there is exactly one replica per server, so each processor is dedicated to its execution. In the case of the semi-active replication protocol, the cost of the communications within every RG, as well as the increasing processor loads, explain the poor performances.

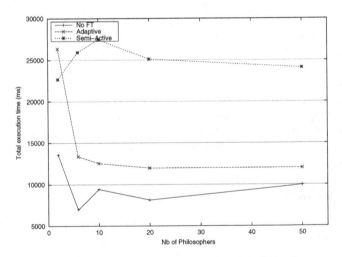

Fig. 7. Comparison of the total execution times with various fault tolerance protocols

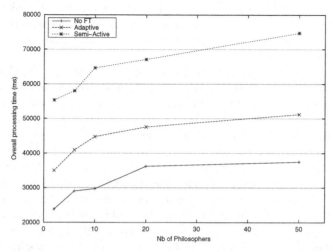

Fig. 8. Comparison of the total processing times with various fault tolerance protocols

It is important to note that, in the case where the strategies inside RGs are switched, failures will not forbid the termination of the application. As long as there is at least one philosopher to keep consuming meals, the application will finish without deadlock. Besides it is possible to simply restart philosophers which weren't replicated, since these replicas had no impact on the rest of the application: no chop-sticks in use, no request for chop-sticks recorded. This is not true in the unreplicated version of the application as failures that occur while chop-sticks are in use will have an impact on the rest of the computation.

Figure 8 accounts for the measured values of the total processing time in each situation. Those results also concur to show that adaptive fault tolerance is a valuable protocol. Of course, the measured times are not as good as in the unreplicated version. But in comparison, the semi-active version induces a lot more processor activity. It ought to be remembered that in this particular application, the switch version is as reliable as the semi-active version in terms of raw fault tolerance: the computation will end correctly. However, the semi-active version obviously implies that the average recovery delays will be much shorter in the event of failures. In such situations, the follower can directly take over. Whereas with the adaptive protocol, the recovery delay depends on the strategy in use: unreplicated philosophers will have to be restarted from scratch and passive standbies will have to be activated before taking over.

6   Conclusion and Perspectives

The framework presented in this paper enables the building of fault-tolerant distributed multi-agent systems. The resulting software is flexible: it possesses the ability to decide which parts of the computation are more critical than the others, and hence should be made to bypass failures through replication. DARX offers control over the way the application safeguards its components, enabling the fault tolerance of the computation to be automatically fine-tuned on the fly. This feature proves to be quite powerful: it allows adaptive fault tolerance whilst preserving software efficiency, as demonstrated by the performances shown in this paper. Moreover, the architecture of the middleware is designed to be scalable.

However, there are still some issues left unsolved: for instance, the observation service mentioned in section 3.4 remains to be integrated in the framework. It works as a stand-alone application, and the API for exchanging commands and data with DARX is set. But the modifications of the DARX classes which shall make use of the observation service are being coded, and the dynamic usage of the observation data is still research material. Hence the current field of investigation is the analysis of the dynamic *criticity* of agents and the adaptation of the replication policy. The heuristics used up to now are mainly driven by the user, due to the lack of a functional observation system. Once it is fully integrated in DARX, that is once the real characteristics of the hosts and of the network are acquired, those heuristics will be enhanced for further efficiency and adequateness. Paving the way for optimal heuristics, [GFB05] presents an extended range of simulations aimed at studying the behaviour of an agent application on top of DARX, as well as its resilience to failures.

In order to validate the work achieved up until now, applications are currently being developed. Those include a basic crisis management system destined to test the viability and the utility of our architecture in terms of such software.

References

[BDC00]   H. Boukachour, C. Duvallet and A. Cardon, "Multiagent systems to prevent technological risks" In *Proceedings of IEA/AIE'2000*, Springer Verlag 2000.

[BGCAMS02]   J.-P. Briot, Z. Guessoum, S. Charpentier, S. Aknine, O. Marin and P. Sens "Dynamic Adaptation of Replication Strategies for Reliable Agents" In *Proc. 2nd Symposium on Adaptive Agents and Multi-Agent Systems (AAMAS-2)*, London, UK, April 2002.

[BMS02]   M. Bertier, O. Marin and P. Sens, "Implementation and performance evaluation of an adaptable failure detector" In *Proc. of the International Conference on Dependable Systems and Networks*, Washington, DC, USA, 2002.

[BMS03]   M. Bertier, O. Marin and P. Sens, "Performance analysis of hierarchical failure detector" To be published in *Proc. of the International Conference on Dependable Systems and Networks*, San Francisco, CA, USA, June 2003.

[CT96]   T. D. Chandra and S. Toueg "Unreliable Failure Detectors for Reliable Distributed Systems" In *Journal of the ACM*, 43:2, March 1996, pp. 225-267.

[FD02]   A. Fedoruk and R. Deters, "Improving Fault-Tolerance by Replicating Agents", In *Proceedings of 1st International Joint Conference on Autonomous Agents and Multi-Agent Systems*, Bologna, Italy, July 2002.

[GB99]   Z. Guessoum and J.-P. Briot, "From active objects to autonomous agents" In *Special Series on Actors and Agents*, edited by Dennis Kafura and Jean-Pierre Briot, IEEE Concurrency, 7(3):68-76, July-September 1999.

[GFB05]   Z. Guessoum, N. Faci and J-P. Briot, "Adaptive Replication of Large-Scale Multi-Agent Systems - Towards a Fault-Tolerant Multi-Agent Platform", In *Software Engineering for Large-Scale Multi-Agent Systems (SELMAS05)*, St. Louis, USA, May 2005.

[GF00]   O. Gutknecht and J.Ferber, "The MadKit agent platform architecture", In
             1st Workshop on Infrastructure for Scalable Multi-Agent Systems, Barcelona,
             Spain, June 2000.
[GS97]   R. Guerraoui and A. Schiper, "Software-Based Replication For Fault Toler-
             ance" In *IEEE Computer*, 30(4):68-74, 1997.
[H96]   Hägg S., "A Sentinel Approach to Fault Handling in Multi-Agent Systems", in
             *Proceedings of the 2nd Australian Workshop on Distributed AI, 4th Pacific Rim
             Int'al Conf. on A.I. (PRICAI'96)*, Cairns, Australia, August 27, 1996.
[H85]   C. A. R. Hoare, "Communicating Sequential Processes", Prentice Hall, 1985.
[KCL00]   Kumar S., Cohen P. R., Levesque H. J., The Adaptive AgentArchitecture:
             Achieving Fault-Tolerance Using Persistent Broker Teams", *4th International
             Conference on Multi-Agent Systems (ICMAS 2000)*, Boston MA, USA, July
             2000.
[KIBW99]   Z. Kalbarczyk, R. K. Iyer, S. Bagchi, K. Whisnant, "Chameleon: A Software
             Infrastructure for Adaptive Fault Tolerance", *IEEE Transactions on Parallel
             and Distributed Systems*, vol. 10, no.6, June 1999, pp. 560-579
[MASIF98]   D. Milojicic et al, "MASIF: The OMG Mobile Agent System Interoperability
             Facility" In *Proc. of the 2nd Int. Workshop on Mobile Agents*, LNCS 1477,
             1998, pp. 50-67.
[MCM99]   D. Martin, A. Cheyer and D. Moran "The Open Agent Architecture: A Frame-
             work for Building Distributed Software Systems" In *Applied Artificial Intelli-
             gence*, 13(1-2):91-128, January-March 1999.
[MSBG01]   O. Marin, P. Sens, J.-P. Briot and Z. Guessoum "Towards Adaptive Fault-
             Tolerance for Distributed Multi-Agent Systems" In *Proceedings of ER-
             SADS'2001*, pp.195-201, Bertinoro, Italy, May 2001.
[NS00]   Niranjan Suri et al.,, "An Overview of the NOMADS Mobile Agent System" In
             Proceedings of ECOOP'2000, Nice, France, 2000.
[PS01]   Stefan Pleisch and André Schiper, "Fatomas - a fault-tolerant mobile agent sys-
             tem based on the agent-dependent approach", In *Proc. of the IEEE Int. Conf.
             on Dependable Systems and Networks*, Goteborg, Sweden, July 2001.
[RBS96]   R. van Renesse, K. Birman, and S. Maffeis, "Horus: A flexible group commu-
             nication system", In *Communications of the ACM*, 39(4):76–83, April 1996.
[SBS99]   M. Strasser, J. Baumann, and M. Schwehm, "An Agent-based Framework for
             the Transparent Distribution of Computations" In *H. Arabnia (ed.), Proc. of
             PDPTA'1999*, Vol I:376-382, Las Vegas, USA, 1999.
[SBS00]   L. Silva, V. Batista, and J. Silva, "Fault-tolerant execution of mobile agents", In
             Proc. of the International Conference on Dependable Systems and Networks,
             pp. 135-143, New York, June 2000.

Nautical Predictive Routing Protocol (NPRP) for the Dynamic Ad-Hoc Nautical Network (DANN)*

Luqi, Valdis Berzins, and William H. Roof

Naval Postgraduate School, Monterey, CA 93943, USA

Abstract. The Carrier Strike Group (CSG) and the Expeditionary Strike Group (ESG) are two common types of US Naval units consisting of multiple ships traveling as a group. All vessels within the CSG/ESG transmit and receive data via satellite, even when those vessels are within radio frequency line of sight (RFLOS). Within the CSG/ESG, satellite communications (SATCOM) are clearly necessary for vessels well forward of the main body, but could be augmented by RFLOS wireless communications for some members of the CSG/ESG. The goal of this research is to identify software technology that minimizes the barriers to employing affordable, commercially available technology (i.e., 802.11x) for ship-to-ship communications at sea. Some of the existing barriers to 802.11x communications at sea result from communication protocols that do not support the varying topologies or human network intervention one would expect to encounter within the CSG/ESG. This paper advances the concept for a predictive routing protocol that proactively addresses the topological and human issues unique to the DANN. Proactive routing will re-route the transmissions prior to interruptions, thus preventing interruption of open communication sessions.

1 CSG/ESG Communications Issues

Currently, passing data from ship-to-ship requires four separate transmissions [1]. Delays associated with signal propagation over long distances, communications protocols, network prioritization, dropped packets and other overhead issues can produce excessive delays and are often inadequate for VTC or VOIP sessions. The challenges and risks associated with some ship-to-ship data communications can be mitigated with predictive routing that eliminates the requirements for SATCOM and associated processing by the remote network operations center (NOC). The challenge of establishing and maintaining RFLOS communications at sea, with an acceptable quality of service, is rather unique. This research uses the Washington State Ferries (WSF) Wireless Internet Project as a baseline and advances that work to address a fully ad-hoc mobile network at sea. WSF research demonstrated the feasibility of pushing 802.11a up to 20 miles over water, identifying 802.11a as the baseline backhaul evaluated for the DANN [2].

---

* This work was supported in part by ARO under project 5NPGARO032 and by AFOSR under project F1ATA05192G001.

F. Kordon and J. Sztipanovits (Eds.): Monterey Workshop 2005, LNCS 4322, pp. 106–120, 2007.

1.1   Problem Modeling

Nautical communication requirements are modeled as a time-dependent graph where each vertex represents a vessel within the CSG/ESG, and each arc represents a communications link. Some of the unique challenges facing the DANN are summarized below.

1.2   Topological Challenges

Vertices move out of range:

- Vessel may move out of range due to course, speed, currents and wind, or to avoid obstacles and localized weather patterns. This could sever a link between vertices or disconnect the entire network.
- Vessels may move out of range in response to direction from the CSG/ESG commander.
- The NPRP will predict when the arc between two vertices will break connectivity, calculate course and speed data needed for vessels to maintain connectivity and find an alternative route for use in case repositioning the vessels is not possible.

Localized Weather Patterns:

- Localized weather patterns and sea states on or near the arc linking two vertices may indicate that more complex routing would provide a higher quality of service.
- The NPRP will calculate the best route around localized weather patterns. If an alternate route does not exist, the NPRP will calculate course and speed data needed for vessels to establish an alternate route.

RF Shadowing:

- Vertices in direct communication with each other may experience a break in signal if both nodes pass on either side of a obstacle, such as an island. This obstacle can cast an RF shadow and block the signal from reaching the vertices.
- Vertices in direct communication with each other may experience a break in signal if a vessel without the ability to relay the wireless traffic passes between the two vertices. The vessel would essentially cast an RF shadow and block the signal.
- Obstacles are modeled as circular regions with a radius 1.10 times the physical radius. The additional ten percent provides an extra measure of security when calculating the time from the arc to the obstruction.
- The NPRP will predict when an obstacle will sever an arc, and determine an alternate route. If an alternate route does not exist, the NRPR will calculate course and speed data needed for vessels to establish an alternate route.

1.3 Human Intervention

DANN performance issues arising from vertices specified "out of service" due to human intervention are summarized below.

- Vessel is in emission control (EMCON) status that prohibits RF communications.
- Vessel is in maintenance status and some communications systems may be shut down for service.
- Vessel is designated "no-relay" by the CBG/ESG Commander to provide additional bandwidth for higher priority communications.
- Vessel is involved in a drill that requires the discontinuation of power to the DANN system.
- If any of these states exist, the NPRP will calculate an alternative route and, if necessary, calculate course and speed corrections for vessels to move them to locations to maintain connectivity.

2 Adaptive and Non-adaptive Protocols

Most mobile ad-hoc network routing protocols are reactive in nature. These protocols are also called "adaptive" because they change routing decisions "on-the-fly" to compensate for network traffic and topology. Adaptive routers receive information from other routers and use this information to adapt routes to the traffic and topology snapshot. An example of such a protocol is the Ad-Hoc On Demand Distance Vector (AODV) [3]. This and other reactive protocols capture variables such as signal strength, signal-to-noise ratio, and number of hops as input to routing algorithms. Data capture of these variables occurs in real-time or near real-time, causing the protocol to re-calculate the optimal routes. Non-adaptive routing protocols, sometimes called static routing protocols, generally do not base routing decisions on measurements, traffic or topology. Non-adaptive routing protocols calculate the route in advance and download the data to the router prior to the router coming on-line. Because static routing protocols are more likely to address fixed topologies, they can be more predictive in nature than adaptive protocols. The predictive nature of the NPRP should assist in maintaining network connectivity. This protocol anticipates and prevents degradations in quality of service (QOS) before they occur. For example, at distances of 20 nautical miles vessel maneuverability, i.e., the ability of a vertex to move to a new location to re-establish connectivity, is relatively slow. Once a vertex loses connectivity, it may take an unacceptable period of time to re-establish RFLOS communications. In anticipation of this state, NPRP has the ability to proactively move a vertex to a new location as it senses an impending break in communications. The system can also provide a vessel (or vessels) with course and speed to re-establish communications within the DANN after a break has occurred. The development and employment of a Nautical Predictive Routing Protocol would compensate for the unique topological and human issues surrounding the DANN. Essentially, NPRP is a hybrid of adaptive and non-adaptive protocol features, and might be called an "adaptive-static" protocol.

3   NPRP Approach

NPRP requires data from the CBG/ESG as a whole, and from each vessel in the group. The essential data available to NPRP is as follows: Each vessel broadcasts unique data to shore facilities via SATCOM. The data includes:

– position in latitude and longitude
– course in degrees
– speed in nautical miles per hour

Additionally, each vessel publishes a plan of the day that often includes planned drills, system maintenance and other activities that would generate an "out of service" state for that vertex. Other data available from the CBG/ESG includes maps showing locations of fixed obstacles and weather information identifying both regional and localized weather patterns. A localized pattern will generally display as a geographic center of activity with an effective radius and a displacement vector.

3.1   DANN Routing Metrics

Each vertex routes the signal based upon information calculated by the DANN application. Each vertex also has full-duplex capability, since transmission is achieved via an amplified sector antenna (eight to fifteen degrees on the main lobe) and reception is via an omnidirectional high-gain antenna. With this infrastructure, each vertex can transmit and receive simultaneously, eliminating the bandwidth degradation normally associated with multi-hop routing. Since the vessels communicate their position, course and speed, each router knows the distance to each vertex, calculated via the Haversine Formula [4]. Standard Great Circle calculations typically apply to distances greater than those found in the CBG/ESG. For very long distances, such as from New York to Los Angeles, an arc more accurately describes the distance. For long distances, spherical trigonometry follows the Law of Cosines:

$$cos(c) = cos(a)cos(b) + sin(a)sin(b)cos(C) \qquad (1)$$

where a, b and c represent three sides of a spherical triangle and C represents the angle opposite side c. For short distances such as those found in the DANN, the Law of Cosines produces a rounding error that can be eliminated by using the Haversine Formula. Since this research addresses linear communication paths (RFLOS), the Haversine Formula provides a realistic and sufficiently accurate distance, d, between two vertices.

In the following equations, R represents the radius of the earth in kilometers.

$$d_{lon} = lon2 - lon1 \qquad (2)$$

$$d_{lat} = lat2 - lat1 \qquad (3)$$

$$a = (sin(dlat/2))^2 + cos(lat1)cos(lat2)sin(d_{lon}/2))^2 \qquad (4)$$

$$c = 2(atan2(\sqrt{a}, \sqrt{1-a})) \qquad (5)$$

$$d = R * c \qquad (6)$$

In some regards, routing within the DANN takes on the appearance of a modified distance vector routing protocol, mainly because each router knows the distance to its neighboring routers. [5] Common metrics found in vector routing protocols, such as delay, are not critical for the DANN. Given two dynamic vertices connected by an arc, a few of the key considerations and metrics for the DANN are given below, expressed in terms of the arc length between the two vertices.

- Is the length of an arc 20 NM or less?
- If the arc length is 20 NM or less, is the length increasing?
- If the length of the arc is increasing, at what time will it reach 20 NM?
- What course and speed corrections should be recommended for which vertex or vertices to ensure the arc remains less than 20 NM?

Given obstacles that might break the arc i.e., land masses, other vessels or localized weather patterns:

- Will the vertices' movements cause them to pass on opposing sides of an obstacle?
- Is the obstacle large enough to cast an RF shadow to break the arc?
- If the obstacle is large enough to break the arc, at what time will this happen?
- If the obstacle is large enough to break the arc, what are the course and speed corrections for which vertex or vertices to avoid having the obstacle break the arc?

Human Intervention.

- Is a vertex scheduled to be unavailable?
- If a vertex is scheduled to be unavailable, at what time will this occur?
- If a vertex is scheduled to be unavailable, what are the course and speed corrections for which vertex or vertices to remain connected?
- If a vertex suddenly becomes unavailable, what are the course and speed corrections for which vertex or vertices to re-establish communications?

In all cases described earlier where the vessel's DANN system is out of service due to human intervention, this intervention is scheduled and generally known by other vessels within the CBG/ESG. Unexpected unavailability generally corresponds to equipment failure. In these cases, the NPRP can track the events and update the routing table to exclude those vertices that will experience out of service conditions. In cases where the out of service vertices are critical to connecting the digraph, NPRP will calculate the next-best routing path and any vertices' course and speed changes necessary to connect the digraph. If there is no next-best solution, the NPRP will identify the vertex or vertices required to connect the digraph and calculate the course/speed changes necessary to position the vertices within backhaul range.

4   The Communication Graph

The dynamic nature of the CBG/ESG subnet is accurately described by three-dimensional vector physics. [6] The formation of vessels forms a communication graph consisting of mobile vertices and arcs that exhibit the topological and human variables described earlier in this paper. Since each vertex reports current location in latitude and longitude, as well as course and speed, the NPRP will calculate when a vertex will move beyond the range of the 802.11a backhaul system. This capability is most important when the vessel moving out of range will disconnect the graph. The NPRP will also calculate a course/speed change that will keep the vessel within range and will also calculate any appropriate course/speed changes for other vertices to provide connectivity redundancy. The communication graph has n vertices numbered 1 to n. Each vertex K has a displacement vector R_K, a velocity vector V_K.

The displacement vector R_K points from an arbitrary origin to the location of the vertex. The selection of the arbitrary origin should attempt to minimize the complexity of the software required to perform the calculations relative to the DANN. Examples of convenient arbitrary origins include the center of the earth, the centroid of the geometric shape formed by the CSB/ESG, or the vertex performing the calculation.

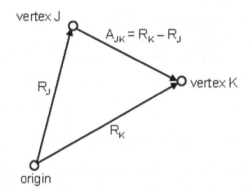

A velocity vector relative to the arbitrary origin for vertex K is defined by

$$V_K = \frac{dR_K}{(dt)} \tag{7}$$

A displacement vector from vertex J to vertex K is

$$A_{JK} = R_K - R_J \tag{8}$$

with an arc length of

$$L_{JK} = |A_{JK}| = \sqrt{A_{JK} \cdot A_{JK}} \tag{9}$$

The derivative of the arc length is

$$\frac{dL_{JK}}{dt} = 1/2 \sqrt[-2]{A_{JK} \cdot A_{JK}} 2A_{JK} \cdot \frac{dA_{JK}}{dt} = \frac{A_{JK}}{|A_{JK}|} \cdot \frac{dA_{JK}}{dt} \tag{10}$$

Using equations (7) and (8), this becomes

$$\frac{dL_{JK}}{dt} = \frac{A_{JK}}{|A_{JK}|} \cdot (V_K - V_J) \tag{11}$$

Within the DANN, the arc length is increasing if

$$\frac{dL_{JK}}{dt} > 0 \tag{12}$$

Based upon WSF research, reliable connectivity between two vertices exists if and only if the length of the arc between the two vertices is less than less than a maximum distance M. For the 802.11x implementation discussed above, M is 20 nautical miles (NM). We can use a linear approximation for short time periods t to express the loss of connectivity condition as

$$M = L_{JK} + \frac{dL_{JK}}{dt} t \tag{13}$$

If expression (11) shows the arc length to be increasing, equation 14 below estimates the time until vertex movement produces an arc of maximum allowable length (i.e., 20 NM) and ends reliable communication along the arc.

$$t = \frac{M - L_{JK}}{\frac{dL_{JK}}{dt}} \tag{14}$$

5   The Obstacle Problem

As an arc between two vertices moves about the ocean's surface, it may move over a land mass that can produce an RF shadow, blocking the signal from reaching the intended receiver. Additionally, other moving vessels passing between two vertices may break the link and cause a loss of communication. These situations will, at a minimum, break RF communications with one vessel, and could disconnect a larger portion of the communication graph. Land masses such as islands and localized weather patterns are depicted both on nautical charts and are visible via radar. Vessels on the ocean's surface are also identified and charted via radar. NPRP will plan for such shadowing conditions and calculate ship movements to compensate for the break in the arc, and to keep the digraph connected. To accomplish this, NPRP must measure and track, over time, the perpendicular distance from the arc to the shadowing object. The algorithm assumes the shadowing object is a sphere, and adds a safety zone of ten percent to the actual radius to ensure the signal can be routed around the shadowing object before the link breaks.

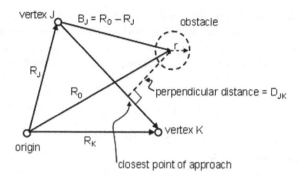

Given two vertices J and K, to calculate the perpendicular distance, let R_O be the displacement vector of an obstacle with radius r, and let $B_J = R_O - R_J$ represent the position of the obstacle relative to vertex J.

Let

$$V_O = \frac{dR_O}{dt} \tag{15}$$

be the velocity of the obstacle. The perpendicular distance from the arc A_{JK} to the obstacle is

$$D_{JK} = |\hat{A}_{JK} \times B_J| = \frac{|A_{JK} \times B_J|}{|A_{JK}|} \tag{16}$$

Where $\hat{A}$ is the unit vector parallel to A_{JK}. The derivative of the perpendicular distance is

$$\frac{dD_{JK}}{dt} = \frac{d}{dt} \frac{|A_{JK} \times B_J|}{|A_{JK}|} = \frac{d}{dt} \sqrt{\frac{(A_{JK} \times B_J) \cdot (A_{JK} \times B_J)}{A_{JK} \cdot A_{JK}}} \tag{17}$$

This equation becomes

$$\frac{2\frac{|A_{JK} \times B_J|}{|A_{JK}|^2} \cdot \frac{d}{dt} A_{JK} \times B_J - 2\frac{|A_{JK} \times B_J|^2}{|A_{JK}|^3} \frac{d}{dt} L_{JK}}{\frac{2|A_{JK} \times B_J|}{|A_{JK}|}} \tag{18}$$

Note:

$$\frac{d}{dt} A_{JK} \times B_J = \frac{dA_{JK}}{dt} \times B_J + A_{JK} \times \frac{dB_J}{dt} = (V_K - V_J) \times B_J + A_{JK} \times (V_O - V_J) \tag{19}$$

Then, based upon the equation

$$\frac{dL_{JK}}{dt} = \frac{A_{JK}}{|A_{JK}|} \cdot (V_K - V_J) \tag{20}$$

$$\frac{d}{dt} D_{JK} = \frac{A_{JK} \times B_J}{|A_{JK} \times B_J|} \cdot \frac{(V_K - V_J) \times B_J + A_{JK} \times (V_O - V_J)}{|A_{JK}|} - \frac{|A_{JK} \times B_J|}{|A_{JK}|^3} A_{JK} \cdot (V_K - V_J) \tag{21}$$

In this equation, all quantities on the right hand side of the equation can be calculated from the positions and velocities of the vertices and obstacle. Occlusions are a concern only when the closest point of the approach to the obstacle is between the end points of the arc. This happens when both of the following conditions hold:

$$(R_K - R_J) \cdot (R_O - R_J) > 0 \qquad (22)$$

$$(R_J - R_K) \cdot (R_O - R_K) > 0 \qquad (23)$$

Using a linear approximation

$$r = D_{JK} + \frac{d}{dt} D_{JK} t \qquad (24)$$

The time to occlusion by the obstacle's edge can be calculated as follows:

$$t + \frac{r - D_{JK}}{\frac{dD_{JK}}{dt}} \qquad (25)$$

Normally, $D_{JK} > r$ and this constraint is only of concern when

$$\frac{d}{dt} D_{JK} < 0 \qquad (26)$$

This means the obstacle is getting closer to the line of sight.

The routing algorithm will perform these calculations periodically and an arc will be dropped from the routing tables if the time t from equation 12 or equation 24 is less than two periods. In order to economize on the hardware, we have proposed a configuration in which each node is connected to its nearest neighbors satisfying the constraints implied by the above, up to a maximum of two connections for each node. If the ships are close enough so that both nearest neighbors satisfy the constraints, this connection policy results in a ring that enables all of the nodes to communicate even if one of the links is severed. Since the constraints are re-evaluated periodically, new connections can be formed when weak connections are dropped, and the identity of the two nearest neighbors can change as the ships change their relative positions, with corresponding changes to the routing patterns.

6   Relevant Research

The research surveyed in this section supports, either directly or indirectly, the NPRP concept. As with any software, NPRP architecture, interoperability, quality of service and reliability must be well-planned and optimal. The research abstracts below provide a window into each graduate's unique research along with a brief explanation of the relevance to NPRP.

6.1   Integrating Stand-Alone Systems

Dr. Paul Young's research identified a method for meeting the need for interoperability among independently developed heterogeneous operating systems, host languages and data models. [7]

The approach articulated in the research has applicability to nautical predictive routing protocol for the dynamic ad-hoc naval network. It is expected that the integrated ships' systems required to host and maintain the NPRP software are likely to be from a variety of independent development contracts and would reflect the developer's strengths, the age of the ship and the technology available at that time. The Object Oriented Method for Interoperability provides a potential methodology for enabling operations among the various systems that may be used in the NPRP and DANN architecture.

Abstract. [7] Meeting future system requirements by integrating existing stand-alone systems is attracting renewed interest. Computer communications advances, functional similarities in related systems, and enhanced information description mechanisms suggest that improved capabilities may be possible; but full realization of this potential can only be achieved if stand-alone systems are fully interoperable. Interoperability among independently developed heterogeneous systems is difficult to achieve: systems often have different architectures, different hardware platforms, different operating systems, different host languages and different data models. The Object-Oriented Method for Interoperability (OOMI) introduced in this dissertation resolves modeling differences in a federation of independently developed heterogeneous systems, thus enabling system interoperation. First a model of the information and operations shared among systems, termed a Federation Interoperability Object Model (FIOM), is defined. Construction of the FIOM is done prior to run-time with the assistance of a specialized toolset, the OOMI Integrated Development Environment (OOMI IDE). Then at runtime OOMI translators utilize the FIOM to automatically resolve differences in exchanged information and in inter-system operation signatures.

6.2   Layered Abstraction Approach

Dr. Michael Dabose proposes a component-based layered abstraction approach to software development that creates an environment for porting software from one platform to another. [8] Given the expected disparity in sensors and computing platforms existing among warships of various classes and vintages, the layered abstraction approach can be considered for the implementation phase following successful proof-of-concept exercises and demonstrations.

Abstract. [8] The current state of the art techniques to describe and implement a hard real time embedded software architecture for missile systems range from inadequate to totally nonexistent. Most of the existing software implementations within such systems consist of hand coded functionality, optimized for speed, with little or no thought to long term maintainability, and extensibility. Utilizing current state of the art software development technology, the first ever software architecture for hard real time missile software has been designed and successfully demonstrated. This component based layered abstraction pattern approach to software architecture revolutionizes reduced development time, cost, provides an order of magnitude decrease in error, and is the first such software architecture to function within the hard time constraints of the most extreme cases related to missile systems. Additionally, componentization of functionality allows for porting of software developed for one missile to any other missile with no modification. Hardware obsolescence is overcome by software abstraction layers which isolate the hardware instance from the software functionality providing a rapid, low cost transition of software from one instance of missile hardware to another. The end result of this research is a software architecture demonstrating the capability of managing complex functionality in an accurate, quantifiable, and cost effective manner.

6.3   Quality of Service Execution Path

The quality of service execution path defined by Dr. John Drummond addresses a weakness in wireless QoS by identifying and mitigating QoS conflicts that occur during program execution. [9] Quality of service goals, such as network latency, jitter and dropped packets may not necessarily result from physical network issues. Improving quality of service is one of the motivations for the DANN. It is important to optimize the program execution path to maximize quality of service prior to adding the network itself to the environment.

Abstract. [9] The substantial complexity and strict requirements of distributed command & control systems creates an environment that places extreme demands upon system resources. Furthermore, inconsistent resource distribution also introduces the distinct possibility of potential errors, and process failures. Many of these potential difficulties can be understood and addressed through a practical analysis of the resource management and distribution procedures employed within these systems. This analysis should include a direct focus upon the essential quality of service that is shared among the software programs that operate within this environment. However, the current approaches to this analysis are lacking in that there is no accurate method to determine precisely what quality of service based conflicts take place during program execution. This problem can be addressed through examination of specific quality of service actions during program execution. To achieve a precise analysis of quality of service actions this dissertation research has implemented an approach to examine the exact quality of service execution path during program operation.

6.4   Architecture Readiness Levels

Dr. Kevin Greaney's research proposes a software architecture based approach for simulation model representations.[10] As the current NPRP simulation model grows in complexity, it is important to ensure its interoperability with other network and communication models. The approach described in Dr. Greaney's dissertation provides a baseline for building simulation models with a higher degree of interoperability certainty.

Abstract. [10] National- and Department-level decision-makers expect credible Department of Defense models and simulations (M&S) to provide them confidence in the simulation results, especially for mission-critical and high-risk decisions supporting National Security. Many of these large-scale, software-intensive simulation systems were autonomously developed over time, and subject to varying degrees of funding, maintenance, and life-cycle management practices, resulting in heterogeneous model representations and data. Systemic problems with distributed interoperability of these non-trivial simulations in federations persist, and current techniques, procedures, and tools have not achieved the desired results. The Software Architecture-Based Product Line for simulation model representations, employing Architecture Readiness Levels presented in this dissertation provides an alternative methodology. The proposed four-layered M&S software architecture-based product line model enables the development of model representations supported by readiness levels. Each layer reflects a division of the software architecture-based product line. The layer represents a horizontal slice through the architecture for organizing viewpoints or views at the same level of abstraction while the software architecture-based product line represents a vertical slice. A layer may maintain multiple views and viewpoints of a software architecture-based product line. A Domain Metadata Repository prescribes the interaction between layers. We introduce the Domain Integrated Product Development Team concept.

6.5   Efficiency and Effectiveness Model

Dr. Grant Jacoby's Intranet efficiency and effectiveness model [11] directly supports the NPRP approach in that NPRP is a predictive routing protocol for a wireless intranet servicing a formation of ships at sea. The evaluation of critical business requirements maps directly to the network "human intervention" described earlier in this paper. A process to identify and measure critical business requirements and their associated variables has the potential to increase intranet quality of service within DANN nodes, as well as throughout other intranet applications.

Abstract. [11] This research provides the first theoretical model – the Intranet Efficiency and Effectiveness Model (IEEM) – for the Family of Measures approach to measure Web activity as well as a holistic framework and multi-disciplinary quality paradigm approach not previously derived in viewing and measuring intranet contributions in the context of a corporations overall critical business requirements. This is accomplished by applying a balanced baseline set of metrics and conversion ratios linked to business processes as they relate to knowledge workers, IT managers and business decision makers seeking to increase value. It also outlines who should conduct these measurements and how in the form of a business intelligence team and provides a means in which to calculate return on intranet metrics investment (ROIMI) with a common unit of analysis for both aggregate and sub-corporate levels through forms of the Knowledge Value Added (KVA) and Activity Based Costing (ABC) methodologies.

6.6   Hoslistic Framework for Software Architecture

Dr. Joseph Puett proposes a software engineering holistic framework that identifies interoperable synergies among software development tools and models.[12] NPRP modeling for the DANN is an essential step towards live testing at sea. The expense associated with live testing must be mitigated by proof-of-concept modeling, and Dr. Puett's research supports enhanced modeling among the various subsystems that will ultimately comprise the DANN. The identification and quantification of synergistic dependencies described in this research provide a potential framework for developing NPRP solutions for multiple topographies.

Abstract. [12] This dissertation presents a Holistic Framework for Software Engineering (HFSE) that establishes collaborative mechanisms by which existing heterogeneous software development tools and models will interoperate. Past research has been conducted with the aim of developing or improving individual aspects of software development; however, this research focuses on establishing a holistic approach over the entire development effort where unrealized synergies and dependencies between all of the tools' artifacts can be visualized and leveraged to produce both improvements in process and product. The HFSE is both a conceptual framework and a software engineering process model (with tool support) where the dependencies between software development artifacts are identified, quantified, tracked, and deployed throughout all artifacts via middleware. Central to the approach is the integration of Quality Function Deployment (QFD) into the Relational Hypergraph (RH) Model of Software Evolution. This integration allows for the dependencies between artifacts to be automatically tracked throughout the hypergraph representation of the development effort, thus assisting the software engineer to isolate subgraphs as needed.

6.7   Software System Safety Index

Dr. Christopher Williamson's research provides a software engineering methodology for identifying software system weaknesses and for preventing potential catastrophic system failures.[13] This correlates directly with NPRP and the DANN in that software system failures in times of armed conflict, although perhaps not catastrophic, may have catastrophic results. Dr. Williamson's approach identifies ways to improve software safety and reliability, both necessary for a system such as that supported by NPRP.

Abstract. [13] The current state of the art techniques of Software Engineering lack a formal method and metric for measuring the safety index of a software system. The lack of such a methodology has resulted in a series of highly publicized and costly catastrophic failures of highassurance software systems. This dissertation introduces a formal method for identifying and evaluating the weaknesses in a software system using a more precise metric, counter to traditional methods of development that have proven unreliable. 'This metric utilizes both a qualitative and quantitative approach employing principles of statistics and probability to determine the level of safety, likelihood of hazardous events, and the economic costbenefit of correcting the flaws through the lifecycle of a software system. This dissertation establishes benefits in the fields of Software Engineering of highassurance systems, improvements in Software Safety and Software Reliability, and an expansion within the discipline of Software Economics and Management.

6.8   Mass-Spring Application to Network Connectivity

Dr. William Roof's research into predictive signal routing and communication graph node positioning inserts mass-spring theory NPRP into the system to maintain node connectivity.[14] This approach decentralizes the network control by identifying a methodology by which each node operates as an independent agent. The distributed approach improves the robustness of the system, relieves network traffic and enhances network quality of service.

Abstract. [14] The truly unique contribution within NPRP is the application of Mass-Spring theory to maintain connectivity between the vertices in the DANN. This is the first ever application of this methodology to mobile ad-hoc wireless networks at sea. The approach, algorithms, and object classes developed to model the approach constitute new contributions as well. The goal of this research is to leave the WiFi standards in place, and to handle key network issues such as load balancing and quality of service by identifying system constraints and by developing software routing that predicts network connection problems and adjusts the topology prior to the problems occurring. The identification of the topology and the hardware constraints that keep the system extremely simple provide a means to model and test low-cost, commercial 802.11x equipment without extensive software engineering rework of the existing protocol stack.

7   Conclusions

The Dynamic Ad-Hoc Nautical Network presents unique challenges to signal routing over a wireless network. The ability to employ a protocol that is predictive, that encompasses the best attributes of both static and dynamic protocols, and that can calculate course and speed to position vertices properly before they lose connectivity, should increase network QOS beyond that available through standard wireless routing protocols.

References

[1] Interview with Tim Hale, SPAWAR PMW-170, San Diego, California, 14 April 2005.

[2] Interview with Nelson D. Ludlow, Washington State Ferries Wireless Internet Project, January 2004.

[3] Chakeres, Ian D, and Belding-Royer, Elizabeth M., AODV Routing Protocol Implementation Design, University of California, Santa Barbara, 1999.

[4] Sinnott, R.W., Virtues of the Haversine, Sky and Telescope, p. 68, 1984.

[5] Tanenbaum, Andrew S., Computer Networks, Fourth Edition, Prentice Hall, p. 357, 2003.

[6] Hecker, Chris, Physics Part 4, The Third Dimension, Behind the Screen, Dec 1995, pp 110.

[7] Young, Paul E., *Heterogeneous Software System Interoperability Through Computer-Aided Resolution of Modeling Differences*, Ph.D. Dissertation, Naval Postgraduate School, Monterey, CA, 2002

[8] DaBose, Michael W., *A Layered Softwre Architecture for Hard Real Time (HRT) Embedded Systems*, Ph.D. Dissertation, Naval Postgraduate School, Monterey, CA, 2002

[9] Drummond, John, *Specifying Quality of Service for Distributed Systems Based Upon Behavior Models*, Ph.D. Dissertation, Naval Postgraduate School, Monterey, CA, 2002

[10] Greaney, Kevin J., *Evolving a Simulation Model Product Line Software Architecture from Heterogeneous Model Representations*, Ph.D. Dissertation, Naval Postgraduate School, Monterey, CA, 2003

[11] Jacoby, Grant A., *A Metric Model for Intranet Portal Business Requirements*, Ph.D. Dissertation, Naval Postgraduate School, Monterey, CA, 2003

[12] Puett, Joseph F. III, *Holistic Framework for Establishing Interoperability of Heterogeneous Software Development Tools*, Ph.D. Dissertation, Naval Postgraduate School, Monterey, CA, 2003

[13] Williamson, Christopher L., *A Formal Application of Safety and Risk Assessmetn in Software Systems*, Ph.D. Dissertation, Naval Postgraduate School, Monterey, CA, 2004

[14] Roof, William H., *Nautical Predictive Routing Protocol (NPRP) for the Dynamic Ad-hoc Naval Network (DANN)*, Ph.D. Dissertation, Naval Postgraduate School, Monterey, CA, 2006

A Factory to Design and Build Tailorable and Verifiable Middleware

Jérôme Hugues[1], Fabrice Kordon[2], Laurent Pautet[1], and Thomas Vergnaud[1]

[1] GET-Télécom Paris – LTCI-UMR 5141 CNRS
46, rue Barrault, F-75634 Paris CEDEX 13, France
jerome.hugues@enst.fr, thomas.vergnaud@enst.fr, laurent.pautet@enst.fr
[2] Université Pierre & Marie Curie, Laboratoire d'Informatique de Paris 6/MoVe 4, place
Jussieu, F-75252 Paris CEDEX 05, France
fabrice.kordon@lip6.fr

Abstract. Heterogeneous non-functional requirements of Distributed Real-Time Embedded (DRE) system put a limit on middleware engineering: the middleware must reflect application requirements, with limited runtime impact. Thus, building an application-tailored middleware is both a requirement and a challenge.

In this paper, we provide an overview of our work on the construction of middleware. We focus on two complementary projects: the definition of middleware that provides strong support for both tailorability and verification of its internals; the definition of a methodology that enables the automatizing of key steps of middleware construction.

We illustrate how our current work on PolyORB, Ocarina and the use of Petri Nets allows designer to build the middleware that precisely matches its application requirements and comes with precise proof of its properties.

1   Introduction

Middleware first emerged as a general solution to build distributed applications. Models and abstractions such as RPC, distributed objects hide the intrinsic of distribution from the user, and provide a programming model close to the local case.

In the meantime, the need for Distributed Real-Time Embedded systems (DRE) increases regularly. Such systems require execution infrastructures that have specific capabilities, some of which conflict with "plain old middleware technology":

– *Distribution* cannot remain hidden from the developer. The semantics of the distribution models must be adapted to real-time application needs. For instance, the application entity should be well adapted to scheduling analysis such as the publish/subscribe model [RGS95]. Besides the impact of runtime entities (e.g. communication channels, memory management) on timeliness or determinism must be fully assessed.
– *Real-Time* engineering guidelines must be supported by the middleware. This middleware follows a clear and precise design so as to guarantee its determinism and its temporal properties; it comes with complete proofs that it does not withdraw the properties of the application [Bud03]. Finally, a methodological guide, support

F. Kordon and J. Sztipanovits (Eds.): Monterey Workshop 2005, LNCS 4322, pp. 121–142, 2007.

tools and Quality of Service (QoS) policies help to tailor the middleware with respect to the application requirements.

- *Embedded* targets that have strong constraints on their resources (e.g. CPU, memory, bandwidth) or limited run-time support by a real-time kernel (no exception, no dynamic memory, limited number of threads, etc). So, middleware must cope with strong limitations; and scale down to small targets. In some cases, new functions or QoS policies are added to cope with platform limitations, e.g. data compression for systems with a narrow bandwidth.

So, there is a need to 1/ make available to the developer some internals of the middleware to allow its tailoring and adaptation; 2/ define a development process and supporting tools to ease this adaptation and ensure its is correct with respect to middleware constraints.

Let us note a DRE is usually composed of several components for with different requirements. Therefore, both functional interoperability and compatibility of non-functional policies must be contemplated. Such assessment capability is seldom contemplated by middleware architects.

Another common pitfall when designing DRE is the use of "Commercial Off-The-Shelf" (COTS) components. This allows to reduce costs and potential errors by reusing already tested components. But this puts a strong limit on middleware tuning, verification and performance capabilities.

Engineers of DRE systems require middleware that have good performance (including efficient marshaling), real time (use only deterministic constructs), fit embedded constraints. Besides, they also need to ensure their use of the middleware is correct (no deadlock, deadline are respected, etc). Hence, this calls not only for a middleware, but also for a design process and tools that allow the user to carefully tune the middleware it to needs, instead of selecting a "best effort" middleware.

The objective of the PolyORB project is to elaborate both a middleware and a design process. We propose an innovative architecture that aims at providing better control on the configuration of the middleware, and enables the careful analysis of its properties. This paper presents an overview of our work in this area for the past years.

In the next section, we motivate our work by reviewing major issues when designing middleware for DRE systems, revolving around tailorability and verification concerns. Then, we present our current results in middleware architecture, and how we efficiently address both concerns by defining an original architecture. We note that another limit to the adoption of middleware is the lack of tool support; we then discuss our current research work around Architecture Description Language to build tool that help building and verifying application-specific middleware configurations.

2   Tailorable and Verifiable Middleware: State of the Art

In this section, we discuss limits and trade-offs when considering tailorable and verifiable middleware. Even though both capabilities are of interest for the application designers, we note that there is usually little support provided by the middleware.

2.1 From Tailorability to Verification

The many and heterogeneous constraints of distributed applications deeply impact the development of distribution middleware. Middleware should support developers when designing, implementing and deploying such systems in heterogeneous environments and evaluate so called "non functional" requirements (such as QoS or reliability).

The design and implementation of tailorable middleware is now a (almost) mastered topic. Design patterns, frameworks have proved their value to adapt middleware to a wide family of requirements [SB03].

In the mean time, middleware platforms have shown in various projects they can meet stringent requirements. They are now used in many mission-critical applications, including space, aeronautics and transportation.

Building distribution platform for such systems is a complex task. One has to cope with the restrictions enforced to achieve high integrity standards, or to meet certification requirements, such as DO-178B. Thus, one has to be able to assert middleware properties, e.g. functional behavioral properties such as *absence of deadlocks*, *request fairness*, or *correct resource dimensioning*; but also *temporal* properties.

Hence, verifying middleware is now becoming a stringent requirement in many DRE systems. The developer must ensure beforehand that its application design is compatible with middleware capabilities.

We claim middleware engineering should now provide provisions for some verification mechanisms as defined by the ISO committee [ISO94] as *"[the] confirmation by examination and provision of objective evidence that specified requirements have been fulfilled. Objective evidence is information which can be proved true, based on facts obtained through observation, measurement, test or other means."*

However, we note there is a double combinatorial explosion when considering middleware as a whole: the number of possible execution scenarios for one middleware configuration increases with the interleaving of threads and requests; the number of possible configurations increases with middleware adaptability and versatility. Finally, the behavior of a middleware highly depends on the configuration parameters selected by the user. Thus, verifying a middleware is a complex task.

Some projects consider testing some scenarios, on multiple target platforms. The Skoll Distributed Continuous Q&A project [MPY+04] relies on the concepts of distributed computing to test TAO many configurations and scenarios on computers around the world. This provides some hints on the behavior of the middleware, but cannot serve as a definite proof of its properties.

One may instead contemplate the verification of middleware properties. Yet this is usually done on a limited scale, restricted to the very specific scenarios of the application to be delivered and the semantics of the distribution model used (e.g. RT CORBA), for instance using the Bogor model checker [DDH+03]. But the middleware must be considered as part of the application and must not be discarded from the verification process as a blackbox would be.

However, middleware implementations of the same specifications may behave differently [BSPN00]. Some properties may be withdrawn by implementation issues, such as the use of COTS, that are hidden by this modeling process, or by different interpretation of the same specifications. Besides, such a verification process usually does not take into account implementation-defined configuration options, and target capabilities. Finally, such methods may be limited by combinatorial explosion that arise when building the system state-space.

Thus, we note it is hard (if not infeasible) to verify existing middleware as a whole. One should go forward and integrate verification to the design of middleware.

2.2 Addressing Verification Concerns

The formal-based verification of distributed application behavioral properties is usually the domain of verification-domain experts, using specific verification techniques, e.g. calculi, formal methods. However, such a verification process is usually used only to verify the semantics of the application (e.g. set of correct message sequences) [Jon94].

Turtle-P [AdSSK03] defines a UML profile for the validation of distributed applications, linked with code generation engines and validation tools built around RT-LOTOS [LAA04]. Validation is done either through simulation or verification of timed automata. However, this provides no information on the underlying distribution framework or middleware integrated to the system; and thus reduces the scope of the properties proved for the application under study.

Finally, it should be noted that complex semantics of distribution models is difficult to model and usually reduced: complex request dispatching policies, I/O or memory management are simplified. This reduces verification cost but also interest in the middleware modeled that looses many configuration capabilities.

Thus, we claim the verification process of a distributed application should also focus on the middleware as a building block, and thus middleware architecture should be made verification-ready so as to ease this process, without impeding its configurability.

Still, this increases the complexity of the verification process: one should focus on the actual configuration being used. This means that models of the configuration should be built "on demand", and that a strong link between model and implementation exists.

From the previous analysis, we conclude that a dedicated process to build and verify tailorable middleware is required. This process should be defined around well-grounded engineering methods and foster reusable and tailorable software components. Besides, verification techniques should be included in the process to assert strong properties of complex configurations, using the most suitable methods, depending on the nature of the property (causal, time, dependability, etc.).

3   The Schizophrenic Architecture: A Tailorable and Verifiable Middleware

In this section, we discuss our approach to design middleware dedicated to the requirements of a given application. This approach can be viewed as a co-design between the application and its supporting middleware. As an illustration of the feasibility of this design process, we provide a highly generic middleware architecture (also known as the "schizophrenic" architecture) and a methodological guide to instantiate it.

3.1 From System Requirements to a Dedicated Middleware

Actual middleware has to fulfill the system requirements. Some solutions are based on standardized "rigid" specifications; this is the case for most CORBA implementations and its many extensions (RT-, FT-, minimum CORBA...). Such middleware architectures are targeted to a certain application domain, and usually add many configuration parameters to partially control its resource or request processing policies.

Yet, implementations are not as efficient as specifically designed middleware [KP05]. The cost to deploy specific features is high due to the API to manipulate. Many optimization options cannot be implemented because of the heterogeneity of requirements and the number of (possibly useless) functions to support. Besides, verification or testing is not addressed and under the control of the middleware vendor. It is a direct consequence of the absence of a "one size fits all" middleware architecture.

Therefore, one should not contemplate middleware as a whole, but instead design middleware components and the process to combine them as a safe and affordable solution to system requirements. Thus, it becomes possible to build the distribution infrastructure built for specific requirements.

In the following, we describe the different steps we followed to define one such process built around a highly tailorable middleware architecture, a set of middleware components.

3.2 Defining a New Tailorable Middleware Architecture

Solutions have been proposed to design tailorable middleware. *Configurable* middleware defines an architecture centered on a given distribution model [SLM98] (e.g. distributed objects, message passing, etc.); this architecture can be tuned (tasking policy, etc.). *Generic* middleware [DHTS98] provides a general framework, which components have to be instantiated to create middleware implementations. Those implementations are called *personalities*. Generic middleware is not bound to a particular middleware model; however, various personalities seldom share a large amount of code.

Generic functions propose a coarse grain parametrization (selection of components). Configuration is fine grain parametrization (customization of a component). Verification is possible through behavioral descriptions (attached to components).

Configurable and generic middleware architectures address the tailorability issue, as they ease middleware adaptation. However, they do not provide complete solutions, as they are either restricted to a class of distribution model; or their adaptation requires many implementation levels, thus becomes too expensive.

3.3 Decoupling Middleware Components

To enhance middleware adaptation at a reduced implementation cost, we proposed the "schizophrenic middleware architecture" [VHPK04]. Its architecture separates concerns between distribution models, API, communication protocols, and their implementations by refining the definition and role of personalities.

The schizophrenic architecture consists of three layers: *application* and *protocol* personalities built around a *neutral* core. Application interacts with application personalities; protocol personalities operate with the network.

Application personalities constitute the adaptation layer between application components and middleware through a dedicated API or code generator. They provide APIs to interface application components with the core middleware; they interact with the core layer in order to allow the exchange of requests between entities. Application personalities can either support specifications such as CORBA, the Java Message Service (JMS), etc. or dedicated API for specific needs.

Protocol personalities handle the mapping of personality-neutral requests (representing interactions between application entities) onto messages exchanged using a chosen communication network and protocol. Protocol personalities can instantiate middleware protocols such as IIOP (for CORBA), SOAP (for Web Services), etc.

The neutral core layer acts as an adaptation layer between application and protocol personalities. It manages execution resources and provides the necessary abstractions to transparently pass requests between protocol and application personalities in a neutral way. It is completely independent from both application and protocol personalities.

The neutral core layer enables the selection of any combination of application and/or protocol personalities. Several personalities can be collocated and cooperate in a given middleware instance, leading to its "schizophrenic" nature.

3.4   PolyORB, a Schizophrenic Middleware

In [VHPK04], we present PolyORB our implementation of a schizophrenic middleware. PolyORB a free software middleware supported by AdaCore[1], PolyORB's research activities are hosted by the ObjectWeb consortium[2].

We assessed its suitability as a middleware platform to support general specifications (CORBA, DDS, Ada Distributed Systems Annex, Web Applications, Ada Messaging Service close to Sun's JMS) as well as profiled personalities (RT-CORBA, FT-CORBA) and as a COTS for industry projects.

In the remainder of this section, we provide a review of the key elements of PolyORB's architecture, implementation, and its capabilities to address middleware tailorability and verification.

3.5   A Canonical Middleware Architecture

Our experiments show that a reduced set of services can describe various distribution models. We identify seven steps in the processing of a request, each of which is defined as one fundamental service. Services are generic components for which a basic implementation is provided. Alternate implementation may be used to match more precise semantics. Such an implementation may also come with its behavioural description for verification purposes. Each middleware instance is one coherent assembling of these entities. The μBroker component coordinates the services : it is responsible for the correct propagation of the request in the middleware instance. Figure 1 illustrates the cooperation between PolyORB services.

---

[1] http://www.adacore.com
[2] http://polyorb.objectweb.org

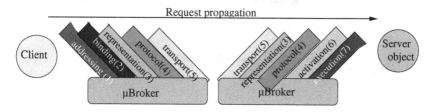

Fig. 1. Request propagation in the schizophrenic middleware architecture

First, the client looks up server's reference using the *addressing* service (1), a dictionary. Then, it uses the *binding* factory (2) to establish a connection with the server, using one communication channels (e.g. sockets, protocol stack).

Request parameters are mapped onto a representation suitable for transmission over network, using the *representation* service (3), this is a mathematical mapping that convert a data into a byte stream (e.g. CORBA CDR).

A *protocol* (4) supports transmissions between the two nodes, through the *transport* (5) service; it establishes a communication channel between the two nodes. Both can be reduced to *finite-state automata*. Then the request is sent through the network and unmarshalled by the server.

Upon the reception of a request, the middleware instance ensures that a concrete entity is available to execute the request, using the *activation* service (6). Finally, the *execution* service (7) assigns execution resources to process the request. These services rely on the *factory* and *resource management* patterns.

Hence, services in our middleware architecture are *pipes and filters*: they compute a value and pass it to another component. Our experiments with PolyORB showed all implementations follow the same semantics, they are only adapted to match precise specifications. They can be reduced to well-known abstractions.

The µBroker handles the coordination of these services: it allocates resources and ensures the propagation of data through middleware. Besides, it is the only component that controls the whole middleware: it manipulates critical resources such as tasks and I/Os or global locks. It holds middleware behavioral properties.

Hence, the schizophrenic middleware architecture provides a comprehensive description of middleware. This architecture separates a set of generic services dedicated to request processing from the µBroker.

3.6 µBroker: Core of the Schizophrenic Architecture

The µBroker component is the core of the PolyORB middleware. It is a refinement of the Broker architectural pattern defined in [BMR+96]. The Broker pattern defines the architecture of a middleware, describing all elements from protocol stack to request processing and servant registration.

The µBroker relies on a narrower view of middleware internals: the µBroker cooperates with other middleware services to achieve request processing. It interacts with the *addressing* and *binding* services to route the request. It receives incoming requests from remote nodes through the *transport* service; *activation* and *execution* services ensure request completion.

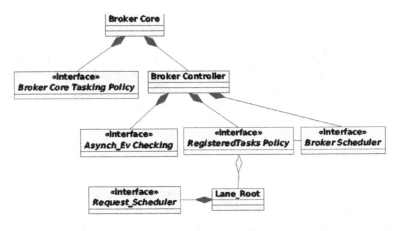

Fig. 2. Overview of the μBroker

Hence, the μBroker *manages resources and coordinates middleware services to enable communication between nodes and the processing of incoming requests.* Specific middleware functions are delegated to the seven services we presented in previous section. The μBroker is the dispatcher of our middleware architecture.

Several "strategies" have been defined to create and use middleware resources: in [PSCS01], the authors present different request processing policies implemented in TAO; the CARISM project [KP04], allows for the dynamic reconfiguration of communication channels. Accordingly, the μBroker is configurable and provides a clear design to enable verification. Figure 2 describes the basic elements of the μBroker.

The *μBroker Core API* handles interactions with other middleware services.

The *μBroker Tasking Policy* controls task creation in response to specific events within the middleware, e.g. new connection, incoming requests;

The *μBroker Controller* manages the state automaton associated to the μBroker. It grants access to middleware internals (tasks, I/O and queues) and schedules tasks to process requests or run functions in the *μBroker Core*. Several policies control it: the *Asynchronous Event Checking* policy sets up the polling and data read strategies to retrieve events from I/O sources; the *Broker Scheduler* schedules tasks to process middleware jobs (polling, processing an event on a source or a request). The *Request Scheduler* controls the specific scheduling of requests; the *Lane_Root* controls request queueing; the *Request Scheduler* controls thread dispatching to execute requests.

These elements are defined by their interface and a common high-level behavioral contract. They may have multiple instances, each of which refines their behavior, allowing for fine tuning. We implemented several instances of these policies to support well-known synchronization patterns.

The schizophrenic middleware architecture proposes one comprehensive view of one middleware architecture. This architecture is defined around a set of canonical components, one per key middleware's function, and the μBroker component that coordinate and allocates resources to actually execute them.

This allows for an iterative process to build new distribution feature and support new models: one can build new services and bind them to the μBroker. These services form

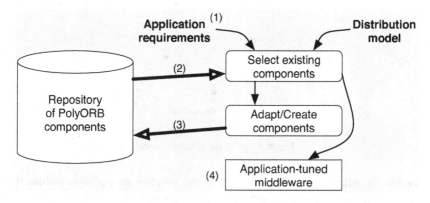

Fig. 3. Designing new personalities

the root of the distribution feature, exported to the user through dedicated API or code generator. We detail the later in the next section.

3.7 A Methodology to Design New Personalities

A methodological guide details the different steps to instantiate PolyORB (figure 3) from a specific set of application requirements and the implied distribution model (step 1). It is intended to give the user the proper knowledge to tailor PolyORB. There are several ways to adapt PolyORB to the application requirements (step 2):

- Use an existing personality. PolyORB already comes with CORBA, RT-CORBA, DSA, MOMA (Ada-like JMS), DDS and the existing configuration parameters;
- Design a new personality: design or refine some of the fundamental components, by re-using fundamental components already developed from existing personalities or from the neutral core; overloading them or designing new variant of fundamental components from scratch.

  Note that when a new personality is designed, we get back to the generic architecture (step 3) to decide whether the new features would be useful for other personalities. In this case, there are two possible policies:
- This feature has a simple and generic enough implementation that can be reused by other personalities, then the feature is integrated in the pool of neutral core layer components, e.g. concurrency policies, low-level transport;
- This feature is intrinsically specific to a personality, the implementation enhancement is kept at the level of the protocol or application personalities, e.g. GIOP message management, DDS specific API.

Finally the user derives one assembly of components: the fine-tuned middleware adapted to its initial needs (step 4).

This procedure may also be repeated to adapt more precisely components, allowing for evolving design of some core elements without impeding the whole assembly.

In this section, we have defined the middleware architecture and associated methodology used to implement middleware. We enforce a strong separation of concerns

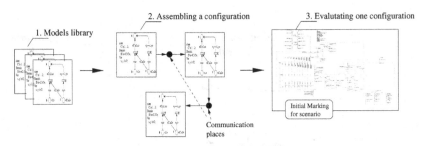

Fig. 4. Steps of the μBroker modeling

between the different functions involved in the middleware and we combine them to form the required implementation. Such a process proved its efficiency when implementing DDS on top of PolyORB [HKP06].

3.8   Formal Verification

In this section, we discuss the formal techniques used to model the μBroker, and then verify some of its expected properties using model-checking.

Modeling one middleware configuration. We propose to use formal methods to model and then verify our system. We selected *Well-formed colored Petri nets* [CDFH91] as an input language for model checking. They are high-level Petri nets, in which tokens are typed data holders. This allows for a concise and parametric definition of a system, while preserving its semantics. Using these methods, we can now model our architecture using Petri nets as a language for system modeling and verification (figure 4).

Step 1: we build one Petri net for each middleware components variation. Petri net transitions represent atomic actions; Petri net places are either middleware states or resources. Common places between different modules define interactions between Petri nets modules, they act as *channel places* [Sou89].

Step 2: for one configuration of the μBroker, some Petri net modules are selected to produce the complete model. Communications places (outlined in black) represent links to other μBroker functions or to middleware services.

Step 3: the selected modules are merged to produce a global model, it represents one middleware configuration. This model and one initial marking enable the verification of the middleware properties.

Then, middleware functions can be separately verified and then combined to form the complete Petri net model. Many models can be assembled from a common library of models. Thus, we can test for specific conditions (policies and settings).

The initial marking of the Petri Net defines available resources (e.g. threads, I/Os); or sets up internal counters. Its state space covers all possible interleaving of atomic actions; thus all possible execution orders are tested.

μBroker configurations and models. In this section, we review the key parameters that characterize the μBroker, and some of the properties one might expect from such a component.

The μBroker is defined by the set of policies and the resources it uses. These settings are common to a large class of applications. We consider one middleware instance, in server mode, that processes all incoming requests. We study two configurations of the μBroker: *Mono-Tasking* (one main environment task) and *Multi-Tasking* (multiple tasks, using the Leader/Followers policy described in [PSCS01]). The latter allows for parallel request processing.

We assume that middleware resources are pre-allocated: we consider a static pool of threads; a bounded number of I/O sources and one pre-allocated memory pool to store requests. This hypothesis is acceptable: it corresponds to typical engineering practices in the context of critical systems. Our implementations and the corresponding models are controlled by three parameters:

S_{max} is the upper bound of I/O Sources listening for incoming data;

T_{max} is the number of Threads available within the middleware;

B_{size} is the size of the Buffer allocated to read data from I/O sources.

S_{max} and T_{max} define a workload profile for the middleware node, B_{size} defines constraints on the memory allocated by the μBroker to process requests. These parameters control middleware throughput and execution correctness.

We list three essential properties of our component. They represent basic key properties our component must verify to fulfill its role.

$P1$, *no deadlock* the system process all incoming requests;

$P2$, *consistency* there is no buffer overflow;

$P3$, *fairness* every event on a source is detected and processed.

$P1$, $P3$ are difficult to verify only through the execution of some test cases: one has to examine all possible execution orders. This may not be affordable or even possible due to threads and requests interleaving. Besides, the adequate dimensioning of static resources to ensure consistency ($P2$) is a strong requirement for DRE systems, yet it is a hard problem for open systems such as middleware. Thus, we propose to verify them for some configuration of the μBroker: each property is expressed as a LTL formula, then verified by model-checker tools.

Achieving formal analysis. One known limit to the use of Petri Nets as model checker is the combinatorial explosion when exploring the system's state space.

We tackle this issue using recent works carried out at the LIP6. By detecting of the symmetries of a system [TMDM03], and exploiting the symmetries allowed by a property [BHI04]. In most favorable cases, these methods require exponentially smaller memory space than traditional method based on full enumeration, and thus more amenable to computations within reasonable delays.

Thus, we claim that the analysis of PolyORB could not have been performed without the use of model checking because of the large number of states. As an illustration, even for common middleware configurations (up to 17 threads) the system presents over 6.56×10^{17} states, but we could compute and evaluate its properties on the model using advanced tools.

This verification experience is a proof of feasibility. New tools are a prerequisite to ease the structuring, and production of a formal specification of a middleware dedicated to application requirements. Such a specification would enable both the verification and the code generation the corresponding implementation.

In the following, we illustrate how an architecture definition language such as the AADL enables us to define such a process and support tools.

4   A Process to Build Tailorable and Verifiable Middleware

The schizophrenic architecture allows for a fine tailoring of the middleware. It also permits formal verification on a given middleware instance. In order to help the configuration of the middleware, we need a way to capture the application needs and then build the corresponding middleware. In this section we explain our methodology to design and build a distributed application with its particular middleware, using the AADL.

4.1   Overview of the AADL

A few ADLs explicitly deal with real-time systems. Examples are ROOM [RSRS99] and AADL [Lew03]. An AADL model can incorporate non-architectural elements: embedded real-time characteristics of the components (execution time, memory footprint...), behavioral descriptions, etc. Hence it is possible to use AADL as a backbone to describe all the aspects of a system.

"AADL" stands for Architecture Analysis & Design Language. It aims at describing DRE systems [FLV00] by assembling blocks separately developed. In this section we describe the AADL and show how it can be used to describe application components.

The AADL [SAE04b] allows for the description of both software and hardware parts of a system. It focuses on the definition of clear block interfaces, and separates the implementations from these interfaces. It can be expressed using graphical and textual syntaxes; an XML representations is also defined to ease the interoperability between tools.

An AADL description is made of *components*. The AADL standard defines software components (data, threads, thread groups, subprograms, processes), execution platform components (memory, buses, processors, devices) and hybrid components (systems). Components model well identified elements of the actual architecture. *Subprograms* model procedures like in C or Ada. *Threads* model the active part of an application (such as POSIX threads). *Processes* are memory spaces that contain the *threads*. *Thread groups* are used to create a hierarchy among threads. *Processors* model micro-processors and a minimal operating system (mainly a scheduler). *Memories* model hard disks, RAMs, etc. *Buses* model all kinds of networks, wires, etc. *Devices* model sensors, etc. Unlike other components, *systems* do not represent anything concrete; they actually create building blocks to help structure the description.

Component declarations have to be instantiated into subcomponents of other components in order to model an architecture. At the top-level, a system contains all the component instances. Most components can have subcomponents, so that an AADL description is hierarchical. A complete AADL description must provide a top-level system that will contain the other components, thus providing the root of the architecture tree. The architecture in itself is the instantiation of this system.

The interface of a component is called *component type*. It provides *features* (e.g. communication ports). Components communicate one with another by *connecting* their features. To a given component type correspond zero or several implementations. Each of them describe the internals of the components: subcomponents, connections between those subcomponents, etc. An implementation of a thread or a subprogram can specify *call sequences* to other subprograms, thus describing the execution flows in the architecture. Since there can be different implementations of a given component type, it is possible to select the actual components to put into the architecture, without having to change the other components, thus providing a convenient approach to configure applications.

The AADL defines the notion of *properties* that can be attached to most elements (components, connections, features, etc.). Properties are attributes used to specify constraints or characteristics that apply to the elements of the architecture: clock frequency of a processor, execution time of a thread, bandwidth of a bus, etc. Some standard properties are defined; but it is possible to define one's own properties.

Refining Architectures. The AADL syntax allows for great flexibility in the precision of the descriptions. In the listing 1.1, we describe a process that receives messages (modeled by an event data port). Such a description is very vague, since we do not give any details about the actual structure of the process (e.g. how many threads?). Yet it is perfectly correct regarding the AADL syntax, and provides a first outline of the architecture specification.

```
1  data message
2  end message;
3
4  process receiver_process
5  features
6    msg : in event data port message;
7  end receiver_process;
```

Listing 1.1. Simple example of an AADL description

We can refine the architecture by providing an implementation of the process. Here we choose a very simple implementation, with one single thread that calls the user application (listing 1.2). We use an AADL standard property to indicate that the thread is dispatched aperiodically. The thread is to be executed upon the reception of a message.

We could also define other implementations, with several threads to process the incoming messages or perform other tasks. This facilitates the refinement of a given architecture: We can start by defining the outline of the architecture (listing 1.1), and then create implementations of the components (listing 1.2).

```
9   process implementation receiver_process.implem
10  subcomponents
11    thr1 : thread receiver_thread.implem;
12  connections
13    connect1 : event data port msg -> thr1.msg;
14  end receiver_process.implem;
15
16  thread receiver_thread
17  features
18    msg : in event data port message;
```

```
19 properties
20   dispatch_protocol => aperiodic;
21 end receiver_thread;
22
23 thread implementation receiver_thread.implem
24 calls
25   {user_app : subprogram application};
26 connections
27   parameter msg -> user_app.msg;
28 end receiver_thread.implem;
29
30 subprogram application
31 features
32   msg : in parameter message;
33 end application;
```

Listing 1.2. Implementation of the process

Our model is partial and does not include any hardware component: we do not specify on what processor the process is running, etc. Such information should be provided when designing the complete architecture: the processes that send messages, the processors, associated memories and potential buses if there are several processors. The model is precise enough for the scope of this paper, though. In the following sections, we focus on the receiver thread.

4.2   Overview of the Methodology

Given its ability to describe both software and hardware components, the AADL perfectly fits our needs. We can use it to completely describe distributed architectures and capture all the necessary parameters. In addition, it has the ability to support a step-by-step design process based on the refinement of architecture. Thus it allows for a progressive approach in the architecture modeling.

The figure 5 illustrates our approach to design the middleware. We use the AADL to describe the application. From the application description, we can deduce the required

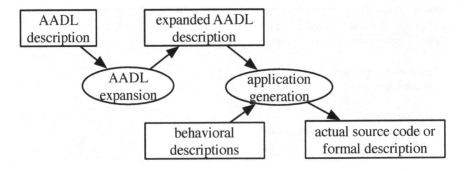

Fig. 5. Application generation based on the AADL

parameters for the middleware (scheduling policy, data types, etc.) and extract an adequate configuration; it is then possible to create an AADL description of the underlying middleware. We can then generate formal description from the AADL model and perform model checking. Once verifications have been performed, we can generate the code for the application and the middleware.

4.3   Modeling the Middleware Architecture Using the AADL

The schizophrenic architecture provides a clear structure to create tailorable middleware. A notation such as the AADL syntax can be used to describe a schizophrenic middleware instance, in order to rapidly configure and deploy a tailored middleware that meets the application requirements.

Architectural description of the middleware components. Middleware is the lower part of an application; it can be viewed as a software component (or a set of software components) on which the user application relies. Given its modular structure, the schizophrenic architecture shall be modeled by a set of AADL software components.

Overall design. Middleware is a part of the application. Hence a middleware architecture shall be described using software components: a set of *subprograms* called by one or more *threads* (depending on the middleware configuration); *data* components model the data structures exchanged between the subprograms.

The subprograms should be organized so that they reflect the seven canonical services and the μBroker of the schizophrenic architecture.

Subprograms cannot be subcomponents of a system, since they do not model "autonomous" components. Hence the schizophrenic architecture cannot be represented as a set of systems. Consequently, the description is to be organized as a collection of packages containing subprograms and data; the packages should reflect the logical organization of the architecture.

Basically, the model should then have seven packages containing the subprograms associated with the seven basic services; the components of the μBroker, which constitutes the middleware "heart", should also be materialized as a package. Finally, the different subprograms and data modeling the personalities should be defined into separate packages. Other "tools", such as socket managers, could be defined into separate packages.

Each service can actually be modeled as a few main subprograms that are called from other parts of the architecture. Such subprograms shall be placed into the public sections of the packages, while more internal subprograms shall be defined into the private part.

Middleware configuration. The middleware configuration is either given by its architectural description, or by some properties associated to the components.

The personalities to use for a given configuration are materialized by the actual packages and components used to describe the architecture. The actual number of threads to use is set by describing them in the architecture.

Some configuration elements such as the tasking policy deal with the behavioral description of the system, not its architecture; yet it is possible to specify them within the μBroker, using user-defined properties.

The configuration of some services can be specified by providing a particular component implementation. For example, the activation service can either be a mere list associating references to procedures, or or more evolved mechanism with priorities, like CORBA's POA. Those two possibilities correspond to two different implementations of the same subprogram type.

4.4   Using AADL to Verify the Middleware

We now explain how to convert the AADL description into a Petri net and in source code; we show how to integrate existing behavioral descriptions associated with AADL components into the generated Petri net.

Using the AADL to support the construction of verifiable systems. The AADL in itself only focuses on the description of the system architectures. Hence, unlike the UML, it does not aim at providing a complete and integrated set of syntaxes to describe all aspects of a model. Instead, the AADL facilitates the integration of other description paradigms within the architectural description, the latter one providing containers for the former ones. This allows for the reuse of "legacy" paradigms instead of imposing a specific syntax.

The integration of third-party languages within the AADL is done through properties or annexes. We privilege the use of AADL properties since it facilitates the use of a repository of behavioral descriptions that can be referenced by the AADL components. This allows for a clear separation between the architectural and behavioral descriptions.

Mappings must be defined in order to describe how to merge behavioral description into the AADL elements. The AADL standard defines mappings for Ada and C languages [SAE04a]. Translations have also been defined between the AADL error model and Petri nets [RKK06], thus allowing the use of existing verification and dependability evaluation tools.

Our approach focuses on the integration of behavioral descriptions within AADL architectures. Thus, behavioral implementations are controlled by the runtime built from AADL descriptions, which helps ensure the consistency between AADL model and resulting application. The figure 6 illustrates the principles of our mappings: behavioral

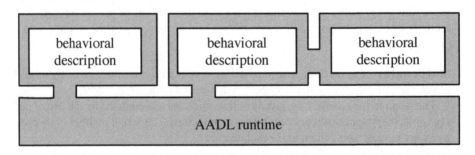

Fig. 6. Principle of an architecture-driven mapping for the AADL

descriptions (in white) are encapsulated by a runtime generated from the AADL description (in grey). We now give an overview of a mapping from AADL constructions to Petri nets and Ada.

Mapping AADL constructions to Petri Nets and source code. We aim at using the AADL to coordinate formal verification and code generation. To do so, we defined rules to produce a Petri net or Ada code from AADL descriptions. Using these mappings we can generate a complete Petri net from the assembly of AADL components, each of them characterized by its own Petri net (such the nets described in section 3.8); once we ensure the architectural constructions are valid, we can generate the corresponding source code. This allows to perform verification on the whole system before code generation.

The AADL elements to map into Petri nets are the software components. Indeed, execution platform components are used to model the deployment of the software components; such deployment information is not to in the scope of Petri nets. AADL threads and AADL subprograms are the most important components, since they describe the actual execution flows in the architecture. AADL processes and systems are actually boxes containing threads or other components, and do not provide any "active" semantics; data components are not active components either.

The mapping for source code takes the same components into account. However, some components, such as AADL threads and processes, represent the AADL runtime. Thus they do not exactly correspond to code generation; the configuration of the AADL runtime is set from the information provided by these components. The table 1 lists the main rules of the mappings.

The Petri net mapping mainly consists of translating the AADL execution flows. Components that do not have any subcomponents nor call sequences are modeled by a transition that consumes inputs and produces outputs. Component features are modeled by places.

We model a place per feature. This systematic approach help the user identify the translation between AADL models and corresponding Petri nets. In addition, it facilitates the expansions of the feature places. For example, we might want to describe the queue protocols defined by the AADL properties: in this case we would replace each place by Petri nets modeling FIFOs or whatever type of queue is specified by the AADL properties.

Connections between features are modeled by transitions. We distinguish connections between subprograms parameters and between other component ports.

Tokens stored in input features are to be consumed by component or connection transitions; tokens produced by component or connection transitions are stored in output features. Components that have subcomponents are modeled by merging the component transition with the subcomponent nets.

If an AADL port is connected to several other ports at a time, the Petri net transition shall be connected to all the corresponding places: a token will be sent to each target place, thus modeling the fact that each destination port receives the output of the initial port.

Call sequences are made of subprograms that are connected. We use an extra token to model the execution control. There is a single execution control token in each thread or subprogram, thus reflecting the fact that there is no concurrency in call sequences, and in threads and subprograms in general.

Table 1. Main patterns of the mapping between the AADL Petri nets and source code

AADL	corresponding Petri net	corresponding Ada code
data data_type end data_type;	not translated in Petri nets	type data_type is null record;

subprogram a_subprogram
features
  input_1 : in parameter;
  input_2 : in parameter;
  output : out parameter;
end a_subprogram;
	control_entry input_1 input_2
	
	component_operation
	
	control_exit output
		procedure a_subprogram
		  (input_1 : in data_type;
		  input_2 : in data_type;
		  output : out data type)
		is
		begin
		  null;
		end;

process a_process
features
  input_1 : in data port data_type;
  input_2 : in data port data_type;
  output : out data port data_type;
end a_process;
	input_1 input_2
	
	component_operation
	
	output
		correspond to a middleware instance

connection : data port output –> input;	output connection input	handled by the middleware
connection : connect : parameter output –> input;	subprogram output output_var connection input	–– procedure subprogram_a (output: out data_type); –– procedure subprogram_b (input: in data_type); subprogram_a (connect); subprogram_b (connect);

It is important to note that this mapping only provides a solution to transform AADL construction into Petri nets. Therefore it cannot produce accurate description of the behaviors of the components, since it is out of the scope of the AADL. Proper behavioral description is achieved by inserting existing Petri nets into the framework generated from the AADL description. It consists of merging the descriptions of the components and the net generated, thus merging the transitions and places of the AADL threads and subprograms with the ones contained in the behavioral Petri net. The Petri net descriptions that corresponds to the behaviors of the AADL components should be set using AADL properties.

Defining a mapping between AADL constructions and Petri nets allows to perform verification on the structure of the architecture. Yet, it is mandatory to ensure the actual source code of the system will conform to the Petri net. This implies that the mapping between AADL and programming languages must be consistent with the Petri net mapping.

To ensure this consistency, the mapping we provide for source code relies on the same principles as for Petri nets [VZ06]. We only only give a very brief and incomplete overview of it in table 1. The source code mapping is basically a translation between the AADL subprogram constructions and Ada. Using both mappings in conjunction ensure that the Petri net used for the model checking of the AADL architecture effectively reflects the actual source code implementation of the architecture.

4.5   Using AADL to Generate the Middleware

We showed how the AADL and the definition of mappings from AADL to formal notations allow us to define a prototyping-based process of DRE system conception.

The initial AADL description can then be refined, according to the feedback provided by the model checking performed on the Petri nets. Once the behavior has been validated, we can generate the corresponding source code and then perform tests on the actual system. The AADL architecture can again be refined, according to the results of the tests.

In order to validate our approach, we created a complete AADL tool suite, Ocarina [VZ06], which can be used as a compiler for the AADL. As a support tool for verifying AADL model, Ocarina can take AADL descriptions as input and perform various operations, such as the expansion of architectural descriptions or the generation of Petri net description as well as compilable source code. It can also be integrated within other applications to provide AADL functionalities.

The code generator of Ocarina can produce Petri net models described in PetriScript [HR]. PetriScript is a text language that facilitates the description of Petri nets and allows to automate building operations, such as fusion of places or transitions, etc.

Ocarina can generate Ada source code that can be run by an instance of PolyORB. It also generates a tailored application personality and configures PolyORB to embed all the required features. We use PolyORB as an AADL runtime and allows one to build distributed applications defined as an AADL model.

Hence, Ocarina helps us to support the generation of tailored middleware, as illustrated on figure 5: from the AADL description of a distributed application, we can infer the description of the middleware instances for each application node, and then produce the corresponding Petri net and source code.

5   Conclusions and Perspectives

Although middleware is now a well-established technology that eases the development of distributed applications, many challenges remain opened. We noted that two key issues are the tailorability of the middleware to versatile application requirements, and the capability of the middleware to provide full proofs of its properties. In this paper, we provided an overview of our ongoing research work on these two aspects.

We first noted that middleware architecture impedes tailorability and verification. Therefore, we proposed and validated the "schizophrenic" middleware architecture. This architecture is a high-level model of middleware that gathers key concepts in middleware, addressing the definition of the key functions and the way to combine them.

Its genericity allows one to derive specific distribution models. PolyORB, our implementation demonstrates how this architecture can help designer to easily build middleware. This middleware is now used as a COTS in industrial projects, providing support for CORBA, DDS and still providing a high level of tailorability.

A methodological guide exists to help this adaptation work. Our measures show that the performance of the adapted middleware are close to existing middleware. Besides, the adaptation work is greatly reduced by the high-level of code reuse.

Finally, the schizophrenic architecture allows formal verification techniques. We illustrated how Petri nets allowed us to provide the first formal proofs of the behavioral properties of our COTS middleware. We consider that The middleware is not a blackbox that should be discarded from the verification process.

However, this remains a complex task that belongs to middleware or verification expert domains. Then, we noted that tools are required to conduct these two important steps in building tailored middleware.

We chose the AADL as a backbone language to help the user specify its application requirements. Dedicated tools are applied to the model to 1/ verify it is correct, 2/ generate the corresponding code and configuration of the support middleware. This provides a first step towards the definition of a "middleware factory" that would enable application designers to instantiate the middleware they actually need. This would reduce complexity in the design of distributed applications by removing the complexity in configuring and using middleware APIs.

Future work will complete and evaluate the benefits of such middleware factory as a supporting process to build specific middleware configuration for DRE systems.

References

[AdSSK03] L. Apvrille, P. de Saqui-Sannes, and F. Khendek. TURTLE-P: Un profil UML pour la validation d'architectures distribuees. In *Colloque Francophone sur l'Ingénierie des Protocoles (CFIP)*, Pparis, France, October 2003. Hermes.

[BHI04] Soheib Baarir, Serge Haddad, and Jean-Michel Ilié. Exploiting Partial Symmetries in Well-formed nets for the Reachability and the linear Time Model Checking Problems. In *Proceedings of the 7th Workshop on Discrete Event Systems (WODES'04)*, Reims, France, septembre 2004.

[BMR+96] Frank Buschmann, Regine Meunier, Hans Rohnert, Peter Sommerlad, and Michael Stal. *Pattern-Oriented Software Architecture: A System of Patterns*. John Wiley & Sons, New York, 1996.

[BSPN00] R. Bastide, O. Sy, P. Palanque, and D. Navarre. Formal specifications of corba services: Experience and lessons learned. In *Proceedings of the ACM Conference on Object-Oriented Programmng, Systems, Languages and Applications (OOPSLA'2000)*, Minneapolis, Minnesota, USA, 2000.

[Bud03] T. J. Budden. Decision Point: Will Using a COTS Component Help or Hinder Your DO-178B Certification Effort. *STSC CrossTalk, The Journal of Defense Software Engineering*, November 2003.

[CDFH91] G. Chiola, C. Dutheillet, G. Franceschini, and S. Haddad. On Well-Formed Coloured Nets and their Symbolic Reachability Graph. *High-Level Petri Nets. Theory and Application, LNCS*, 1991.

[DDH+03] William Deng, Matthew B. Dwyer, John Hatcliff, Georg Jung, Robby, and Gurdip Singh. Model-checking middleware-based event-driven real-time embedded software. In *Proceedings of the First International Symposium on Formal Methods for Components and Objects (FMCO 2002)*, March 2003.

[DHTS98] B. Dumant, F. Horn, F. Dang Tran, and J-B. Stefani. Jonathan: an open distributed processing environment in java. In *Proceedings of the IFIP International Conference on Distributed Systems Platforms and Open Distributed Processing*. Springer-Verlag, 1998.

[FLV00]   P. H. Feiler, B. Lewis, and S. Vestal. Improving predictability in embedded real-time systems. Technical Report CMU/SEI-2000-SR-011, université Carnegie Mellon, December 2000. http://la.sei.cmu.edu/publications.

[HKP06]   Jérôme Hugues, Fabrice Kordon, and Laurent Pautet. A framework for DRE middleware, an application to DDS. In *Proceedings of the 9th IEEE International Symposium on Object-oriented Real-time distributed Computing (ISORC'06)*, pages 224–231, Gyeongju, Korea, Avril 2006. IEEE.

[HR]   A. Hamez and X. Renault.   *PetriScript Reference Manual*.   LIP6, http://www-src.lip6.fr/logiciels/mars/CPNAMI/MANUAL_SERV.

[ISO94]   ISO. *Quality management and quality assurance - vocabulary*. ISO, 1994. ISO 8402:1994.

[Jon94]   Bengt Jonsson. Compositional specification and verification of distributed systems. 1994.

[KP04]   M. Kaddour and L. Pautet. A middleware for supporting disconnections and multi-network access in mobile environments. In *Proceedings of the Perware workshop at the 2nd Conference on Pervasive Computing (Percom)*, Orlando, Florida, USA, March 2004.

[KP05]   F. Kordon and L. Pautet. Toward next-generation toward next-generation middleware? *IEEE Distributed Systems Online*, 5(1), 2005.

[LAA04]   LAAS. The RT-LOTOS Project, 2004. http://www.laas.fr/RT-LOTOS.

[Lew03]   B. Lewis. architecture based model driven software and system development for real-time embedded systems, 2003. available at http://la.sei.cmu.edu/aadlinfosite/LinkedDocuments/.

[MPY$^+$04] Atif Memon, Adam Porter, Cemal Yilmaz, Adithya Nagarajan, Douglas C. Schmidt, and Bala Natarajan. Skoll: Distributed Continuous Quality Assurance. In *Proceedings of the 26th IEEE/ACM International Conference on Software Engineering (ICSE)*, Edinburgh, Scotland, May 2004.

[PSCS01]   I. Pyarali, M. Spivak, R. Cytron, and D. C. Schmidt. Evaluating and Optimizing Thread Pool Strategies for RT-CORBA. In *Proceedings of the ACM SIGPLAN workshop on Languages, compilers and tools for embedded systems*. ACM, 2001.

[RGS95]   R. Rajkumar, M. Gagliardi, and L. Sha. The Real-Time Publisher/Subscriber Inter-Process Communication Model for Distributed Real-Time Systems: Design and Implementation. In *Proceeding of the 1st IEEE Real-Time Technology and Applications Symposium*, Denver, Colorado, USA, May 1995.

[RKK06]   A.-E. Rugina, K. Kanoun, and M. Kaâniche. Aadl-based dependability modelling. Technical Report 06209, LAAS-CNRS, apr 2006.

[RSRS99]   B. Rumpe, M. Schoenmakers, A. Radermacher, and A. Schürr. UML + ROOM as a standard ADL? In *Proc. ICECCS'99 Fifth IEEE International Conference on Engineering of Complex Computer Systems*, 1999.

[SAE04a]   SAE. Aadl, annex d: Language compliance and application program interface. available at http://www.sae.org, sep 2004.

[SAE04b]   SAE. Architecture Analysis & Design Language (AS5506). available at http://www.sae.org, sep 2004.

[SB03]   D.C. Schmidt and F. Buschmann. Patterns frameworks and middleware: Their synergistic relationships. In *Proceedings of the 25th International Conference on Software Engineer ing*, 2003.

[SLM98]   D. Schmidt, D. Levine, and S. Mungee. The design and performance of real-time object request brokers. *Computer Communications*, 21, april 1998.

[Sou89]   Y. Soussy. Compositions of Nets via a communication medium. In *10th International Conference on Application and theory of Petri Nets*, Bonn, Germany, June 1989.

[TMDM03]   Y. Thierry-Mieg, C. Dutheillet, and I. Mounier. Automatic symmetry detection in well-formed nets. In *Proc. of ICATPN 2003*, volume 2679 of *Lecture Notes in Computer Science*, pages 82–101. Springer Verlag, juin 2003.

[VHPK04]   T. Vergnaud, J. Hugues, L. Pautet, and F. Kordon. PolyORB: a schizophrenic middleware to build versatile reliable distributed applications. In *Proceedings of the 9th International Conference on Reliable Software Techologies Ada-Europe 2004 (RST'04)*, Palma de Mallorca, Spain, June 2004.

[VZ06]   T. Vergnaud and B. Zalila. Ocarina: a Compiler for the AADL. Technical report, Télécom Paris, 2006. available at `http://ocarina.enst.fr`.

A Concurrency Abstraction for Reliable Sensor Network Applications

János Sallai[1], Miklós Maróti[2], and Ákos Lédeczi[1]

[1] Institute for Software Integrated Systems, Vanderbilt University,
2015 Terrace Place, Nashville, TN 37203, USA
{sallai,akos}@isis.vanderbilt.edu
[2] Bolyai Institute, University of Szeged, Szeged, Hungary
mmaroti@math.u-szeged.hu

Abstract. The prevailing paradigm in the regime of resource-constrained embedded devices is event-driven programming. It offers a lightweight yet powerful concurrency model without multiple stacks resulting in reduced memory usage compared to multi-threading. However, event-driven programs need to be implemented as explicit state machines, often with no or limited support from the development tools, resulting in ad-hoc and unstructured code that is error-prone and hard to debug. This paper presents TinyVT, an extension of the nesC language that provides a virtual threading abstraction on top of the event-driven execution model of TinyOS with minimal penalty in memory usage. TinyVT employs a simple continuation mechanism to permit blocking wait, thus allowing split-phase operations within C control structures without relying on multiple stacks. Furthermore, it provides fine-grained scoping of variables shared between event handlers resulting in safer code and allowing for optimizations in compile-time memory allocation. TinyVT source code is mapped to nesC with a source-to-source translator, using synchronous communicating state machines as an intermediate representation.

1 Introduction

Most programming environments for wireless sensor nodes are based on one of the two dominating programming abstractions for networked embedded systems: event-driven or multi-threaded programming. In the event-driven paradigm, programs consist of a set of actions that are triggered by events from the environment or from other software components. Actions are implemented as event handlers: functions that perform a computation and then return to the caller. Event handlers run to completion without blocking, hence, they are never interrupted by other event handlers. This eliminates the need for locking, since event handlers are atomic with respect to each other. Furthermore, because of run-to-completion semantics, all event handlers can use a single shared stack.

In the multithreaded approach, execution units are separate threads with independent, linear control flow. Threads can block, yielding control to other threads that execute concurrently. Since the execution of threads is interleaved,

F. Kordon and J. Sztipanovits (Eds.): Monterey Workshop 2005, LNCS 4322, pp. 143–160, 2007.
© Springer-Verlag Berlin Heidelberg 2007

data structures that are accessed by multiple threads may need locking. Each thread has its own stack and administrative data structures (thread state, stack pointer, etc.) resulting in memory usage overhead which may become prohibitive in resource-constrained systems.

Although the two abstractions were shown to be duals [1], there has been a lot of discussion about the advantages and drawbacks of both approaches in the literature [2][3][4]. Multithreading, especially preemptive multithreading, is commonly criticized for the nondeterministic interleaved execution of conceptually concurrent threads [5]. Various locking techniques are used to reduce (or eliminate) nondeterminism from multithreaded programs. Unfortunately, identifying critical sections, as well as choosing the appropriate lock implementations for the critical sections are error prone tasks. Suboptimal locking may lead to performance degradation, while omitting locks or using the wrong kind of locks result in bugs that are notoriously hard to find.

The most compelling advantage of multithreading is that the thread abstraction offers a natural way to express sequential program execution. Since threads can be suspended and resumed, blocking calls are supported: when a long-running operation is invoked, the thread is suspended until the operation completes and the results are available. The event-driven approach, in contrast, does not have this feature. Consequently, sequential execution involving multiple event handler invocation contexts is hard to express, and the corresponding event-driven code is hard to read.

The sensor network community is slightly biased toward the event-driven paradigm. The reason behind this tendency is twofold. First, the event-driven model reflects intrinsic properties of the domain: sensor nodes are driven by interaction with the environment in the sense that they react to changes in the environment, rather than being interactive or batch oriented. Second, the limited physical memory inhibits the use of per thread stacks, thus limiting the applicability of the multi-threaded approach. It is important to note here that Moore's law has an unorthodox interpretation here: it is applied toward reduced size and cost, rather than increase in capability, therefore, the amount of available physical resources is not expected to change as the technology advances.

The event-driven paradigm, nevertheless, has its caveats [2]. Real-time response to interrupts is not possible in traditional event-driven systems, since events cannot be preempted, thus interrupts must be stored and executed later. Relaxing this requirement would violate the atomicity of events, and could introduce race conditions necessitating locking. Events are required to complete quickly, because long-running computations can deteriorate the responsiveness of the system. To avoid this, complex CPU-intensive operations have to be split up into multiple event handlers. This constraint, however, hinders the portability of code that is not written in this event-aware style.

We have identified three issues that can have significant implications on the reliability and maintainability of event-driven code. First of all, unlike the thread abstraction, the event-driven paradigm does not offer linear control flow. The program execution is split up into actions that are executed in response to events.

It is often required, however, that an event triggers different actions depending on the program state. Traditional programming languages do not support dispatching different actions depending on *both* event type *and* program state. To tackle this issue, programs have to be implemented as state machines. Without explicit language support, these state machines are implemented in an unstructured, ad-hoc manner. As a result, the program code is often incomprehensible, error-prone and hard to debug. Second, sharing information between actions also lacks language support, and hence, programmers tend to use global variables, which is also error-prone and often suboptimal with respect to static memory usage. Third, since the event-driven paradigm does not allow blocking wait, complex operations must be implemented in a *split-phase* style: an operation request is a function that typically returns immediately, and the completion is signaled via a callback. This separation of request and completion, however, renders the use of split-phase operations impossible from within C control structures (such as if, while, etc.).

To address the above limitations, this paper introduces TinyVT, an extension of the nesC [6] language that provides a thread-like programming abstraction on top of the execution model of TinyOS [7]. The novelty of this approach is that threading is "compiled away:" programs that are expressed in a linear, thread-like fashion are compiled into event-driven nesC code. TinyVT has several important features that increase the expressiveness of the code and help improve the reliability of TinyOS components and applications:

Threads. The thread abstraction allows programs to be written in a linear fashion without sequencing event handler executions via explicit state machines. TinyVT threads are static in the sense that they are defined compile-time and they cannot be dynamically spawned. TinyVT threads are non-reentrant and stackless, thus very lightweight: only one byte is required to store the current state of the thread.

Blocking Wait. TinyVT employs a simple continuation mechanism, allowing threads to block on events. Blocking is also allowed within C control structures. Blocking on an event yields control to other threads or to the TinyOS scheduler, therefore, the execution of multiple concurrent threads is interleaved. Note that TinyVT does not require any scheduler other than the standard one provided by TinyOS.

Automatic Variable Allocation. TinyVT offers C-style scoping and automatic allocation of variables local to a thread, eliminating the need for global variables for information sharing between related actions. TinyVT does not require per thread stacks: local variables within a scope that includes at least one yield point (i.e. blocking wait) are statically allocated, while automatic local variables that are not shared between event handlers are allocated on the (single, shared) stack. To optimize memory usage, statically allocated shared variables use the same memory area if their lifetimes do not overlap.

Synergy with NesC. Since TinyVT is an extension of the nesC language, mixing nesC code and threading code is allowed. The TinyVT compiler, a source-to-source translator that maps TinyVT code to the nesC language, only processes the threading code within the modules, leaving any event-based nesC code unmodified. The generated code is subject to static analysis (data-race detection) and optimization by the nesC compiler.

Static Program Analysis. TinyVT code, due to the static nature of the language, lends itself to program analysis. The TinyVT compiler decomposes the threading code into communicating finite state machines. This FSM-style decomposition allows for static checking of safety properties, such as deadlock-freeness.

Run-Time Safety. Depending on the program state, some input events may not always be enabled. While nesC does not explicitly offer language support to manage component state, TinyVT does address this issue: the TinyVT compiler knows which events are enabled at a given point of program execution. If an unexpected event occurs, an exception handler is invoked. If no exception handler is specified, the execution of the program is halted to avoid nondeterministic behavior.

The rest of the paper is structured as follows. Section 2 provides a brief overview of TinyOS and nesC, introducing the terminology used in subsequent sections and setting the context for the rest of the paper. Then, we present the motivation of our work showing that the inherent complexity of event-driven software is difficult to manage. In section 4 we introduce the syntax of TinyVT and demonstrate the expressiveness of the threading abstraction through an example. Section 5 discusses how threading code is mapped to the event-based execution model of TinyOS. Since there is a large semantic gap between the levels of abstraction, the mapping is implemented in two phases. We describe an intermediate representation of component-based event-driven programs using synchronous communicating state machines as a vehicle, and explain how it maps to nesC. Then, we describe the challenges of translating threading code to the intermediate representation. Finally, we discuss the advantages, as well as the limitations of our approach, comparing it to related work in the field of sensor network operating systems.

2   TinyOS and the NesC Language

This section describes TinyOS [7], a representative event-driven operating system for networked embedded systems, and its implementation language, nesC [6]. NesC and TinyOS have been adopted by many research groups worldwide. TinyOS has been ported to a dozen hardware platforms, and a rich collection of software components is available. TinyOS and nesC provide low-level access to hardware, a flexible, event-based concurrency model, and a component-based architecture promoting modularization and reuse.

2.1   Concurrency Model

Though TinyOS is and event-based operating system, its concurrency model differs from that of the traditional event-driven paradigm. Based on the observation that data processing and event arrival from the environment are intrinsically concurrent activities in sensor nodes, TinyOS models concurrency with *tasks* and *events*. A task represents deferred computation that runs to completion without being interrupted by other tasks. Events represent interrupt contexts: they can preempt tasks as well as other events. Tasks are scheduled by a FIFO scheduler. Posting tasks is allowed from both task and event contexts.

Obviously, the two levels of parallelism in TinyOS may result in race conditions, and thus, variables that are accessed from interrupt context may need locking. However, the static nature of the nesC language (i.e. no function pointers or dynamic memory allocation is allowed) allows for compile-time data-race detection providing an adequate solution to this issue.

2.2 Component-Oriented Architecture

TinyOS provides a set of reusable system *components*, with well-defined, bidirectional interfaces. Common OS services are factored out into software components, which allows applications to include only those services that are needed In fact, the core OS requires just a few hundred bytes of RAM. There are two kinds of components in nesC: *modules* and *configurations*. Modules contain executable code, while configurations define composition by specifying encapsulated components and static bindings between them. A nesC application is defined as a top-level configuration.

Bidirectional *interfaces* provide a means to define a set of related (possibly split-phase) operations. Interfaces declare *commands* and *events*, both of which are essentially function declarations. A component *providing* an interface must provide the implementations of the interface's commands, and may signal events through the interface. A component that *uses* an interface can call the commands, and must implement callback functions for the events.

3 Managing the Complexity in Event-Driven Software Development

To demonstrate the inherent complexity of event-oriented programming, we present two examples. The first example, a packet-level I^2C driver, shows that managing control flow manually can be challenging, even in simple applications. The second example, a matrix multiplication, suggests that it is nontrivial to port code that implements a long-running computation, such as encryption key generation or data compression, to an event-driven platform.

3.1 Example: I2C Packet Level Interface

Let us consider the implementation of a packet-level interface for the I2C bus that operates above the byte-oriented hardware interface. The corresponding module should provide split-phase operations to write a packet to, and to read a packet from the bus. We only present packet sending; reading a packet works analogously.

The hardware interface provides the following operations. Starting of the send operation is requested with the **sendStart** command, to which the hardware responds with a **sendStartDone** event. Sending a byte is also implemented in a split-phase style: the hardware signals the completion of the write command with a **writeDone** event. After all the bytes are written, the bus has to be relinquished with a **sendEnd** command, the completion of which is acknowledged with the **sendEndDone** event.

The following pseudocode describes the procedure that writes a variable-length packet to the bus, using the byte-oriented hardware interface:

Algorithm 1. Pseudocode of the **writePacket** command in a packet-level I^2C interface

---
```
 1: procedure I2CPACKET.WRITEPACKET(length, data)
 2:     call I2C.sendStart
 3:     wait for I2C.sendStartDone
 4:     for index = 0 to length do
 5:         call I2C.write(data[index])
 6:         wait for I2C.writeDone
 7:         index = index + 1
 8:     end for
 9:     call I2C.sendEnd
10:     wait for I2C.sendEndDone
11:     signal writePacketDone
12: end procedure
```

Expressing this behavior in a linear fashion, however, is not possible in an event-driven system. The code must be broken up into a **writePacket** command and three event handlers, and the control flow must be managed manually. Variables that are accessed from more than one event handlers (**length**, **data**, and **index**) must be global and statically allocated. Typically, manual control flow is implemented with a state machine: a global static variable stores the component state, while the transitions of the state machine are coded into the event handlers. Commonly, only a restricted subset of input events is allowed at a given point of execution. Because of this, actions in the event handlers must be protected against improper invocation patterns (e.g. **writePacket** can only be called again after the previous packet sending is finished).

Manual management of control flow can become particularly tedious and error-prone as the complexity of the task increases. Breaking up the code into event handlers inhibit the use of loops and conditionals with blocking wait. As a result, even a simple control flow that can be expressed linearly with a few nested loops, may result in very complex state machines. Moreover, the resulting event-driven code will most probably be suboptimal, unclear, hard to debug, and often incorrect.

Efficient allocation of variables that are shared between multiple event handlers is also a challenging task in the presence of resource constraints. Notice that variables associated with sending a packet, and variables used when reading a packet might never be used at the same time. In a thread-oriented programming model, such variables are created on the local stack, and destroyed when they go out of scope. A similar, manual stack management approach appears in some event-driven components: variables with non-overlapping lifetime can be placed into a union allocated in static memory, thus the component consumes no more static memory than the memory required by the maximal set of concurrently used variables. However, such optimizations can be extremely tedious when the component logic is complex.

3.2   Example: Matrix Multiplication

Long-running computations may deteriorate the responsiveness of event-driven systems, since events are atomic with respect to each other and cannot be preempted.

This problem also manifests itself in cooperative multi-threading, however, such systems commonly provide a yield operation, by which the running computation may relinquish control and let other threads execute. This, however, is not possible in an event-driven programming paradigm.

Consider the multiplication of two fairly large matrices, a computation that is prohibitive in an event-driven system that has to handle various other events (e.g. message routing) concurrently. The most straightforward solution to this problem is to break up the outermost loop of the matrix multiplication algorithm, and to manage the control flow with a state machine emulating the loop.

This workaround, although typically tedious, will always work. However, this has serious implications: since it is cumbersome to emulate yield in event-driven systems, existing code which is not structured in an event-aware fashion can be extremely complex to port. This applies to computationally intensive algorithms, such as encryption key generation or data compression.

4   The TinyVT Language

In this section we overview the syntax and operational semantics of TinyVT, and through an example, we illustrate how TinyVT simplifies the development of event-driven applications.

4.1   Language Constructs

TinyVT extends the nesC language with two basic construct: *threads* and blocking *await* statements. Threads describe sequential blocks of computation with independent, linear control flow. The execution of concurrent threads is interleaved. A thread may pass control to another thread by signaling an event on which the other thread blocks, or, in TinyVT terminology, upon which the other thread *awaits*. Blocking wait can be expressed with the *await* statement. The await statement specifies one or more events, with the corresponding event handling code inlined, on which the thread blocks. Await has *OR* semantics: if the thread blocks on multiple events, the occurrence of any one of them resumes the execution of the thread. Thread execution continues with the execution of the body of the event handler of the triggering event, and the thread keeps running the code following the event handler till the next blocking statement is reached.

Event handlers cannot contain blocking code. The body of the event handler must be a valid nesC compound statement (i.e. function body), with the exception that either *dreturn* or *ireturn* should be used instead of the standard C *return* statement. Deferred return, or *dreturn*, means that after the execution of the event handler finishes, the control is *not* passed immediately back to the caller, instead, the thread continues running until the next blocking statement. In contrast, immediate return, or *ireturn*, returns to the caller "almost immediately": before actually returning, it posts a task which when scheduled, resumes the execution of the thread with the code following the await statement in which the event handler resides. Hence, *ireturn* defines an implicit yield point after the await statement. Using both deferred and immediate return is allowed within the same event handler. For clarity, it is required that functions with no return value should explicitly specify their return style with deferred or immediate return statement(s).

Threads may contain *yield* statements that explicitly transfer the control back to the caller of the event that invoked the currently running computation. Yield is syntactic sugar: it is essentially equivalent to posting a task and then blocking on it.

Threads react to events from the environment by executing a series of actions until the execution reaches a yield point (*await*, *yield* or *ireturn* statement). With each accepted event, the execution of the thread progresses. In fact, TinyVT threads can be thought of as state machines that are described in a linear, thread-like fashion, where the states are associated with yield points, and actions are associated with the code between them.

Since actions run in the execution contexts of the triggering events, there is no dedicated execution context associated with a TinyVT thread. In traditional multi-threading, there is a stack associated with each thread. In contrast, TinyVT threads use a common, shared stack, which is unrolled every time the thread blocks. Because of this, variables with lifetime spanning multiple actions must be statically allocated. TinyVT shields this from the programmer: automatic variables are allowed within threads and allocated in static memory. Because of the static nature of the language, call graphs are known compile time, thus further optimizations are possible: automatic variables that cannot be active concurrently are allocated at the same memory area.

TinyVT threads are not reentrant. A thread reacts an event only if it explicitly blocks on it. If an event is received when the thread is executing an action, or, if the thread is blocked, but the input event is not among the ones the thread is awaiting, an exception occurs. The default behavior on an exception is to halt the execution of the program, in order to prevent nondeterministic behavior. However, the programmer can implement a custom exception handler per event type, and may choose to recover from the error. This behavior may seem as a restriction, but it is in face equivalent to the behavior of event-driven systems: without extra logic, a program cannot handle a new message, for example, while the previous one is still being processed.

Structurally, threads reside within nesC modules. One module may contain multiple threads. Threads can access the local state of the module (i.e. global variables), can invoke functions at the module scope as well as through the module's interfaces (in nesC terminology: *call commands* and *signal events*), and can react to function calls through the interfaces. Threads are static in the sense that they are known at compile time, and cannot be dynamically spawned. Hence, threads are statically instantiated when the application starts. Instead of transferring control to the threads immediately after the application is bootstrapped, we require that the first statement in a thread be an await statement. This way, modules containing threading code are not bound to using a TinyVT specific interface. As a result, the fact that a module contains threading code is not visible from outside: they can be used in component specifications equivalently to standard nesC modules. This limitation reflects the event driven programming practice that components do not start executing immediately at boot-up time, instead, they initialize in response to an *init* command.

4.2 Example

We illustrate the expressiveness of TinyVT by rewriting the I2C packet-level interface example using the thread abstraction.

In the idle state, i.e. when no client request is being processed, the thread blocks on the `writePacket` command. If a client request comes in, the inlined implementation of the command is executed, requesting access to the bus by calling the `sendStart` command. The thread blocks as the next await statement is reached. The occurrence of the `sendStartDone` event, signaled by the byte-level hardware interface, resumes the thread execution. Since the corresponding event handler returns with a deferred return statement, the return value will be saved in an automatic temporary variable, and the same event context will continue running the code up to the next blocking statement. That is, the initialization of the index variable, the evaluation of the loop condition, as well as writing the first byte to the I2C bus will take place before the thread blocks again.

Notice that the execution of the thread is driven by the incoming events. TinyVT generalizes the concept of events to nesC commands, TinyOS tasks, as well as to local functions: a thread can block on any of these. Mixing multiple event types in one await statement is also allowed.

TinyVT supports run-time safety checking through exception handlers. For example, if a `writePacket` call comes in from the client while there is another packet being processed, the control is passed to an exception handler. The default behavior of the exception handler is to halt the execution of the application. However, the programmer may define custom exception handling code. In this example, we can assume that the hardware adheres to the contract defined by the I2C interface, but we need to prepare for handling client calls at any time.

```
uint8_t *packet_data; uint8_t packet_length; uint8_t index;
await result_t command I2CPacket.writePacket(
                uint8_t length, uint8_t* data)
{
    packet_data = data;
    packet_length = length;
    call I2C.sendStart();
    dreturn SUCCESS;
}
await result_t event I2CP.sendStartDone() {
    dreturn SUCCESS;
}
for(index=0; index<packet_length; ++index) {
    call I2C.write(packet_data[index]);
    await result_t event I2C.writeDone()
    {
        dreturn SUCCESS;
    }
}
call I2C.sendEnd();
await result_t event I2C.sendEndDone() {
    dreturn SUCCESS;
}
signal I2CPacket.writePacketDone(SUCCESS);
```

Fig. 1. Excerpt from the packet-level I2C interface module implemented with TinyVT threads. Notice how this code resembles the pseudocode presented in Alg. 1.

Therefore, the thread has to be protected with an exception handler, which is a nesC function definition with the *unexpected* qualifier:

```
unexpected result_t command I2CPacket.writePacket(
                uint8_t length, uint8_t* data)
{
    return FAIL;
}
```

Fig. 2. Exception handler in TinyVT

5 Mapping of the Threading Abstraction to Event-Driven Code

Although TinyVT offers a thread-like programming abstraction capable of expressing linear control flow, it is important to note that TinyVT threads are very much *unlike* threads in the traditional sense: there is no explicit execution context associated with a thread. Furthermore, the resulting event-driven code requires no multi-threading OS support nor does it introduce dependence upon a threading library. TinyVT threads are *virtual* in the sense that they only exist as an abstraction to express event-driven computation in a sequential fashion, and are transformed into (non-sequential) event-driven code by the TinyVT compiler.

While in traditional threading, context management and continuation support comes from the operating system or from the hardware essentially for free, TinyVT has to address these issues at the compiler level. Since there is a significant semantic gap between the thread abstraction and event driven-code, we introduce an intermediate representation, based on synchronous communicating state machines, that establishes an execution model on top of an event-driven system, and serves as a compilation target for the TinyVT compiler.

5.1 Operational Semantics of the Intermediate Representation

The execution model of TinyVT is based on tightly coupled, synchronous communicating state machines (SCSM), providing an expressive vehicle to capture the structure, the control flow, the state, and the communication patterns of event-driven software components. Although the SCSM representation is influenced by communicating finite state machines [8], instead of being a modeling language with well-defined denotational semantics, it primarily focuses on executability of the model rather than providing a mathematically sound foundation for creating correct-by-construction systems. As SCSMs are used exclusively as an intermediate representation, we do not define a concrete syntax for the language here.

An SCSM is defined by a finite set of *states*, *input events*, and *transitions* that map states and events to other states. Transitions are associated with *actions*, which are units of computation defined in the host language. To reduce state space, SCSM allows for the definition of *state variables*, which, depending on their scope, may be accessed from multiple actions. Actions typically read and update shared state variables, and generate *output events*.

It is valid to omit the triggering event from the definition of a transition. If the event is omitted, the transition fires immediately after the source state of the transition is entered. Transitions without events are allowed to have *guard* conditions, which are predicates over the state variables and are evaluated when the source state of the transition is reached. A transition can fire only if the predicate holds. SCSM does not allow specifying both a guard and a triggering event for a transition. Furthermore, mixing event-triggered and guarded output transitions from the same state is also not allowed: for any given state in a well-formed SCSM, either all or none of the output transitions are defined with events. These limitations partition the states into two sets: *blocking states*, in which the state machine is waiting for an external event, and *transitory states*, that are immediately exited after being entered.

SCSMs are deterministic: if a state has multiple out-transitions the same event cannot be assigned to more than one transition. Alternatively, for transitory states, the guards corresponding to the transition must be mutually exclusive.

Unlike traditional FSM models, SCSM does not assume that transitions are instantaneous. Therefore, input events are disabled during the execution of actions, and are re-enabled only after the action completes and the target state is reached. If an input event occurs when the state machine cannot handle it (referred to as an *exception*), the state machine immediately transitions to a (terminal) error state.

SCSMs communicate with their environment through input and output events. Communication between state machines is synchronous: if an action in machine **A** generates an output event which is accepted by machine **B**, **B** starts executing, and the action in **A** that generated the event blocks until **B** relinquishes control. That is, control flow is synchronously passed between communicating state machines. Multiple state machines may react to the same event. The execution of the corresponding event handlers is serialized, but their execution sequence is undefined.

The SCSM language supports hierarchical composition. The composition of state machines **A** and **B** is defined as a SCSM, such that the state set of the composite state machine is the Cartesian product of the states of **A** and **B**, and the input and output events of the constituent state machines are matched by name. Composition allows for event renaming, thus supporting arbitrary associations of input and output events, including fan-in and fan-out. Furthermore, it allows for event hiding, forbidding the propagation of the hidden input or output events over the composite state machine's boundary.

5.2   Mapping the State Machine Model to Event-Driven Code

The SCSM representation is conceptually an extension of the event-driven execution model of TinyOS, with a structure that resembles that of component-oriented nesC programs.

The nave way of implementing an SCSM in nesC is as follows. The state is stored in a global integer variable. Actions are implemented as functions at the nesC module scope. The transition system, i.e. the control logic that maps events and state to actions, is factored out to a scheduler function. When an input event occurs, to which the state machine reacts, it is handled by a generated event handler that calls the scheduler with the event type as a parameter. The scheduler decides which action to call depending on the event type and the current state. After the event handler completes, the scheduler updates the state. If the new state is a transitory state, the scheduler evaluates the guard conditions and invokes an action accordingly, again, updating the state when the action completes. This is iterated until a blocking state is reached. After entering a blocking state, the scheduler returns control to the generated event handler, which then returns to its caller.

The mapping of SCSM to nesC, as described above, is simple, it has limitations. Events commonly have formal parameters, as well as a return value. Passing parameters and return values between the generated event handlers and the actions is cumbersome, because every call has to go through the scheduler function, which has a fixed signature. Instead of trying to find a workaround for this issue (e.g. packing parameters into a variable length untyped array), we factored out the scheduler functionality into the generated event handlers and into the actions.

The generated event handler does the dispatching depending on the value of the state variable. Since the signature of the generated event handler and the corresponding actions are identical, the issue of parameter passing is eliminated. After the action returns, the generated event handler saves the returned value into a temporary local variable, and updates the state. If the resulting state is transitory, the actions and the state updates are executed iteratively, until a blocking state is reached. Then the generated event handler returns with the return value that was saved in the temporary variable.

5.3 Transforming Threading Code to the Intermediate Representation

TinyVT threads that do not declare automatic variables nor use branching or loops (i.e. C control constructs such as if, while, etc.) can easily be translated into SCSM. Await statements mark blocking states, the inlined event handlers are the corresponding actions. Immediate return statements in the event handlers are translated into three statements: setting a global thread-specific return type flag to IRETURN, posting the thread-specific continuation task, and a standard C return statement with the given return value. In the case of deferred returns, the return type flag is set to DRETURN, no continuation task is posted, and the standard C return statement is generated. The next state for all event handlers is a transitional state with two output transitions guarded by the return type flag: on IRETURN, the next state is a blocking state, awaiting the thread specific continuation task, which when executed, transitions the state machine into a transient join state. On DRETURN, the next state is the join state. Code following the await statement but before the next blocking statement is wrapped into an action, which is assigned to a transition from the join state to the blocking state marked by the next blocking statement.

C control structures that contain blocking statements are implemented with transient states branching based on the evaluated condition expression. We explain the translation of the while statement; other control structures (for, if, etc.) are implemented similarly. The while statement is translated to a transitory initial state that unconditionally transitions to a branching state, executing an action that evaluates the loop condition. The branching state is a transitory state that transitions to the transitory join state with an empty action if the loop condition evaluated to FALSE. On TRUE, the next state is the initial state of the state machine that corresponds to the body of the while loop. The final state of the enclosed state machine is linked to the initial state of the while statement with an empty action. The body of the while loop is processed recursively: the corresponding SCSM is built similarly as described a paragraph earlier, resolving C control structures if needed.

It is important to note that not all C control structures need to be converted to SCSM representation. If a control structure does not include any blocking code, it can be treated as a *primitive* statement, which is allowed within actions.

The compiler can decide if a control structure has blocking code by post-order traversing the abstract syntax tree and marking the nodes of statements with blocking descendants.

Automatic local variables declared within primitives can be allocated on the shared stack, since their lifetime is limited to a compound statement that will execute within one event context. However, if the scope of the variable is a compound statement that contains blocking code, the variable has to be allocated in static memory, since the shared stack is unrolled every time the thread blocks.

It is easy to see that compiler-managed variables with non-overlapping scopes can be allocated at the same static memory address. The compiler solves this by creating a `struct` for each compound statement, which contains the local variables, and a `union` containing the `struct`-s of non-overlapping child scopes, recursively.

6   Discussion and Future Work

We believe that the execution model of TinyOS coupled with the nesC programming model is a good level of abstraction for developing sensor node applications. In the presence of severe resource constraints, language support for low-level interfacing with the hardware is imperative. Although nesC provides a sophisticated component-oriented programming model that helps manage the structural complexity of sensor node applications, the inherent complexity of event-driven control flow may persist at the module level.

The virtual threading that TinyVT provides helps mitigate this complexity. It must be emphasized, however, that the goal of TinyVT is *not* to provide an abstraction that shields the event-driven nature of the OS from the programmer. Instead, it serves as a tool that improves code readability, reduces development time, yet retains the low-level hardware access and flexible control of resources provided by the host language. Indeed, it is imperative that the programmer be aware that a TinyVT thread is just a virtual thread, and have an understanding of the compilation process.

TinyVT is not a silver bullet. It is widely known that not all patterns of sequential control flow can be expressed in a thread-like fashion. Analogously, the behavior of some nesC modules is cumbersome, if not impossible, to express in TinyVT. This particularly holds for components operating on top of a hardware presentation layer with nested interrupts. Since TinyVT threads are not reentrant, the programmer has to assure that asynchronous events are handled in a timely manner, alternately, unexpected events have to be handled adequately. Nevertheless, the programmer can always fall back to using plain event-driven nesC code in such cases, and write TinyVT modules only when it is convenient.

Our compiler prototype, though it processes the whole application to resolve symbols and wirings, considers only the scope of the shared variables when optimizing memory allocation, and does not detect if variables in different threads (or modules) can be allocated to the same memory address. That is, the optimization is local to a thread. Extending this functionality with whole-program analysis to facilitate global optimization is subject of further research.

Currently, we do not support all nesC features in TinyVT threads. For example, `goto` is not allowed, and `switch` statements containing blocking code are also not handled. It is primarily because the C standard is very permissive regarding labels, and the compilation of such code can be complicated. We consider eliminating these limitations in the future only if there is a demand for the currently unsupported language features.

Another exciting future direction is extending the compiler with a more thorough interface compatibility checking, based on the communication patterns exhibited/supported by the components through their interfaces. Since TinyVT threads express computation in a linear fashion, the communication patterns of modules are encoded in the control flow. Though TinyVT actions allow for data-dependent behavior, we suspect that some errors, such as violations initialize-before-use constraints, might be able to be detected via static analysis.

7 Related Work

Contiki [9] is a multitasking operating system for memory-constrained devices built around a small event-driven kernel. Unlike traditional operating systems, the Contiki kernel does not provide explicit support for multithreading. Instead, multithreading is implemented as an external library, which is linked into the application only if explicitly needed. Since each thread requires its own stack, traditional multithreading is expensive on memory-constrained platforms. As an alternative, Contiki promotes the use of protothreads [10]. Protothreads achieve threading without per thread stacks using a lightweight continuation mechanism, called local continuations, implemented as a set of C macros. The use of continuations is limited to a C function block, consequently, protothreads cannot span multiple functions. Protothreads in Contiki are similar to threads in TinyVT in that both approaches provide a threading context on top of an event-driven execution model. Protothreads take an opportunistic approach by exploiting esoteric or non-standard features of the C language, while in the TinyVT language a thread is a first class object with explicit compiler support. In contrast to TinyVT, automatic local variables in a protothread are not preserved when the protothread blocks, which can result in potentially unsafe code.

MANTIS [11] is a multithreaded operating system for wireless sensors built around classical concepts, such as preemptive scheduling with time slicing, kernel-level support for synchronization, etc. MANTIS provides a familiar API which is easy to use, making it particularly suitable for experimentation with new algorithms or rapid prototyping of sensor network applications. However, because of the need for per thread stacks, traditional multithreading is costly: MANTIS trades RAM usage for flexibility and ease of use.

TinyOS [7] is probably the most popular operating system in the wireless sensor networks domain. In TinyOS, the event-driven model was chosen over the multithreaded approach due to the memory overhead of the threads. TinyOS defines two kinds of execution contexts: tasks and events. Tasks are scheduled by a FIFO scheduler, have run-to-completion semantics, and are atomic with respect to other tasks. TinyOS models interrupt service requests as asynchronous events: events can interrupt tasks, as well as other asynchronous computations. This duality provides a flexible concurrency model, and easy interfacing with the hardware, however, it can introduce race conditions and may necessitate locking.

nesC [6], the implementation language of TinyOS addresses this issue by providing language support for atomic sections and by limiting the use of potentially "harmful" C language features, such as function pointers and dynamic memory allocation. nesC is a "static" language in the sense that program structure, including the static call graph and statically allocated variables, are known compile time, allowing for whole-program analysis and compile-time data-race detection. TinyVT inherits these features from nesC, while extending the language with support for threading and blocking wait. TinyVT overcomes the problem that complex operations have to be implemented using explicit state machines in nesC, hence, improving code maintainability and safety. nesC has a component oriented design that allows partitioning the applications, which is largely orthogonal to the execution model of TinyOS. This gives flexibility to the programmer and promotes reuse.

TinyGALS [12] defines a globally asynchronous and locally synchronous a programming model for event-driven systems. Software components are composed locally through synchronous method calls to form modules, modules communicate through asynchronous message passing. Local synchrony within a module refers to the flow of control being instantaneously transferred from caller to callee, while asynchrony means that the control flow between modules is serialized through the use of FIFO queues. However, if modules are decoupled through message passing, sharing global state asynchronously would incur performance penalties. To tackle this, the TinyGALS programming model defines guarded synchronous variables that are read synchronously and updated asynchronously.

The galsC [13] language, an extension of nesC, provides high-level construct, such as ports and message queues, to express TinyGALS concepts. TinyGALS/galsC and our approach attack the same substantial problem, namely that managing concurrency with the event-driven paradigm lacks explicit language support. TinyGALS ensures safety through model semantics. In contrast, TinyVT promotes static analysis and runtime safety checking instead. While in TinyGALS modules are decoupled through message passing, and synchronous control flow is limited to the module scope, TinyVT does not impose limitations on the allowable communication styles. We believe that our approach gives more flexibility to the programmer with respect to choosing the right structural decomposition for a problem, whereas galsC could impose limitations on the program structure. For example, control flow from an interrupt context cannot propagate outside the module: hence, all tasks that are timing critical must be implemented within the module.

SOS [14] is a general-purpose operating system for sensor nodes with an event-driven kernel and dynamically loadable modules. SOS strictly adheres to the event-driven paradigm: events are atomic with respect to each other. To handle interrupts in a timely manner without operating in an interrupt context, the SOS kernel uses priority queues to schedule the serialized execution of events. Since interrupt contexts do not propagate into application code, applications can fully leverage the benefits of the atomicity assumption. SOS, similarly to TinyOS, would be an ideal compilation target for TinyVT.

The Object State Model (OSM) [15] employs attributed state machines to express event-based program behavior. The application of FSM concepts is a natural choice for the domain: actions are executed depending on the input event and the actual state, whereas imperative languages, such as C, lack explicit support to associate actions with both events and program state. OSM specification is translated to Esterel [16], a synchronous language, which then can be compiled into efficient C code by the Esterel compiler. The most significant contribution of OSM, however, is that it offers efficient allocation of shared variables based on their lifetime making this approach particularly suitable for programming resource-constrained devices. TinyVT employs a similar approach to allocate automatic local variables. An important difference is that our language constructs do not allow explicit association of shared variables with states (since the state machine model is used only as an intermediate representation, and the concrete syntax is less expressive), hence OSM can achieve slightly better memory usage. However, our approach offers excellent code readability, while OSM should rather be used as a target for automatic code generation.

8   Conclusion

The novelty of this work is that it provides language support to describe event-based computation in a well structured, linear fashion without compromising the expressiveness of the implementation language. The event-driven execution model of TinyOS remains exposed to the TinyVT programmer, along with all the features of the nesC language from supporting component-oriented programming to compile time data-race detection.

The "virtual thread" that TinyVT introduces is a simple language extension that provides a means to express linear control flow and blocking operations. Yet, these threads do not suffer from the problem of nondeterminacy which multithreading is commonly criticized for. First, TinyVT implements a variant of non-preemptive multithreading by sequencing the execution of atomic event handlers. Non-preemptive multithreading offers significantly more determinism and better analyzability than its preemptive counterpart. Second, the syntax of TinyVT ensures that the programmer is aware of the control flow between conceptually concurrent threads. Calls to split phase operations explicitly state which thread the control is passed to; similarly, the *await* statement explicitly specifies the thread which the control is received from. This stands in contrast to the approach of general-purpose multithreading, where control flow is governed by the scheduling policies of the operating system or a user-space threading library, and the programmer has no insight into inter-thread control flow (except for locking decisions).

The TinyVT compiler automates the tasks that programmers traditionally do manually. As the complexity of applications keeps growing even in the sensor network domain, such tasks are becoming hard to manage. However, the TinyVT compiler can easily cope with this complexity, and thus, produce better quality and more reliable code than an average programmer.

References

1. Laurer, H.C., Needham, R.M.: On the duality of operating system structures. SIGOPS Operating Systems Review **13** (1979) 3–19
2. v. Behren, R., Condit, J., Brewer, E.: Why events are a bad idea (for high-concurrency servers). HotOS IX (2003)
3. Lee, E.: What's ahead for embedded software? IEEE Computer (2000) 16–26
4. Adya, A., Howell, J., Theimer, M., Bolosky, W.J., , Douceur, J.R.: Cooperative task management without manual stack management. Proceedings of the USENIX Annual Technical Conference (2002) 289–302
5. Lee, E.: The problem with threads. IEEE Computer (2006) 33–42
6. Gay, D., Levis, P., v. Behren, R., Welsh, M., Brewer, E., Culler, D.: The nesc language: A holistic approach to networked embedded systems. SIGPLAN (2003)
7. Hill, J., Szewczyk, R., Woo, A., Hollar, S., Culler, D., , Pister, K.: System architecture directions for network sensors. Proc. of the 9th International Conference on Architectural Support for Programming Languages and Operating Systems (ASPLOS-IX) (2000)
8. Brand, D., Zafiropulo, P.: On communicating finite state machines. Journal of the ACM **30** (1983) 323–242
9. Dunkels, A., Grnvall, B., Voigt, T.: Contiki - a lightweight and flexible operating system for tiny networked sensors. EmNetSI (2004)
10. Dunkels, A., Schmidt, O., Voigt, T.: Using protothreads for sensor node programming. The Workshop on Real-World Wireless Sensor Networks (2005)
11. et al, H.A.: Mantis: system support for multimodal networks of in-situ sensors. WSNA (2003) 50–59
12. Cheong, E., Liebman, J., Liu, J., , Zhao, F.: Tinygals: A programming model for event-driven embedded systems. Proceedings of the 18th Annual ACM Symposium on Applied Computing (SAC'03) (2003)
13. Cheong, E., Liu, J.: galsc: a language for event-driven embedded systems. Proceedigs of Design, Automation and Test in Europe **2** (2005) 1050–1055
14. Han, C., Kumar, R., Shea, R., Kohler, E., Srivastava, M.: A dynamic operating system for sensor nodes. In Proceedings of the 3rd international Conference on Mobile Systems, Applications, and Services (2005) 163–176
15. Kasten, O., Rmer, K.: Beyond event handlers: Programming wireless sensors with attributed state machines. The Fourth International Conference on Information Processing in Sensor Networks (IPSN) (2005)
16. Berry, G., Gonthier, G.: The esterel synchronous programming language: Design, semantics, implementation. Science of Computer Programming **19** (1992) 87–152

Outdoor Distributed Computing with Split Smart Messages

Nishkam Ravi and Liviu Iftode

Department of Computer Science, Rutgers University
{nravi, iftode}@cs.rutgers.edu

Abstract. In this paper, we exemplify outdoor distributed computing and point out the key challenges. We present Split Smart Messages, a lightweight, portable, network failure resilient and relatively secure middleware that enables a large subset of outdoor distributed computing applications. We also present a Service Discovery, Interaction and Payment Protocol (SDIPP) tailored for mobile phones. We evaluate our middleware and protocol on Sony Ericsson P900 phones and present experimental results.

1 Introduction

Traditional distributed computing techniques were designed specifically for the client/server paradigm. In this approach, a connection is established with one or more stationary servers and messages are exchanged to complete a task. The connection needs to be maintained during the entire lifetime of a task. The computation is distributed among the different servers for the purpose of optimizing performance. The key properties of typical distributed systems are resource sharing, concurrency, scalability and openness. The machines and the underlying networking medium are assumed to be fairly robust and trustworthy. Failures are treated as anomalies. Consequently, distributed systems are designed with a robust, secure and fairly static infrastructure in mind. While failures and disconnections are taken care of, they are not considered part of normal operation.

In contrast, outdoor distributed computing systems have to be designed to cope with frequently occurring failures and disconnections due to dynamically changing topologies. Failures have to be treated as part of normal operation and therefore, systems have to be designed with a weakly connected challenged network in mind. This network is typically composed of heterogeneous nodes that join and leave the network dynamically and are better identified by properties than by statically assigned names (e.g IP addresses). Nodes typically act as both clients and servers, and can potentially exhibit malicious behavior. Ad-hoc wireless connections with short life-times are dominant. Mobility is common. Prior knowledge of the configuration of the system is limited. While the goal of resource sharing is common with traditional distributed computing, the kind of resources that are shared and the mechanisms used for sharing those resources are quite different.

F. Kordon and J. Sztipanovits (Eds.): Monterey Workshop 2005, LNCS 4322, pp. 161–183, 2007.

Properties apart, the goals of outdoor distributed computing are fundamentally different from the goals of traditional distributed computing. While traditional distributed computing is focused primarily on optimization of performance through sharing of resources, outdoor distributed computing enables new functionalities and applications. In this paper, we identify the set of applications that define this new form of computing (Section 2.1) and point out the challenges common to most applications (Section 2.2). We then present the design and implementation of a middleware for outdoor distributed computing (Sections 3 and 4).

2   Outdoor Distributed Computing

What is outdoor distributed computing? We answer this question by identifying the set of applications that motivate this new form of computing and identifying the challenges synonymous with this class of applications.

2.1   Motivating Applications

Vehicular Computing. There is growing interest in equipping vehicles with portable computers to enable applications such as real-time congestion estimation, collision avoidance, route planning, content sharing, etc. Vehicles form a mobile ad-hoc network and disseminate information among themselves. Various data propagation models can be conceived, such as broadcast, geographical routing and publish/subscribe. Vehicles typically exchange information about each other (e.g location and speed) and about the environment (e.g accidents and signs). The information can be exchanged proactively (e.g through broadcast) or queried on demand and routed between the source and destination. Furthermore, the information can be collected and dissipated incrementally using store-and-forward mechanisms.

Social Networking. Akin to vehicular computing, which involves information exchange in a mobile ad-hoc network of vehicles, social networking involves information exchange in a mobile ad-hoc network of people. For example, researchers at a conference may wish to exchange profiles, or invite people with similar research interests for lunch. A distributed application that executes on the handhelds of researchers and finds people with similar research interests is a typical example of a social networking application. Yet another example is *ad-hoc carpooling*, where a user initiates a request to carpool to a certain destination and his neighbors answer the query if they are interested. We can extend this class of applications to include distributed information exchange between handhelds of soldiers on a battlefield, or firemen on duty.

Location-based Services. There is great value in making information services highly personalized. Using location information is one of the best ways of personalizing services. Emergency services led by E911 in North America and E112 in Europe have motivated the wireless carriers to deploy localization technologies.

Tracking personnel (e.g patients in a hospital) and assets (e.g objects in a store) using location is predicted to become fairly popular. A typical example is a *friend-tracking* application, where a group of friends keep track of each other's locations using their handhelds while traveling or when in a museum. Provisioning information to the user's handheld (such as list of restaurants) or sending notifications (such as a sale on men's suits in the proximity) based on user's location can enable new business models. Location-based billing is yet another example. A user can establish personal zones, such as a home zone or work zone and arrange preferential billing with his wireless service provider. Similarly, telematics-centered location-based services can aid traffic monitoring and congestion avoidance. It is speculated that location-based services will create a multi-billion dollar market.

Environment Query. Deployment of sensors that gather information about the environment has already begun. Cameras on New York streets, temperature sensors in forests of California, pressure sensors in bridges are just a few examples. RFID tags and readers are commonly used today in many applications. Networking these sensors and then linking them to more powerful devices such as car PCs or handhelds can enable plethora of distributed computing applications.

2.2   Challenges and Requirements

Numerous research challenges need to be overcome in order to realize the applications described above. In this section, we point out some of the key challenges that are common to these applications.

Opportunistic Networking. Mobility leads to periods of disconnection. Networking infrastructure may only be intermittently available. This makes the design of outdoor distributed computing applications challenging. An ideal design should treat disconnection as part of normal operation, and look for *opportunities* to pass information/data along. IP is clearly insufficient; delay tolerant networking solutions [28], store-and-forward mechanisms, and opportunistic routing algorithms [34] are needed. Since the network is not pre-configured, protocols are needed for resource and service discovery [14,43,16,4]. For this to happen, new naming conventions are needed to uniquely identify resources and services, as IP addresses do not scale well to highly dynamic scenarios.

Portable Middleware. Devices over which distributed computing applications execute will range from tiny sensor nodes to mobile phones to car PCs. In other words, we are looking at a network of nodes with different operating systems, varying computation power and heterogeneous networking capabilities. For such heteregeneous devices to successfully cooperate in the execution of a common task, there is a pressing need for designing middleware that can hide the underlying software abstractions from the applications and create a homogeneous virtual environment for applications to execute in [56]. At the same time, such middleware should be easily portable to different operating systems in order to maximize code reuse and minimize development effort. For performance reasons, the middleware should impose low computation and networking overheads.

Context Awareness. User context can be helpful in personalizing services and applications [57]. Examples of context information include location, time of day, user activity, user profile, available networking interfaces, environment, etc. There are numerous challenges in creating context-awareness for outdoor distributed computing applications. Active research is being carried out in sensing user activity and location [61,50,18,54,20,52]. Context information from different sensors needs to be fused and reasoned with to obtain directly usable information. Ontologies are being developed to reason with context information [9,25]. Practical problems, such as storage and retrieval of context, cannot be overlooked.

Security and Privacy. Outdoor distributed computing relies on cooperation between alien devices. Some of these devices would interact with each other for a few seconds, a few minutes at the most, and would likely not cross paths again ever after. Personal data in the form of context information would be heavily shared. In such a computing model, both user devices and data are prone to attacks. Reputation-based security schemes are hard to devise, due to the ad-hoc nature of the network. Also, reputation schemes require strong identities which exacerbate the privacy problem. Novel security models that induce trust in the network are needed. Privacy mechanisms that restrict flow of sensitive information need to be devised. Location information, in particular, is very sensitive. Users would not like their location to be known to others all the time. The US government realized the seriousness of the this problem and released the *Location Privacy Protection Act* [5] in 2001. Since then, there has been some research focused on safeguarding location privacy [32,53].

Energy Optimization. Due to mobility, majority of the devices on which outdoor distributed computing applications execute, are battery powered. This includes mobile phones, laptops, PDAs and sensors. Battery has a limited lifetime, and therefore energy optimization mechanisms need to be applied at all levels, including hardware, operating system and compiler. The applications themselves need to be designed with this constraint in mind and should be inherently *lightweight*. One way to accomplish this is to offload computing to a wall-powered server whenever opportunities to connect to the server are available. This approach is called *cyber foraging* [19]. Another approach is to trade the fidelity of applications for energy [44]. Such mechanisms need to be applied during application design phase, as opposed to compiler or OS based energy optimization mechanisms, which are hidden from the applications.

Incentive for Cooperation. Cooperation is the key to outdoor distributed computing applications. Why should devices cooperate? Why should a device forward packets for another device? What if a device exhibits selfish, reserved or parasitic behavior? Although the symbiotic nature of these applications promotes cooperation, there is a need for devising incentive models so that devices can benefit from cooperating with other nodes, even if other nodes refuse to cooperate. Such models will drive the equilibrium towards cooperation. A good starting point is to follow the design of reputation-based schemes, which are used to promote trust in peer-to-peer networks, and tailor them to work for short-lived interactions.

Human-Computer Interaction. Human-computer interaction issues will play a big role in the success or failure of these applications. Since user attention is a limited resource, the complexity of using and interacting with such applications has to be minimized. Novel user interfaces are needed. Speech recognition, gesture recognition and vision-based solutions can be very helpful. The applications have to be robust and reliable even in the presence of network failures to ensure satisfactory user experience.

Bootstrapping. Bootstrapping of outdoor distributed applications is a hard problem, and there are numerous reasons for it. First, while these applications are assumed to be ad-hoc in nature, there is a minimal amount of configuration required on every device to bootstrap these applications. The configuration effort may outweigh the convenience that a user gets in return. There is a need to hide this configuration effort from the users. Second, the users have to carry with them a minimal amount of hardware and software to avail of such services and applications. This contradicts the spontaneous nature of these applications. The solutions should be designed around hardware that users already carry. Also, the software layer required for bootstrapping these applications should be bare minimum. Third, a certain amount of infrastructure is required to support many of these applications/services. For such an infrastructure to exist, right economic models are needed. While these applications have a lot of utility, users must be willing to pay a price for using these applications. There is a need to minimize the infrastructure requirement to improve chances of deployment. Fourth, due to the fact that these applications rely on cooperation between devices, a user may not be convinced about paying a price for a technology that he/she cannot use unless others have it too. The dependencies need to be minimized. Fifth, technology is not matured enough to support robust, secure and distraction-free distributed applications in ad-hoc networks. The research challenges pointed out in this section need to be overcome before such applications can become a reality.

2.3   Technology Enablers

As mentioned before, in order to make bootstrapping easier, it is important to design solutions around devices that have the greatest potential of becoming ubiquitous. Here we identify such devices.

Mobile Phones. Mobile phones are carried by almost everyone. Hitherto, they were mostly used for the purpose of making and taking phone calls on the move. With advances in hardware and improving storage trends, mobile phones are evolving into personal computing devices. Sony Ericsson P900, which is a commonly used phone today, runs Symbian OS, an operating system designed specifically for mobile phones, and comes equipped with two different versions of Java: Personal Java [10] and J2ME CLDC/MIDP [1]. It also supports C++ in order to provide low-level access to the system. The phone has 16MB of internal memory and upto 128MB external flash memory, which is small compared to newer phones that have GBs of storage capacity. What is particularly noteworthy about these phones, is the hybrid wireless networking capabilities that they come equipped with, which includes Bluetooth, WLAN, IR and internet connectivity via GPRS. These phones can serve as personal computers for all practical purposes, if only the display could be made bigger and battery lifetime improved. There is already some research initiative in exploring the potential of mobile phones as next generation personal computers [35,55].

Car PCs. Cars have carried on-board computers for decades and modern mobile microprocessors control everything from engine performance to car's instrument cluster. There is ongoing effort in making car PCs more popular and sophisticated than they are today. There are numerous vendors that assemble and sell car PCs (e.g Xenarc, Logisys etc). Several cars already come equipped with full car PCs that run Windows XP (e.g Nissan 350Z and Peugeot 307 XSi). So far these systems are used for stand-alone applications such as navigation systems. DSRC is a block of spectrum in the 5.850 to 5.925 GHz band allocated by US FCC to enable communication between cars. Several car manufacturers, including Toyota, Daimler Chrysler and GM are funding research for the development of distributed applications based on car-to-car communication.

Sensors. GPS, thermometer, calorimeter, multi-meter, magnetic compass, barometer, RADAR sensor, infra-red sensor, RFID reader, camera are just a few examples of sensors that we use in our daily life. Sensors are the "eyes and ears" of outdoor distributed computing applications. They gather information about the environment, which serves as context and aids in provisioning services to the user. Location sensors, activity sensors, RFID readers, temperature sensors, cameras, are some of the more directly usable sensors for distributed applications. The size of these sensors varies and so does their cost and utility. Many of these sensors are programmable and can be networked together and linked to more powerful computing devices to enable many interesting outdoor distributed computing applications. While some of them are meant to be wall-powered, others are meant to be scattered in the environment and survive on batteries.

3   Split Smart Messages: A Middleware for Outdoor Distributed Computing

In this section, we describe the design of Split Smart Messages, a middleware for outdoor distributed computing. Split Smart Messages is an extension of the Smart Message [37] model and has been tailored to suit the requirements of resource constrained devices such as Smart Phones which come with a pre-installed JVM. In the design of SSM, we have payed special attention to opportunistic networking, portability, security and lightweightness.

The design of Split Smart Messages has been inspired by mobile agents. A Split Smart Message (SSM) is a user-defined application whose execution is distributed over a series of nodes using execution migration. The nodes on which SSMs execute, called *nodes of interest*, are named by properties and discovered dynamically using application controlled routing. To move between two nodes of interest, an

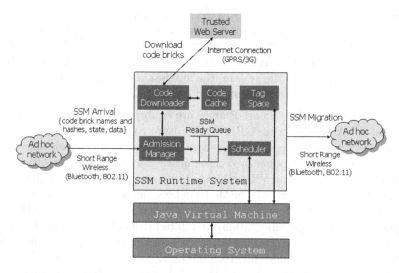

Fig. 1. Split Smart Messages Architecture

SSM calls explicitly for execution migration, and routes itself without any underlying routing support. An SSM consists of *code bricks*(e.g Java class files) and *data
bricks*(e.g Java objects which store data and execution state). SSMs in addition to
being lightweight, provide the functionality to support service execution, discovery, and migration in highly volatile mobile ad hoc networks. SSMs are resilient to
network failures, as they carry the code for routing themselves, and can therefore
store-and-forward themselves opportunistically.

3.1 SSM Middleware Architecture and Implementation

Every participating node has to be equipped with the SSM middleware. The
SSM middleware is written completely in Java (using J2ME CDC and CLDC),
and can be ported to the common JVMs. It consists of the following components
(as shown in Figure 1):

Tag Space. Tag space is name-based virtual memory. It is composed of tags
which are *(name, data)* pairs. These tags are Java objects that can be created,
deleted, read from, or written into by SSMs. Nodes are identified by properties
that are stored in tags. Also, services running on these nodes create tags for
advertising themselves. Tags are, therefore, integral to content-based routing
and service discovery over SSMs.

In addition to providing storage, tags also provide inter-SSM communication
and synchronization. Commonly, a blocked SSM is woken up by the interpreter
when the tag is written by another SSM. Each time an SSM blocks on a tag, its
corresponding Java thread is terminated. Each time an SSM is unblocked (and
consequently dispatched for execution), a new Java thread is created for it.

Admission Manager. The admission manager is responsible for receiving and admitting incoming SSMs over different network interfaces. Our admission manager listens on the TCP/IP socket interface (for receiving SMs over 802.11b) as well as Bluetooth L2CAP interface (for receiving SMs over Bluetooth). While admitting SSMs into the system, the admission manager verifies the data bricks and state against certain verification policies.

Code Downloader. Smart Phones are equipped with multiple network interfaces: WLAN, Bluetooth, GPRS/3G. Future car PCs are believed to have multiple network interfaces too. By virtue of these hybrid networking capabilities, these devices are capable of communicating with each other over short-range wireless (Bluetooth or WLAN), while being connected to the internet at the same time (via GPRS/3G). SSMs have been designed with this feature in mind.

As mentioned before, an SSM is composed of: code bricks (which are Java class files in our implementation) and data bricks (which are Java objects in our implementation). During migration, if internet connectivity is available, only data bricks are transferred across the local network (using WLAN/Bluetooth), while code bricks are uploaded to and downloaded from a trusted web server (using GPRS/3G)[1]. This helps security as described later in this section. If internet connectivity is not available, then code bricks are transported along with data bricks.

The component that downloads code from the trusted web server is implemented as a MIDlet that runs over MIDP [1]. MIDP supports OTA (Over-The-Air) Provisioning, which is used for implementing dynamic downloading of code. The code downloader is invoked by the Admission Manager everytime code needs to be downloaded.

Code Cache. Code cache stores frequently used code bricks. In order to implement Code cache, we exploit Java's classloader. The Java dynamic class loading mechanism is used to load a class representing a code brick. In the process, a new *Class* instance of the corresponding class is created. The classloader will not unload the class as long as there is a live reference to the *Class* instance. References to the cached classes are stored such that these classes are not unloaded by the classloader. When the caching policy chooses a class for eviction, we just remove the stored reference for that class.

Scheduler. The scheduler is responsible for dispatching SSMs (from the SSM ready queue) for execution on the JVM. The SSM scheduler is implemented as a Java thread that extracts an SSM from the ready queue in FIFO order, dispatches it for execution as a Java thread, and goes to sleep. When the SSM completes its execution, it wakes up the scheduler using the Java's thread synchronization mechanism.

3.2 Example

To illustrate the SSM distributed computing model, let us consider a network of handhelds belonging to people attending a conference. At the beginning of the

---

[1] Hence, the name *Split* Smart Messages.

```
i=0;    /* i stored in data brick */
while(i<N){
  migrate("Ubiquitous");
  /* ask attendee to join */
  if (readTag("Joined"))
    i++;
}
migrate("Initiator");
```

Fig. 2. Example of Split Smart Message Code: Ad hoc Creation of a Research Discussion Group at a Conference

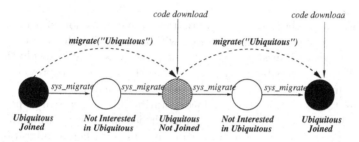

Fig. 3. Execution Path for the Split Smart Message Presented in Figure 2

conference, people download on their handhelds a simple SSM that creates tags for their research interests. These tags can be used by other SSMs to identify people with certain research interests. For instance, a certain person can download an SSM that sets up a discussion with N people interested in ubiquitous computing (i.e., identified by a tag named *Ubiquitous*) or invites them to have lunch together. This SSM works in an ad hoc fashion over short range wireless links and achieves its task even if the attendees do not know each other beforehand.

Each time an attendee wants to start a discussion on a given research topic, or invite people for lunch, she injects this SSM in the network from her handheld. The SSM migrates through the network until it finds N people willing to have such a discussion or meet for lunch. Once the group is set, it returns and informs the initiator. For instance, Figure 2 presents the code for an SSM that creates a group discussion for *Ubiquitous* computing. Figure 3 depicts the execution path of this SSM over five nodes.

The key operation in the SSM programming model is migration, which implements content-based routing using tags [21]. An SSM names the nodes of interest by tags, and then calls *migrate* to route itself to a node that has the desired tags. In our example, *migrate("Ubiquitous")* routes the SSM to people interested in ubiquitous computing using other handhelds (i.e., belonging to people who may or may not be interested in ubiquitous computing), as intermediate nodes. The *migrate* function uses the *sys_migrate* primitive for transferring the SM to the next hop. After migration, the SM resumes from the next instruction following the migrate call.

3.3   Portability

For implementing migratory applications or services, it is important that they be portable and transferable with minimal overhead. The original Smart Message architecture [37] was implemented by modifying Sun's Java Kilobyte virtual machine (KVM). The whole architecture was implemented inside the VM because of the need for VM support in capturing the execution state and restoring it at destination to resume the execution. This implementation, although powerful and efficient, is not portable. Since devices like Smart Phones and Smart Watches come with a pre-installed Java VM, (and most of the time users do not want to or cannot modify the system software on their devices), we have designed SSM middleware such that it can execute on top of unmodified Java virtual machines.

The main issue to be solved in a pure Java implementation of a migration-based middleware is performing migration without requiring the VM to capture and restore the execution state. The execution state is located inside the VM and is not directly accessible to the external world. In order to provide migration without modifying the VM, we have designed a mechanism for capturing and restoring the execution state by incorporating all the necessary operations in the SSM itself. The heart of our approach lies in instrumenting the SSM bytecode in such a way that the SSM can save its state before migration and restore it before resumption with a minimal overhead. Using this mechanism, the state is encoded in the data bricks, and no explicit state information is shipped. Being resource and bandwidth constrained, mobile ad hoc networks impose constraints on the amount of data that can be transferred for reliable communication. With this in mind, we have focussed on making the migration mechanism extremely lightweight and efficient. Our Java bytecode instrumentation mechanism increases the Java bytecode size by only 3% as opposed to previously proposed portable Java migration mechanisms, which increase the bytecode size by as much as 400%. The mechanism is generally applicable to any system based on execution migration of Java programs For details on our instrumentation mechanism, refer to [45].

3.4   Security

The security issues associated with SSMs are the same as those associated with mobile agents. As mentioned in [36], the security threats for mobile agents can roughly be classified into four categories: *agent to platform, platform to agent, agent to agent, others to agent*. The *others to agent* threat is not specific to mobile agents, but in general applies to any form of data transfer between two untrusted peers. Broadly speaking, the other three categories contain two different security threats: snooping/changing/dropping data, and running malicious code. When we look at a mobile agent as composed of code and data, the security threats specific to them involve malicious code running on a certain platform. Protecting data against threats like replay attacks, middleman attacks, snooping or changing data, is a problem common to any form of network communication.

Therefore, we assume that state-of-the-art solutions can be applied to protect mobile agents' data, and in the following, we focus on protecting against malicious code.

The agent-to-platform category represents the set of threats in which agents exploit security weaknesses of an agent platform or launch attacks against an agent platform. This set of threats includes denial of service or unauthorized access. Mobile agents can launch denial of service attacks by consuming an excessive amount of the agent platform's computing resources. Mobile agents can gain unauthorized access to confidential data on the platform if they can bypass the platform's security policy. Several techniques have been proposed for protecting the agent platform, namely Signed Code [22], Proof Carrying Code [42], Path Histories [46], Authorization Certificates [59], Safe Code Interpretation [47], State Appraisal [29], and Software-based Fault Isolation [60]. Some of these techniques aim at authenticating the mobile agent or the source of the agent, while others are focused on safe code execution.

The solution that we propose for SSM aims at inducing trust between the agent and the platform by establishing trust between the target platform and the agent source. As mentioned before, devices such as Smart Phones and Car PCs support *dual connectivity*. Dual connectivity provides a simple infrastructure for establishing trust in the local ad hoc network. An SSM is composed of two essential components: data bricks (Java objects) and code bricks (Java class files). To protect devices against malicious code, the SSM middleware transfers data bricks over the ad hoc network, while code bricks are downloaded from a trusted web server (when internet connectivity is available). Trusted code bricks ensure a certain level of security, which can be improved upon by using one of the aforementioned techniques in conjunction.

Downloading code from a trusted web server is safer than relying on authentication certificates presented by an incoming SSM because the SSM could have been tampered with. No safe assumptions can be made about the data/code coming from a machine, unless the machine follows the trusted computing model [17].

In our current architecture, the code bricks are uploaded to the web server beforehand. The web server would make the code available after suitable authentication, which may involve manual analysis or abstract interpretation of the code to ensure that it is safe. To support on-the-fly uploading of code bricks, Proof-carrying-code technique or Microsoft's Authenticode [7] could be employed. We assume the existence of an authentication web service.

There are many reasons for not migrating the whole SSM over the internet. First, our current design is opportunistic in nature and exploits a web service only when available, but does not depend on it. If the web service is not available, the code bricks can be fetched from the source over short range wireless. Having an architecture that migrates the whole SSM over the internet would make it strongly coupled with internet availability. Second, code bricks can be uploaded to the web server beforehand offline and downloaded on demand, because an SSM always uses the same code bricks. This is an upload-once-download-many strategy. Data bricks keep growing and shrinking in size and number as the SSMs travel across the network. Uploading and downloading data bricks from a web server on the fly, restricts the level of authentication that can be provided by the web server. Third, it is important to minimize internet usage as there is a cost associated with downloading data from the internet. Many 3G/GPRS service providers charge an amount proportional to the amount of data downloaded from the internet.

3.5   Performance

We evaluated the SSM middleware on Smart Phones as well as HP iPAQs to get an insight into the performance of SSMs on resource constrained devices. Our goals in conducting the experimental evaluation were threefold : (1) quantify the impact of bytecode instrumentation on the SSM bytecode size, (2) compare the costs of basic SSM operations on Smart Phones with that on HP iPAQs, (3) compare single-hop round-trip time of an SSM on Smart Phones with that on HP iPAQs to get an estimate of communication costs. Our testbed consists of Sony Ericsson P800 and P900 phones communicating over Bluetooth, and HP iPAQs communicating over 802.11b.

Table 1 shows the increase in bytecode size as a result of instrumenting four of our SSM test cases. We have used Soot1.2.5 [2] to do off-line bytecode instrumentation. On average, we observe an increase of 2.9% in the bytecode size, which is negligible as compared to existing approaches (see Section 5 for details).

Table 2 shows the cost of tag space operations. Table 3 compares the cost of SSM execution (including migration) on Smart Phones with that on HP iPAQs. The results indicate that for establishing a Bluetooth connection it takes on an average a constant of 1 second, and the round-trip time varies from 300ms to 1600ms(excluding the cost of establishing a Bluetooth connection) as data brick size is varied from 1KB to 16KB. For all practical purposes, this is good

Table 1. Increase in SSM Bytecode Size Due to Instrumentation

Unmodified Byte-code(KB)	Modified Byte-code(KB)
1084	1122
1230	1266
1527	1564
2330	2395

Table 2. Cost of SSM Tag Space Operations

Operation	Time(μs)	
	HP iPAQ	Sony Ericsson P800/P900
readTag	78	188
createTag	89	578
writeTag	71	203
deleteTag	98	156

Table 3. Effect of Data Brick Size on Single-Hop SSM Round-Trip Time

Size(Bytes)	Round-Trip Time(ms)	
	HP iPAQ	Sony Ericsson P800/P900
1044	150	1450
2088	177	1600
4056	196	1790
8010	234	2120
16010	301	2630

performance. The performance on iPAQs is much better compared to that on Smart Phones, which is expected because iPAQs have more computation power than Smart Phones and 802.11b offers a much higher bandwidth than Bluetooth. The cost of downloading code from the web server has a lower bound of 3 seconds, which is determined by the size of the corresponding *jad* file, which is at least 250 bytes.

4   SDIPP: Service Discovery, Interaction and Payment Protocol

In this section, we describe the design and implementation of a protocol for provisioning services on devices with dual connectivity (e.g smart phones). The services execute on top of the SSM middleware as *Service SSMs*, and can therefore migrate themselves. For advertising themselves, the services create tags on the nodes they execute on, which can be discovered using *Discovery SSMs*. In addition, they register themselves with a web server that is publicly known. When Bluetooth is available on the device, the services can also be discovered using the Bluetooth Service Discovery Protocol(SDP).

4.1   Architecture

Bluetooth engine, GPRS Engine and *Cache* are the building blocks of the protocols. Bluetooth Engine is invoked by the protocols to discover or interact with the services in the proximity. It is a layer above the Bluetooth stack and provides a convenient Java API similar to JSR-82 for accessing the Bluetooth stack. *GPRS Engine* is invoked to carry out the communication with the web services over GPRS.

Cache is persistent storage. The personal information of the user along with her preferences regarding services are stored in the cache. Personal information of the user may include name, age, address, credit card number etc. Storing personal information serves two purposes: first, it provides a way of identifying the user and authenticating her if need be; second, personal information along with preferences and location help in identifying the best suited service for the user during service discovery phase thereby making SDIPP context-aware. Cache also stores the interface/protocol downloaded by the interaction protocol and the data needed across protocols or across sessions.

Fig. 4. SDIPP Discovery Model

4.2   Discovery Protocol

Bluetooth SDP provides service browsing without apriori knowledge of the service characteristics. It does not include functionality for accessing services, however, it can be used in conjunction with some other protocol for accessing services. Our discovery protocol is hierarchical in nature, and is a 3-step process as summarized below:

One-hop Discovery. Services in the proximity (one-hop) are discovered using Bluetooth SDP. If the list of services discovered by Bluetooth SDP includes the desired service, the discovery phase is over. If it does not include the desired service, but instead lists a Service Discovery Service(SDS), the SDS is invoked to locate the desired service in a multi-hop fashion.

Multi-hop Discovery. In our implementation, SDS is implemented using Split Smart Messages. Discovery SSMs broadcast themselves in the ad-hoc network and look for tags with the desired properties. These tags are created by services for the purpose of advertising themselves. When a desired tag (i.e service) is found, the requester is informed.

Web-Based Discovery. Services also register themselves with a public web service and periodically update their information. If internet connectivity via GPRS is available, the public web service is contacted and requested for information about the desired service (e.g location).

4.3   Interaction Protocol

In outdoor distributed computing scenarios, the interaction of the user with a service is assumed to be spontaneous, and therefore the protocol for interacting with the service would need to be learnt on the fly. Our interaction protocol is inspired by Jini [4]. Every service registers itself with a web server, which assigns it a unique id and stores the interface which can be downloaded for interacting with the service. Figure 5 shows the interaction protocol. The protocol can be summarized as follows:

- The device lists the services discovered during discovery phase. The desired service is requested for its id over short-range wireless.
- The service responds with its id.

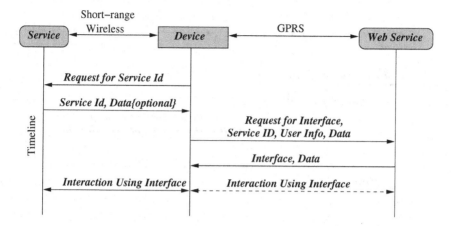

Fig. 5. SDIPP Interaction Protocol

- The id along with the personal information of the user stored on the device is sent over to a trusted web server over the GPRS connection. The personal information of the user would be used for authenticating them if the service requires that.
- The web server, after authenticating the request, responds with the code and data needed for interacting with the service. The code is a Java program that contains the protocol and interface for interacting with the service.
- Since the code is obtained from a trusted server it is assumed to be safe and is dispatched for execution on the device. All further communication between the device and the service takes place as a result of executing the downloaded code.

Note that the web server(s) for storing the downloadable interface for the services may be different from the web server(s) that act as service directories. We implement downloading of code from the internet using OTA (Over-The-Air) provisioning [8].

4.4 Payment Protocol

Our protocol for paying services is based on the electronic cash representation proposed by the Millicent protocol [30]. Millicent proposes the idea of using accounts based on scrip and brokers to sell scrip. A piece of scrip represents an account the user has established with a vendor. At any given time, a vendor has outstanding scrip (open accounts) with the recently a users. The balance of the account is kept as the value of the scrip. When the customer makes a purchase with scrip, the cost of the purchase is deducted from the scrip's value and new scrip (with the new value/account balance) is returned as When the user has completed a series of transactions, he can "cash in" the remaining value of the scrip (close the account). Brokers serve as accounting intermediaries

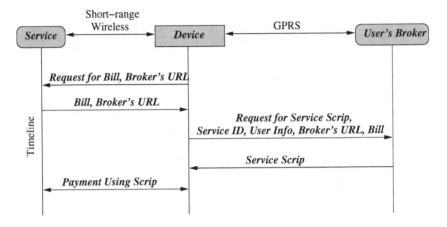

Fig. 6. SDIPP Payment Protocol

between users and vendors. Customers enter into long-term relationships with broke the same way as they would enter into an agreement with a bank, credit card company, or internet service provider. Brokers buy vendor scrip as a service to users and vendors. Broker scrip serves as a common currency for customers to use when buying vendor scrip, and for vendors to give as a refund for unspent scrip.

We try to satisfy the design principals described in [48]. In our model, the broker is a web service that the user already has an account with. The vendor is the service that the user wishes to use and pay for.

Figure 6 illustrates the payment protocol. It as can be summarized as following:

- The device requests the service for its broker's URL and the bill over short-range wireless.
- The service responds with its broker's URL and the bill.
- The service id, broker's URL and bill amount is sent over to the user's broker over GPRS along with the personal information of the user stored on the device.
- User's broker buys service scrip from service's broker on user's behalf. The amount of scrip bought is greater than or equal to the bill amount.
- User's broker responds to the device with the service scrip .
- User pays the service using the service scrip.

Brokers are assumed to be trusted services that have service providers as their clients and other brokers as their peers. Even if the broker tries to cheat, the customer and the service provider can independently check the scrip and detect broker fraud. Service provider fraud consists of not providing service for valid scrip or deducting more amount from the scrip than is valid. If the service provider tries to cheat, the customer can detect the fraud and complain to the broker who will take care of it.

If the customer is cheating, then the service provider's only loss is the cost of detecting the bad scrip and denying service. Every transaction requires that the customer knows the secret associated with the scrip. The protocol never sends the secret in the clear, so there is no risk due to eavesdropping. No piece of scrip can be reused, so a replay attack will fail. Each request is signed with the secret, so there is no way to intercept scrip and use the scrip to make a different request.

This payment protocol provides a security model that is well suited for profit-based services, where the service and the user need to be authenticated to each other and anonymity maintained at the same time.

4.5   Evaluation

The SDIPP protocol was implemented and tested on Sony Ericsson P900 phones which have both Personal Java and MIDP in addition to C++. We used MIDP and JSR-82 (Java Bluetooth API) to implement the architecture. Table 4 shows the time of completion for the different phases of the SDIPP protocol. The time of completion of the Interaction Protocol depends on the size of the code downloaded from the internet. The lower bound is determined by the size of the *jad* file of the corresponding code which is typically 250 Bytes. The time of completion of the ad-hoc service discovery over Split Smart Messages depends on the number of nodes (hops) involved.

Table 4. Performance Evaluation of SDIPP

Operation	Average Time of Completion
Bluetooth Service Discovery	22.5 sec
Ad-hoc Service Discovery	2 sec × No. of Hops
Web directory lookup	2.5 sec
Interaction Protocol(Lower Bound)	3 sec
Payment Protocol	6 sec

We have implemented and tested a few applications on top of this protocol. We have also gained some experience in the process. For details refer to [55].

5   Related Work

Split Smart Messages (SSMs) share the idea of code migration with mobile agents [38,31], and active networks [26,41], as well as the security and portability issues.

Unlike mobile agents, SSMs are defined to be responsible for their own routing in a network. This feature combined with content-based routing allows SSMs to adapt quickly to changes that may occur both in the network topology and the availability of resources at nodes. Furthermore, the SSM system architecture is lightweight and defines a node architecture suitable for resource constrained devices. Services can be executed, discovered and migrated on top of the SSM middleware.

SSMs differ from active networks (AN) in several key features. Primary difference comes from the problems they try to solve: AN target improved performance for end-to-end data transfers in relatively stable networks, while SSMs help the development of distributed applications on top of a new computing infrastructure that is unreliable and under-utilized due to the lack of programmability. Unlike AN, we define a computing model whereby several SSMs can cooperate, exchange data, and synchronize with each other through the tag space. In terms of migration, AN do not transfer the execution state from node to node whereas the SSM model does.

Tag Space bears resemblance with tuple spaces [24,40]. While both offer persistent shared memory for applications, the essential difference is that the tag space is local to every node.

To implement execution migration (i.e., transfer of the execution state), two approaches can be used: VM-based or compiler-based. The first approach implies designing new VMs or modifying existing ones to support the capturing and restoring of the execution state. The second approach works for unmodified VMs, but it involves either a modified compiler, or other tools that insert new pieces of code in the source code or directly in the executable program in order to capture and restore the execution state.

Similar to the original SM implementation, a number of systems [51,49,23] have modified the Java VM (JVM) to provide the required state capturing and restoring. Unlike SMs, which were designed specifically for networks of resource constrained devices, these systems are too heavy for devices such as cell-phones or PDAs.

Numerous service discovery protocols(SDPs) have been proposed. Each has its own infrastructure requirements and target audiences. Bluetooth SDP [14] follows the client-service model and enables nearby devices to discover services on each other. Bluetooth is a low power protocol making it suitable for energy-constrained devices. Bluetooth SDP is query based, which means that clients query for available services rather than services pro-actively announcing their presence. It uses unicast and broadcast as the communication mechanism and does not provide any service invocation mechanism. DEAPspace [43] proposed by IBM research, is aimed for single-hop ad hoc environments. Nodes cache service information and periodically broadcast it to share the information with each other. DEAPspace follows the client-service model. INS [16] is a hierarchical resource discovery and service location protocol that uses a late binding mechanism to provide resilience against name-to-location mapping changes. INS follows the client-service-directory model where the directory is distributed. INS is scalable and targets peer-to-peer networks.

Salutation [13] follows the client-service-directory model and uses RPC for service invocation. Salutation provides a transport-independent interface to applications making it very flexible. Effort has been made to map Salutation

APIs to Bluetooth Service Discovery Layer [27]. Service Location Protocol [33] is a lightweight protocol that targets service discovery within a site. It uses URL-based service invocation mechanism. Directories are optional. SLP supports both service announcements and client queries. Universal Plug and Play(UPnP) [6] is a device oriented service discovery protocol that targets home and office environments. UPnP follows the client-service model and uses XML for service invocation. UPnP is being actively advocated by Microsoft. Splendor [62] follows a *client-service-proxy-directory* model, where *proxy* is used to achieve privacy, authentication and load-sharing. Jini [4] follows client-service-directory model, where the directory not only provides service look-up but also downloadable Java code/objects for interacting with the service using RMI. Jini targets enterprise environments. UDDI [12] uses a web-based distributed directory that enables profit-based web services to list themselves on the internet and discover each other, similar to *yellow pages*.

Aalto et al [15] describe a system for Bluetooth and WAP Push based advertising for Smart Phones. They utilize Bluetooth for positioning the end-user's handheld and obtaining the Bluetooth address. The advertisements are then pushed to the phone over WAP. Scott et al [58] propose machine readable *visual tags* for bypassing Bluetooth service discovery on phones. Visual tags can be recognized by phone cameras and can improve device discovery time. However, this restricts discovery to only devices that are visible and increases human-intervention (for scanning the environment with phone camera).

Cooltown [39] and Splendor [62] utilize the idea of associating devices and services with the web. UDDI [12] is a web-based distributed directory that enables profit-based web services to list themselves on the internet and discover each other, similar to *yellow pages*. NTT DoCoMo's I-mode [3] makes web service provisioning on Smart Phones easier. Recently, they adopted Sony's contactless smart card technology called Felica [11], which can be used for electronic payment. Felica implements RF functions for wireless communication and is therefore extremely short-range.

6   Conclusions

In this paper, we exemplified outdoor distributed computing and identified the key challenges. We presented a middleware, called Split Smart Messages, that enables a large subset of outdoor distributed computing applications. We evaluated it on a testbed of HP iPAQs and Sony Ericsson P900 phones and found it lightweight, portable, resilient to network failures and relatively secure. We also presented a protocol, called SDIPP, which exploits dual connectivity on devices (e.g smart phones) for service provisioning (discovery, interaction and payment); and evaluated its performance on Sony Ericsson P900 phones.

Acknowledgements. This material is based upon work supported by NSF under grants ANI-0121416 and CNS-0520123.

References

1. MIDP Profile. http://wireless.java.sun.com/midp/.
2. Soot: a Java Optimization Framework. http://www.sable.mcgill.ca/soot/.
3. i-mode. http://www.nttdocomo.com/corebiz/imode.
4. Jini Network Technology. http://wwws.sun.com/software/jini.
5. Location privacy protection act, 2001. http://www.theorator.com/bills107.
6. Microsoft Upnp Specification.
7. Miscrosoft Authenticode Technology.
   http://msdn.microsoft.com/library/default.asp.
8. OTA Provisioning. http://java.sun.com/products/midp.
9. Owl web ontology language. http://www.w3.org/TR/owl-features/.
10. PersonalJava. http://java.sun.com/j2me/.
11. Sony Felica Technology. www.sony.net/Products/felica.
12. UDDI. http://www.uddi.org.
13. White Paper : Salutation Architecture, 1998.
    http://www.salutation.org/whitepaper/originalwp.pdf.
14. Bluetooth Specification Part E. Service Discovery Protocol (SDP), 1999.
    http://www.bluetooth.com.
15. L. Aalto, N. Gothlin, J. Korhonen, and T. Ojala. Bluetooth and wap push based location-aware mobile advertising system. In *Proceedings of the 2nd international conference on Mobile systems, applications, and services*, pages 49–58, Boston, MA, June 2004.
16. W. Adjie-Winoto, E. Schwartz, H. Balakrishnan, and J. Lilley. The design and implementation of an intentional naming system. In *Proceedings of the seventeenth ACM symposium on Operating systems principles*, pages 186–201, Charleston, SC, December 1999.
17. W. Arbaugh, D. Farber, and J. Smith. A secure and reliable bootstrap architecture. In *IEEE Symposium on Security and Privacy*, pages 65–71, Oakland, CA, May 1997.
18. P. Bahl and V. N. Padmanabhan. RADAR: An in-building RF-based user location and tracking system. In *INFOCOM (2)*, Tel-Aviv, Israel, March 2000.
19. R. Balan, J. Flinn, M. Satyanarayanan, S. Sin, and H. Yang. The case for cyber foraging. In *Proceedings of 10th ACM SIGOPS European Workshop*, Saint Emilion, France, September 2002.
20. L. Bao and S. S. Intille. Activity recognition from user-annotated acceleration data. In *Proceedings of the 2nd International Conference on Pervasive Computing*, Vienna, Austria, April 2004.
21. C. Borcea, C. Intanagonwiwat, A. Saxena, and L. Iftode. Self-Routing in Pervasive Computing Environments using Smart Messages. In *Proceedings of the 1st IEEE International Conference on Pervasive Computing and Communications (PerCom)*, pages 87–96, Dallas-Fort Worth, Texas, March 2003.
22. N. Borisov and E. Brewer. Active certificates: A framework for delegation, 2000.
23. S. Bouchenak and D. Hagimont. Pickling threads state in the java system. In *Proceedings of the Technology of Object-Oriented Languages and Systems (TOOLS 33)*, Santa Barbara, CA, August 2000.
24. N. Carriero and D. Gelernter. Linda in Context. *Communications of the ACM*, 32(4):444–458, April 1989.
25. H. Chen, T. Finin, and A. Joshi. An ontology for context-aware pervasive computing environments. *Special Issue on Ontologies for Distributed Systems, Knowledge Engineering Review*, 18(3):197–207, 2003.

26. D. Wetherall. Active Network Vision Reality: Lessons from a Capsule-based System. In *Proceedings of the 17th ACM Symposium on Operating Systems Principles (SOSP)*, pages 64–79, Charleston, SC, December 1999.

27. C. Dabrowski, K. Mills, and J. Elder. Understanding consistency maintenance in service discovery architectures during communication failure. In *Proceedings of the third international workshop on Software and performance*, pages 168–178, Rome, Italy, July 2002.

28. K. Fall. A delay tolerant network architecture for challenged internets. In *Proceedings of SIGCOMM*, Karlsruhe, Germany, August 2003.

29. W. M. Farmer, J. D. Guttman, and V. Swarup. Security for mobile agents: Authentication and state appraisal. In *Proceedings of the Fourth European Symposium on Research in Computer Security*, Rome, Italy, September 1996.

30. S. Glassman, M. Manasse, M. Abadi, P. Gauthier, and P. Sobalvarro. The Millicent protocol for inexpensive electronic commerce. In *Proceedings of the 4th World Wide Web Conference* , pages 603–618, Boston, MA, December 1995.

31. R. Gray, G. Cybenko, D. Kotz, and D. Rus. Mobile agents: Motivations and state of the art. In J. Bradshaw, editor, *Handbook of Agent Technology*. AAAI/MIT Press, 2002.

32. M. Gruteser and D. Grunwald. Anonymous usage of location-based services through spatial and temporal cloaking. In *Proceedings of the First International Conference on Mobile Systems, Applications, and Services (MobiSys)*, San Fransisco, CA, May 2003.

33. E. Guttman. Service location protocol: Automatic discovery of ip network services. *IEEE Internet Computing*, 3(4):71–80, 1999.

34. P. Hui, A. Chaintreau, J. Scott, R. Gass, J. Crowcroft, and C. Diot. Pocket switched networks and human mobility in conference environments. In *WDTN '05: Proceeding of the 2005 ACM SIGCOMM workshop on Delay-tolerant networking*, Philadelphia, PA, August 2005.

35. L. Iftode, C. Borcea, N. Ravi, P. Kang, and P. Zhou. Smart phone: An embedded system for universal interactions. In *Smart phone: An embedded system for universal interactions. In Proceedings of the tenth International Workshop on Future Trends in Distributed Computing Systems*, Suzhou, China, May 2004.

36. W. Jansen and T. Karygiannis. Nist special publication 800-19 - mobile agent security, 2000.

37. P. Kang, C. Borcea, G. Xu, A. Saxena, U. Kremer, and L. Iftode. Smart Messages: A Distributed Computing Platform for Networks of Embedded Systems. *The Computer Journal, Special Focus-Mobile and Pervasive Computing*, 47(4):475–494, 2004.

38. N. Karnik and A. Tripathi. Agent Server Architecture for the Ajanta Mobile-Agent System. In *Proceedings of the 1998 International Conference on Parallel and Distributed Processing Techniques and Applications (PDPTA)*, pages 66–73, Las Vegas, NV, July 1998.

39. T. Kindberg, J. Barton, J. Morgan, G. Becker, D. Caswell, P. Debaty, G. Gopal, M. Frid, V. Krishnan, H. Morris, J. Schettino, B. Serra, and M. Spasojevic. People, places, things: Web presence for the real world.

40. T. Lehman, A. Cozzi, Y. Xiong, J. Gottschalk, V. Vasudevan, S. Landis, P. Davis, B. Khavar, and P. Bowman. Hitting the distributed computing sweet spot with tspaces. *Computer Networks: The International Journal of Computer and Telecommunications Networking*, 35(4):457–472, March 2001.

41. J. Moore, M. Hicks, and S. Nettles. Practical Programmable Packets. In *Proceedings of the 20th Annual Joint Conference of the IEEE Computer and Communications Societies (INFOCOM)*, pages 41–50, Anchorage, AK, April 2001.

42. G. C. Necula. Proof-carrying code. In *Conference Record of POPL '97: The 24th ACM SIGPLAN-SIGACT Symposium on Principles of Programming Languages*, Paris, France, January 1997.

43. M. Nidd. Service Discovery in DEAPspace. In *IEEE Personal Communications*, August 2001.

44. B. D. Noble, M. Satyanarayanan, D. Narayanan, J. E. Tilton, J. Flinn, and K. R. Walker. Agile application-aware adaptation for mobility. In *SOSP '97: Proceedings of the sixteenth ACM symposium on Operating systems principles*, St Malo, France, October 1997.

45. N.Ravi, C. Borcea, P. Kang, , and L. Iftode. Portable Smart Messages for Ubiquitous Java-enabled Devices. In *The First Annual International Conference on Mobile and Ubiquitous Systems: Networking and Services (MobiQuitous)*, Boston, MA, August 2004.

46. J. J. Ordille. When agents roam, who can you trust? In *First Conference on Emerging Technologies and Applications in Communications (etaCOM)*, Portland, OR, May 1996.

47. J. K. Ousterhout, J. Y. Levy, and B. M. Walsh. The Safe-Tcl Security Model. Technical Report SMLI TR-97-60, Sun Microsystems, 1997.

48. P.Boddupalli, F.Al-Bin-Ali, N.Davies, A.Friday, O.Storz, and M.Wu. Payment support in ubiquitous computing environments. In *Proceedings of the IEEE Workshop on Mobile Computing Systems and Applications*, Monterey, CA, October 2003.

49. H. Peine and T. Stolpmann. The Architecture of the Ara Platform for Mobile Agents. In *First International Workshop on Mobile Agents MA*, pages 50–61, April 1997.

50. N. B. Priyantha, A. Chakraborty, and H. Balakrishnan. The cricket location-support system. In *MobiCom '00: Proceedings of the 6th annual international conference on Mobile computing and networking*, Boston, MA, August 2000.

51. M. Ranganathan, A. Acharya, S. Sharma, and J. Saltz. Network-aware Mobile Programs. In *Proceedings of the USENIX 1997 Annual Technical Conference*, pages 91–104, Anaheim, CA, January 1997.

52. N. Ravi, N. Dandekar, P. Mysore, and M. Littman. Activity recognition from accelerometer data. In *Proceedings of the Seventeenth Conference on Innovative Applications of Artificial Intelligence(IAAI)*, Pittsburgh, PA, July 2005.

53. N. Ravi, M. Gruteser, and L. Iftode. Non-inference: An information flow control model for location-based services. In *Proceedings of the Third International Conference on Mobile and Ubiquitous Systems (Mobiquitous)*, San Jose, CA, July 2006.

54. N. Ravi, P. Shankar, A. Frankel, A. Elgammal, and L. Iftode. Indoor localization using camera phones. In *Proceedings of the Workshop on Mobile Computing Systems and Applications(WMCSA)*, Washington, USA, April 2006.

55. N. Ravi, P. Stern, N. Desai, and L. Iftode. Accessing ubiquitous services using smart phones. In *Third International Conference on Pervasive Computing and Communications*, Kauai, Hawaii, March 2005.

56. M. Roman and R. Campbell. Gaia: Enabling active spaces. In *Proceedings of 9th ACM SIGOPS European Workshop*, Kolding, Denmark, September 2000.

57. D. Salber, A. K. Dey, and G. D. Abowd. The context toolkit: Aiding the development of context-enabled applications. In *Proceedings of CHI*, Pittsburgh, PA, May 1999.

58. D. Scott, R. Sharp, A. Madhavapeddy, and E. Upton. Using visual tags to bypass bluetooth device discovery. *SIGMOBILE Mobile Computing and Communications Review*, 9(1):41–53, January 2005.

59. M. Thompson, W. Johnston, S. Mudumbai, G. Hoo, K. Jackson, and A. Essiari. Certificate-based access control for widely distributed resources. In *Proceedings of the Eighth USENIX Security Symposium*, Monterey, CA, June 1999.

60. R. Wahbe, S. Lucco, T. E. Anderson, and S. L. Graham. Efficient software-based fault isolation. In *SOSP '93: Proceedings of the fourteenth ACM symposium on Operating systems principles*, pages 203–216, Asheville, NC, December 1993.

61. R. Want, A. Hopper, V. Falco, and J. Gibbons. The active badge location system. *ACM Transactions on Information Systems*, 10(1):91–102, December 1992.

62. F. Zhu, M. Mutka, and L. Ni. Splendor: A secure, private, and location-aware service discovery protocol supporting mobile services. In *First International Conference on Pervasive Computing and Communications*, Dallas-Fort Worth, Texas, March 2003.

Towards a Real-Time Coordination Model for Mobile Computing

Gregory Hackmann, Christopher Gill, and Gruia-Catalin Roman

Department of Computer Science and Engineering
Washington University, St. Louis, MO, USA
{gwh2, cdgill, roman}@cse.wustl.edu

Abstract. Current coordination models offer limited support for applications in which mobile hosts not only must coordinate their actions, but must also coordinate when those actions will be taken. This paper describes the design of TNM, a new coordination model based on *timed futures* — a novel extension to current coordination models through which mobile hosts can propose and negotiate which actions they will take and when. We discuss the use and advantages of this new coordination model in the context of the automatic motorway application challenge problem posed for the 2005 Monterey Workshop.

1   Introduction

Mobile computing has experienced rapid growth in recent years due to both advances in technology and societal trends toward greater adoption of technology into peoples daily lives. These trends are occurring both on the individual scale, with mobile devices becoming the norm for personal communication, data storage and processing, and entertainment; and on larger scales as mobile network centric architectures are being designed to replace previously monolithic segments of transportation systems [1], military command and control systems [2], and other critical infrastructure.

The physical mobility of *agents*, which are people or programs performing actions that unless otherwise constrained are asynchronous and autonomous with respect to the actions of other agents in the system, is of particular importance in these systems. Physical mobility results in ad hoc networks, which create many challenges for application developers. These challenges include:

- frequent unannounced disconnections,
- message delay and loss, and
- intermittent connectivity between hosts.

To address these challenges, a number of coordination models have been developed to decouple the interactions between agents from the computations and other actions performed by each agent. This decoupling promotes rapid application development, flexible application deployment, and formal reasoning about interactions between mobile hosts. However, for some mobile computing applications (e.g., the transportation and military command and control systems mentioned above), these capabilities are not enough: the timing of actions by the mobile hosts is also critical to their correct operation, and new coordination models are needed to support temporal coordination of agents actions explicitly.

F. Kordon and J. Sztipanovits (Eds.): Monterey Workshop 2005, LNCS 4322, pp. 184–202, 2007.

This paper presents the design of TNM[1], a new coordination model that facilitates negotiation and execution of time-constrained actions across logically mobile agents and physically mobile hosts. TNM extends previous coordination models by providing new primitive tuple space operations and semantics for negotiating temporal actions, while preserving application flexibility and ease of deployment. TNM first provides future operation primitives to allow agents to propose and negotiate the future creation and removal of information from a shared tuple space. TNM then refines the semantics of those future operation primitives to include a quantitative notion of time under which explicit timing of actions can be asserted and requested. Finally, TNM defines semantics for binding proposals to requests, semantics for determining when proposals and requests for actions have been satisfied, and semantics for whether (and if so how) proposals and requests can be retracted if necessary.

The rest of this paper is structured as follows. Section 2 surveys previous related work on centralized, distributed, and timed coordination models upon which TNM builds, and which TNM extends. Section 3 describes a motivating example from the 2005 Monterey Workshop automatic motorway challenge problem, and highlights several challenges that previous coordination models do not address. Section 4 presents the TNM coordination model in detail, and identifies the main contributions of our approach: support for futures, timed futures, and semantics for satisfaction and retraction. Section 5 discusses how the TNM coordination model can address the challenges posed by the motivating example discussed in Section 3, through an example scenario. Finally, Section 6 offers concluding remarks and summarizes remaining open problems for future work.

2   Related Work

We now summarize related research on coordination models that precedes our work on TNM, explain how TNM builds upon and extends those previous advances, and highlight the novel aspects of our approach within that context. We first consider centralized coordination models in which agents interact through a single common tuple space that has no quantitative notion of time, in Section 2.1. In Section 2.2, we describe coordination models that add support for coordination in distributed and mobile settings. Finally, in Section 2.3 we consider coordination models that add notions of relative and absolute time. Taken together, these coordination models form the foundation upon which which we have developed our extensions in the TNM model, which we discuss in greater detail in Section 4.

2.1   Centralized Coordination Models

First, we consider the coordination primitives needed for centralized communication without consideration of time. The basic tuple space operations provided by LINDA [3] are:

- **out(t)**, which places *tuple* t into the tuple space;
- **in(p)**, which removes a tuple matching *pattern* p from the tuple space and returns it to the agent that issued the in operation; and

---

[1] TNM is an abbreviation of the Latin phrase *tempus neminem manet*, which translates into English as *time waits for no one*.

- **rd(p)**, which copies a tuple matching pattern p but does not remove the tuple from the tuple space, and returns the copy to the agent that issued the rd operation.

If no matching tuple is present when an in or rd operation is issued, the call to the operation will not return until a matching tuple is added to the tuple space. Therefore, both in and rd are *blocking* operations from the perspective of an agent invoking them.

A **react(p,s)** primitive is provided by LIME [4]. This primitive offers a natural extension to the operation primitives provided by the LINDA coordination model, in which a *reaction* containing pattern p and code fragment s is registered with the tuple space, and the call to the react operation then returns. When a tuple matching pattern p subsequently appears in the tuple space, the code fragment s is invoked. Reactions allow tuples to be handled asynchronously from the actions of the agents that register the reactions. Reactions help to protect agents from unbounded blocking.

2.2 Distributed and Mobile Coordination Models

Many distributed and mobile applications require bounds on blocking times and/or the ability to determine the success or failure of tuple space operations. A variety of coordination models have added variations on the in and rd primitives that are better suited to distributed coordination such as *probing* operations **inp(p)** and **rdp(p)**, which return null if no tuple matching pattern p is found; *group* blocking primitives **ing(p)** and **rdg(p)**, which return all tuples matching pattern p as opposed to only returning one matching tuple; and probing group operations **ingp(p)** and **rdgp(p)**, which return either all matching tuples or null if none are found.

LIME [4] also extends the centralized coordination model discussed in Section 2.1 by supporting transiently shared tuple spaces, to accommodate mobility of agents and hosts. LIMONE [5] adds a policy-driven acquaintance list so that agents can share tuple spaces selectively with other agents.

Again, while these extensions address many of the concerns of distributed and mobile coordination, they do not support reasoning about *whether* a particular tuple, once produced by an agent, will be visible to another agent. The TNM coordination model extends current distributed and mobile coordination models to include the ability to reason about when a proposal or request has been satisfied, as well as whether a proposal or request can be retracted if necessary.

2.3 Timed Coordination Models

Quantitative notions of relative and absolute time have appeared in several coordination models [6,7,8,9]. In these models, time is explicitly represented in the expression of tuples, patterns, and other coordination model features. For example, [6] defines the equivalent of an **out(t,d)** operation[2], in which the appearance of tuple t in the tuple space is subject to a relative *delay* d from when the operation is invoked.

---

[2] The operation signature notation we use in this paper assumes that a language that supports overloading, such as Java or C++, is used to specify a different operation definition for each distinct operation signature. In languages that do not support overloading, the same effect can be achieved through mangling of the operation names.

These timed coordination models also add further semantics to operation primitives, based on the explicit representation of time. For example, time-outs are used in the equivalent of a **rdp(p,w)** operation provided by *Timed Linda* [7] where parameter w determines how long the operation will wait before returning either a tuple matching pattern p, or null if no matching tuple appears before the time-out.

The CAST [9] coordination model provides operation primitives that take into account hosts motions in space and time. Our extensions in the TNM coordination model (described in Section 4) are based on the operations in the CAST coordination model, but only consider time and not space. To simplify discussion in the rest of this paper, we therefore abstract the CAST operations as follows:

- **out(t,start,end)**, which places *tuple* t into the tuple space — start and end are times that delimit the lifetime of tuple t in the tuple space;
- **in(p,start,end)**, which removes a tuple matching *pattern* p from the tuple space and returns it to the agent that issued the in operation — start is the time at which the operation will first attempt to match a tuple in the tuple space, and end is the time at which the operation will return null if it has not matched a tuple before then;
- **rd(p,start,end)**, which copies a tuple matching pattern p (but does not remove the tuple from the tuple space) and returns the copy to the agent that issued the rd operation — start is the time at which the operation will first attempt to match a tuple in the tuple space, and end is the time at which the operation will return null if it has not matched a tuple before then;
- **ing(p,start,end)**, which has the same semantics as in(p,start,end) except that it removes and returns all matching tuples if any are present;
- **rdg(p,start,end)**, which has the same semantics as rd(p,start,end) except that it returns copies of all matching tuples if any are present; and
- **react(p,s,start,end)**, which at time start registers a reaction containing pattern p and code fragment s with the tuple space and at time end unregisters that same reaction.

Adding quantitative time to coordination models is an important first step towards real-time coordination, as it makes it possible to reason about *when* tuples can be matched (if at all). However, these timed coordination models are still unable to reason about *whether* tuples will be matched. The TNM coordination model addresses this limitation by extending current timed coordination models to include *timed futures* that can be *bound* to other timed futures and to timed tuples, and thus can be used to reason about (and make guarantees regarding) whether tuples will be produced, read, and consumed (and if so, when).

3   Motivating Example

The automatic motorway application presented in the 2005 Monterey Workshop challenge problems [10] is an important example that serves to illustrate the motivation for, and potential impact of, our work on TNM. It also serves to establish criteria for determining where features provided by TNM are needed, versus where features of other existing coordination models are sufficient.

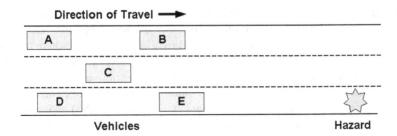

Fig. 1. Vehicles Approaching a Hazard

In this application, vehicles enter and leave an automatic motorway through regular entrances and exits, and navigate autonomously along the motorway[3] To support this activity safely and with suitable performance, the vehicles' on-board computing and communication capabilities must be used to coordinate lane changes and other actions with nearby vehicles, and to propagate information about congestion, obstacles and other contextual features to other vehicles throughout the motorway.

A key problem for this system is how to ensure that traffic moves steadily throughout the system while avoiding collisions between vehicles. Consider for example a scenario illustrated in Figure 1 in which five vehicles are traveling as a *platoon* [11], occupying all three lanes of a segment of an automatic motorway. A software agent hosted by the leading vehicle in one of the lanes (vehicle E in Figure 1) detects hazards, such as a large piece of debris or other obstacle, ahead in its lane. When a hazard is detected, this agent immediately alerts software agents hosted on the other vehicles and considers actions that will allow it to avoid a collision with the hazard.

The difficulty is that an agent's appropriate actions may depend not only on current spatio-temporal factors (such as its vehicle's speed, the trajectories of the lanes in the motorway, the distance to the hazard, and the relative positions and speeds of the other cars in the platoon) but also on the potential future actions of the other agents. For example, vehicle E may be unable to move left one lane unless vehicle C decelerates, providing room for vehicle E to merge into the middle lane. However, vehicle C's deceleration may inhibit vehicle D's ability to merge left as well, to avoid the hazard. To avoid collisions (the primary concern) while preferring a smooth flow of the vehicles around the hazard (an important secondary concern), the vehicles' respective agents must therefore coordinate which actions each will take, and also at what times they will take them.

The rest of this section considers how such coordination can be realized in the context of this example scenario. In Section 3.1 we first describe relevant assumptions we make about the motorway example itself. In Section 3.2 we discuss to what extent existing coordination models address this example scenario. In Section 3.3 we then describe the remaining unaddressed issues posed by this application, which motivate the TNM coordination model that is discussed in detail in Section 4.

---

[3] The original application scenario proposes a two-lane motorway. We generalize this problem to have three or more lanes, in order to highlight TNM's handling of more complex coordination scenarios.

3.1   Assumptions About the Automatic Motorway Example

As a foundation for discussion in the rest of this paper, we now note and justify relevant assumptions we make about the automatic motorway example itself. First, we assume that accurate information about the speed and position of each vehicle can be obtained and communicated among the vehicles within a local region. Obtaining accurate positioning information is a challenging problem in its own right; but since this capability is fundamental to the safe operation of such an automatic motorway, we assume that it can be addressed through other techniques, as in [11].

Second, as stated in [10], we assume that it will not be cost-effective to deploy servers and other fixed infrastructure along the entire stretch of the motorway. For example, the cost of placing servers at motorway entrances and exits may be justified by the safety-critical nature of those junctures and by the potential for cost recovery, e.g., through collecting tolls at those servers. However, it is neither possible to anticipate all places along the motorway that a hazard could occur (e.g., where a vehicle might lose a portion of its cargo) nor would it be affordable to deploy enough servers for complete coverage of the motorway.

Third, we assume that an accurate and consistently defined view of time is available to every agent within each context: i.e., end-to-end among the servers deployed at crucial motorway intersections, within a platoon of vehicles moving along the motorway, etc. Scenarios in which previously distinct contexts merge (e.g., a platoon of cars reaches an intersection where a server is deployed) will necessarily require additional mechanisms (e.g., clock synchronization protocols) to merge the relative views of time. However, a detailed discussion of those issues is beyond the scope of this paper.

3.2   Applicability of Existing Coordination Models

We now consider the applicability of existing coordination models to the automatic roadway example. We first examine which features of centralized coordination models can be applied to this example. We then examine which features of distributed and mobile coordination models are required by the example, and finally which features of timed coordination models are also necessary.

Centralized coordination models. A server at each on-ramp and off-ramp could provide a tuple space through which agents hosted on vehicles entering and departing the motorway can exchange information through wireless communication. For example, the server at an on-ramp could provide and update a standard set of tuples describing known hazards in the motorway, current weather conditions, etc., into the tuple space. Vehicles entering the roadway could then perform rd operations to obtain that information, and as they encounter other servers along the motorway issue subsequent rd operations to refresh that information.

Agents hosted on vehicles exiting the motorway could also perform out operations to report information they have obtained while in transit. For example, an agent that has observed a hazard in the motorway could report it to the server. Each server registers reactions for various important kinds of information, such as hazard reports; when a tuple is injected into the tuple space, the associated code fragment can perform additional necessary actions (such as corroborating hazard reports, or notifying other servers along the affected segment of the motorway).

Distributed and mobile coordination models. In addition to the tuple space maintained on each server, we assume each vehicle would also have one or more tuple spaces (e.g., one private tuple space and one public tuple space) of its own. When a vehicle comes into wireless range of a server or another vehicle, their public tuple spaces would be federated automatically (as in LIME) so that tuples would be pooled among all connected agents. Note that for brevity we do not consider security issues, which are beyond the scope of this paper. For a sample treatment of password protection for tuples and tuple spaces and other relevant issues, we refer to our previous work on secure service provision in ad hoc networks [12].

Federating tuple spaces provides a way for vehicles to exchange information among themselves either directly or through copying tuples into the server's tuple space. For example, agents on vehicles in the roadway may supplement server-provided information with "gossip" from other vehicles. For example, uncorroborated hazard reports, which though they might be treated with lower confidence than a corroborated report issued by the server itself, would allow an agent to prepare for the possibility that a given report is in fact correct.

Furthermore, servers may themselves offer additional "quality of experience" services such as downloading information feeds for news and entertainment media from the wired network to a vehicle. Because vehicles may not know of these services *a priori*, the server could advertise these services by placing additional advertisement tuples in its tuple space. When the server's tuple space is federated with vehicles tuple spaces, those advertisements would become available to those vehicles' agents.

Other features of distributed and mobile coordination models are also needed to support the automatic motorway example. For example, the rdp operation primitive allows agents to query for tuples without blocking, which is necessary when matching tuples may or may not be present in the tuple space. Furthermore, for service discovery an agent may want to obtain the entire set of service advertisement tuples matching a service request pattern, which requires operation primitives such as rdgp.

Timed coordination models. The discussion so far has focused on coordination models that do not offer an explicit representation of time. However, there are many cases where the ability to represent the lifetimes of tuples, and to support timeouts and other features of operation primitives that depend on an explicit representation of time, is useful. For example, reports of current weather conditions are time sensitive, so bounding the lifetimes of tuples that report those conditions can help to avoid agents receiving out-of-date information.

Also, as vehicles move along the motorway their tuple spaces will be federated with tuple spaces on servers and other vehicles for finite intervals during which the appearance of new information may be of interest. Instead of using blocking rd or rdg operations, or transient rdp or rdgp operations, an agent on the vehicle could specify a wait time during which it would like to receive information matching a given pattern, using the timed rdp or rdgp operations.

Servers may also use timed operations to control when information is added to or removed from their tuple spaces. For example, a news feed service may be priced higher during peak hours than during off-peak hours, so that the server would specify different lifetimes for tuples advertising peak and off-peak versions of a service. The server could also schedule the creation of service advertisement tuples by using timed out operations, which delay the tuple's creation until a specified time.

3.3   Remaining Challenges

Although a number of important coordination requirements for the automatic motorway can be met, as we have discussed in Section 3.2, several challenges still remain for which current coordination models do not offer adequate support. Specifically, agents need to be able to propose and request future actions, to be notified when proposals and requests are bound, to reason about when those actions will occur, and to manage retraction of proposals if subsequently available information reveals them to be infeasible or sub-optimal.

Representing sequences of operations. Although service discovery is supported by current coordination models, agents have no way to propose to provide a certain piece of information in the future. This constrains the scope of possible interactions significantly, as all aspects of an interaction between two agents must be handled one operation at a time, rather than allowing agents to coordinate entire sequences of operations.

For example, in the scenario presented in Figure 1, it would be at least inefficient — and due to time constraints on making decisions could possibly lead to a collision — if the vehicles had to coordinate sequentially. For example, consider the following partially ordered sequence of operations, in which the operations within each step are executed concurrently but all changes to the tuple space by those operations are completed before the next step begins:

1. Vehicle E injects a tuple alerting other vehicles to a detected hazard, and also injects a tuple with its proposal to move left one lane.
2. Vehicle D reads the alert tuple, and injects a tuple with its own proposal to move left one lane; vehicle C reads the proposal from vehicle E, determines that it must decelerate to avoid a collision with vehicle E, and injects a tuple with its proposal to decelerate.
3. Upon seeing the proposal from vehicle D, vehicle C determines that if it decelerates vehicle D may collide with it, retracts its proposal to decelerate and injects a new proposal to move left one lane.
4. Vehicle A detects that if it accelerates or maintains its velocity vehicle C may collide with it, and injects a tuple with its proposal to decelerate; vehicle B detects that if it decelerates or maintains its velocity vehicle C may collide with it, and injects a tuple with its proposal to accelerate.
5. All vehicles determine that the proposed actions will avoid collisions and the vehicles take their proposed actions.

Timing data. Even if agents were able to coordinate entire sequences of operations concurrently, the coordination model still would not provide a means for them to reason about whether a given sequence of operations would complete within a specified time limit (e.g., before vehicle E came too close to the hazard to be able to steer around it). To perform this kind of reasoning, agents must be able to propose not only sequences of actions to be taken, but the times at which each of the actions in a sequence would be taken. Therefore, the coordination model needs to incorporate an explicit quantitative representation of time into its support for coordinating sequences of actions.

Proposals, requests, and binding. While it is necessary for vehicles to add timing *data* to the tuples they inject, this alone is not sufficient to allow efficient and reliable coordination. For example, if during step 1 vehicle A had decided to change lanes (e.g., to be able to exit the roadway at an upcoming exit) and during step 2 read vehicle C's proposal to decelerate, then vehicle C's retraction of its proposal to decelerate would violate vehicle A's dependence on that proposal and furthermore vehicle C would have no indication of that violation. What is needed, therefore, is a way for timed tuples to be both *proposed* and *requested*, and for proposals and requests to be *bound* so that reliable coordination involving inter-dependent sequences of operations can be achieved.

Retraction. Anticipating and addressing all combinations of events that may have significant consequences is notoriously difficult in complex inter-connected applications, even within a single mobile host, as the Mars Pathfinder [13] example demonstrates. Should an unanticipated condition arise on a host during coordination involving sequences of actions, an agent may need to retract a proposed sequence of actions. However, the implications of such a retraction must be handled carefully since other agents may have made their own decisions based on the assumption that the proposed sequence of operations would occur. Two distinct forms of retraction are needed:

– *strong retractions* in which the proposed sequence of operations is retracted unconditionally (e.g., if a vehicle enters a mode of failure after which it is impossible for it to perform an expected action); and
– *weak retractions* in which the proposed sequence of operations is retracted only if another agent does not depend on the sequence already (e.g., if a vehicle discovers a potential optimization to an already sufficient maneuver that it has proposed).

Although the addition of timing data to tuples has been achieved in other coordination models as we have discussed in Section 2, explicit mechanisms for proposing, requesting, binding, and retracting future operations are still needed. In Section 4 we discuss our proposed approach to address these outstanding issues.

4   The TNM Coordination Model

This section describes the main contributions of this work, which address the unmet challenges described in Section 3.3: (1) extending coordination models with *future* primitives to let agents propose and request the future availability of information within a shared tuple space, which we discuss in Section 4.1; (2) extending untimed futures to include a quantitative notion of time, which we discuss in Section 4.2, so that explicit real-time constraints can be asserted, evaluated, and assured; and (3) extending the semantics of untimed and timed futures to address when futures are *bound* and when futures may or may not be *retracted*, which we discuss in Sections 4.3 and 4.4, respectively.

4.1 Futures

We first provide a new extension to existing coordination models: "future" primitives that propose and request basic tuple-space operations which would take place in the future. Five future primitives are provided by the TNM coordination model, which agents can use to propose to inject, remove, or copy tuples into or from the tuple space:

- **future_out(p)** proposes to put a tuple matching pattern p into the tuple space at some point in the future;
- **future_in(p)** requests to remove a tuple matching pattern p from the tuple space at some point in the future;
- **future_rd(p)** requests to copy a tuple matching pattern p from the tuple space at some point in the future;
- **future_ing(p)** requests to remove all tuples matching pattern p from the tuple space at some point in the future; and
- **future_rdg(p)** requests to copy all tuples matching pattern p from the tuple space at some point in the future.

Each of these operations puts a special *future* tuple of the form

```
<future_type, id, pattern, bound_list>
```

into the tuple space. The future_type field indicates what type of future it is (i.e., future_out, future_in, future_rd, future_ing, or future_rdg). The id field contains a unique identifier that is assigned automatically to that tuple by the tuple space. The pattern field contains a copy of the pattern that was passed as a parameter to the future operation. The bound_list field is initially empty and is updated automatically according to the binding rules discussed in Section 4.3. After the tuple is placed in the tuple space and its id and bound_list fields are filled in, each of these future operations then returns a copy of the newly created and initialized future tuple. The agent may then use that tuple's identifier at a later time to request retraction of that future tuple, as we discuss in Section 4.4.

4.2 Timed Futures

As we discussed in Section 3.3, not only must a real-time coordination model support agents' ability to reason about sequences of actions, but it must also allow them to reason about *when* those actions would occur. To provide this capability, the TNM coordination model includes explicit representations of time in the future operations, and adds temporal semantics to the binding and preference rules for timed futures.

We first introduce timed versions of the future_in, future_rd, and future_out primitives. These primitives are similar to the corresponding untimed future operation primitives, except that they specify temporal parameters in addition to a pattern:

- **timed_future_out(p,start,end)**, proposes that a timed out operation will put a timed tuple matching pattern p into the tuple space — the lifetime of the tuple will be delimited by the times given by the start and end parameters to the timed future out operation;

- **timed_future_in(p,start,end)**, requests a timed in operation that will attempt to remove a tuple matching pattern p from the tuple space at the time given by the start parameter, and will wait until the time given by the end parameter before returning null if no tuple is matched by then;
- **timed_future_rd(p,start,end)**, requests that a timed rd operation will attempt to copy a tuple matching pattern p from the tuple space at the time given by the start parameter, and wait until the time given by the end parameter before returning null if no tuple is matched by then;
- **timed_future_ing(p,start,end)**, requests a timed ing operation that will attempt to remove all tuples matching pattern p from the tuple space at the time given by the start parameter, and will wait until the time given by the end parameter before returning null if no tuple is matched by then; and
- **timed_future_rdg(p,start,end)**, requests that a timed rdg operation will attempt to copy all tuples matching pattern p from the tuple space at the time given by the start parameter, and will wait until the time given by the end parameter before returning null if no tuple is matched by then.

Each of these operations puts a special *future* tuple of the form

```
<future_type, start, end, id, pattern, bound_list>
```

into the tuple space. The future_type field again indicates what type of future it is (i.e., timed_future_out, timed_future_in, timed_future_rd, timed_future_ing, or timed_future_rdg). The start and end fields contain the values of the temporal parameters passed to the timed future operation primitive. The id, pattern, and bound_list fields are equivalent to the corresponding fields in the untimed future tuples, and uniqueness of id field values is maintained across both timed and untimed future tuples.

4.3 Binding

A novel and important feature of the TNM coordination model is its support for binding future tuples so that dependences of requested tuples on proposed tuples can be represented and reasoned about. We first consider the semantics of binding untimed futures, and then discuss the semantics of binding timed futures. For both untimed and timed futures, we present rules for which tuples can be bound and then present preference rules which govern the order in which tuple bindings are performed among those that can be bound.

Semantics of binding. We say that a future_in, future_ing, future_rd or future_rdg tuple with a pattern p, and a future_out tuple with a pattern p', can be *bound* automatically by the tuple space if p is no more specific than p', i.e., $\{t \mid t \text{ matches } p'\} \subseteq \{t \mid t \text{ matches } p\}$. A bound future_in, future_ing, future_rd or future_rdg tuple with pattern p constitutes a guarantee that a subsequent in, ing, rd, or rdg operation (respectively) with pattern parameter q will succeed as long as pattern q is no more specific than pattern p. In fact, the operation can succeed if any future_out operation produces a tuple that matches pattern q. However, it is impossible to *reason* about such a guarantee unless q is no more specific than p.

Timed future tuples can be used to determine if there will be a timed out operation that is guaranteed to satisfy a timed in, ing, rd, or rdg operation, and to bind
timed future tuples in a manner similar to the binding of untimed future tuples. We
say that a timed_future_in tuple, a timed_future_ing tuple, a timed_future_rd tuple, or
timed_future_rdg tuple, with a pattern p and start time s and end time e, and a
timed_future_out tuple with a pattern p' and start time s' and end time e', can be *bound*
automatically by the tuple space if p is no more specific than p', and the time interval delimited by s and e overlaps the time interval delimited by s' and e'. We define
the *temporal intersection* of two timed future tuples to be the intersection of the time
intervals delimited by their respective start and end fields.

Binding rules. Binding of untimed future tuples is a directed relation from future_out
tuples to future_in, future_rd, future_ing, and future_rdg tuples. The list in the bound_list
field of a future_out tuple may only contain identifiers of other kinds of future tuples,
and the list in the bound_list field of all other kinds of future tuples may only contain
identifiers of future_out tuples. Because it is possible for multiple future tuples to have
patterns matching the pattern in a newly injected future tuple, the tuple space respects
the following rules when binding future tuples, to preserve appropriate semantics of the
future operations.

- A future_in or future_rd tuple may be bound by exactly one future_out tuple.
- A future_ing or future_rdg tuple may be bound by any number of future_out tuples.
- A future_out tuple that is bound to a future_in or future_ing tuple may not be bound
  to any other future tuple.
- A future_out tuple may be bound to any number of future_rd or future_rdg tuples.

The binding rules for timed future tuples are similar to those for untimed future
tuples, but with the addition of temporal semantics. With timed future tuples binding
is a directed relation from timed_future_out tuples to timed_future_in, timed_future_rd,
timed_future_ing, and timed_future_rdg tuples.

- A timed_future_in or timed_future_rd tuple may be bound by exactly one
  timed_future_out tuple.
- A timed_future_ing or timed_future_rdg tuple may be bound by any number of
  timed_future_out tuples.
- A timed_future_out tuple that is bound to a timed_future_in or timed_future_ing tuple may not be bound to another timed_future_in or timed_future_ing tuple.
- A timed_future_out tuple can only be bound to future_rd or future_rdg tuples whose
  end times are earlier than the start time of any timed_future_in or timed_future_ing
  tuple to which the timed_future_out tuple is bound, but the timed_future_out tuple
  can be bound to any number of such future_rd or future_rdg tuples.

Preference Rules. When a new future tuple is injected into the tuple space, the tuple
space will perform a sequence of tuple bindings made one-at-a-time according to the
rules given above, until no more allowed bindings can be made. At each step of that
sequence, the following preference rules are applied (in the order they are given) to the
set of all allowed bindings, to choose the next binding to be made by the tuple space.

- Preference is first given for binding a future_out tuple to a future_in, future_rd, future_ing or future_rdg whose pattern is no less specific to its pattern than any other future_in, future_rd, future_ing or future_rdg tuple. This preference rule is designed to increase specificity of the bindings performed.
- Preference is then given for binding a future_out tuple to an unbound future_in, future_rd, future_ing or future_rdg tuple over binding it to an already bound future_ing or future_rdg tuple. This preference rule is designed to decrease the number of unbound requests for tuples.
- Preference is then given for binding a future_out tuple to an unbound future_rd or future_rdg tuple over binding it to an unbound future_in or future_ing tuple. This preference rule is designed to increase the number of requests that can be satisfied by each proposal by binding it preferentially to requests that leave the tuple available to other requests rather than consuming it.
- If more than one binding has been selected after the previous preference rules have been applied, then one binding is chosen non-deterministically from that selected set. This preference rule is designed to ensure that binding progresses even when the preceding preferences have not distinguished a unique binding.

Preference rules for timed future operation primitives are similar to those for untimed future operation primitives, though both pattern specificity and temporal specificity are considered.

- The first preference is for binding a timed_future_out tuple to a timed_future-_in, timed_future_rd, timed_future_ing or timed_future_rdg whose pattern is no less specific to its pattern than any other matching timed_future_in, timed-_future_rd, timed_future_ing or timed_future_rdg tuple. Like the corresponding preference rule for untimed futures, this preference rule is designed to increase specificity of the bindings performed in terms of the tuples' *patterns*.
- The next preference is to bind a timed_future_out tuple to a timed_future_in, timed_future_rd, timed_future_ing or timed_future_rdg whose temporal intersection no smaller than that for any other matching timed_future_in, timed_-future_rd, timed_future_ing or timed_future_rdg tuple. This preference rule is designed to increase specificity of the bindings performed in terms of the tuples' *temporal intervals*.
- Preference is then given for binding a timed_future_out tuple to an unbound timed_future_in, timed_future_rd, timed_future_ing or timed_future_rdg tuple over binding it to an already bound timed_future_ing or timed_future_rdg tuple. Like the corresponding preference rule for untimed futures, this preference rule is designed to decrease the number of unbound requests for tuples.
- Preference is then given for binding a timed_future_out tuple to an unbound timed_future_rd or timed_future_rdg tuple over binding it to an unbound timed_future_in or timed_future_ing tuple. Like the corresponding preference rule for untimed futures, this preference rule is designed to increase the number of requests that can be satisfied by each proposal by binding it preferentially to requests that leave the tuple available to other requests rather than consuming it.
- If more than one binding has been selected after the previous preference rules have been applied, then one binding is chosen non-deterministically from that selected

set. Like the corresponding preference rule for untimed futures, this preference rule is designed to ensure that binding progresses even when the preceding preferences have not distinguished a unique binding.

4.4   Satisfaction and Retraction

Because each future tuple represents a proposed future operation on the tuple space, two additional concerns must be addressed: when is a future considered to have been satisfied by another operation on the tuple space, and when may a future tuple that has not been satisfied be retracted from the tuple space by the agent that proposed it? We augment the structure of timed and untimed future tuples to contain two additional boolean fields labeled *satisfied* and *retracted*, which are both valued false when the future tuple is created. The satisfied field indicates whether or not a future tuple has been satisfied by a subsequent basic tuple space operation, and the retracted field indicates whether or not a future tuple has been retracted by an agent.

Satisfaction. Each basic tuple space operation can satisfy only one previously unsatisfied future tuple corresponding to that operation type: an out operation can only satisfy a future_out or timed_future_out tuple, an in operation can only satisfy a future_in or timed_future_in tuple, and so on. Furthermore, a basic tuple space operation can only satisfy a future tuple whose pattern is no more specific than the pattern or tuple it was given, and can only satisfy a timed future tuple whose start and end times delimit an interval within which the basic tuple space operation was performed.

If multiple future tuples could be satisfied by a basic tuple space operation, the following rules are applied (in the order they are given) to determine which future tuple is marked as being satisfied, taking into account the pattern and temporal specificity of the basic tuple space operation to the future tuples that it could potentially satisfy.

- Preference is given first to future tuples whose pattern is most specific to the pattern or tuple given to the basic tuple space operation.
- Preference is then given to timed future tuples over untimed future tuples and to timed future tuples with an earlier end time over timed tuples with a later end time.
- If more than one future tuple has been selected after the previous satisfaction rules have been applied, then one future tuple is chosen non-deterministically from that selected set.

The future tuple thus selected is then updated automatically by the tuple space by setting the tuple's satisfied field to true.

Retraction. The final issue we address in the TNM coordination model is the ability for agents to retract future tuples. This ability supports re-negotiation of (timed or untimed) sequences of actions among agents, to allow sequences that are no longer feasible to be discarded, or to allow more optimal sequences to be chosen, as the agents' operating contexts change, or as agents obtain more accurate information about their operating contexts, over time.

However, the ability of an agent to retract a proposed operation has important implications for other agents whose actions depend on the operation that would be retracted.

For example, retracting a future_out tuple takes back the proposal it has made that a suitable tuple would be provided by a subsequent out operation, upon which another operation requested by a future_in, future_ing, future_rd or future_rdg operation may depend. This can have cascading effects on agents expecting the no-longer-guaranteed tuples to be available which could then prevent them from providing tuples they had proposed. Despite the potentially adverse consequences of retraction, possibilities such as the anticipated failure of a host[4] motivate having operation primitives for both strong and weak forms of retraction in the TNM coordination model:

- **retract(id)**, where the future tuple whose unique id field value matches the passed id parameter is simply marked as having been retracted, if it is present in the tuple space; and
- **retractp(id)**, where the matching future tuple is only marked as having been retracted if that will not affect other agents, i.e., if it has already been satisfied or its bound_list field is empty.

The **retract(id)** operation returns a copy of the future tuple that was marked as having been retracted, or null if no tuple with the given id was present in the tuple space. The **retractp(id)** operation returns a copy of the future tuple that was marked as having been retracted, or null if no future tuple with the given id was present in the tuple space or if the tuple was bound to any other tuples.

To ensure that appropriate semantics for the future tuples can be enforced entirely within the future and retraction operation primitives, we place one restriction on the out, in, and ing tuple space operations of the TNM coordination model: they can be applied to any kind of tuple *except* the timed and untimed future tuples described in Sections 4.1 and 4.2. An out operation that is given a tuple whose first field contains a future tuple type will simply return without modifying the tuple space. An in or ing operation with a pattern that can match a future tuple will ignore all future tuples. The rd and rdg operations have the same semantics for future tuples as they would to any other tuples, however, so that an agent may query for copies of future tuples existing in the tuple space.

5   Discussion

A crucial feature of the TNM coordination model is that agents can propose and request when tuples will be produced, read, and consumed, which can be mapped directly onto spatio-temporal properties of the context within which agents will propose and take their actions. For example, in the hazard avoidance scenario shown in Figure 1 and discussed in Section 3, agents running on each vehicle could propose timed future out operations and request timed future rd operations for tuples describing timed sequences of acceleration, deceleration, and lane change actions. In the following discussion we assume that agents exchange information about the vehicles' motions frequently, so that

---

[4] For the sake of discussion we assume hosts can detect and announce their failure prior to its occurrence - this assumption can be weakened in practice through periodic heartbeats, failure detectors, and other means.

each maintains an accurate picture of the spatio-temporal structure of the platoon, and can compute potential actions accordingly.

When the agents on the vehicles in the platoon receive the hazard alert from the agent on vehicle E, each generates plausible sequences of actions that it could take to make room for other vehicles, or to avoid the hazard itself. The crux of negotiating a plausible maneuver that will avoid collisions is the position of vehicle C among the other vehicles, and the inter-dependence of vehicles actions that this entails. For example, one plausible sequence of actions would be for vehicle C to accelerate and for vehicles D and E to decelerate and then change lanes, with the resulting configuration of the platoon illustrated in Figure 2. Another plausible sequence of actions would be for vehicle C to maintain its current trajectory, for vehicle E to accelerate and change one lane left ahead of vehicle C, and for vehicle D to decelerate and change one lane left behind vehicle C, with the resulting configuration of the platoon shown in Figure 3. A third plausible sequence of actions would be for vehicle A to decelerate and for vehicle B to accelerate, and for vehicles C, D, and E to change one lane left, resulting in the configuration of the platoon shown in Figure 4. Figure 5 summarizes the set of possible maneuvers by each of the vehicles, combinations of which produce the platoon configurations illustrated in Figures 2 through 4:

1. vehicle A would decelerate until time t_1;
2. vehicle B would accelerate until time t_1;
3. vehicle C would decelerate until time $t_2 > t_1$;
4. vehicle C would maintain velocity until time t_1 and then change one lane left;
5. vehicle C would accelerate until time $t_2 > t_1$;
6. vehicle D would decelerate until time t_2 and then change one lane left;

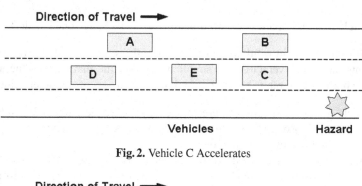

Fig. 2. Vehicle C Accelerates

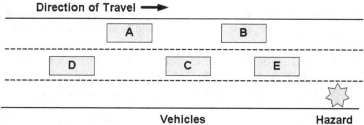

Fig. 3. Vehicle C Maintains Trajectory

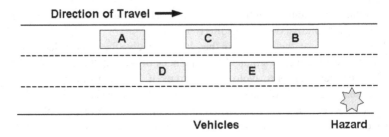

Fig. 4. Vehicle C Moves Left

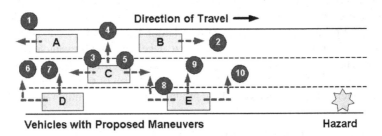

Fig. 5. Proposed Vehicle Maneuvers

7. vehicle D would maintain velocity until time t_2 and then change one lane left;
8. vehicle E would decelerate until time $t_2 > t_1$ and then change one lane left;
9. vehicle E would maintain velocity until time $t_2 > t_1$ and then change one lane left; and
10. vehicle E would accelerate until time $t_2 > t_1$ then change one lane left.

Each vehicle's agent would propose its own actions, and would also request actions by agents on nearby vehicles. For simplicity we assume that each of the agents can compute both its own plausible actions and those of the agents on other vehicles[5]:

- vehicle A would use timed_future_rd operations to request action 2 of vehicle B (i), and actions 3 through 5 of vehicle C (ii); vehicle A would then propose action 1 by using a timed_future_out operation (iii);
- vehicle B would use timed_future_rd operations to request action 1 of vehicle A (iv, which would be bound by vehicle A's timed_future_out operation from iii), and actions 3 through 5 of vehicle C (v); vehicle B would then propose action 2 by using a timed_future_out operation (vi, which would bind to vehicle A's timed_future_rd from i);
- vehicle C would use timed_future_rd operations to request action 1 of vehicle A (vii, which would be bound by vehicle A's timed_future_out operation from iii), action 2 of vehicle B (viii, which would be bound by vehicle B's timed_future_out operation

from vi), actions 6 and 7 of vehicle D (ix), and actions 8 through 10 vehicle E (x); vehicle C would use timed_future_out operations to propose actions 3 through 5 (xi, which would bind to vehicle A's and vehicle B's timed_future_rd operations from ii and v);

- vehicle D would use timed_future_rd operations to request actions 3 through 5 of vehicle C (xii, which would be bound by vehicle C's timed_future_out operations from xi) and actions 8 through 10 of vehicle E (xiii); vehicle D would use timed_future_out operations to propose actions 6 and 7 (xiv, which would bind to vehicle C's timed_future_rd operations from ix);
- vehicle E would use timed_future_rd operations to request actions 3 through 5 of vehicle C (xv, which would be bound by vehicle C's timed_future_out operations from xi) and actions 6 and 7 of vehicle D (xvi, which would be bound by vehicle D's timed_future_out operations from xiv); vehicle E would use timed_future_out operations to propose actions 8 through 10 (xvii, which would bind to vehicle C's and vehicle D's timed_future_rd operations from x and xiii).

Each vehicle would issue reactions for bound timed future tuples corresponding to the actions it has proposed and requested. When an agent's proposal or request is bound, the agent can use weak retraction to remove other proposed or requested actions from consideration, though agents may wait until at least one complete plausible sequence of inter-dependent actions by all vehicles is decided before pruning the set of potential sequences by retracting requests or proposals.

6 Concluding Remarks

In this paper we have presented the TNM coordination model, which offers novel coordination features including futures, timed futures, binding, and satisfaction and retraction semantics, which allow agents to negotiate timed and untimed sequences of actions explicitly. We have shown how these features can help to address challenges posed by the 2005 Monterey Workshop automatic motorway example, which other coordination models do not address. As our experience with avionics mission computing applications we have studied in previous research [14,15,16] indicates, automating vehicle functions (including real-time coordination among moving vehicles) to increase each agent's situational awareness and responsiveness is likely to be beneficial in practice.

As future work we will examine how the tuple space can automatically rebind future tuples to preserve guarantees that would otherwise be disrupted by strong retraction semantics, and will study whether this automatic rebinding capability could allow weak retraction to be realized under a wider set of circumstances, e.g., for automatic optimization under control of the tuple space as new future tuples are proposed and retracted. We will also investigate the complex scheduling issues which arise from placing timing constraints on tuple-space operations. Many metrics that are used in real-time scheduling, such as per-process priorities, have limited applicability in ad-hoc networks of mobile hosts. Furthermore, centralized scheduling algorithms would be impractical to use in mobile ad-hoc networks, as hosts move into and out of contact with each other. Therefore, we plan to investigate new scheduling algorithms for timed future coordination, to provide resource-limited timing guarantees in a decentralized fashion.

References

1. Caltrans, the Institute of Transportation Studies at UC Berkely: California partners for advanced transit and highways (path). (http://www-path.eecs.berkeley.edu)
2. Army, U.S.: Future combat systems (fcs). (http://www.army.mil/fcs/)
3. Gelernter, D.: Generative communication in Linda. ACM Trans. Program. Lang. Syst. **7**(1) (1985) 80–112
4. Picco, G., Murphy, A., Roman, G.C.: LIME: Linda meets mobility. In: Proc. of the 21st Int'l. Conf. on Software Engineering. (1999)
5. Fok, C.L., Roman, G.C., Hackmann, G.: A lightweight coordination middleware for mobile computing. In: 6th International Conference on Coordination Models and Languages (Coordination '04). (2004) 135–151
6. Jacquet, J.M., Bosschere, K.D., Brogi, A.: On timed coordination languages. In: 4th International Conference on Coordination Languages and Models (Coordination '00), London, UK, Springer-Verlag (2000) 81–98
7. de Boer, F.S., Gabbrielli, M., Meo, M.C.: A denotational semantics for timed linda. In: 3rd ACM SIGPLAN international conference on Principles and practice of declarative programming (PPDP '01), New York, NY, USA, ACM Press (2001) 28–36
8. Mousavi, M.R., Reniers, M., Basten, T., Chaudron, M.: Separation of concerns in the formal design of real-time shared data-space systems. In: Third International Conference on Application of Concurrency to System Design (ACSD '03), IEEE Computer Society (2003)
9. Roman, G.C., Handorean, R., Sen, R.: Tuple space coordination across space and time. In: 8th International Conference on Coordination Languages and Models (Coordination '06), Bologna, Italy, Springer LNCS 4038 (2006) 266–280
10. Kordon, F., Sztipanovits, J.: The monterey workshop series (2005 theme: Workshop on networked systems: realization of reliable systems on top of unreliable networked platforms). http://www-src.lip6.fr/homepages/Fabrice.Kordon/Monterey/objectives.html (2005)
11. Horowitz, R., Varaiya, P.: Control design of an automated highway system. Proceedings of the IEEE **88**(7) (2000) 913–925
12. Handorean, R., Roman, G.C.: Secure Service Provision in Ad Hoc Networks. In: Proceedings of the First International Conference on Service Oriented Computing (ICSOC 2003). (2003)
13. Jones, M.: What really happened on Mars? www.research.microsoft.com/~mbj/Mars_Pathfinder/Mars_Pathfinder.html (1997)
14. Doerr, B.S., Venturella, T., Jha, R., Gill, C.D., Schmidt, D.C.: Adaptive Scheduling for Real-time, Embedded Information Systems. In: Proceedings of the 18th IEEE/AIAA Digital Avionics Systems Conference (DASC). (1999)
15. Gill, C., Schmidt, D.C., Cytron, R.: Multi-Paradigm Scheduling for Distributed Real-time Embedded Computing. IEEE Proceedings, Special Issue on Modeling and Design of Embedded Software **91**(1) (2003)
16. Gill, C.D., Gossett, J.M., Corman, D., Loyall, J.P., Schantz, R.E., Atighetchi, M., Schmidt, D.C.: Integrated Adaptive QoS Management in Middleware: An Empirical Case Study. Journal of Real-time Systems **24** (2005)

Dynamic System Reconfiguration Via Service Composition for Dependable Computing

W.T. Tsai[1], Weiwei Song[1], Yinong Chen[1], and Ray Paul[2]

[1] Department of Computer Science and Engineering, Arizona State University, Tempe AZ, 85287 USA
[2] Department of Defense, Washington DC

Abstract. Dependable service-oriented computing is challenging because it faces an open, heterogeneous, and dynamic computing environment. In a service-oriented computing system, services developed by different vendors on different platforms and in different programming languages perform computations collaboratively through open standard protocols. This paper presents an innovative dynamic reconfiguration technology that can be embedded into a service-oriented application to make the application reconfigurable. Traditional reconfiguration algorithm assumes each component can independently switch without collaboration. The proposed reconfiguration agents are embedded in different services, and they communicate via a collaborative reconfiguration protocol to achieve a consistent reconfiguration decision. In addition, the reconfiguration protocol itself is fault-tolerant.

Keywords: Service-oriented architecture, self-reconfiguration, dynamic composition, and fault tolerance.

1 Introduction

Dependability is the trustworthiness of a computer system such that reliance can justifiably be placed on the service it delivers [3]. The service delivered by a system is its behavior, as it is perceived by its users. A user is another system (human or device) which interacts with the former. Dependability is often measured by a set of system properties such as reliability, availability, safety, and security.

A system is dependable if it can complete its mission in a timely manner in the event of component failures and runtime environment changes. In particular, dependable service-oriented computing refers to the capability of providing essential services and functions in the presence of runtime environment changes, failures, and unavailability of component services. Service-oriented system will not be reliable if it cannot reconfigure adaptively and dynamically. In this paper, we focus on the fail-silent failure [14] of the services and components instead of the arbitrary failures such as Byzantine failures.

Service-Oriented Architecture (SOA) has received significant attention recently as major computer and software companies such as HP, IBM, Intel, Microsoft, and SAP, have all embraced SOA, as well as government agencies such

F. Kordon and J. Sztipanovits (Eds.): Monterey Workshop 2005, LNCS 4322, pp. 203–224, 2007.

as DoD (US Department of Defense). The initial focus on SOA has been the development of interoperability standards and protocols, such as WSDL, SOAP, UDDI, and recently numerous SOA standards have been proposed including ebSOA, ebXML, CPP, CPA, BPEL, OWL-S, and RDF.

SOA based computing is emerging as computing paradigm and is changing the way software and even hardware is developed [9] [29], including

- Service-oriented requirement engineering (model-based, architecture-based, reuse-oriented, framework-oriented analysis, simulation-based analysis with formal analysis);
- Service-oriented architecture and design (enterprise computing, dynamic collaboration, system composition, dynamic system analysis);
- Service-oriented programming languages (model-based development, support automated code generation);
- Service-oriented implementation (by dynamic discovery, composition, and model-based architecture, and automated code generation);
- Dynamic testing, verification, evaluation, simulation, reliability analysis of services;
- Dynamic policy construction, verification, simulation, enforcement of security and other policies using formal policy languages;
- System maintenance and update will be via service re-composition and possibly architectural reconfiguration.

SOA may look inherently reliable because it has a loosely coupled architecture, and any service can be replaced by another service if a former fails or becomes unavailable. The replacement in theory is just like a re-composition process. Furthermore, it looks like possible to replace a collection of services and change the overall application architecture at runtime. However, this is actually much more complex than it appears to be.

This paper introduces a Development and Runtime Service (DRS) framework for developing reconfigurable applications in a SOA via service composition [27]. The services are coordinated by a collaboration protocol which enables the runtime distributed reconfiguration and re-composition.

The applications are specified and composed with the PSML model [26][28]. The model defines the service composition logic as well as the reconfiguration rules, which can be modified and evolved at runtime to adapt to new situations.

The DRS framework includes a closed feedback control loop for runtime monitoring, evaluation, and management to support fault-tolerant computing through reconfiguration. Furthermore, the reconfiguration mechanism proposed is concurrent and collaborative:

- **Concurrent:** The reconfiguration is concurrent because multiple reconfigurations can interleave and execute simultaneously. They also compete against each other for the shared resources.
- **Collaborative:** Collaboration and interoperability are important characteristics of SOA systems between services and services, as well as between services and applications. During the reconfiguration, participants involved

will be locked and thus cannot be interrupted by other reconfigurations or service requests for reconfiguration integrity. Reconfiguration participants must be coordinated to perform the dynamic reconfiguration, in such a way that reconfigurations involving multiple collaborative participants either all succeed or none succeed.

In addition, the reconfiguration protocols and services must be fault-tolerant too. To do this, the reconfiguration protocol is designed so that failures during the reconfiguration process, including failures of reconfiguration participants, are handled. The novelty of the proposed DRS includes a collaboration protocol to address reconfiguration concurrency and collaboration.

The reconfiguration protocol handles fail-silent failures of application services and DRS agents during reconfiguration. We prove that the system can converge to a stable state within a short time period if no service fails in the time period. Analytical results are given to estimate for the convergence time.

The rest of the paper is organized as follows: Section 2 gives an overview of the proposed approach. Section 3 describes the DRS collaboration protocol and elaborates the fault-tolerant design for the reconfiguration protocol. Section 4 evaluates and discusses the performance of the proposed protocol. Section 5 discusses the related work and section 6 concludes the paper.

2   Approach Overview

2.1   Characteristics of Service-Oriented Architecture

SOA participants can be divided into three parties: the application builders (service requesters), the service brokers (service publishers), and the service providers (service developers). Service providers develop services independent of potential applications by following open protocols and standards. Service brokers publish the available services to the public so that the application builders can look up desired services and compose the target application using the services. Thus a target application is built through service discovery and service composing instead of traditional process of designing and coding software.

SOA has the following characteristics that are different from traditional software:

- Standard-based Interoperability: SOA emphasizes on stand-based interface, protocols, communication, coordination, workflow, discovery, collaboration, and publishing. These standards allow services developed in different computing platforms to interoperate with each other with the knowledge of service specifications only.
- Dynamic Composition via Discovery: SOA provides a new way of application development by composing services just discovered. Furthermore, the composition and discovery can be carried out at runtime.
- Dynamic Governance and Orchestration: Execution of services needs to be controlled and several mechanisms are available for execution control. One is

service governance by policy. Specifically, policies can be specified, checked, and enforced during both SOA development time and runtime to ensure the system complies with the organization requirements. The other is orchestration where process execution will be coordinated by a central controller and it is responsible for scheduling the execution of services that may be distributed across a connectivity network such as ESB (Enterprise Service Bus).

Dynamic reconfiguration in SOA is different from traditional reconfiguration as shown in table 1.

Table 1. SOA versus traditional distributed systems

Features	SOA systems	Distributed systems
Interoperability	Open standard protocols.	May use any protocols.
Alternative components	Potentially unlimited as new services may be developed by any service providers and made available at any time.	Limited backup spares are specified at design time.
Service discovery	Backup services can be discovered and the collaboration protocols between the services can be negotiated at runtime.	Backup spares and their interactions to the system are known at design time.
Verification & Validation (V&V)	Atomic services can be pre-verified by suppliers, but dynamic composition need to be verified at runtime.	Reconfiguration is verified as a part of the initial design with limited support of dynamic V&V.
Decision making in reconfiguration	The algorithm can be changed.	Often pre-determined by a reconfiguration algorithm.

SOA systems need specific mechanisms to handle reconfiguration including an overall new strategy to perform dynamic reconfiguration as well as new supporting technologies.

2.2   Roadmap of Reconfiguration

The dynamic reconfiguration can be classified into three phases:

1. Rebinding with Standby: Rebinding is an action of substituting a standby service for a service currently running. The standby and current services must be equivalent, in other words, both must satisfy the same service specification (including all the interfaces such as parameters and method names, and computation logic as specified in a service specification language such as OWL-S), and one can replace the other in all applications, i.e., have identical service interfaces and functionalities. The reconfiguration action is to use the

URI (Universal Resource Identifier) or URL (Universal Resource Locator) of a standby service to replace that of the current service. For example, a client may request to switch to a replacement encryption service that provides identical 64-bit encryption algorithm after it detects failure of the current service.

2. Re-composition with Collaboration: A more complicated situation occurs when there are no semantically equivalent services available for rebinding. In such a case, it will be necessary to use a different service, with different types and/or semantics, to replace an exiting service. In other words, the application functionality will be different because a different service with different functionality is now used. The type of re-composition may change the internal business logic, the partnership and collaboration among the participating services. For example, a client and a server both are required to switch from a 64-bit encryption algorithm to a 128-bit encryption algorithm.

3. Fault-tolerant Reconfiguration: In the course of reconfiguration, if the reconfiguration mechanism is not fault proof from the failure of the reconfiguration agents, then the application can suffer from the double failures, i.e., the failure of the application services and that of the underlying reconfiguration mechanism. To make a SOA system dependable, the dynamic reconfiguration platform must also be dependable. Thus, one of the important goals of the reconfiguration consensus protocol is to make it fault-tolerant. This is shown in Fig. 1.

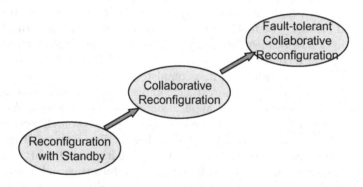

Fig. 1. Reconfiguration Roadmap

2.3 Reconfiguration Strategies and Infrastructure for SOA

The overall strategy for SOA dynamic reconfiguring can be based on the following considerations:

1. **Runtime Reconfiguration Infrastructure:** It is necessary to develop an infrastructure to support SOA dynamic reconfiguration, and this infrastructure may have significant overhead compared to those conventional SOA infrastructures without dynamic reconfiguration. The overhead comes from monitoring, distributed reconfiguration protocols, and evaluation mechanisms.

2. **Policy-Driven Reconfiguration:** SOA applications are often governed by policies so that applications can be monitored and managed at runtime [28]. This mechanism requires a policy engine to continuously monitor, schedule, and enforce appropriate actions at runtime according to pre-specific policies. In some SOA systems, even the policies can be updated at runtime. As dynamic reconfiguration is runtime behavior, policy-driven reconfiguration is a logical choice, however, this will require another computing infrastructure to support policy specification, analysis, simulation, verification, enforcement, and evaluation.

3. **Distributed Reconfiguration Protocols:** In some SOA applications, service orchestration is centralized even though distributed services are used. In other words, these distributed SOA applications are still managed in a centralized manner. These applications are certainly easier to manage than distributed SOA applications with distributed orchestration. Similarly, dynamic reconfiguration in SOA can be centrally managed so that it is easier to manage various dynamic reconfiguration activities such as monitoring, planning, execution, and evaluation. But dynamic reconfiguration with centralized management has a single point of failure. On the other hand, distributed reconfiguration protocol is important for system reliability, scalability and maintainability but distributed algorithms are often more complex than their centralized counterparts.

Dynamic reconfiguration based on the first two considerations have been developed earlier [27], and this paper proposes dynamic SOA reconfiguration with distributed control. The first two considerations already demand runtime monitoring, situation assessment, and distributed agents to perform dynamic reconfiguration. The third consideration requires these distributed agents to collaborate and coordinate with each other in a completely distributed manner.

An SOA application can be rather complex already, and even adding the first two considerations into the application can be a enormous tasks. This can be illustrated using a common 5-layered SOA application architecture [2]. This 5-layered architectural is as illustrated in Fig. 2: Presentation, Business Process Choreography, Services, Enterprise Components, and Operational Systems, and two supporting mechanisms: Integration Architecture and Management & Monitoring. The supporting mechanisms can be applied to each of the five layers. The dynamic reconfiguration mechanism added can be the 3rd supporting mechanism, and can be applied to most of these five layers if needed.

The 5-layered architecture is not the only SOA application architecture, numerous other architectures have been proposed including IBM SOA Foundation architecture [2] [14][25][32], Microsoft's .Net 2005 (Whitehorse)[24], SAP's NetWeaver [33], OASIS's FERA [6], enterprise SOA applications such as Enterprise SOA [18] and Service-Oriented Enterprise (SOE) [11] , and self healing architecture PKUAS [22].

Dynamic reconfiguration can be added into different aspects of SOA too. For example, it can be added to ESB (Enterprise Service Bus) to make ESB fault-tolerant, or it can be added to various SOA controllers such as orchestration/

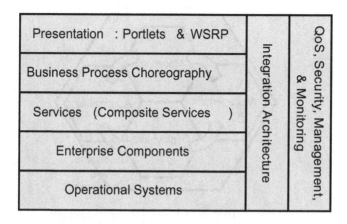

Fig. 2. Layered Architecture of SOA

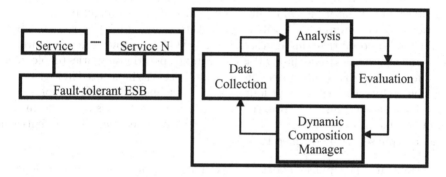

Fig. 3. Layers of Fault-tolerant Mechanisms

policy engines to make them fault tolerant [30].This is interesting because as dynamic reconfiguration is added to ESB and orchestration and/or policy engines, an SOA application can have a layer of fault-tolerant mechanisms starting at the application level down to the infrastructure level, and each layer can has its own reconfiguration policies. This can be shown by Fig. 3 where the right hand side shows the SOA engine controller with its own dynamic reconfiguration, and the communication backbone as the ESB which can be fault-tolerant too, and the applications running using service 1 to service n can have its own fault-tolerant architecture too.

Another interesting fact of SOA and SOA infrastructure is that in SOA, the lifecycle management can be embedded in the operation infrastructure to facilitate dynamic software composition. In this way, the SOA application development infrastructure and operation infrastructure can be merged together in a single and unified SOA infrastructure. A development infrastructure may include: modeling, function and policy specification, analysis, design, code generation, verification and validation such as model checking and testing. An

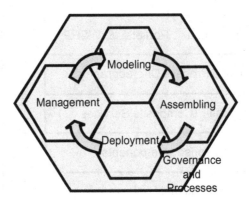

Fig. 4. IBM SOA Foundation Architecture

operation infrastructure may include: code deployment, code execution, policy enforcement, monitoring, communication, and system reconfiguration.

In an SOA environment, it will include features from both infrastructures. Both IBM and Microsoft take this approach. In IBM SOA Foundation Architecture, development activities (modeling and assembly) and operation activities (deployment and management) are integrated into a single process as illustrated in Fig. 4.

The architecture consists of four phases: modeling, assembling, deployment, and management. Furthermore, runtime governance activities are performed to provide guidance and oversight for the target SOA application. The activities in the four phases are performed iteratively.

- Modeling: This phase models the user requirements in a system model with a set of services.
- Assembling: This phase composes applications using services that have been created or discovered at runtime according the model specified in the previous phase.
- Deployment: In this phase, the runtime environment is configured to meet the application's requirements, and the application is loaded into that environment for execution.
- Management: After the application is deployed, the services used in the application are monitored. Information is collected to prevent, diagnose, isolate, and fix any problem that might occur during execution. These activities in management phase will provide the designer with better knowledge to make future application better.
- Governance and processes: The entire process will be controlled and orchestrated by policies.

IBM SOA Foundation Architecture is based on a model-driven application development process. This back looping process along with the governance and other processes can be delivered together with the target SOA application to the user. When there is a need of changing the application architecture, the

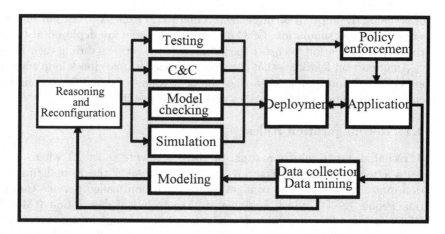

Fig. 5. Process Embedded Service Oriented Reference Architecture for Dynamic Reconfiguration

user needs only to re-specify the system model and the application will be re-assembled and re-deployed.

Fig. 5 shows an overall framework of combining operation infrastructure and development infrastructure with dynamic reconfiguration for an SOA application. The framework needs the following services:

- Dynamic reconfiguration services,
- Monitoring services,
- Code generation service,
- Deployment services,
- Dynamic V&V (Simulation, Model checking, Consistence and Completeness etc), and
- Dynamic assessment and analysis services.

The Code generation service generates the application and system code once the application model is generated. The Deployment service allows the application developer to specify the system configuration and then deploys the generated application service together with infrastructural services according to specified configuration. The Monitoring service monitors the activities of the services and their collaboration via ESB reference. The collected data is send to Assessment service for further evaluation. The Assessment service assesses the data collected from monitoring service according to service dependability properties such as reliability, performance, and security as well as properties of interest. The result will send to reconfiguration service for service reconfiguration decision making. The Reconfiguration service reconfigures the service at runtime according to the assessment of service situation as well as recomposes the application for newly introduced specifications. Before reconfiguration takes place, the readily installed service configuration and specification are sent to the verification services to verify the interoperability and integrity of the configuration so that it reduces the risk of breaking the application after the reconfiguration. The Verification and testing services such as simulation, C&C and model checking are deployed at the same time with application to ensure the integrity of the services during their lifecycle.

An important feature is that the whole process has a feedback loop where data are collected and evaluated so that the next round of dynamic reconfiguration can take advantages of latest data and analysis results.

2.4   Reconfiguration Rules

A reconfiguration rule is a tuple of three elements (e, a, c) where e represents a reconfiguration triggering event, a represents the reconfiguration action, and c represents the configuration description, called Service Configuration Profile (SCP), which is similar to the technical description (tModel) in UDDI service directory [31] of available services found by querying the service directory. The service reconfiguration profile includes the fields of type, service, ID, and reconfiguration indicator of configuration dependency. Two services with the same reconfiguration indicator can mutually replace each other without breaking the application integrity. For example, table 2 shows the reconfiguration rules for the encryption/decryption services, where 64-bit encryption service has the reconfiguration indicator to that of 64-bit decryption service. The reconfiguration rules are initially defined during the application modeling process and are deployed to each individual DRS agent. They can be updated as data are collected and evaluated with respect to the previous configuration.

Table 2. Reconfiguration Rules

Event	Encryption service failure
Action	Replace service
tModel	Redundancy: encryption service 64bit: serviceID : 0 Recomposing: encryption service 128bit : serviceID:1
Event	Decryption service failure
Action	Replace service
tModel	Redundancy: decryption service 64bit: serviceID: 0 Recomposing: decryption service 128bit : serviceID:1

Depending on the Service Configuration Profile, the reconfiguration of an encryption service may replace only the failed service with its standby or redundant service, or it may cause a re-composition of the encryption service, which is coordinated by the collaboration algorithm that ensures the decryption algorithm at the other side of the communication channel will be recomposed properly. This is illustrated in the following Fig. 6.

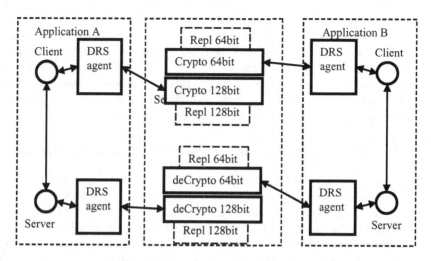

Fig. 6. DRS and Application Architecture

2.5   Reconfiguration Event Registration and Subscription

In SOA, services can be registered and published, and the DRS agent can take advantage of this to look up replacement services. During the service registration, services are categorized accordingly based on their semantic information and interface definition to form the reconfiguration service farm.

In SOA with dynamic reconfiguration, in addition to services, reconfiguration events can be registered and published. This is needed because DRS agents are distributed agents, and they need to receive the news of the reconfiguration

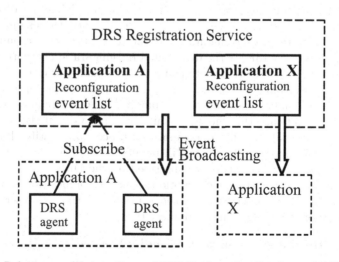

Fig. 7. Relations and Interactions of DRS Registration Service and DRS agents

triggering events. With registration and publishing of reconfiguration events, DRS can subscribe to these events and received update as new events arrives. Monitoring agents and deployment agents are responsible to send update to the broker that maintain the list, and send to appropriate DRS agents so that they can trigger appropriate reconfiguration. This also requires that DRS agents register with brokers with specific reconfiguration events so that they can receive the update when the event arrives. This is illustrated in Fig. 7.

3   DRS Reconfiguration and Collaboration Protocol

DRS reconfiguration collaboration protocol ensures reconfiguration integrity in a distributed environment. It is based on a consensus protocol with no centralized control. Due to the space limitation, only the major outline of the protocol will be presented in this section. The distributed consensus problem is a fundamental problem in distributed systems [19]. It covers a wide variety of situations in which processors/agents/players communicate through messages and they must obtain a consensus regardless of the behaviors of participants. A participant can display different kinds of failures including fail-silent where a failed component will simply stop working and will not produce any output after it fails to the Byzantine failure where a malicious component may generate misleading signals to disrupt the operation.

The consensus problem needs to address the following properties [7]:

Agreement: No two correct processes decide on different values.
Termination: All correct processes eventually decide.
Validity: Any decision value is the initial value of some processes.

This paper addresses the fail-silent failure model. A failed participant can be recovered and rejoin the system later. As aforementioned, the DRS agents are notified of the need to reconfigure after receiving the broadcast of registered reconfiguration event. The broadcasting message also includes the list of subscribers to this reconfiguration event. The aim of the reconfiguration collaboration is to coordinate the distributed reconfiguration activities of DRS agents. They must reach consensus to complete the reconfiguration.

During reconfiguration, a DRS agent tries to look up for a redundant service first for rebinding, because this re-binding approach requires the least amount of effort and thus this should be initiated first. Only if the rebinding fails, the DRS agent will start the re-composition process and notify all the participants. Meanwhile, more DRS agents will be affected. For example, encryption service reconfiguration event is only subscribed by the DRS agent that interacts with the encryption service, an encryption service re-composition event are subscribed by both DRS agents that talk to encryption and decryption services because the change of either algorithm will affect these parties.

3.1   Reconfiguration with Standby Service

DRS agent sends heartbeat signals periodically to monitor the status of controlled services and their standby services. Whenever an active service crash

Algorithm 1. Thread 1: Service monitoring thread where H is the threshold for probing cycles

---

while true **do**
    for all service in Services set **do**
        Send heartbeat message to services
        if no reply from service for **H** consecutive cycles **then**
            trigger reconfiguration process
            wake up reconfiguration thread
            insert event into event queue
        end if
    end for
    Sleep cycle_timeout
end while

Algorithm 2. Thread 2: Reconfiguration process

---

while true **do**
    if reconfiguration_event queue is not empty **then**
        Grab the event from reconfiguration event queue
        Select candidate service
        Switch and bind to new service
    end if
end while

Algorithm 3. Collaboration Algorithm

---

if there are standby services available **then**
    use standby service
    exit
end if{otherwise start consensus process}
Request the configuration vector from all other DRS agents in the group
if configuration vector is not empty **then**
    for all configuration key **do**
        if the configuration vector has the same configuration key **then**
            configuration counter increments 1
        else
            set the configuration counter to zero
        end if
    end for
end if
sort configuration array by counter from max to minimum.
{ The following boolean expression evaluates if every configuration vector contains this value. }
if configuration counter value of the first element equals to the size of group **then**
    select the configuration key of the first element as the candidate service
    perform configuration
else
    No agreement reached, fail to perform reconfiguration.
end if

event is detected, the controlling DRS agent reconfigures the failed service with their standby services. In this case, no collaboration is needed. The pseudo code for a basic reconfiguration agent is listed as in Algorithm 1 and Algorithm 2.

3.2   Collaborative Reconfiguration with Consensus Protocol

In a unreliable environment, it is likely that the current active service fails and none of the standby services can replace the failed service. Furthermore, it is possible that a new service should replace an existing service as the new service may have new algorithms and/or performance. In both cases, the application needs to incorporate a different service to continue. This needs to be done with close collaboration of DRS agents.

The consensus protocol within a group of DRS agents forces the participating DRS agents to reach an agreement before they start the reconfiguration process. The consensus protocol is shown in Algorithm 3.

3.3   Fault-Tolerant Consensus Protocol

During the reconfiguration, if a DRS agent fails, the above algorithm will fail as no fault-tolerant mechanism is available. To be able to cope with agent failures, it is important to understand when and how a distributed agent can fail. As far as the reconfiguration alogrithm is concerned, a DRS agent can fail at three critical points:

1. It fails before the reconfiguration event is broadcasted, in this case a new DRS agent can replace the failed one and continue the operation.
2. It fails after the reconfiguration event is broadcasted but before any tModel information is sent out to others.
3. It fails after the decision is made but before it performs the binding action and broadcasts its final results.

In addition, the consensus protocol is also vulnerable to the failure of the messages between DRS agents and between DRS agents and services where they can be delayed, corrupted or even dropped.

It is important that the reconfiguration consensus protocol can tolerate these failures. This paper proposes a fault-tolerant reconfiguration consensus protocol with the following components:

– Both active and standby DRS agents are available. A DRS agent is active if it engages in the reconfiguration process and monitors other services. A DRS agent is standby if it monitors only the status of active DRS agents. Note that active and standby services may both fail during the reconfiguration process.
– Application log which is a stable storage associated with each application. It records the critical states for the each DRS agent that serves the application.
– Registration log which is a stable storage in Pool Registry that records the monitoring association between standby DRS agents and active DRS agents.

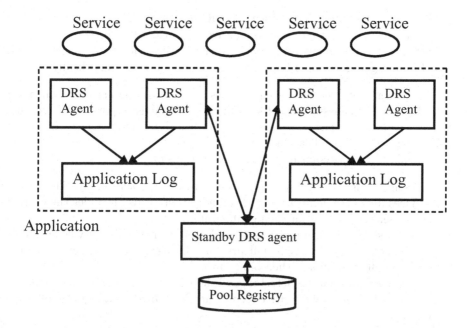

Fig. 8. DRS Fault-tolerant Platform Architecture

Figure 8 shows the fault-tolerant design of the reconfiguration platform. It consists of the DRS registry, Standby DRS agent pool and Application log.

The protocol has a pool of standby DRS agents, and the standby agents are ready to participate in reconfiguration if an active DRS agent fails.

1. All standby DRS agents are created and maintained in this pool.
2. The pool contains a predefined number of standby processes. Whenever a standby DRS agent becomes active, or a standby DRS agent fails, a new standby agent is instantiated and put into the pool.
3. Once a standby DRS agent becomes active, it will be removed from the Standby Agent Pool until it fails or deactivated upon application termination.
4. Standby DRS agent monitors active DRS agent for failure detection. One DRS agent sends heartbeat messages to a few active DRS agents at a predefined time interval. Once it detects the failure of an active agent, it substitutes itself for the failed agent.
5. The list of active DRS agents monitored by a standby DRS agent is stored in the Pool registry. The replacement standby DRS agent reads from the Pool Registry for the list and then monitors the agents in the list.

The fault-tolerant design of reconfiguration consensus protocol includes failure-detection, failure-recovery and critical reconfiguration state checkpointing.

The failure detection consists of service monitoring, active DRS agent monitoring and failure status checkpointing.

- DRS agent monitors the services that it configures.
- Standby DRS agent monitors the active DRS agent it will replace.
- Standby DRS agent monitors each other for failure detection of themselves.
- Monitoring is performed by sending heartbeat message periodically

The critical state checkpointing involves a set of logging activities whenever the DRS agent reaches a critical state identified that is important to recovery correctly the reconfiguration consensus protocol. Each DRS agent will log its own states into the Application log.

Critical state checkpointing includes the actions of:

- DRS agent logs its current configuration to the application log. That is the services under its monitoring and configuration. It also includes the current active service binding for each configuration.
- When a service failure is detected, and there is a standby service available. The controlling DRS agent will first log the newly selected service as the active configuration and then bind to that service.
- When a service failure is detected, and there is no a standby service available. Thus it triggers a collaborative reconfiguration. DRS agent logs the following events:

    Notification. It sends the reconfiguration event to register service to initiate a broadcasting of the reconfiguration event.

    Computing. It receives the configuration information from all other agents inside of the group

    Reached. It reaches an agreement and they agreed upon configuration value.

    Rebinding. It changes the current configuration and switches to new configuration.

    Failed. It fails to reach an agreement.

    Ready. The agreement is verified by all the members of the group by querying

Based on the above design, the new agent monitoring algorithm and configuration algorithm are shown in Algorithm 4 and Algorithm 5 respectively.

3.4   Failure Recovery

The failure recovery includes two recovery processes: the recovery from the failed active DRS agent and the recovery from the failed standby DRS agent. The former is a critical recovery process because it involves the failure of active DRS agent that is in charge of reconfiguration consensus protocol. The recovering process reads the recovery information of the failed DRS agent from the application log. This process can be classified into the following cases:

- If a DRS agent fails before it logs the selected service, the replacement agent will read old information stored and then it will detect the failure of the agent, thus proceeds to reconfiguration.

Algorithm 4. DRS agent fault-tolerant monitoring algorithm

```
while true do
    if logstatus ≠ READY then
        print "Agent is now performing reconfiguration"
    else if currentid = INVALID then
        print "Agent does not have a current service"
    else if status = STANDBY then
        for i = 0 to i < NumofAgent do
            agent.getconfigdata()
            if status ≠ ACTIVE then
                getagentlog()
                if logstatus = NOTIFY then
                    print "Move to state : NOTIFY"
                    queue.queue(logdata)
                else if logstatus = COMPUTING then
                    print "Move to state : COMPUTING"
                else if logstatus = READY then
                    print "Move to state : Ready"
                else if logstatus = REBINDING then
                    print "Move to state : REBINDING"
                end if
            end if
        end for
    else if status = ACTIVE then
        if server[currentid] ≠ ACTIVE then
            print "Current service is no longer active. Performing reconfiguration"
            long time = System.currentTimeMillis()
            String mytoken=time+":"+config.id
            queue.queue(mytoken);
            print "Move to state : NOTIFY"
        else
            print "Current service is running OK!"
        end if
    end if
    t.sleep(TIMEOUT);
end while
```

– If a DRS agent fails after it logs the new configuration, the replacement agent reads the updated information, and then continues its operation as replacement.
– If the DRS agent fails before it logs the broadcasting of the reconfiguration events. The replacement agent reads in the configuration, and find out it needs to broadcast a reconfiguration event. It will do so, and continue its operation as replacement.
– If the DRS agent fails after it logs the reconfiguration event but before it logs the agreement results, which means it fails in the middle of collecting tModel information. The replacement agent remedies the failure by resending the query for tModel information and proceeds normally.

Algorithm 5. DRS agent fault-tolerant configuration algorithm

```
while true do
    if  logstatus = READY then
        if  queue.isNotEmpty() then
            logstatus = NOTIFY;
        else
            print  "Nothing to Reconfig"
            t.sleep(TIMEOUT)
        end if
    else if logstatus = NOTIFY then
        for  i = 0 to i < NumofAgent  do
            if i ≠ id then
                if status = ACTIVE then
                    agent.startconfig(token)
                else
                    continue
                end if
            end if
        end for
        print  "Move to state : COMPUTING"
        logstatus = COMPUTING;
        queue.dequeue()
    else if logstatus = COMPUTING then
        bNotfound = true
        for i = 0 to i < NumofServer do
            bNotfound = false
            for  j = 0 to j < NumofAgent do
                if  agent[j].server[i] = INACTIVE  then
                    bNotfound = true;
                    break;
                end if
            end for
        end for
        if !bNotfound then
            logstatus = REBINDING;
            logdata = i;
            print  "Moving to state : REBINDING"
        else
            logstatus = READY;
            print  "Moving to state : Ready"
        end if
    else if logstatus =REBINDING then
        logstatus = READY;
        print  "Moving to state : Ready"
    end if
end while
```

– If the DRS agent fails after it logs the reconfiguration agreement result. If the result is "no agreement reached", it takes no further remedy action. If the result shows the agreed upon configuration, it will continue to operate as the replacement using the information logged.

The latter is a less critical because it replaces only a failed standby DRS agent. The recovery process reads the recovery information of the failed standby DRS agent from the registration log. The Pool Registry records the IDs of the active DRS agents that a standby DRS agent monitors. Once a standby DRS agent fails, it will be replaced by another standby DRS agent. The replacement standby agent reads data from the Pool Registry and start to monitor the DRS agent that was monitored by the failed standby agent.

The proof of correctness is omitted due to the space limitation. Major steps in the proof will show that the proposed protocol can tolerate arbitrary failures in services and DRS agents including active and standby agents.

4   Evaluation and Analysis

4.1   Algorithm Complexity

Let the number of DRS agents be n, the number of average different configurations for a DRS agent m. The best case for consensus algorithm to reach an agreement is:

$$O(n * m + m * \log m) \tag{1}$$

Which is the sum of the time it takes for each individual DRS agent of the group to collect the configuration information from each other and the time that it takes to process the information by sorting. The best case scenario is when there is no lose or delay of communications between the participants and there are no failures of DRS agent. The worse case could be infinite if the system suffers constant failures before it ever stabilizes. Note that no system can recover from constant failures.

4.2   Timing Analysis

Timing analysis determines quantitatively the time span that the system takes to stable itself after the occurrence of the last failure within the system either it is a service failure or an active DRS agent failure.

– Let the worst time needed to complete a reconfiguration without failure be Δt;
– Let μ be the time of the occurrence of the last system failure (either a service failure or an agent failure). We assume that to replace a failed DRS agent takes no time.
– System detects the failure after $2T$.
– Let p represents the condition that no further system reconfiguration is required.

Then we can have a formula in the form of LTL

$$p <> \cup(\mu + \Delta t + 2T) \qquad (2)$$

The LTL expression means that eventually the system will reach to a stable state with no reconfigurations after the elapse of $\Delta t + 2T$ from the time that the last failure of the system occurs.

5   Related Work

Recently, several studies have focused on dynamic software architecture, i.e., the software architecture that modifies its structure during execution [4]. The current research focuses on the formal specification techniques that can be used to reason and analyze dynamic architectures. A variety of reconfiguration rules such as graph rewriting rules, process algebra (such as CCS and CSP), predicate calculus, and architecture modification language (AML) [10] have been proposed to specify and analyze dynamic architectures. However, these studies have not focused on the dynamic SOA yet. One significant difference between existing dynamic architecture and SOA is that the dynamic architecture of SOA is fully integrated with many aspect of software development, such as service composition, code generation, and deployment.

Many studies have been conducted to build dynamic reconfigurable system for fault tolerance. The existing approaches include software architecture based systems such as Darwin [21], Dynamic ACME [13], Dynamic Wright [1], Rapide [20], OpenRec [16], C2 [23]. However, they focus on traditional component-based systems and can not be readily extended to support service-oriented application.

Gravity [8] is a service-oriented component model that introduces auto adaptive behavior at runtime as defined in the application composition. However, once the composition is changed, it cannot dynamic recompose the application.

The Open Grid Services Architecture (OGSA) [12] is a Grid system architecture based on Web services concepts and technologies. OGSA is a grid solution created to allow applications to share data and computing resources, as well as to access them across multiple organizations in an efficient way. Similar to OGSA, DRS shares the same high-level control loop for service management. The DRS supplements the OGSI to provide a solution for dependable Grid services.

6   Conclusion

This paper discussed dynamic reconfiguration strategies for SOA systems and applications. Dynamic reconfiguration in SOA is different from traditional dynamic reconfiguration because SOA systems involve dynamic composition, dynamic modeling, deployment, policy enforcement, and dynamic architecture. This paper then outlines a distributed protocol to perform distributed dynamic reconfiguration in an SOA environment.. This protocol is supported by a set of DRS agents.

References

1. R. Allen, R. Douence, and D. Garlan, "Specifying and Analyzing Dynamic Software Architectures", Proceedings of the 1998 Conference on Fundamental Approaches to Software Engineering (FASE'98) Lisbon, Portugal, March 1998.
2. A. Arsanjani, "Service-Oriented Modeling and Architecture: How to Identify, Specify, and Realize Services for Your SOA", whitepaper from IBM, Nov 2004, available at: http://www-128.ibm.com/developerworks/webservices/library/ws-soa-design1/
3. A. Avizienis, J. C. Laprie, B. Randell and C. Landwehr. Basic Concepts and Taxonomy of Dependable and Secure Computing. IEEE Transactions on Dependable and Secure Computing, Vol.1, No.1, 2004, pp 11-33.
4. J. Bradbury, J. Cordy, J. Dingel, and M. Wermelinger, "A Survey of Self-Management in Dynamic Architecture Specifications", Proc. of International Workshop on Self-Management Systems, 2004
5. G. Brown and R. Carpenter, "Successful Application of Service-Oriented Architecture across the Enterprise and Beyond", Intel Technology Journal, Nov 2004. Available at: http://www.intel.com/technology/itj/2004/ volume08issue04/art09_successful/p07_references.htm.
6. B. Carmeli, etc. "High throughput reliable message dissemination", Proceedings of the 2004 ACM Symposium on Applied Computing, 2004, pp. 322-327.
7. T. Chandra, and S. Toueg. "Unreliable Failure Detectors for Reliable Distributed Systems," Journal of the ACM, 43(2), Mar., 1996, pp. 245-267.
8. H. Cervantes and R.S. Hall: "Autonomous Adaptation to Dynamic Availability Using a Service-Oriented Component Model," ICSE 26th , 2004, pp. 614-623.
9. Y. Chen, W.T. Tsai, Introduction to programming languages: Programming in C, C++, Scheme, Prolog, C#, and SOA, second edition, Kendall/Hunt Publishing Company, 2006.
10. J. Dowling and V. Cahill, "Dynamic Software Evolution and the K-Component Model", Proc. of Workshop on Software Evolution, OOPSLA, 2001
11. T. Erl, Service-Oriented Architecture: A Field Guide to Integrating XML and Web Services, New York: Prentice Hall PTR, 2004.
12. I. Foster, C. Kesselman, J. M. Nick and S. Tuecke, "The Physiology of Grid: An Open Grid Services Architecture for Distributed Systems Integration", Feb.17 2002, http://www.globus.org/ogsa/.
13. D. Garlan, R. T. Monroe, and D. Wile, "Acme: Architectural Description of Component-Based Systems". Foundations of Component-Based Systems. G.T. Leavens, and M. Sitaraman (eds). Cambridge University Press, 2000 pp. 47-68.
14. M. Fischer, "The Consensus Problem in Unreliable Distributed Systems", Foundations of Computation Theory, volume 158 of Lecture Notes in Computer Science, 1983, pp. 127-140.
15. R. High, S. Kinder and S. Graham, "IBM SOA Foundation: An Architectural Introduction and Overview, Version 1.0", 2005
16. J. Hillman and I. Warren,"An Open Framework for Dynamic Reconfiguration", ICSE 26th 2004, Vol. 00, pp. 594-603.
17. G. J. Holzmann, The SPIN Model Checker: Primer and Reference Manual, Addison-Wesley Professional, 2003.
18. D. Krafzig, K. Banke and D. Slama, Enterprise SOA: Service-Oriented Architecture Best Practices, New York:vPrentice Hall, PTR, 2005.

19. L. Lamport, R. E. Shostak and M. Pease, "The Byzantine Generals Problem", ACM Transactions on Programing Languages and Systems, 4(3), July, 1982, pp. 382-401.

20. D. C. Luckham, "Specification and Analysis of System Architecture Using Rapide", IEEE Transactions on Software Engineering 21 (4), 1995, pp. 336-355.

21. J. Magee, N. Dulay, S. Eisenbach, and J. Kramer, "Specifying Distributed Software Architectures", Proc. the 5th European Software Engineering Conference (ESEC '95), September 1995 pp. 137-153.

22. H. Mei, G. Huang and W. Tsai, "Towards Self-Healing Systems via Dependable Architecture and Reflective Middleware," 10th IEEE International Workshop on Object-oriented Real-time Dependable Systems, Sedona, February 2005, 337 - 344.

23. P. Oreizy, M. M. Gorlick, R. N. Taylor, D. Heimbigner, G. Johnson, N. Medvidovic, A. Quilici, D. S. Rosenblum, and A. L. Wolf. "An Architecture-Based Approach to Self-Adaptive Software", IEEE Intelligent Systems, Vol. 14, No. 3, May/June 1999, pp. 54-62.

24. B. Randell and R. Lhotka, "Bridge the Gap between Development and Operations with Whitehorse", MSDN magazine, July 2005, http://msdn.microsoft.com/msdnmag/issues/04/07/whitehorse/default.aspx.

25. S. Simmons, "Introducing the WebSphere Integration Reference Architecture: A Service-based Foundation for Enterprise-Level Business Integration", IBM WebSphere Developer Technical Journal, Aug. 17, 2005, http://www-128.ibm.com/developerworks/websphere/techjournal/0508_simmons/0508_simmons.html

26. W.T. Tsai, R. Paul, B. Xiao, Z. Cao and Y. Chen, "PSML-S: A Process Specification and Modeling Language for Service Oriented Computing", IASTED 9th , 2005, pp. 160-167

27. W. T. Tsai, W. Song, R. Paul, Z. Cao, and H. Huang, "Services-Oriented Dynamic Reconfiguration Framework for Dependable Distributed Computing", COMPSAC 2004, pp. 554-559.

28. W. T. Tsai, X. Liu, Y. Chen, and R. Paul, "Simulation Verification and Validation by Dynamic Policy Enforcement", Proc. of Annual Simulation Symposium, 2005, pp. 91-98.

29. W. T. Tsai, "Service-Oriented System Engineering: A New Paradigm," IEEE International Workshop on Service-Oriented System Engineering (SOSE), October 2005, pp. 3 - 8.

30. W. T. Tsai, C. Fan, Y. Chen, R. Paul, and J. Y. Chung, "Architecture Classification for SOA-based Applications", Proc. of IEEE International Symposium on Object and Component-Oriented Real-Time Distributed Computing (ISORC), 2006, pp. 295-302.

31. OASIS UDDI Standard: http://www.uddi.org/

32. IBM Developers Works, "New to SOA and Web services", available at: http://www-128.ibm.com/developerworks/webservices/newto/.

33. SAP NetWeaver product introduction, available at: http://www.sap.com/solutions/netweaver/index.epx.

A Component-Based Approach for Constructing High-Confidence Distributed Real-Time and Embedded Systems

Shih-Hsi Liu[1], Barrett R. Bryant[1], Mikhail Auguston[2], Jeff Gray[1], Rajeev Raje[3], and Mihran Tuceryan[3]

[1] University of Alabama at Birmingham
{liush, bryant, gray}@cis.uab.edu
[2] Naval Postgraduate School
auguston@cs.nps.navy.mil
[3] Indiana University Purdue University Indianapolis
{rraje, tuceryan}@cs.iupui.edu

Abstract. In applying Component-Based Software Engineering (CBSE) techniques to the domain of Distributed Real-time and Embedded (DRE) Systems, there are five critical challenges: 1) discovery of relevant components and resources, 2) specification and modeling of components, 3) exploration and elimination of design assembly options, 4) automated generation of heterogeneous component bridges, and 5) validation of context-related embedded systems. To address these challenges, this paper introduces four core techniques to facilitate high-confidence DRE system construction from components: 1) A component and resource discovery technique promotes component searching based on rich and precise descriptions of components and context; 2) A timed colored Petri Net-based modeling toolkit enables design and analysis on DRE systems, as well as reduces unnecessary later work by eliminating infeasible design options; 3) A formal specification language describes all specifications consistently and automatically generates component bridges for seamless system integration; and 4) A grammar-based formalism specifies context behaviors and validates integrated systems using sufficient context-related test cases. The success of these ongoing techniques may not only accelerate the software development pace and reduce unnecessary development cost, but also facilitate high-confidence DRE system construction using different formalisms over the entire software life-cycle.

1 Introduction

As the complexity of Distributed Real-Time Embedded (DRE) software systems continues to increase [11], there is a need to facilitate the construction of such systems from reusable components that can be configured for the particular implementation being constructed. Component-Based Software Engineering (CBSE) [8] addresses this issue, providing the mechanism to leverage existing artifacts and resources rather than handcraft DRE systems from scratch, as is often observed in current practice. CBSE techniques, however, only partially fulfill the objective of software development. For example, to meet both longevity

F. Kordon and J. Sztipanovits (Eds.): Monterey Workshop 2005, LNCS 4322, pp. 225–247, 2007.
© Springer-Verlag Berlin Heidelberg 2007

and changeability requirements demands continuous optimizations to the configuration of the component interactions and application logic. Furthermore, end users' demands on confidential, high quality, and time-to-market software products have not yet been completely addressed. Endeavoring to redeem the promises to both organizations and end users leads to five core challenges:

- **Discovery of relevant components and resources:** Amid a repository of available components, discovering relevant components is non-trivial. Particularly, DRE systems not only require stringent demands on functional correctness, but also non-functional (i.e., Quality of Service (QoS)) satisfaction. Such QoS demands, however, are not purely influenced by standalone systems composed by selected components - the context of the system under development also has a major influence. For example, there may be several implementations of the same functional component with different run-time features (e.g., battery consumption versus throughput). Additionally, two components may also have functional and/or QoS dependencies between each other that lead to mutual influence. A manual discovery process by embedded system engineers may be time consuming and error prone. An automated and unified resource discovery process based on component specifications, component dependencies, and context specifications may accelerate search speed as well as select the best component for specific DRE system construction.
- **Specification and modeling of components and their relevant properties:** As described in the first challenge, in order to discover an appropriate component, that component must be entered into the repository with an appropriate specification and model that can be detected by the discovery service. The specification indicates the relevant functional and non-functional (i.e., QoS) properties of the component and dependencies between components. The model indicates the domain the component belongs to in order to narrow and expedite the search to the appropriate application domain. A consistent and understandable specification syntax and semantics may reduce possible accidental complexity during DRE software development.
- **Exploration and elimination of design assembly:** Different challenges faced by embedded systems developers require effective design and fine tuning, crosscutting multiple layers of infrastructure and system logic. Such challenges result from diverse configuration possibilities, numerous appropriate component candidates for composition, and highly complex component dependencies in embedded systems. The combination of these challenges results in abundant design alternatives. Embedded systems engineers must be able to examine and deploy various design alternatives quickly and easily amid possible configurations, component candidates, and component dependencies.
- **Automatic generation of correct component bridges:** Some of the available components may be applicable only to specific technology platforms, requiring an approach that operates in a heterogeneous manner. The generation of component wrappers from formally specified behavioral characteristics may offer assistance in verifying the correctness of component

interactions that are more difficult or impossible to perform in handcrafted solutions. Furthermore, the specifications of component properties provides a capability to check if a set of components are assembled in a valid and legal manner. For example, adjustments made at one layer of the infrastructure may lead to unforeseen consequences at some other layer of the infrastructure, or may adversely affect application logic.

- **Validation of context-related embedded systems:** The factors of validation emerge from component specifications, component dependencies, component configurations and system logics, and heterogeneous component bridges. Such factors are, in fact, all context-related, and thus require the knowledge of different contexts and sufficient random test cases to cover all possible states under each given context. For a large number of test cases in different contexts, efficiently managing and reusing them to address the regression test problem are required. Cohesively tieing such test cases to the artifacts of the earlier software life-cycle to cover the quantitative and qualitative validation of context-related embedded systems are also imperative.

Although CBSE techniques lift the abstraction to a higher level and use interface description languages to specify the characteristics of composition units [8], these five accidental complexities still arise. This paper introduces four core techniques to facilitate high-confidence DRE system construction in the vision of the UniFrame project [20]: 1) A component and resource discovery technique promotes component searching based on multi-level descriptions of components and context; 2) A timed colored Petri Net-based modeling toolkit enables design and analysis of DRE systems and eliminates infeasible design options to avoid unnecessary later work; 3) A formal specification language consistently describes all specifications and automatically generates component bridges for seamless system integration; and 4) A grammar-based formalism specifies context behaviors and validates integrated systems using sufficient context-related test cases. The success of these progressive techniques may not only accelerate software development pace and reduce unnecessary development cost, but also enable high-confidence DRE system construction by formalizing the static and dynamic properties of a DRE system, and facilitating validation of the functional and QoS requirements of the system at component, service, and system levels.

The rest of the paper is organized as follows. Section 2 introduces UniFrame, the application domain in this paper, and its case study. In Section 3, four core techniques to address the five challenges are presented. Section 4 discusses the current CBSE techniques in the DRE domain. Section 5 concludes the paper and discusses future work stemming from current limitations.

2   Background

This section offers an overview of the UniFrame process and the domain of mobile augmented reality [22]. A case study, called the Battlefield Training System (BTS), is also described and applied to four techniques in the later sections.

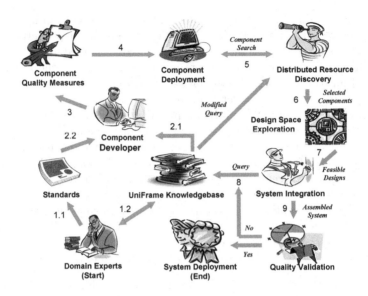

Fig. 1. The Overview of the UniFrame Process

2.1   UniFrame

UniFrame is a knowledge-based framework that offers techniques and tools for composing distributed systems from possibly heterogeneous components [21]. Figure 1 is an overview of the UniFrame process. The process starts from acquiring knowledge from domain experts. As shown in arrows 1.1 and 1.2, UniFrame engineers collaborate with domain experts to obtain sufficient backgrounds and knowledge on the application domain, components, component assemblies, component dependencies, and their functional and non-functional requirements and standards. Such information may be converted into an executable formal specification and stored in the knowledgebase [13]. Component quality measures concentrate on the evaluation of components according to their functional and non-functional requirements. Validated components are deployed to the distributed environment for future acquisition and assembly. Please note that the descriptions of the deployment environment context are stored in the knowledgebase for the searching procedure. The distributed resource discovery procedure searches and locates relevant components using the Unified Meta-component Model (UMM) [20]. QoS-UniFrame [16], as a design space exploration and elimination toolkit, utilizes timed colored Petri Nets [9] to model possible designs of DRE systems and analyzes the feasibility of design artifacts in compliance with their QoS requirements. During the system integration procedure, Two-Level Grammar (TLG) [4] formally and seamlessly bridges heterogenous components. Lastly, Attributed Event Grammar (AEG) [1] specifies possible event traces and provides a uniform method for automatically generating and executing test cases for quality validation purposes. This paper concentrates on the last four procedures (the right half of Figure 1) for high-confidence DRE system construction during the entire software life-cycle. Such procedures may reduce possible accidental complexity and increase confidence of the software development.

2.2   Mobile Augmented Reality Systems

An augmented reality system [7] enriches the environment by merging real and virtual objects in a real environment. The real-time interactions and the registration (alignment) for real and virtual objects with each other are also required. The integrated concepts of augmented reality, mobile computing, wearable computing and ubiquitous computing systems enable research into Mobile Augmented Reality Systems (MARSs) [22].

Generally, a MARS consists of six subsystems: computation, presentation, tracking and registration, geographical model, interaction, and wireless communication [22]. The computation subsystem performs specific computational tasks for the application. The presentation (rendering) subsystem computes and depicts virtual multimedia objects. The geographical model stores the geometrical and detailed hierarchical 3D information of the environment where a demonstrator works. The interaction subsystem offers a user friendly interface that allows a demonstrator to conveniently input the data for processing as well as see the output generated by the presentation subsystem. Wireless communication provides the mobile communication between the subsystems. The tracking and registration subsystem tracks a user's (or an object's) position and orientation using trackers or sensors and registers virtual objects in compliance with the tracking results. The tracking data can be used both by the rendering and presentation subsystem to generate the 3D graphics properly aligned with the physical world, and also could be utilized by the computing subsystem for various tasks such as spatial queries for location-aware computational tasks.

There are numerous off-the-shelf or custom-built hardware solutions to tracking. These often consist of sensors that provide position (2 or 3 dimensions), orientation (2 or 3 Degrees of Freedom), or a combination. They utilize a variety of technologies (magnetic, ultrasound, vision-based, infra-red, wireless, ultra-wide-band, mechanical) to achieve the tracking and have various QoS properties such as resolution, accuracy, and range. For example, Global Positioning System (GPS) is a 2-dimensional position tracker that has a world-wide range, but has a resolution on the order of 1 meter. The Inertia-Cube^{TM} from Intersense Technologies[1], is a self-contained (sourceless) inertial orientation tracker that outputs three orientation angles and has a 1 degree yaw[2] accuracy and 0.25 degree accuracy in pitch and roll angles. In a mobile augmented reality system that covers a wide area, many such trackers may need to be deployed in various locations.

Many challenges exist in utilizing the trackers in such an environment that contains multiple trackers with different characteristics (heterogeneity) and spread over large spaces, with possible redundancies in their sensing modalities. The first challenge is the discovery by the tracked object of all the sensors available in a

---

[1] http://www.intersense.com/company/whatismotion.htm

[2] Yaw corresponds to how far the object is pointing away from its direction of travel due to rotation about its vertical axis.

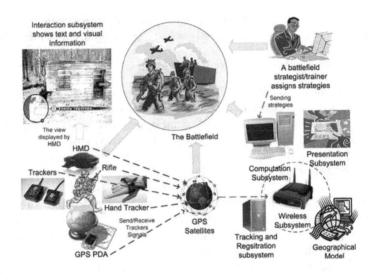

Fig. 2. The Battlefield Training System Example

given location. The next challenge is to select a subset to be utilized. Finally, the last challenge is to utilize the selected sensors to fuse the data and provide a single, high quality measurement of the pose (position and orientation) of the tracked object. UniFrame is used to accomplish the discovery and selection tasks.

In order to demonstrate the advantages of the UniFrame process over high-confidence component-based DRE system construction, a Battlefield Training System (BTS) example is introduced. Figure 2 shows an overview of the BTS example.

The following description is an example scenario for the BTS system. Imagine a soldier who is walking on the street to rescue a virtual hostage hidden in one of the buildings. The position and orientation sensors on his body send back the 6 Degrees of Freedom (6DOF) data to the tracking subsystem every half-second. When the soldier is in a certain position and is looking in a particular direction, the rendering subsystem will display enemy soldiers in certain 3D positions according to a training scenario generated by the computational subsystem. This rendering of enemy soldiers, therefore, is intimately tied to the position and orientation information coming from the tracking subsystem. The soldier has to shoot the enemies using a specialized rifle whose pose is also tracked. By computing the bullet trajectory, the system computes if the enemy is killed and updates the view of the soldier accordingly. The soldier can communicate with the command center via his headphone. The information of each building and the soldier's current position can be displayed on the Head Mounted Display (HMD) by text. Several movement, light, audio and temperature sensors will periodically send the physical conditions of the battlefield back to the computation subsystem. All of this simulation, computation, and rendering depends greatly on accurate tracking of the various objects such as the soldier, the HMD, and the rifle.

Several high-level functional and QoS requirements are required to establish a satisfactory BTS.

- **Functional Requirements**
  - (F1) A soldier should wear both position and orientation sensors on his body to obtain 6 Degrees of Freedom (6DOF) results: 3 for position and 3 for orientation. The soldier should also wear a hand tracker on his hand to sense the 6DOF of the hand.
  - (F2) Each rifle should contain position and orientation sensors to the 6DOF of an objective that the soldier may target.
  - (F3) Audio input and output devices should be provided to the soldier for communicating with his teammates.
  - (F4) An optical see-through Head Mounted Display (HMD) should provide the interaction subsystem that displays both text and visual objects. This could be a one-eye, monocular system that leaves the second eye unobstructed for other tasks.
  - (F5) The computation subsystem should compute the scenarios and strategies for training a soldier.
  - (F6) The geographical model should store all the necessary geographical and geometrical information of the battlefield. Such geographical information should be hierarchical in compliance with the three dimensions of the battlefield.
  - (F7) A GPS PDA (Personal Data Assistant) should provide the up-to-date geographical information of the battlefield obtained from the geographical model.
  - (F8) GPS satellites and relevant wireless communication devices should transfer tracking results and registered virtual objects between tracking and registration, geographical model, and computation subsystems.
  - (F9) A battlefield training system strategist/trainer should assign training strategies and adaptable scenarios to the computation subsystem.
- **Quality of Service Requirements**
  - (Q1) Each visual object should be displayed on the correct coordinates of the HMD. The coordinate inaccuracy should not exceed 5mm.
  - (Q2) Each visual object should be displayed and continuously updated on the HMD. The sampling frequency of each object should be at least 24Hz. The residual visual object that misses the hard deadline should not be displayed to confuse the soldier.
  - (Q3) Each text object should be displayed on the correct coordinates of the HMD. The coordinate inaccuracy should not exceed 5mm.
  - (Q4) Each text object should be displayed on the HMD in real-time. The sampling frequency of such an object should be at least 24Hz. The residual text object that misses the hard deadline should not be displayed to confuse the soldier.
  - (Q5) Each audio signal should be transmitted to the soldier in real-time. The sampling frequency of each signal should be at least 44Hz.

- (Q6) Each position sensor and orientation sensor on the soldier, the rifle, and the hand should send at least 120 6DOF sampling information back to the computation subsystem every second.
- (Q7) The interaction subsystem should display text and visual objects with a reasonable resolution (e.g., resolutions for position and orientation sensors should be respectively at least 0.75mm and 0.05 degrees).
- (Q8) The presentation/rendering subsystem should not provide obscure text and visual objects to the interaction subsystem. For example, 12-point (or more) proportional spaced bitmap fonts should be provided.
- (Q9) The geographical model should provide the geographical information in time upon the request from other subsystems. The query processing time of each geographical information should not exceed 0.01 second.

The listed functional and QoS requirements can be classified into three abstraction levels in UniFrame: component, service, and system. Functional or QoS requirements at the component level mean that a specific component correctly performs a functional task and satisfies *how well* it should perform as specified in the corresponding QoS requirements. F1, F2, F4, F6, Q7, and Q8 are examples of such requirements. To perform a service obeying its functional requirements at the service level, a sequence of components (i.e., a functional path [30]) collaborates with each other in a specific order. Each component carries out a specific task (e.g., rendering) and the combination of these tasks fulfills the overall requirements. Regarding QoS requirements, a QoS path quantitatively describes how well the corresponding functional path can be satisfied [30]. For F3, F7, F9, Q1, Q2, Q3, Q4, Q5, and Q6, each of which is achieved by comprising at least two components that interact with each other. F5 and Q9, however, can be mistakenly classified into the component level because of the brief descriptions. From the perspective of the component level, F5 and Q9 are realized by the computation or the geographical model subsystem. Such a classification, in fact, does not consider the entire picture of the BTS example. After obtaining the training strategies, the computation subsystem should compute and then assign specific tasks to other appropriate subsystems. Such tasks may request some collaborations among different subsystems. Additionally, because there may be more than one virtual object displayed on the interaction subsystem, the computation, tracking and registration, presentation, and wireless subsystems frequently interact with the geographical model subsystem to access the geographical results. Therefore, F5 and Q9 are regarded as system level requirements.

3   The UniFrame Approach

To tackle accidental complexities as mentioned in Section 1, UniFrame offers four kernel techniques in the requirements, analysis, design, implementation, and testing workflows.

3.1   Distributed Discovery of Components

As indicated previously, the underlying model for the UniFrame approach is the Unified Meta-component Model (UMM) [20]. The UMM has three parts: a) Components, b) Service and associated guarantees, and c) Infrastructure [19]. Components in UniFrame are units of independent development and deployment and offer specific services with associated guarantees about the QoS. The infrastructure provides the environment for deploying such independently developed components and discovering them via the UniFrame Resource Discovery System (URDS), which is a pro-active and hierarchical discovery service [23].

UniFrame Resource Discovery System (URDS). URDS consists of three levels: a) registration level, b) pro-active search level, and c) user interaction and administration level. The registration level is realized by active registries, which are enhanced versions of the basic publication mechanisms provided by different component deployment environments (e.g., the built-in registry in Java-RMI[3]). The enhancement is in the form of an ability for these basic mechanisms to actively listen and communicate with the head-hunters (described shortly). Component developers are required to use the UniFrame knowledgebase (as indicated in Figure 1) and create, in addition to the implementation of the components, comprehensive specifications called the UMM-Specifications. An example of such a specification is shown in the next section. Once the component and its associated specification is ready, both of these are published with the corresponding local active registry and deployed on the network.

The pro-active search level is implemented by head-hunters. These are specialized components who are entrusted with the task of pro-actively gathering component specifications from various active registries. Head-hunters store these specifications in their local store, called a meta-repository. Head-hunters, in addition to gathering specifications, carry out the task of matching specifications stored in their meta-repositories with incoming queries. It is quite conceivable that any single head-hunter may not contain all the specifications that are deployed over a network, and hence, head-hunters may collaborate with one another to cover a much larger search space. Various techniques for the collaboration between head-hunters have been experimented with. These include random, long-term, short-term, and profile-based. Results of these experiments [24] demonstrate that such a collaboration allows a selective search, as compared to an exhaustive search (which may be costly in a large setup), without substantially sacrificing the quality of the selected components.

The top level of URDS is achieved by the Internet Component Broker, which is made up of the Domain Security Manager, Query Manager, Link Manager, and Adapter Manager. The Internet Component Broker is responsible for authenticating head-hunters and active registries (via the Domain Security Manager), receiving incoming queries and returning results (via the Query Manager) to the system integrator, for linking different Internet Component Brokers (via the

---

[3] Remote Method Invocation - http://java.sun.com/products/jdk/rmi

Link Manager), and providing adapter components for bridging the technological heterogeneities (via the Adapter Manager).

UMM Specification and Discovery of Components. The UMM specification of components is in accordance with the concept of multi-level specification [2]. The UMM specification of a component, in addition to its name, type and informal description, consists of computational attributes, cooperation attributes, auxiliary attributes, QoS attributes, and deployment attributes.

The computational attributes describe the functional characteristics of a component. These include inherent attributes, which contain the book keeping information (such as the ID and version) of that component and functional attributes. The functional attributes contain the syntactical, semantical, and the synchronization contracts, along with a few additional fields such as technology of implementation and the algorithm (if any) used. The cooperation attribute indicates possible collaborators of a component. The auxiliary attributes provide information about special features that may be incorporated in a component such as security. The QoS attributes, which are critical in the case of DRE systems such as MARS, contain information about the QoS parameters (e.g., latency), their values (or a range), associated costs and the levels of quality that a component provides. The deployment attributes indicate the execution environment needed for that component and the effects of the environment on the QoS characteristics of the component. For example, the partial UMM specification of an *IS-PCTracker* that can be used in the MARS environment for providing the position and orientation information (6DOF) is shown below (an example of a complete UMM specification is found in [19]):

```
Component Name: IS-PCTracker Domain Name: Distributed Tracking
Informal Description: Provides the position and orientation
information.

Computational Attributes
    Inherent Attributes:
        Id: cs.iupui.edu/ISPCTracker;
        ...
        Validity: 12/1/07
        Registration: pegasus.cs.iupui.edu/HH1
        Technology: CORBA

    Functional Attributes:
        Functional Description: Provides the position and
                                orientation of a tracked object.
        Algorithm: Kalman Filter;
        Complexity: O(n^6)

        Syntactical Contract:
            Vector getPosition();
            Vector getOrientation();
```

```
Semantic Contract:
    Pre-condition: {calibrated (PCTracker)== true}
    Post-condition: {sizeof (posVector) == 3) &&
                     sizeof (orientationVector) == 3}
Synchronization Contract:
    Policy: Mutual Exclusion
    Implementation Mechanism: semaphore
. . . .


Quality of Service Attributes
    QoS Metrics: tracking_volume, resolution_pos,
                 resolution_orientation, accuracy_pos,
                 accuracy_pitch, accuracy_yaw,
                 accuracy_roll, sampling_freq

                 tracking_volume: 2mx2mx3m
                 resolution_pos: 0.75mm
                 resolution_orientation: 0.05 degrees
                 accuracy_pos: 2-3mm
                 accuracy_pitch: 0.25 degrees
                 accuracy_yaw: 0.5 degrees
                 accuracy_roll: 0.25 degrees
                 sampling_freq: 100-130 Hz

    . . .
```

The above specification indicates various important factors: a) it is comprehensive and embodies the multi-level specification concepts, b) it places an emphasis on functional as well as non-functional (QoS) features of a component, and c) it is consistent with the concepts of service-oriented approaches for developing DRE systems. Due to its comprehensive nature and multi-levels, the UMM specification of a component (such as an *IS-PCTracker*) allows complicated matching techniques during the discovery process of the URDS for appropriate components. For example, a system integrator may specify a subset of typical attributes (e.g., the type, the syntactical attributes, pre- and post-conditions associated with the interface, and QoS parameters with specific values) for an *IS-PCTracker*. Once this query is received by the Query Manager, it will pass it on to a subset of the head-hunters to search for appropriate components. URDS uses multi-level matching, i.e., depending upon the level, a different technique is used to match the corresponding part of the incoming query with the specifications stored in the local meta-repository. This approach is an enhancement of the one discussed in [32]. For example, matchings such as type and technology use keyword match, syntactical matching uses type relations, semantical matching uses theorem provers, synchronization matching uses keywords and temporal logic, and QoS matching uses numerical relationships. Thus, the multi-level matching is more comprehensive than simple attribute-based matching. Also, different head-hunters may use different algorithms for discovering components that match the given query from their local meta-repository. Once appropriate components are discovered, they are presented back to the system integrator who can select an appropriate one for his/her current needs.

3.2   Design Space Exploration and Elimination

UniFrame advocates the principles of CBSE [8], design by contract[4], and multi-level contracts [2]. Such principles facilitate URDS to discover relevant components from the repository in compliance with their functional and QoS requirements. The complexity and magnitude of a design space increases exponentially as more appropriate components are found for a distributed embedded system. QoS-UniFrame [16] is a two-level modeling toolkit for designing and analyzing distributed embedded systems. Such a toolkit explores and eliminates the design space of a DRE system and assures its QoS requirements. At the first level, QoS-UniFrame performs design space exploration and elimination using the formalism of timed colored Petri Nets [9]. A Petri Net graph visually achieves design space exploration by depicting all relevant components (places in a Petri Net graph) and design decisions (transitions in a Petri Net graph). Design space elimination is accomplished by a reachability tree construction of the Petri Net graph. Such a reachability tree comprises a number of sequences of states (i.e., markings) that represent selected component status and dynamic behaviors regarding QoS at given points of execution. A QoS-UniFrame interpreter implements the tree construction that obeys the formalisms of timed colored Petri Nets and the static and dynamic properties embedded in the Petri Net graph.

Besides the formalisms, an aspect-oriented programming approach using AspectJ [10] is utilized to insert (i.e., weave) statements into the interpreter for analyzing and/or asserting static or strict QoS requirements regarding components, execution paths, and the system [16]. If the inserted statements are not fulfilled, QoS-UniFrame stops constructing new nodes in the reachability tree whereas all the leaves generated are the design space that satisfies static and strict QoS requirements. Because dynamic QoS information accordingly relates to the deployment environment, a statistical and stochastic approach is exploited at the second level [16]. The previous state and observations of components can be accessed from the knowledgebase for the evaluation of dynamic QoS requirements. QoS-UniFrame utilizes a meta-programmable approach, called PPCEA (Programmable Parameter Control for Evolutionary Algorithms) [14], that prunes off less probable design alternatives by means of statistic and stochastic evolutionary algorithms.

Figure 3 (a) shows a partial high-level design of the BTS example represented by a Petri Net graph using QoS-UniFrame. It describes three execution paths that perform rendering text on the Head Mounted Display (HMD), rendering a three dimensional graph on the HMD, and speech processing. White circles (i.e., places) are the hardware (e.g., *hmd*) or software components (e.g., *renderProcessing*) selected for the design; light colored circles are notations (called stub

---

[4] http://archive.eiffel.com/doc/manuals/technology/contract

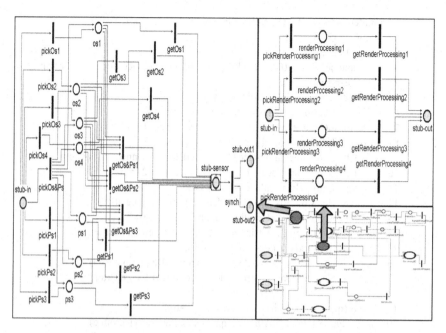

Fig. 3. (a) Timed Colored Petri Net Graph of BTS (at bottom right) (b) Design exploration for *IS-PCTracker* (at left) and (c) for *renderProcessing* (at top right)

places) for decision making complying with the syntax of timed colored Petri Nets; black bars are the functions performed along the execution paths (e.g., *getTrackResult*) or selection actions exploring the design space (e.g., *pickOs4* of Figure 3 (b)); and arrows are the direction of the execution paths (e.g., all arrows in Figure 3 (a)) or design decisions (e.g., all arrows in Figure 3 (b) and (c)).

Figure 3 (a) describes the behavioral view of software architecture of the BTS. The enlarged view of Figure 3 (a) and its details may be found in [17]. Figure 3 (b) is a containment component of Figure 3 (a) that represents all possible design alternatives of the *IS-PCTracker* derived from selecting different combinations of orientation sensors (OS) and position sensors (PS). Because of the non-deterministism of timed colored Petri Nets, tokens flowing along the *stub-in* place can be directed to any of seven transitions without preference. Transitions *pickOs1* to *pickOs4* and *pickPs1* to *pickPs3* mean that only one of the sensors is selected. Transition *pickOs&Ps* forces all seven sensors to be possible candidates, and transitions *getOs&Ps1* to *getOs&Ps3* choose two sensors from OS and PS, respectively. There are twelve design alternatives generated due to the non-deterministism. Figure 3 (c) is also a containment component in Figure 3 (a) that shows four *renderProcessing* components appropriate for constructing the BTS. To guarantee high-confidence DRE system construction, analysis and assertion statements, treated as pre-conditions and/or post-conditions of component composition, are written in AspectJ following QoS requirements and woven into the source code of the QoS-UniFrame interpreter, as shown in Figure 4.

```
1   pointcut analyzeQoS() : call(public void *.enableTrans(..)) &&
        args(QoSPar qos);
2   after (QoSPar qos) : analyzeQoS(qos){
3       double qosValue=0.0;    double [] compValue, serviceValue, systemValue;
4       boolean flag = false;
5       Object [] obj = thisJoinPoint.getArgs();
6       JBuilderAtom tran = (JBuilderAtom)obj[0];
7       Vector inConn = tran.getInConnections("Place2Trans");
8       for (int i=0;i<inConn.size();i++){
9           JBuilderConnection place2Trans = (JBuilderConnection)inConn.get(i);
10          JBuilderModel place = (JBuilderModel)place2Trans.getSource();
11          Vector myToken = place.getAtoms(qos.getName());
12          JBuilderAtom token = (JBuilderAtom)myToken.get(0);
13          if (qos.getAnalysisLevel("component")==true){
14             flag = token.getAttribute(qos.getName(), compValue);
15             if (flag) qosValue = compValue[0];
16             if (qosValue > qos.getStrictComponentRequirements())
17                flag = Global.storeEnableTran.removeElement(tran);
18          }
19          if (qos.getAnalysisLevel("service")==true){
20             flag = token.getAttribute(qos.getName(), serviceValue);
21             if (flag) qosValue = serviceValue[0] +
                   token.getAttribute("CurrentService",serviceValue);
22             if (qosValue > qos.getStrictServiceRequirements())
23                flag = Global.storeEnableTrans.removeElement(tran);
24             else token.setAttribute("CurrentService",qosValue);
25          }
26          if (qos.getAnalysisLevel("system")==true)
27          {   /*...similar to the analysis at the service level..*/   }
28  }}
```

Fig. 4. An AspectJ example to analyze and assert QoS requirements

Figure 4 asserts the satisfaction of the lower bound of a QoS parameter at the component, service, and system levels. *enableTrans* is a function that verifies if a transition is enabled to facilitate the reachability tree generation. All enabled transitions are stored in a global vector, called *storeEnableTrans*. The loop from lines 8 to 28 examines all the places connected to the transition. Lines 13 to 18 assure a requirement of the QoS parameter at the component level. If the requirement is not met, the enabled transition will be removed from the vector, as shown in line 17. For the service level QoS requirements analysis, line 21 is the QoS formula computing *how well* the corresponding functional task performs. If the requirement is met, the current value of the QoS parameter is updated (line 24). Conversely, line 23 deletes the transition such that the reachability tree will not generate new nodes related to this transition.

QoS-UniFrame performs design space exploration and elimination during a DRE system construction. The design space exploration approach visually depicts the behavioral view of software architecture at the higher abstraction level. The design space elimination approach analyzes all kinds of QoS requirements by passing various types of QoS parameters (i.e., *QoSPar*) into Figure 4 and by revising the QoS formulae accordingly. Due to the space considerations, please refer to [16] for the stochastic design space elimination using PPCᴇᴀ .

3.3   System Integration

In UniFrame, application domains described in the knowledgebase are assumed to be formalized using a Generative Domain Model [6]. A key aspect of a GDM is the presence of generative *rules* which formalize its structure. GDM's may be constructed for various domains according to the standards. Furthermore, components developed for that domain will also follow these standards. We use Two-Level Grammar (TLG) [4] to express the GDM since TLG's class hierarchy allows convenient expression of abstract component hierarchies and TLG rules may be used to express the generative rules required by the GDM [5]. TLG may be used to provide attribute evaluation and transformation, syntax and semantics processing of languages, parsing, and code generation. All of these are required to use TLG as a specification language for components and domain-specific generative rules.

An example TLG for a sound sensor GDM is:

```
class SoundSensor is subclass of Sensor.
    SoundLocation :: Location.
    SoundVolume :: Float.
    AlarmThreshold :: Float.
    SafeArea :: {Location}*.
    alarm : SoundVolume > AlarmThreshold,
                        SoundLocation not in SafeArea.
end class Sensor.
```

SoundSensor inherits various **Sensor** properties such as the location of the sensor itself and adds additional properties such as the location and volume of the sound detected, the threshold at which an alarm should be sounded, and a safe range to ignore sounds. These type declarations are established by the first level of the TLG and correspond to context-free grammar rules (the : : corresponds to the : : = in traditional BNF notation). Note that **SafeArea** is a set of 0 or more locations. The second level of the grammar contains rules (e.g., in the above TLG, alarm will be true if the sound volume exceeds the alarm threshold and the sound location is not in the set of safe area locations). Additional rules may establish pre-conditions, post-conditions, and invariants, including QoS constraints.

The component development and deployment process starts with a UMM requirements specification of a component, following the established GDM for a particular domain. The UMM specification is informal and indicates the functional (i.e., computational, cooperative and auxiliary aspects) and non-functional (i.e., QoS constraints) features of the component. This informal specification may also be formalized using TLG to provide additional semantics such as rules for validating the component and pre and post-conditions. Validated components are deployed on the network for potential discovery by the URDS. If the component does not meet the requirement specifications then the developer refines either the UMM requirements specification or the design.

MDA[5] Platform Independent Models (PIM's) are based upon the domains and associated logic for the given application. TLG allows these relationships to be expressed via inheritance. If a software engineer wants to design a server component to be used in a distributed embedded system, then he/she should write an informal requirements specification in the form of a UMM describing the characteristics of that component. We use the UMM and domain knowledge base to generate platform independent and platform-specific UMM specifications expressed in TLG (which we will refer to as UMM-PI and UMM-PS, respectively). UMM-PI describes the bulk of the information needed to progress to component implementation. UMM-PS merely indicates the technology of choice (e.g., CORBA[6]). These effectively customize the component model by inheriting from the TLG classes representing the domain with new functionality added as desired. In addition to new functionality, we also impose end-to-end Quality-of-Service expectations for our components (e.g., a specification of the minimum frame-rate in a distributed video streaming application). Both the added functionality and QoS requirements are expressed in TLG so there is a unified notation for expressing all the needed information about components. A translation tool [12] may be used to translate UMM-PI into a PIM represented by a combination of UML and TLG. Note that TLG is needed as an augmentation of standard modeling languages such as UML to define domain logic and other rules that may not be convenient to express in UML directly.

A Platform Specific Model (PSM) is an integration of the PIM with technology domain-specific operations (e.g., in CORBA, J2EE[7], or .NET[8]). These technology domain classes also are expressed in TLG. Each domain contains rules that are specific to that technology, including how to construct glue code for components implemented with that technology. Architectural considerations are also specified, such as how to distinguish client code from server code. PSMs may be expressed in TLG as an inheritance from PIM TLG classes and technology domain TLG classes. This means that PSMs will contain not only the application-domain-specific rules, but also the technology-domain-specific rules. The PSM also maintains the QoS characteristics expressed at the PIM level. Because the model is expressed in TLG, it is executable in the sense that it may be translated into executable code in a high-level language. Furthermore, it supports changes at the model level, or even requirements level if the model is not refined following its derivation from the requirements, because the code generation itself is automated.

---

[5] Model Driven Architecture - http://www.omg.org/mda

[6] Common Object Request Broker Architecture - http://www.omg.org/corba

[7] Java 2 Enterprise Edition - http://java.sun.com/javaee

[8] http://www.microsoft.com/net

An example of high-level rules to generate connector code between client-side and server-side operations is given below:

```
ClientUMM, ServerUMM :: UMM.
ClientOperations, ServerOperations :: {Interface}*.
```

Here it is assumed that UMM specifications exist for both the client and server and that the operations of each are represented as a syntactic interface (although we may wish to include semantic information in practice). The second level of the grammar provides for generating code to map the client operations to the server operations according to a specific component model. Additional rules would specify the details of these mappings. Such rules may use both application-specific and technology-specific domain knowledge.

3.4   Quality Validation

After system integration, a validation procedure demonstrates the functional-ity correctness and quality satisfaction of a DRE system. The Attributed Event Grammar (AEG) approach [1], as shown in Figure 5, is introduced for creat-ing and running test cases in automated black-box testing of real-time reactive systems (e.g., reactive behaviors of triggering rifles).

The purpose of the attribute event grammar is to provide a vehicle for gen-erating event traces (Step 1 in Figure 5). An *event* is any detectable *action* in the environment that could be relevant to the operation of the System Under Test (SUT). For example, an event may be a time interval or a group of sensors triggered by a soldier that has a beginning, an end, and duration. There are two basic relations defined for events: two events may be ordered or one event may appear inside another event. The behavior of the environment (i.e., *event trace*) can be represented as a set of events with these two basic relations de-fined for them. Two events can happen concurrently as well. An event may have attributes associated with it. Each event type may have a different attribute set. Event grammar rules can be decorated with attribute evaluation rules. The

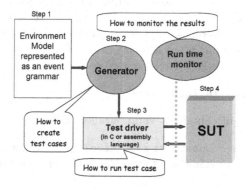

Fig. 5. An Overview of the AEG approach

action is performed immediately after the preceding event is completed. Events usually have timing attributes like begin_time, end_time, and duration. Some of those attributes can be defined in the grammar by appropriate actions, while others may be calculated by appropriate default rules. For example, for a sequence of two events, the begin time of the second event should be generated larger than the end time of the preceding event.

The event traces generated by the generator (Step 2) are not completely random since they fulfill constraints embedded in the environment model. Event attributes provide inputs to the SUT, and the event trace structure facilitates the necessary timing constraints. The test driver (e.g., a C program) can be derived from the given event trace (Step 3). Generated test drivers may interact with the system and adjust the evolving event trace based on the results of that interaction. The environment model can contain descriptions of hazardous states in which SUT could arrive. Thus, it becomes possible to conduct experiments with the SUT in the simulated environment and gather statistical data about the behavior of SUT in order to estimate operational effectiveness, safety and other dependability properties of the SUT (Step 4). By changing the values of parameters of the environment model (e.g., adjusting frequencies of some events in the model and running experiments with the adjusted model), the dependencies between environment parameters and the behavior of the system can be identified. This approach integrates the SUT into the environment model, and uses the model for both testing of the SUT in the simulated environment and assessing risks posed by the SUT. Such an approach may also be applied to a wide range of reactive systems, where environment models can be defined to specify typical scenarios and functional profiles.

The following (oversimplified) example of a missile defense scenario of the BTS demonstrates how to incorporate an interaction with the SUT into AEG. We assume the SUT tracks the launched missile by receiving specific geographical data from the orientation and position sensors of *IS-PCTracker* on the soldier (*send_sensor_signal*() action in the model simulates sensor inputs to the SUT), and at a certain moment makes a decision to fire an anti-missile (i.e., *interceptor*) by generating an output to a corresponding actuator (*SUT_launch_interceptor*()). The catch construct represents an external event generated at runtime by the SUT. The external event listener is active during the execution of a test driver obtained from the generated event trace. This particular external event is broadcast to all corresponding event listeners. The following event grammar specifies a particular set of scenarios for testing purposes.

```
Attack::= { Missile_launch } *
```

The Attack event contains several parallel Missile_launch events.

```
Missile_launch::= Boost_stage / Middle_stage.completed := True/
                  Middle_stage  WHEN (Middle_stage.completed) Boom
```

The Boom event (which happens if the interception attempts have failed) represents an environment event, which the SUT in this case should try to avoid.

```
Middle_stage::= ((CATCH  SUT_launch_interception(hit_coordinates)
                 WHEN(hit_coordinates == Middle_stage.coordinates)
                  [ p(0.1) interception
                    / Middle_stage.completed := False;
                    send_hit_input(Middle_stage .coordinates);
                    BREAK; /   ] END_CATCH   |  move )
                ) *
```

The sequence of move events within Middle_stage may be interrupted by receiving an external event *SUT_launch_counterattack* (*hit_coordinates*) from the SUT. This will suspend the move event sequence and will either continue with event counterattack (with probability 0.1), which simulates the enemy-counterattack event triggered by the SUT, followed by the BREAK command, which terminates the event iteration, or will resume the move sequence. This model allows several counterattack attempts through the same missile launch event. For simplicity it is assumed that there is no delay between receiving the external event and the possible counterattack event.

```
move ::= /adjust( ENCLOSING Middle_stage .coordinates) ;
              send_sensor_signal(ENCLOSING Middle_stage.coordinates);
              move.duration:= 1 sec /
```

This rule provides attribute calculations and sends an input to the SUT. In general, external events (i.e., events generated by the SUT) may be broadcast to several event listeners in the AEG, or may be declared as exclusive and will be consumed by just one of the listeners. If there is not a listener available when an external event arrives, there may be an error in the environment model, which can be detected and reported at the test execution time. To alleviate this problem, AEG may contain a mechanism similar to an exception handler for processing external events which have missed regular event listeners.

The environment model defined by AEG can be used to generate (pseudo) random event traces, where events will have attribute values attached, including time attributes. The events can be sorted according to the timing attributes and the trace may be converted into a test driver, which feeds the SUT with inputs and captures SUT outputs. The functionality of this generated test driver is limited to feeding the SUT inputs and receiving outputs and may be implemented as an efficient C or even assembly language program that meets strict real-time requirements. Only send and catch actions obtained from the event trace are needed to construct the test driver; the rest of the events in the event trace are used as "scaffolds" to obtain the ordering, timing and other attributes of these actions. The generator takes as input the AEG model and outputs random event traces. Necessary actions are then extracted from the trace and assembled into a test driver.

The main advantages of the approach are as follows: 1) The environment model provides for automated generation of a large number of random test drivers; 2) It addresses the regression testing problem: generated test drivers can be saved and reused; 3) The generated test driver contains only a sequence of calls to the SUT, external event listeners for receiving the outputs from SUT, and time delays where needed to fulfill timing constraints, hence it is quite efficient and could be used for real-time test cases; 4) Different environment models for different purposes can be designed; 5) Experiments with the environment model running with the SUT provide a constructive method for quantitative and qualitative software risk assessment [28]; and 6) Environment models can be designed in early stages, before the system design is complete and can be used as an environment simulation tool for tuning the requirements and prototyping efforts. The generated event traces can be considered as use cases that may be used for requirements specification on early stages of system design.

4   Related Work

In recent years, there have been multiple research theories and industrial standards proposed for DRE systems (e.g., TAO [25]). Because various kinds of complexities are omni-present in DRE systems, there are many possible solutions to such complexities that have been introduced at different abstraction levels. Among many tools presented by different institutes or vendors, the following are relevant to UniFrame.

- **RAPIDware:** RAPIDware [18] is a project for component-based development of adaptable and dependable middleware. It uses rigorous software development methods to support interactive applications executed across heterogeneous networked environments throughout the entire software life-cycle. RAPIDware consists of three major techniques to fulfill its objectives: in terms of the design workflow, adaptable design techniques are utilized to design components that comprise crosscutting concerns (e.g., QoS and security); a programming paradigm is introduced to specify QoS requirements, evaluate the system accommodation in terms of different configurations and contexts, and validate functional and non-functional properties via automated checking; and a middleware development toolkit that assists software engineers in implementing and selecting components and composing the entire system.
- **APEX:** Advanced Programming Environment for Embedded Computing Systems (APEX) [29] is a promising infrastructure for software development in the domain of embedded systems, especially for digital signal processing. Similar to UniFrame, APEX consists of five core techniques that cover the entire software life-cycle: the Online Repository for Embedded Software is a web-based repository systems to facilitate component management and retrieval; the COTS Aware Requirement Engineering methodology adapts and analyzes product requirements for any possible artifact reuse during the software development; the Design for Independent Composition and Evaluation techniques decomposes an embedded system into a set of independent subsystems in the design workflow for better modularization; the Automated Modification and Integration of Components utilities compose and customize components by generating glue code using existing design patterns and class

templates, respectively; and the Environment for Automated Simulation and Quality Analysis toolkit simulates the embedded systems and performs the coverage and performance analysis.

There are three key differences between APEX, RAPIDware, and UniFrame. First, UniFrame and RAPIDware are promising in seamlessly integrating a system from homogeneous and heterogeneous components by respectively using automated glue/wrapper code generation and middleware techniques. APEX has not explicitly discussed this issue [29]. Second, in order to reuse components effectively and efficiently, UniFrame introduces a QoS-driven Product Line (QoSPL) [17] framework to assist in constructing a set of DRE systems that share common features in the design and analysis workflows. RAPIDware introduces a middleware development toolkit for selecting and integrating components. APEX mainly concentrates on the reusability analysis at the requirements workflow and exploits the analysis results to the following workflows. Finally, to our best knowledge, the formalisms (e.g., stochastic Petri Nets) that APEX applies mostly concentrate on performance analysis and validation. The usage of formalisms is relatively less mentioned in other workflows. Conversely, both UniFrame and RAPIDware use formalisms throughout the software development.

5   Conclusion and Future Work

Rapid advances in hardware, software, and networking technologies are enabling an unprecedented growth in the capabilities of complex DRE systems. However, the traditional development pressures continue to force the introduction of creative ways to develop systems more rapidly and with less cost. For years, many such creative ways have been derived from the concepts of essential and accidental complexities [3]. UniFrame addresses such complexity by utilizing a unified component and resource discovery technique, a timed colored Petri Nets modeling toolkit, an automatic code generation paradigm, and an event trace approach. Additionally, the last formal method technique enhances the confidence of DRE system construction by specifying event traces, generating and executing test cases, and validating quality issues.

Currently, various prototypes of URDS have been constructed and experimented with. These prototypes contain the features of pro-active discovery, multi-level matching (matching restricted to only a few levels), and customization based on reinforcement learning principles. The results of these experimentations are promising and hence, efforts are underway to customize the URDS to the domain of MARS. The scope of design space exploration and elimination that QoS-UniFrame covers is mostly on software and hardware issues. Design and analysis paradigms to address network latencies are under the situation of local area network communication such that the latencies can be ignored. Enriching the notations of timed colored Petri Nets to comprise various communication approaches and heterogeneous protocols over network is our current plan. In addition, as a part of the prototype of the product line engineering framework, QoS-UniFrame is planned to cohesively collaborate with QoS-driven TLG [15] for DRE product line construction. As for AEG, the first prototype of the test driver generator has been implemented at Naval Postgraduate School and used for several case studies. In the area of AR, extensive work has been done on the registration and calibration aspects that relate the coordinate systems, including those of trackers [26][27][31].

References

1. Auguston, M., Michael, J. B., Shing, M.-T.: Environment Behavior Models for Scenario Generation and Testing Automation. Proc. ICSE Workshop Advances in Model-Based Software Testing (2005)
2. Beugnard, A., et al.:Making Components Contract Aware. IEEE Computer (1999) **32**(7) 38–45
3. Brooks, F. P.: No Silver Bullet: Essence and Accidents of Software Engineering. IEEE Computer (1987) **20** 10–19
4. Bryant, B. R., Lee, B.-S.: Two-Level Grammar as an Object-Oriented Requirements Specification Language. Proc. 35th Hawaii Intl. Conf. System Sciences (2002), `http://www.hicss.hawaii.edu/HICSS_35/HICSSpapers/PDFdocuments/STDSL01.pdf`
5. Bryant, B. R., et al.: Formal Specification of Generative Component Assembly Using Two-Level Grammar. Proc. 14th Intl. Conf. Software Engineering and Knowledge Engineering (2002) 209–212
6. Czarnecki, K., Eisenecker, U. W.: Generative Programming: Methods, Tools, and Applications. Addison-Wesley (2000)
7. Klinker, G. J., et al.: Confluence of Computer Vision and Interactive Graphics for Augmented Reality. Presence: Teleoperators and Virtual Environments (1997) **6**(4) 433–451
8. Heineman, G., Councill, W. T.: Component-Based Software Engineering. Addison-Wesley (2001)
9. Jensen, K.: Coloured Petri Nets V Basic Concepts, Analysis Methods and Practical Use, Volume 1, Basic Concepts. Monographs in Theoretical Computer Science. Springer-Verlag (1997)
10. Kiczales, G., et al.: Getting Started with AspectJ. Communication of the ACM (2001) **44**(10) 59–65
11. Kordon, F., Lemoine, M., eds.: Formal Methods for Embedded Distributed Systems: How to Master the Complexity. Springer-Verlag (2004)
12. Lee, B.-S., Bryant, B. R.: Automation of Software System Development Using Natural Language Processing and Two-Level Grammar. Proc. 2002 Monterey Workshop on Radical Innovations of Software and Systems Engeering in the Future. Springer-Verlag Lecture Notes in Computer Sciences (2004) **2941** 219–223
13. Lee, B.-S., Bryant, B. R.: Applying XML Technology for Implementation of Natural Language Specifications. Intl. Journal of Computer Systems, Science and Engineering (2003) **5** 3–24
14. Liu, S.-H., Mernik, M., Bryant, B. R.: Parameter Control in Evolutionary Algorithms by Domain-Specific Scripting Language PPCEA. Proc. Intl. Conf. Bioinspired Optimization Methods and their Applications (2004) 41–50
15. Liu, S.-H., et al.: Quality of Service-Driven Requirements Analyses for Component Composition: A Two-Level Grammar++ Approach. Proc. 17th Intl. Conf. Software Engineering and Knowledge Engineering (2005) 731–734

16. Liu, S.-H., et al.: QoS-UniFrame: A Petri Net-Based Modeling Approach to Assure QoS Requirements of Distributed Real-time and Embedded Systems. Proc. 12th IEEE Intl. Conf. and Workshop Engineering of Computer Based Systems (2005) 202–209

17. Liu, S.-H., et al.: QoSPL: A QoS-Driven Software Product Line Engineering Framework for Distributed Real-time and Embedded Systems. Proc. 18th Intl. Conf. Software Engineering and Knowledge Engineering (2006) 724–729

18. Michigan State University. RAPIDWare: Component-Based Development of Adaptable and Dependable Middleware. (2006) http://www.cse.msu.edu/rapidware

19. Olson, A. M., et al.: UniFrame: A Unified Framework for Developing Service-Oriented, Component-Based Distributed Software Systems. Service-Oriented Software System Engineering: Challenges and Practices, eds. Stojanovic Z., Dahanayake, A., Idea Group Inc. (2005) 68–87

20. Raje, R. R., et al.: A Unified Approach for the Integration of Distributed Heterogeneous Software Components. Proc. 2001 Monterey Workshop Engineering Automation for Software Intensive System Integration (2001) 109–119

21. Raje, R., et al.: A QoS-based Framework for Creating Distributed and Heterogeneous Software Components. Concurrency and Computation: Practice and Experience (2002) **14** 1009–1034

22. Reicher, T.: A Framework for Dynamically Adaptable Augmented Reality Systems. Doctoral Dissertation, Institutfür Informatik. Technische Universität München (2004)

23. Siram, N. N., et al.: An Architecture for the UniFrame Resource Discovery Service. Proc. 3rd Intl. Workshop Software Engineering and Middleware (2002) 20–35

24. Siram, N. N.: An Architecture for the UniFrame Resource Discovery Service. Master Thesis, Dept. of CIS. Indiana Univ.-Purdue Univ. Indianapolis (2002)

25. TAO (The ACE ORB). Distributed Object Computing (DOC) Group for Distributed Real-time and Embedded Systems. (2006) http://www.cs.wustl.edu/~schmidt/TAO.html

26. Tuceryan, M., Genc, Y., Navab, N.: Single Point Active Alignment Method (SPAAM) for Optical See-through HMD Calibration for Augmented Reality. Presence: Teleoperators and Virtual Environments (2002) **11**(3) 259–276

27. Tuceryan, M., et al.: Calibration Requirements and Procedures for a Monitor-based Augmented Reality System. IEEE Trans. on Visualization and Computer Graphics (1995) **1**(3) 255–273

28. Tummala, H. et al.: Implementation and Analysis of Environment Behavior Models as a Tool for Testing Real-Time, Reactive System. Proc. 2006 IEEE Intl. Conf. on System of Systems Engineering (2006) 260–265

29. University of Texas at Dallas. APEX: Advanced Programming Environment for Embedded Computing Systems. (2006) http://www.utdallas.edu/research/esc

30. Wang, N., et al.: QoS-enabled Middleware. Middleware for Communications. Wiley and Sons (2003)

31. Whitaker, R., et al.: Object Calibration for Augmented Reality. Proc. Eurographics '95 (1995) 15–27

32. Zaremski, A. Wing, J.: Specification Matching of Software Components. ACM Trans. on Software Engineering (1995) **6**(4) 333–369

Providing Dependable Services with Unreliable SoCs—The DECOS Approach

Hermann Kopetz

Institut für Technische Informatik
Vienna University of Technology
A1040 Wien, Treitlstraße 3, Austria
hk@vmars.tuwien.ac.at

Abstract. DECOS (Dependable Components and Systems) is an EU-funded integrated research project (IP) with the goal to develop a framework and an associated design methodology for the component-based design of dependable embedded systems. The core of DECOS is based on the Time-Triggered Architecture (TTA), a distributed architecture for high-dependability real-time applications. In the first part of this paper the design flow of DECOS from the Platform Independent Model (PIM) to the Platform Specific Model (PSM) is discussed and the DECOS execution environment is introduced. In the second part the fault-tolerance mechanisms of DECOS are explained. After a deliberation of the fault hypothesis, the support for the implementation of triple-modular redundancy (TMR) is presented.

Keywords: Dependable Systems, Time-triggered Architecture, Embedded Systems, Design Methodology, Fault Tolerance.

1 Introduction

DECOS (Dependable Components and Systems) is an Integrated Research Project of the sixth European Framework program. It is the objective of DECOS to develop an *integrated* architecture and an associated design methodology for the component-based design and implementation of large dependable embedded systems. The interactions of the components are realized by the exchange of time-triggered and event-triggered messages across interfaces to a real-time communication system.

DECOS is based on the Time-Triggered Architecture (TTA), which has been developed at the *Institut für Technische Informatik* of the Vienna University of Technology during the past twenty years. The TTA [1] is an *integrated distributed* computer architecture, designed to provide a continuous *timely* service with an MBTF of better than 10^9 hours in the presence of component failures, *provided that* the occurrences of component failures are in agreement with the stated fault hypothesis. The TTA is intended for applications that require utmost availability even in the presence of an arbitrary fault in any of its components: examples of such applications are the control of a nuclear power plant, the flight control

F. Kordon and J. Sztipanovits (Eds.): Monterey Workshop 2005, LNCS 4322, pp. 248–257, 2007.

system of an airplane, or a computer-based brake-control system within an automobile that does not contain a mechanical backup. Such a high reliability can only be achieved by the provision of redundancy in the hardware, since the observed component (chip) failure rates are orders of magnitudes lower[2] than the required system reliability. Every redundancy scheme is based on a number of assumptions — the *fault hypothesis* — about the types and frequency of faults that the system is supposed to handle. In case that all fault-handling mechanisms are perfect and cover all scenarios that are listed in the fault hypothesis, the probability of system failure is reduced to *assumption coverage*[3], i.e., the probability that the assumptions made in the fault hypothesis are met by reality. The fault hypothesis of any fault-tolerant system is thus a critical document in the design process.

One common technique to implement fault-masking by redundancy is *triple-modular redundancy* (TMR). In the TMR approach three synchronized deterministic replicas of every critical component form a new unit — the fault-tolerant unit (FTU) — that masks the arbitrary failure of any one of its three components. An incoming message is distributed to all three units of the FTU and the result message (and the internal state) is output to three voters that make majority decisions based on at least two identical results. If one of the components produces no result or a result that is different from the result of the other two components, this component is considered to have failed. TMR structures will only succeed if the redundant components are synchronized and fail *independently*. Correlated failures can occur because of external causes (a single external event, e.g., a lightning stroke that causes the failure of more than one component) or by error propagation, i.e. an erroneous component sends a faulty message to an up to that instant correctly operating component and thus corrupts the internal state of this component. The issues of fault isolation and error propagation of replicated components are thus of critical importance in the design of an architecture that is intended to support fault-masking by TMR.

This paper is structured as follows. In the next Section two we introduce the model-driven design methodology developed in DECOS. DECOS starts by decomposing a large application into a number of nearly autonomous *Distributed Application Subsystems* (DAS). The Platform Independent Model (PIM) of a DAS is then transformed into the Platform Specific Model (PSM) and allocated to the DECOS execution environment. Section three presents the DECOS execution environment, which is based on the TTA. Section four focuses on the fault-tolerance mechanisms of DECOS and explains how the implementation of triple-modular redundancy is supported by DECOS.

2   Model-Driven Design in DECOS

In DECOS we assume that a large real-time application can be decomposed into many different nearly autonomous *Distributed Application Subsystems* (DAS). Examples of a DAS in the automotive context are: the DAS that performs vehicle dynamics control, the entertainment DAS or the DAS for the body electronics control functions (e.g. controlling the light, access control, air conditioning, etc.). From the functional point of view every DAS can be considered to be nearly independent from every other DAS. The communication among DASes, if needed, is realized via well-defined interfaces, the inter-DAS gateways. In many automotive applications, every DAS is provided with its own dedicated hardware base — we call such an architecture a *federated architecture*. In a federated architecture there is minimal sharing of hardware resources among DASes. As a consequence of this *non-sharing of hardware resources* there are today more than fifty different electronic control units (ECUs) in a premium car. An architecture which is intended to support the sharing of hardware resources among the nearly independent DASes is called an *integrated architecture*. DECOS is intended to provide such an integrated execution environment, where a physical ECU can support more than one DAS.

2.1   The Platform Independent Model (PIM)

The design methodology of DECOS assumes that in a first step an application is partitioned into the set of its nearly independent distributed application subsystems(DAS). Each DAS is developed independently from any other DAS and represented as a network, where the nodes are considered to be computational units (we call them *jobs*) that have an internal state, and accept and produce messages, while the links are communication channels for the timely transport of messages between the jobs. A DAS can be represented at different levels of abstractions. The *Platform Independent Model* (PIM) of a DAS is a high-level abstract representation that does not make any assumption about the physical execution environment or about the physical communication links among jobs. We call a job at the PIM level an *I-job*.

Since jobs must meet deadlines and can contain state, a model of time must be part of any job representation. In DECOS we use a *single model of time*, the *physical sparse real-time*[4] of the TTA, and use this model of time for all representations of jobs. The PIM model of a job, the I-job, must thus express all timing information,such as the instant of expecting a message or the instant of sending a message in the metric of physical real-time. The interface where a job provides its services to other jobs is called the linking interface (LIF). The LIF specification of all I-jobs of task consists of the operational specification and the meta-level specification, as discussed in [5]. The operational specification contains the syntactic message specification in the value domain and the temporal domain, while the meta-level specification assigns meaning to the information chunks that have been established by the operational specification.

2.2   The Platform Specific Model (PSM)

In order to be able to execute a job and to estimate the concrete hardware resources (processing, memory) for the execution of a job, a concrete hardware platform, the target platform, must be selected. In the next phase the *I-job* must be transformed into a representation that can be executed on the selected target platform. We call this platform-specific model of a job the *S-job* representation.

The concrete form of the S-job representation depends on the resource characteristics of the selected target platform. If this target platform consists of a CPU with a given operating system and middleware that supports a specific application program interface (API) then the S-job must contain the commands that can be executed by this specific CPU and must communicate with its environment across the given API. If the selected hardware platform is an FPGA, then the S-Job will be represented in a form that can be loaded directly into the FPGA.

As soon as the S-job representation of a job is available, the concrete hardware requirements (processing time, memory) for the execution of the job are available. These concrete hardware requirements are needed in order to be able to allocate the S-job to a given node.

3   The DECOS Execution Environment

A physical DECOS micro-component consists of a host subsystem, a communication controller to a time-triggered core network and a local interface subsystem to the environment as depicted in Fig. 1. The host-subsystem can be a computer with a real-time operating system, middleware and the application software, an FPGA or a dedicated hardware subsystem a shown in Fig. 2. In the TTA no assumptions are made about the internal structure of a micro-component. Only the (message) interfaces of the micro-components to the TT network musts be fully specified in the domains of time and value

The temporal properties and the value properties of the Platform Message Interface (PMI) are independent of the concrete implementation of the micro-component. It is thus possible to exchange one implementation option by another without any modification of the interface properties of the micro-component.

The host subsystem of the node is connected to the *inner port* of the communication controller, as shown in Fig. 1. A communication channel of the time-triggered core network ends at an *outer port* of the *communication controller* of a micro-component. The communication controller contains a memory for the storage of incoming and outgoing event (queue) and state messages realized as

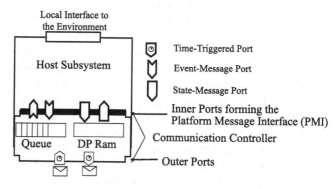

Fig. 1. DECOS micro-component with host subsystemand communication controller

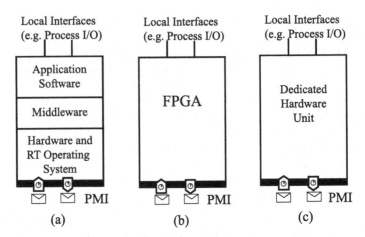

Fig. 2. Different implementation options for a Micro-component

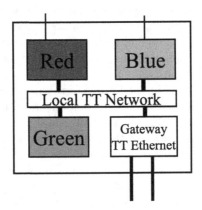

Fig. 3. Multi-core node of the TTA, consisting of four micro-components (including a gateway to TT Ethernet)

dual-ported RAM module. Whenever the global time reaches a (periodic) instant that has been assigned to the outer port, a pending message will be sent to the time-triggered core network. Incoming messages are delivered to the host across the inner ports either in the *information push mode* (by raising an interrupt) or in the *information pull mode* after the host has send a request for the delivery of the next message. The interface between the host computer and the inner ports of the communication interface subsystem is called the *Platform Message Interface* (PMI). The PMI is the most important interface of the DECOS architecture.

The communication channel between the different I-jobs of a task is realized by an overlay network on top a time-triggered core network. The time-triggered core network guarantees non-interference (in the temporal domain) of the communication channels allocated to different DASes.

Since a DECOS node will normally provide the resources for a number of S-jobs from different nearly independent DASes, a DECOS host must provide an encapsulated partition for every S-job and a (virtual) communication channel with known temporal properties for the communication among the S-jobs of a given DAS. The partitioned execution environment within a DECOS node can be furnished either by a real-time operating system on a scalar processor that provides protected partitions and *a priori* fixed processor capacity for the timely execution of each S-job or by a given dedicated core (CPU and memory) of a multi-core physical node. We call such a dedicated core a micro-component. The communication among the micro-components of a multi-core physical node can be realized by another time-triggered network, as depicted in Figure 3. Eventually, such a node can be implemented as a single system-on-a-chip (SoC).

4 Fault Tolerance in DECOS

In the following paragraphs we discuss the fault-masking mechanisms of DECOS with respect to hardware faults. Since DECOS is based on TTA [1], the fault-tolerance mechanisms of DECOS rely on the fault-tolerance mechanisms of the TTA. In the TTA it is assumed that the hardware design and the basic fault-handling mechanisms are free of design faults.

4.1 Fault-Containment Regions

The first step in the specification of a fault hypothesis is concerned with the establishment of a the fault-containment regions (FCR), i.e. the units of failure. An FCR is a subsystem that is considered to fail independently from any other FCR. If we must tolerate the physical destruction of a hardware component (e.g., in an accident), then different FCRs must be in different physical locations, i.e. the computer system must be distributed. In the TTA we assume that every node of the distributed system forms an FCR.

4.2 Failure Modes and Frequency of Faults

In the next step we must specify the *critical failure modes* of FCRs. Any restriction of the tolerated failure modes must be considered as an additional assumption that has a negative effect on the assumption coverage. In the optimal case no restriction of the failure modes are made, i.e., a failing component can manifest an arbitrary behavior. We consider a failure mode of an FCR as *critical*, if it impacts the remaining correct nodes of the distributed system in such a way that the functionality or the consistency of the distributed computing base among the nodes that are outside the affected FCR is lost. We focus on a single fault during a fault-recovery interval Δd. After the recovery interval Δd the architecture has recovered from the consequences of this fault and can tolerate a further fault (provided enough resources remain operational). We define a set of nodes as Δd-*consistent* if Δd time units after the occurrence of failure all remaining correct nodes have the same view about this failure event.

Permanent Failures: In the TTA it is assumed that a single node, which can be implemented on a single SoC, can fail in an arbitrary failure mode without disturbing the correct operation of the other nodes that are not affected by the fault. A restricted failure-mode model would require two independent FCRs (one FCR monitoring the behavior of the other FCR) which cannot be housed on the same die because of the many common mode elements of a single die such as power supply, mask, production process, physical space. If the fault is transient, then the failed node is assumed to recover within a given recovery interval.

Massive Transient Disturbances: Another important fault class in a distributed embedded system, particularly in the automotive domain, is concerned with massive transient disturbances, e.g., those caused by electromagnetic emission (EMI). A massive transient disturbance can cause the temporary loss of communication among otherwise correct nodes that reside in different FCRs or cause state-corruptions within more than one node. Based on available failure data [2] it is reasonable to assume that the multiple correlated faults produced by a massive transient disturbance are transient, i.e., that the hardware is not faulted by the massive transient disturbance. In such a situation the TTA provides the core service of prompt error detection in order that the nodes may take some local corrective action until the transient disturbance has disappeared and the communication service and the consistency of the nodes is reestablished by a fast restart. For example, [6] report that in an automotive environment a temporary loss of communication of up to 50 msec can be tolerated by freezing the actuators in the positions that were taken before the onset of the transient disturbance. The probability of occurrence of massive transient disturbances must be reduced by proper quality engineering, e.g., by shielding the cables or installing fiber optics instead of copper. In a safety-critical distributed system massive transient disturbances must be rare events. From the point of view of the communication system, fast detection of a transient disturbance and fast recovery after the transient has disappeared are important.

Frequency of Faults: The assumptions about the frequency of fault occurrence are depicted in Table 1. We distinguish between transient failures and permanent failures as well as between fail-silent failures and Byzantine failures.

Whereas the data in the first row — permanent failures — is derived from extensive field data,the assumptions of row two, three and four are not as well

Table 1. Assumed failure rates

Type of Failure	Failure Rate	Source
permanent fail silent	< 100 FIT (MTTF > 1 000 000 hours)	Field data from the automotive industry[2]
transient fail silent	< 100 000 FIT (MTTF > 1000 hours)	SEUs caused by neutrons[7]
permanent Byzantine	< 2 FIT (MTTF > 5 000 000 hours)	Fault injection experiments[8]
transient Byzantine	< 2 000 FIT (MTTF > 50 000 hours)	Fault injection experiments[8]

supported by experimental data and field evidence. In particular it is very difficult to find a good estimate for the transient failure rates, because these failure
are very dependent upon the environmental conditions (e.g., geometry of the
setup determines the susceptibility with respect to EMI, geographical position
and altitude determines the rate of SEUs etc..) of the unit under observation.
The failure rates of Table 1 are our best estimates and are used in our reliability
models to calculate the service availability of the TTA.

4.3 Fault Masking by Triple-Modular Redundancy (TMR)

DECOS, which is based on the TTA [1], performs error handling in the time
domain at the architecture level and error handling in the value domain by
triple modular redundancy (TMR) of the host-subsystems.

The architecture-level error handling in the temporal domain is enabled by the
a priori knowledge about the permitted sending instants of the nodes, which is
a characteristic element of the time-trigged architecture. Whenever a node sends
a message at an instant which is not in agreement with the predefined sending
schedule, the node is classified as faulty. The communication system contains
a special device, a *guardian*, which contains knowledge about the predefined
sending schedules and blocks any untimely message (In Fig. 4 the guardian is
part of the TT Ethernet [9] switch). The guardian thus transforms an untimely
message into an omitted message, i.e., an omission failure, which is a fail-silent
failure.

Figure 4 depicts a triple-modular redundant (TMR) configuration of five nodes
of DECOS. Each node supports a number of different DASes. For example the
first node supports a pink, a blue and a green DAS and a gateway to TT Ethernet. Let us assume that the services of two DASes, the blue DAS and the red
DAS , are safety-critical and have to protected by TMR. We will instantiate the
replicated micro-components of these safety-critical DASes on three nodes (on
node one, two, and four for the blue DAS, and on nodes three, four, and five
for the red DAS) under the assumption that each node forms an independent

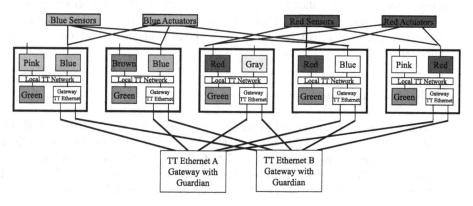

Fig. 4. TMR configuration in the TTA with the nodes depicted in Fig. 2

fault-containment region[10]. The communication between the nodes is realized by two replicated external deterministic communication channels via the TT service of an external network, e.g., TT Ethernet[9]. It is assumed that the internal state of each red DAS micro-component is periodically distributed to the other two red DAS micro-components for the purpose of outvoting a transient error in the internal state. The same must hold true for the blue DAS. The duration of the period of the internal state distribution determines the repair time after the occurrence of a transient fault and is an important parameter of any reliability model. Replicated sensors input the information from the environment to the respective micro-components. In order to establish a consistent view of the environment at all replicas, an agreement protocol has be executed that establishes an agreed value at an agreed point of the sparse time base[4] for every replicated input data element. The output is delivered to fault-tolerant voting actuators. In the depicted configuration, the failure of any single device (input, output, SoC, and any one of the two communication subsystems) is tolerated. A prerequisite for such a fault-tolerant structure to mask an error in any one fault-containment region is the availability of a global notion of time and the timely and deterministic behavior of the communication service among the SoCs.

There is an additional benefit in such an architecture approach if the nodes are formed by giga-scale SoCs. It is expected that in technologies beyond 90nm feature size, single-event upsets (SEU) will severely impact field-level product reliability, not only for embedded memory, but for logic and latches as well[11,12]. This effect can be mitigated by providing a triple-modular redundant structure, consisting of three SoCs, for masking transient, intermittent, and permanent SoC faults.

5   Conclusion

DECOS provides the framework for the component-based implementation of large distributed system, starting with the platform independent model of a distributed application subsystem and supporting the transforming to the platform specific model and the allocation to the given distributed execution environment. The architecture inherent mechanisms for fault-masking by triple modular redundancy enable the component-based implementation of high-dependability applications.

Acknowledgments

This work has been supported in part the European Integrated Project DECOS under project number IST-511764, by the Austrian FIT IT project on TT Ethernet under project number 808197/1729-KA/HN, by the European Network of Excellence ARTIST II under project number IST-004527. Many discussions with within our research group at the TU Vienna are warmly acknowledged.

References

1. H. Kopetz and G. Bauer. The time-triggered architecture. In *Proceedings of the IEEE*, volume 91, pages 112–126, January 2003.
2. B. Pauli, A. Meyna, and P. Heitmann. Reliability of electronic components and control units in motor vehicle applications. VDI-Bericht 1415, Verein Deutscher Ingenieure (VDI), Düsseldorf, 1998.
3. D. Powell. Failure mode assumptions and assumption coverage. In *Int. Symp. on Fault-Tolerant Computing (FTCS-22)*, Boston, MA, 1992.
4. H. Kopetz. Sparse time versus dense time in distributed real-time systems. In *Proceedings of the 12th International Conference on Distributed Computing Systems*, Yokohama, Japan, June 1992.
5. H. Kopetz and N. Suri. Compositional design of RT systems: A conceptual basis for specification of linking interfaces. *6th IEEE International Symposium on Object-Oriented Real-Time Computing (ISORC03), May 14 - 16, 2003, Hokkaido, Japan*, May. 2003.
6. G. Heiner and T. Thurner. Time-triggered architecture for safety-related distributed real-time systems in transportation systems. In *Proceedings of the The 28th Annual Fault Tolerant Computing Symposium (FTCS 28)*, page 402, Munich, Germany, 1998.
7. P. Hazucha and C. Svensson. Impact of CMOS technology scaling on the atmospheric neutron soft error rate. *IEEE Transactions on Nuclear Science*, 47(6):2586–2594, 2000.
8. A. Ademaj, G. Bauer, H. Sivencrona, and J. Torin. Evaluation of fault handling of the time-triggered architecture with bus and star topology. In *IEEE International Conference on Dependable Systems and Networks (DSN 2003)*, pages 123–132, San Francisco, USA, June 2003.
9. H. Kopetz, A. Ademaj, P. Grillinger, and K. Steinhammer. The Time-Triggered Ethernet (TTE) design. In *Proceedings of the 8rd International Symposium on Object-Oriented Real-Time Distributed Computing (ISORC)*, pages 22–33, Seattle, WA, USA, May 2005.
10. H. Kopetz. Fault containment and error detection in the time-triggered architecture. *The Sixth International Symposium on Autonomous Decentralized Systems (ISADS 2003)*, pages 139–146, April 2002.
11. C. Constantinescu. Impact of deep submicron technology on dependability of vlsi circuits. In *IEEE International Conference on Dependable Systems and Networks (DSN 2002)*, pages 205–214, June 2002.
12. Semiconductor Industry Association. International technology roadmap for semiconductors, 2003. 2003 edition.

Modeling and Verification of Cooperative Self-adaptive Mechatronic Systems*

Holger Giese**

Software Engineering Group, University of Paderborn
Warburger Str. 100, D-33098 Paderborn, Germany
hg@upb.de

Abstract. The advanced mechatronic systems of the next generation are expected to behave more intelligently than today's systems by building communities of autonomous agents which exploit local and global networking to enhance their functionality. Such mechatronic systems will therefore include dynamic structural adaptation at the network level and complex real-time coordination protocols to adjust their behavior to the changing system goals leading to cooperative self-adaptation in a safe and coordinated manner. In this paper the Mechatronic UML approach and its concepts for compositional modeling and verification of crucial safety properties for cooperative self-adaptive mechatronic systems are outlined. Based on former results for the compositional verification of the real-time coordination and safe rule-based dynamic structural adaptation, we present in this paper a systematic compositional verification scheme which permits to verify the safety of real-time systems with compositional adaptation and an *a priori* unbounded number of structural configurations.

1 Introduction

Advanced mechatronic systems [1] today start to combine traditional mechanical and electrical engineering with technologies from software engineering in order to provide reliable technical solutions for complex real-world problems.

The advanced mechatronic systems of the next generation are expected to behave more intelligently than today's systems by building communities of autonomous agents which exploit local and global networking to enhance their functionality in a scalable and fault tolerant manner.

Such advanced networked mechatronic systems will include dynamic structural adaptation of the networking topology and complex real-time coordination which enables them to adjust their behavior at run-time to the changing system goals. These systems thus support the coordinated self-optimization of networked

---

* This work was developed in the course of the Special Research Initiative 614 – Self-optimizing Concepts and Structures in Mechanical Engineering – University of Paderborn, and was published on its behalf and funded by the Deutsche Forschungsgemeinschaft.
** Currently a visiting professor at the Hasso-Plattner-Institut, University of Potsdam.

F. Kordon and J. Sztipanovits (Eds.): Monterey Workshop 2005, LNCS 4322, pp. 258–280, 2007.

systems [2], which goes beyond traditional self-adaptive systems (cf. [3,4,5]) that only operate locally.

The development of self-adaptive systems can be viewed from two perspectives, either top-down when considering an individual system, or bottom-up when considering cooperative systems. Individual self-adaptive systems evaluate their own global behavior and change it when the evaluation indicates that they are not accomplishing what they were intended to do, or when better functionality or performance is possible. Self-adaptive systems can on the other hand also work bottom-up when operating in a cooperative style. Such *cooperative self-adaptive systems* are composed of a large number of components that interact according to local and often rather simple rules (in an extreme form also referred to as self-coordination). The global behavior of the system emerges from these local interactions, and it is difficult to deduce properties of the global system by studying only the local properties of its parts.

One major problem which has to be addressed when developing cooperative self-adaptive mechatronic systems is the real-time coordination and the potentially dynamic structural adaptation of the communication and cooperation structures. As mechatronic systems are often safety-critical applications, the development of software controlling these systems consequently has to undergo a rigorous process including the prevention of faults employing adequate and well-founded modeling concepts and the detection of critical faults due to the verification of crucial safety properties. Thus, we do not only require a suitable solution to model both the integration between the continuous and discrete real-time processing as well as the networking with structural adaptation, but also means for its proper verification.

In order to address the verification of those real-time coordination features that result from the structural adaptation at run-time, techniques such as testing the system in several test environments and in its operation environment are not sufficient any more due to the rather incomplete coverage of possible design faults. Current formal verification approaches, which provide the required more complete coverage at least in principle, on the other hand do not scale for the considered class of systems: While model checking approaches can prove safety properties for models of moderate size only, semi-automatic approaches such as theorem proving require usually not available advanced proof skills.

In this paper the MECHATRONIC UML approach and its concepts for compositional modeling and verification of crucial safety properties for cooperative self-adaptive mechatronic systems are outlined. Based on former results for the compositional verification of the real-time coordination [6] and safe rule-based dynamic structural adaptation [7,8], we present in this paper a systematic compositional verification scheme which permits to verify the safety of real-time systems with compositional adaptation and an *a priori* unbounded number of structural configurations.

We first employ an application example to outline the most important system characteristics as well as resulting challenges for the design of advanced networked mechatronic systems in Section 2. Then the employed MECHATRONIC UML approach is sketched in Section 3 before the modeling of the network part of the application example is outlined in Section 4. We then introduce the underlying formal model in Section 5 and then describe the underlying compositional reasoning scheme in Section 6. The paper closes with an overview about the related work in Section 7 and a final conclusion and outlook on future work.

2   Cooperative Self-adaptive Mechatronic Systems

We introduce in this section the specific characteristics and challenges we have to face when developing cooperative self-adaptive mechatronic systems, starting with a motivating example.

2.1   Application Example: The RailCab System

As a concrete example for an advanced mechatronic system with cooperative self-adaptation, we consider the Paderborn-based RailCab research project (http://www-nbp.upb.de/en), which aims at combining a passive track system with intelligent shuttles that operate individually and make independent and de-centralized operational decisions. The project is funded by a number of German research organizations. It has built a test track in the scale of 1:2.5 such that the ideas of the project can be evaluated in real operation (cf. Fig. 1 (a)).

The vision of the RailCab project is to provide the comfort of individual traffic concerning scheduling and on-demand availability of transportation as well as in-dividually equipped cars on the one hand and the cost and resource effectiveness of public transport on the other hand. The modular railway system combines sophisticated undercarriages with the advantages of new actuation techniques

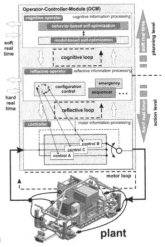

(a)   (b)

Fig. 1. (a) The test track and shuttle prototype of the RailCab project – (b) The OCM architecture and its elements

as employed in the Transrapid (http://www.transrapid.de/en) to increase passenger comfort while still enabling high speed transportation and (re)using the existing railway tracks.

One particular crucial design goal is the minimization of the energy consumption. To be competitive w.r.t. traditional train systems, the shuttles must be able to reduce the energy consumption due to air resistance by building temporary convoys whenever suitable. Such convoys are built on-demand and require a small distance between the different shuttles such that a high reduction of air resistance is achieved.

The coordination between the shuttles is realized with wireless communication. The shuttles have to change their behavior depending on their current position and role within a convoy. A rear shuttle will, for example, hold the distance to the front shuttle on a constant level, while if operating independently the constant velocity would be the control goal. The feedback controller which controls the acceleration of the shuttle has thus to be dynamically exchanged at run-time. A shuttle also has to reduce the intensity of braking when another one drives in a short distance behind it to exclude any rear-end collision when braking.

The design of the shuttles thus has to ensure a safe coordination when building or breaking convoys by dynamic structural adaptation. The switching between different controllers at run-time must guarantee safety and stability. Due to the safety-critical character of the resulting real-time coordination between speed control units of the shuttles, appropriate techniques to provide these guarantees which can be employed when building the control software of the shuttles are required.

The outlined shuttle system is well suited to identify the essential challenges of the future generation of cooperative self-adaptive mechatronic systems and will thus be further employed to outline them and present the proposed approach. For sake of brevity, we will consider only an oversimplified version of the convoy building problem.

2.2 Design Challenges

As illustrated by the building of convoys in the application example, crucial requirements for mechatronic systems are the tight integration of quasi-continuous and discrete control software and that a proper realization of complex real-time coordination and dynamic structural adaptation by the software has to be achieved at the network level. We further explain these challenges looking at the micro- and macro-architecture of networked mechatronic systems.

Micro-Architecture. The typical functions and requirements for a single subsystem in an advanced mechatronic systems can be exemplified using, for example, the internal subsystem architecture named Operator-Controller Model (OCM) depicted in Fig. 1 (b) (cf. [9]).

(1) On the lowest level of the OCM, there is the controller including an arbitrary number of alternative control strategies. Within the OCM's innermost loop, the currently active control strategy processes measurements and produces control signals. As it directly affects the plant, it is called motor loop. The

software processing is necessarily quasi-continuous, including smooth switching between the alternative control strategies which are described with some form of differential equations or difference equations.

(2) The controller is controlled by the reflective operator, in which monitoring and controlling routines are executed. The reflective operator operates in a predominantly event-oriented manner and thus usually includes a control automaton with a number of discrete control states and transitions between them. It does not access the actuators of the system directly, but may modify the controller and initiate the switch between different control strategies. Furthermore it serves as the connecting element to the cognitive level of the OCM. In the top-level OCMs the reflective operator is also responsible for the real-time coordination with other top-level OCMs.

(3) This topmost level of the OCM is called the cognitive operator. On this level, the system can gather information concerning itself and its environment and use it for the improvement of its own behavior. This element is optional and thus might not be present in all subsystems.

Macro-Architecture. In general, the OCM-hierarchy defines locally within a complex, autonomous mechatronic systems a strictly hierarchical control flow, i.e. each level tries to execute control as much as possible locally but whether reconfiguration is to be executed is decided on the next higher level. The OCM hierarchy can be nested, i.e. the each level may include a full-fledged OCM.

No such hierarchy exists anymore when it comes to the level of freely interacting software agents. This is the level above the OCM hierarchy where agents exchange information but no central control is defined. As an example, consider the different shuttles, stations and possibly job brokers of the RailCab project. These agents interact with each other only in a local context and adapt their architecture dynamically as required when building convoys.

Taking the outlined requirements for advanced networked mechatronic systems at the micro- and macro-architecture level into account, we have to address the following main challenges:

(a) A suitable approach for hierarchical structures of OCMs is required which supports besides hybrid behavior also the safe reconfiguration of subsystems in order to support the reliable self-adaptation of the OCMs.

(b) For the level of freely interacting software agents, the approach must in addition provide means to model and analyze the flexible but safe real-time coordination between the autonomous mechatronic agents.

(c) Besides the real-time coordination, at the level of freely interacting software agents, means to specify and analyze the dynamic structural adaptation also have to be provided.

(d) Finally, the approach must integrate the concepts a-c for hierarchical OCM structures, flexible real-time coordination of software agents, and safe dynamic structural adaptation in such a manner that the safe hierarchical reconfiguration, safe real-time coordination, and safe dynamic structural adaptation can still be guaranteed.

3   Mechatronic UML

We outline in this section how we address the identified challenges by the model driven MECHATRONIC UML development approach which combines domain specific modeling and refinement techniques with verification based on compositional model checking of the real-time behavior and the checking of structural inductive invariants for the dynamic structural adaptation.

The MECHATRONIC UML approach addresses the outlined challenges providing the following essential solutions:

(1) It at first suggests modeling the *hierarchical agent structure* of the software within a single mechatronic agent using a refined UML 2.0 component model including the detailed definition of ports which is refined to define a proper integration between discrete and continuous control such that the reconfiguration of hierarchical component systems can be described in a modular manner [10]. A conceptual mapping to a reconfigurable variant of hybrid/timed automata then permits to check in a modular manner that only safe reconfiguration steps are present in a given model [2]. This solution addresses challenge (a).

(2) Our approach in addition addresses the *real-time coordination* (challenge (b)) by supporting a compositional proceeding for modeling and compositional verification of the real-time software when using the UML 2.0 component model with ports and connectors as well as pattern with rigorously defined real-time behavior [6]. Timed automata, a related notion of refinement, and the overlapping of the pattern and component behavior at the ports resp. roles is employed to decompose the verification problem into number of checks which have to be performed for local models only such that scalability is achieved (cf. [11]). At this level, additional means for the compositional safety analysis [12] and constructive improvement of dependability by means of fault tolerance techniques [13] are provided.

(3) The *structural adaptation* of the complex topology of the technical system as outlined in challenge (c) is described by object diagrams. Using an extended notion of UML object diagrams named Story Pattern [14], we can then define the structural adaptation rules for the networked mechatronic agents which operate on their local context only (cf. [15]). The resulting dynamic structural adaptation is formalized by graph transformation systems. Currently the verification of crucial safety properties using model checking for models of moderate size and automatic checking of structural invariants for infinite state system is supported (cf. [7,8]).

The former three modeling and analysis solutions are complemented by support for the generation of code for hard real-time processing for the employed UML concepts [16,17], which guarantees that the high level properties which have been proven in the separate modeling views are preserved by the code generation.

In addition to the provided modeling and analysis solutions, their proper integration into a whole systematic and correct compositional reasoning framework as stressed in challenge (d) is required.

We have addressed the integration of the concepts for hierarchical OCM structures and flexible interaction of software agents that enables the independent verification of the safe hierarchical reconfiguration and the safe real-time coordination in an informal manner already in [18,2].

In this paper we will focus on the formal reasoning framework which allows us to combine the developed solution for the compositional modeling and verification of the real-time coordination and the solution for the verification of structural invariants for the rule-based structural adaptation.

4   Modeling

In the following, we will describe our approach in more detail using the beforehand introduced RailCab example which combines our results about the real-time coordination presented in [6] and the results about the safe rule-based reconfiguration presented in [7,8]. The outlined scheme will then later be generalized into the required compositional reasoning scheme for cooperative self-adaptive mechatronic systems.

4.1   Basic Ontology and Hazard Definition

We at first employ UML class diagrams and UML object diagrams to describe all possible system configurations and possible hazards.

Ontology. We start with an *ontology* model of the considered system using UML class diagrams. For our example, the physical entities of the system in form of shuttle agents and tracks and their relationships are specified in the class diagram depicted in Figure 2. We use tracks to denote short segments with room for only a single Shuttle and their successor association connects them into a directed track layout. The current position of a Shuttle is described by the association on while the go association encodes the potential movement towards a Track which cannot be stopped (due to the physical laws). We do here not further discuss the details of the physical attributes of the Shuttle such as the actual position pos on the Tracks or the physical laws for sake of brevity.

Hazards. UML object diagrams can be used to model concrete configurations as instances of the ontology. We can therefore specify unsafe conditions, i.e., configurations that should not occur during when the system is executed such as *hazards* or *accidents*.

At this stage usually all *hazards* and *accidents* which have to be taken into account have to be defined. We restrict our attention for our example to collisions

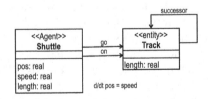

Fig. 2. Class diagram of the example ontology

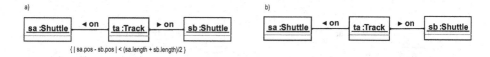

a)   b)

$\{ \, | \, \text{sa.pos} - \text{sb.pos} \, | < (\text{sa.length} + \text{sb.length})/2 \, \}$

Fig. 3. The Collision accident for two shuttles

between shuttles which can be characterized by two shuttles which are located on the same track (see Fig. 3 a)).

Behavior. The continuous behavior is annotated in the ontology of Figure 2 in form of a differential equation $d/dt \, pos = speed$ and define the continuous change of the attributes over time as long as no discrete behavioral step is executed.

To model also the discrete behavior of the system, we employ *Story patterns*, an extension of UML object diagrams based on the theory of graph transformation systems (cf. [14]), which are basically rules which describe the transformation of one instance configuration into another one by two object diagrams specifying partial configuration. The first one is a pre-condition which is expected to be present before the rule can be applied while the second is a post-condition which describe the side-effect relative to the first one. Thus if the pre-condition can be matched, i.e., occurs in a configuration, that occurrence is transformed to correspond to the post-condition.

Appropriate stereotypes are used to extend the object diagrams such that the pre- and post-condition can be compactly specified within a single object diagram: unmarked elements remain constant, elements annotated with the ≪destroy≫ are erased, and elements annotated with the ≪create≫ are created. Crossed out elements belong to the pre-condition and specify that if any of these elements can be matched in a given configuration, the rule is not applicable.

Story patterns are further used to describe all relevant changes of the configuration, e.g., agent behavior, coordination rules, or physical effects. The story patterns in Fig. 4 describes the physical behavior of a Shuttle moving from one Track to the next.

The combination of the continuous and discrete behavior does in fact allow a collision to happen and ensures that the relevant inertia of the moving shuttle is appropriately represented within our model.

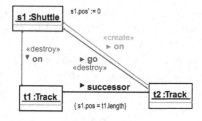

Fig. 4. The move Story Pattern: moving a shuttle to the next track

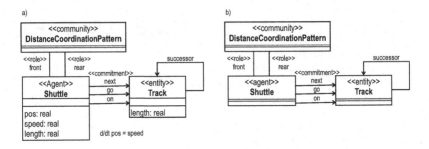

Fig. 5. Class diagram of the ontology with coordination patterns

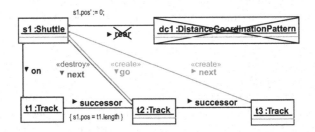

Fig. 6. Behavioral rule: unrestricted movement for a Shuttle

4.2 Dynamic Structural Adaptation

The basic idea to cope with the identified hazards is to employ real-time co-ordination by means of structural adaptation rules and coordination patterns which guarantee that these situations identified as potentially hazardous cannot (or can at least only very unlikely) result in an accident. We employ the design steps outlined later in Section 4.3 to design the detailed local real-time coordination between two shuttles. Beforehand, we have to enhance our model to also reflect these patterns, given commitments, and the adaptation rules.

In a first step the ontology (Fig. 2) is accordingly extended with additional conceptual elements as presented in Fig. 5. These enhancements include a next association, which denotes the commitment to go to that specific Track when the next time a go-Rule is executed. Two shuttles can be group together by the DistanceCoordinationPattern via the two roles rear respectively front.

In addition, behavioral rules to rule the coordination are introduced to ensure that Shuttles respect the commitment expressed by their next association: Fig. 6 describes a solitary Shuttle to move freely.

The required coordination for the collision avoidance is realized by instantiating a DistanceCoordinationPattern which disables the unrestricted rule and enables the provided behavioral rules for coordinated movement when one Shuttle approaches another one.

A special instantiation rule createDC is employed to create the DistanceCoordinationPattern when required: If there is a beforehand unconnected Shuttle on a

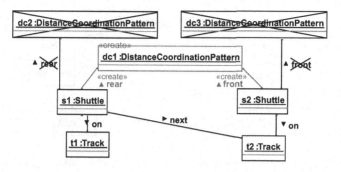

Fig. 7. Instantiation rule: creating a DistanceCoordinationPattern

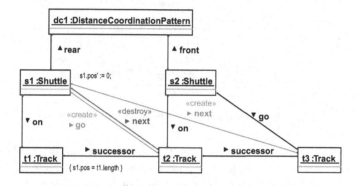

Fig. 8. Behavioral rule: Coordinated movement

Shuttle's next Track (see Fig. 7). The additional rule deleteDC erases the pattern instance when the rear Shuttle is no longer near (has no go or next association to the current location of the front Shuttle).

The additional coordinated behavioral rules goDC1 (see Fig. 8) and goDC2 then only permit the rear Shuttle to move forward when the front Shuttle has already moved which reliably prevents that the moveMultiple rule could result in a collision.

4.3   Real-Time Coordination Pattern

In the domain of cooperative self-adaptive mechatronic systems, an autonomous agent like a shuttle usually operates in a local environment only and thus the interfaces to its environment are strictly local (e.g., a shuttle trying to build a convoy has to interact only with one other shuttle and not with a third one which is a few kilometers away). Due to this domain-specific restriction, we usually only require relative simple coordination patterns, i.e. patterns with simple coordination protocols between roles, limited numbers of input signals, and a fixed number of roles.

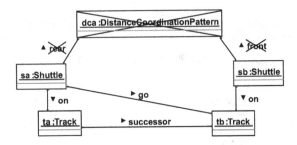

Fig. 9. Invariant: No uncoordinated movement of Shuttles in close proximity

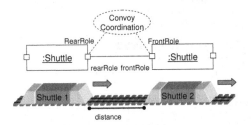

Fig. 10. Component Diagram and Patterns

The real-time coordination between two shuttles for building and maintaining a convoy is one such simple coordination pattern. As depicted in Figure 10, the ConvoyCoordination pattern between two shuttles describe that shuttles build convoys with one another via the dedicated RearRole and FrontRole roles.

The more detailed coordination is then specified in the roles of this pattern (see Figure 11). As the agents (components) in the considered domain must meet hard real-time requirements, we use our real-time variant of UML state machines named *Real-Time Statecharts* [19] for the specification of role behavior. The additionally supported constructs from timed automata [20,21] such as clocks, time guards, time invariants and further annotations like worst case execution times and deadlines enable an automatic and correct implementation on a real physical machine with limited resources which preserve the high level properties of the model (cf. [17,19]).

The following scheme is used for the communication via roles: If an event has the form roleA.message this denotes that the transition is only triggered when message is received via the port related to roleA. The side-effects roleB.message describes the sending of message to the port related to roleB. If we use events where no port is referenced, the message is local and sent resp. received within the same statechart.

As depicted in Figure 11, initially both roles are in their state noConvoy::default, which denotes that they are not in a convoy. The rear role then can non-deterministically choose to propose building a convoy or not. To propose a convoy, a message is sent to the front role of the related shuttle and that front role decides non-deterministically to reject or to accept the proposal.

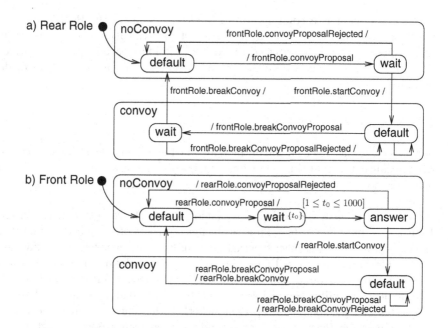

Fig. 11. Real-Time Statechart for roles **RearRole** and **FrontRole** role

If we are in convoy mode, the rear shuttle may non-deterministically choose to propose breaking up the convoy. It then sends a proposal to the front shuttle to do so. The front shuttle may again non-deterministically choose to reject or accept that proposal.

For the connector which represents the communication media in form of a wireless network we do not define the behavior explicitly by means of a Statechart. Instead, we only specify its QoS characteristics such as throughput, maximal delay etc. in the form of connector attributes (it will forward incoming signals with a delay of 1 up to 5 msec.; it operates unreliably in the sense that it might fail completely at any time).

To specify required safety constraints, the following RT-OCL [22] constraint must hold which requires that a combination of role states where the front role is in state noConvoy and the rear role is in state convoy can never be reached. This state is unsafe as the front shuttle could brake with full intensity although another shuttle drives in short distance behind, which may result in a rear-end collision.

```
context DistanceCoordination inv:
    not (self.oclInState(RearRole::Main::convoy) and
         self.oclInState(FrontRole::Main::noConvoy))
```

As shown in [6], properties like the former one can be guaranteed if the pattern are verified and the components correctly refine the related pattern roles. As a component may realize different roles of different patterns (In our example, the

Shuttle component is a combination of refined versions of the RearRole and the FrontRole), the components have to be subject to verification also to ensure that the verified pattern properties still hold (cf. [6]). This reasoning scheme permits to reuse patterns during the construction of other systems as proven and verified building blocks.

4.4   Component Behavior

In this section the specification of the real-time behavior of the single components which realize the real-time coordination pattern roles as outlined in the last section is considered which preserves the verification results by refining the role behaviors.

Figure 12 depicts the real-time behavior of the Shuttle component of Figure 10, taken from [6]. The Real-Time Statechart consists of three orthogonal states FrontRole, RearRole, and Synchronization. FrontRole and RearRole are refinements of the role behaviors from Figure 11 and specify in detail the communication that is required to build and to break convoys. Synchronization coordinates the communication and is responsible for initiating and breaking convoys. The three sub-states of Synchronization represent whether the shuttle is in the convoy at the first position (convoyFront), at second position (convoyRear), or whether no convoy is built at all (noConvoy). The whole statechart is a refinement of both role

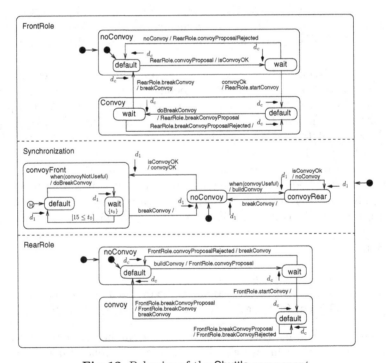

Fig. 12. Behavior of the Shuttle component

descriptions as it just resolves the non-determinism from the roles from Figure 11 and does not add additional behavior.

5 Formal Model

We used graph transformation systems (GTS) [23] with attributes and continuous attribute updates which support hybrid behavior as underlying formal model.

As underlying concept graphs and graph patterns which in addition include negative nodes and edges are employed. A graph pattern P *matches* a graph G, if there exists an isomorphic function *iso* that maps all positive elements of P (P^+) to elements of G and no isomorphic function *iso′* exists which extends *iso* and map at least one negative element of P (P^-) to elements of G.

Graph patterns that are used to describe system properties can be divided into required and forbidden patterns. A *required* pattern must always be fulfilled during system execution (system invariant), whereas a *forbidden* pattern must never be fulfilled (system hazard, accident).

5.1 Graph Transformation Systems

A *graph transformation system* $S = (\mathcal{G}^i, \mathcal{R})$ consists of a set of initial graphs $\mathcal{G}^i$ and a set of graph transformation rules $\mathcal{R}$ (defined by a set of story patterns), defining all possible transformations in the transformation system. The state (configuration) of S is a graph G and we denote all possible configurations of S as $\mathcal{G}_S$.

A rule $r \in \mathcal{R}$ (written $\langle\langle L \rightarrow_r R\rangle\rangle$) is *applicable* to a graph G if G matches L. A *story pattern* defines the two graph patterns L and R as follows: Those elements of the story pattern that are not annotated with ≪create≫ build L. R consists of all elements that are not annotated with ≪destroy≫.

During the *application* of a rule $\langle\langle L \rightarrow_r R\rangle\rangle$ to a graph G, the elements that are in L^+ but not in R^+ are removed from G, and elements that are in R^+ but not in L^+ are added to G. Therefore, the elements annotated with ≪create≫ will be created by the rule and those annotated with ≪destroy≫ will be erased. Elements without annotations are preserved by the application of the rule.

We write $G \Longmapsto_r G'$ if rule r can be applied to graph G and the application results in graph G'. We write $G \Longmapsto^* G'$ if G is transformed into G' by a (possibly empty) sequence of rule applications. For a given graph transformation system $S = (\mathcal{G}^i, \mathcal{R})$ and a graph G, the set of reachable graphs of S starting from G is denoted by $REACH(S, G) = \{G' \mid G \Longmapsto^* G'\}$. All reachable graphs of S are denoted by $REACH(S) = \bigcup_{G \in \mathcal{G}^i} REACH(S, G)$.

5.2 Hybrid Graph Transformation Systems

While graph transformation system permit to model complex discrete models, we have to also support continuous behavior and thus in addition consider the following extensions for *hybrid graph transformation systems* (HGTS): We assign types to all nodes and edges, provide node type specific attributes $a \in \mathcal{V}$, and node type specific continuous behavior for the attributes of that node type. The state of a HGTS therefore consist of a graph G as well as an assignment X which provides for each node n and related attribute a the current value as $X(n, a)$.

Graph patterns are accordingly extended such that they can also contain Boolean constraints over the node attributes. In addition, for the right hand side graph pattern we also permit to employ updates which determine the new attribute values as a function of node attributes of the left hand side.

Due to the additional continuous behavior, we have, like for hybrid automata, two steps for HGTS: (1) At first, the classical GTS step results in a discrete change of the graph which takes place in zero time, in addition, the application of a rule require that the additional Boolean constraints are fulfilled and may also change some of the attribute values of the nodes denotes by related attribute updates in the right hand side of the rule. (2) Secondly, a time consuming continuous step that results for a current state (G, X), a time step $\delta > 0$, and trajectories $\rho : [0, \delta] \to [\mathcal{V} \to \mathbb{R}]$ with $\rho(0)(a) = X(n, a)$ for each node $n \in G$ and attribute $a \in \mathcal{V}$ which conforms to the continuous behavior specification of the type of n results in a state (G, X_δ) for time δ with identical graph G and the continuous state X_δ defined by $X_\delta(n, a) := \rho(\delta)(a)$.

Using this concept, we can, for example, describe the velocity of a vehicle given as a node n using differential equations or real-time behavior by means of clock variables with a constant derivative 1.

Using a rule labeling *alphabet* $\mathcal{A}$ and a corresponding *labelling* for all rules $\alpha : \mathcal{R} \to \mathcal{A}$ we further write $G \xrightarrow{a} G'$ instead of $G \to_r G'$ if $\alpha(r) = a$ and $G \xrightarrow{\tau(\delta)} G'$ for a continuous step. $G \xrightarrow{w}_* G'$ is accordingly defined as the finite sequence of steps $G_i \xrightarrow{a_i} G_{i+1}$ with w the concatenation of the labels $a_1; \ldots; a_n$ with $\tau(\delta_1); \tau(\delta_2)$ is reduced to $\tau(\delta_1 + \delta_2)$.[1] If more appropriate we may also omit the labeling and write $G \to G'$ and $G \to_* G'$.

The *composition* $S \oplus T$ of two HGTS S and T is defined by simply joining the rule sets. We can in addition define the *parallel composition* $S\|T$ of two labeled HGTS S and T by synchronizing always two rules of both HGTSs with the same label. We further require that to build a parallel composition, the combined rules are always identical w.r.t. shared element types. For the parallel composition holds that S as well as T simulate $S\|T$ (see below).

5.3   Simulation and Refinement

A graph pattern P further *matches* a graph pattern P', if there exists an isomorphic function *iso* that maps all positive elements of P to positive elements of P' and all negative elements of P to negative elements of P'. If P matches P', we say that P is a subpattern of P', and write $P \sqsubseteq P'$. In case of conditions for graph pattern refinement must in addition hold, that the conditions of the refined graph pattern P' restricted to all elements also present in P imply the conditions of P'.

---

[1] We ignore here the problem of Zeno behavior which might result from an infinite sequence of classical steps or a not convergent sequence of time steps ($\sum \delta_i \not\to \infty$).

For any graph pattern P_1 and P_2 with $P_2 \sqsubseteq P_1$ holds that for any other graph pattern P that substitution is monotonic w.r.t. refinement $(P[P_2/P_1] \sqsubseteq P)$ Combining both results we get $G \models \neg P \Rightarrow G \models \neg P[P_2/P_1]$.

To ensure that a more detailed HGTS is restricted to the behavior specified in a more abstract one, we employ the following notion of simulation for HGTSs:

Definition 1. *For two HGTS $S = (\mathcal{G}_S^i, \mathcal{R}_S)$ and $T = (\mathcal{G}_T^i, \mathcal{R}_T)$ holds that S is a simulation of T iff S has the same types as T and an $\Omega \in \mathcal{G}_S \times \mathcal{G}_T$ exists with $(G_S, G_T) \in \Omega$ implies $G_S|_T \approx G_T$ and*

$$\forall G_S' \in \mathcal{G}_S : G_S \rightarrow G_S' \quad \exists G_T' \in \mathcal{G}_T : G_T \rightarrow_* G_T' \wedge (G_S', G_T') \in \Omega \qquad (1)$$

for all $G_S \in \mathcal{G}_S^i$ holds $\Omega \cap \{G_S\} \times \mathcal{G}_T^i \neq \emptyset$. We write $S \precsim T$.

For HGTS S_1, S_2, and S_3 with $S_3 = S_1 \| S_2$ holds pre construction that the parallel composition results in simulation $(S_3 \precsim S_1 \wedge S_3 \precsim S_2)$. The strengthening of rule conditions, adding attributes, or extending the LHS of a rule are typical examples of GTS refinement steps which ensure a simulation relationship.

6 Compositional Verification

The idea for the compositional verification of networked mechatronic systems is to employ our approach for the automatic checking for structural invariants for infinite state models [7,8] and combined it with our approach for the compositional model checking of model fragments consisting of patterns and components [6] in order to verify that the crucial safety properties identified during an initial system analysis hold.

6.1 Basic Ontology and Hazard Definition

In Section 4.1, in a first step an ontology S_0 of the system in form of an HGTS which describes all relevant elements, relations, and attributes of the system is developed. This model contains the top-level software components, but will not take the effects of any software control into account.

The proposed steps to the verification efforts are starting with the identification of hazards by means of forbidden graphs. This might be, for example, a collision between two shuttles which can be characterized by a structure where both shuttles are on the same or adjacent tracks and their distance is not sufficient (see Figure 3 a)). We then want to prove the absence of such a hazard G_h described as a graph pattern of the HGTS S_0.

6.2 Structural Adaptation

Instantiation rules, the controlled behavior in case that related coordination patterns are present, and possibly additional structural invariants have to be defined in the next step as described in Section 4.2. Therefore, the ontology given by the HGTS S_0 is then accordingly extended. As the added control via software could in principle not alter the possible system behavior but only restrict it, the resulting HGTS S_1 therefore simulates S_0 ($S_1 \precsim S_0$).

In our example, the HGTS S_1 then further includes a coordination pattern P which should take care of the related coordination problem. The pattern is represented by a special node and can be characterized by a graph pattern G_p such that the graph pattern includes some nodes that also appear in the hazard (usually the pattern roles; e.g., the two shuttles are involved). Therefore, we can assume that a graph isomorphism iso exists such that $G_h \cap iso(G_p)$ is not empty. As both graph pattern are themselves by definition connected graphs, $G_{h+p} := G_h \cup iso(G_p)$ is then also a connected graph pattern.

We accordingly extend the ontology S_0 into an ontology S_1 with attributes, and real-time behavior by adding instantiation rules for the patterns. However, for the employed HGTS formalism currently not techniques exist that can check directly the required properties. Therefore, we propose to use a rough abstraction S_1^a of S_1 in form of a GTS ($S_1 \precsim S_1^a$) instead of the more detailed HGTS S_1 which abstract from all attributes and continuous behavior. To further check the absence of the hazard, we identify its structural part G_h^s (see Figure 3 b)) with $G_h^s \sqsubseteq G_h$ which abstracts from the attributes of the hazard G_h as implied by S_1^a. We do not need an abstract pattern G_p^s for G_p as G_p is already a purely structural pattern with is covered by S_1^a. We can still assume that $G_{h+p}^s := G_h^s \cup iso(G_p^s)$ must be a connected graph as $G_h^s \cap iso(G_p^s)$ is not empty. To describe that the hazard is never present if not also the pattern is present we can use a forbidden graph pattern $P_{h \wedge \neg p}^s$ where G_h^s is the positive part and $iso(G_p) \setminus G_h^s$ denotes the negative part. If $P_{h \wedge \neg p}^s$ is excluded, we know that the hazard is never possible without a related active pattern.

We then have to show that a hazard is only possible if the pattern is also present for the HGTS S_1^a holds:

$$\nexists G' \in \mathsf{REACH}(S_1^a) : G' \models P_{h \wedge \neg p}^s. \tag{2}$$

We can employ our approach for the automatic checking of structural invariants for infinite state models [7,8] to show that condition 2 holds.[2] In our example we can show that a Shuttle will not go to a Track occupied by another Shuttle without having a coordination pattern in place.[3]

As $P_{h \Rightarrow \neg p}$ is a forbidden graph pattern, we simply have to prove that its negation is a structural invariant of S_1^a and can then conclude due to $S_1 \precsim S_1^a$ that also holds:

$$\nexists G' \in \mathsf{REACH}(S_1) : G' \models P_{h \wedge \neg p}^s$$

---

[2] The same approach could have been applied for a rough abstraction S_0^a of the initial ontology S_0 ($S_0 \precsim S_0^a$) if the hazard is *inherently* excluded by the behavior of the not controlled system. However, most often this will not be the case and we have to further add the control functionality to our model as done in the case of S_1.

[3] Even though this invariant is not necessarily required for the operational correctness of the model, this implied condition (see Fig. 9) needs to be made explicit, along with several structural constraints restricting cardinalities, in order for the specification to pass the inductive invariant checking (cf. [7]).

Note that from $G_h \sqsubseteq G_h^s$ follows as outlined in Section 5.3 that we can make the same conclusion for the original hazard for $P_{h \wedge \neg p}$ with positive graph G_h.

$$\nexists G' \in \mathsf{REACH}(S_1) : G' \models P_{h \wedge \neg p}$$

6.3 Real-Time Coordination Pattern

The refinement of the system behavior which results due to the additional control implied by the coordination patterns as described in the last section, has to be realized in form of a real-time coordination pattern as outlined in Section 4.3.

To also verify that an active pattern ensures that the real hazard G_h is not possible, we refine our model further by deriving a HGTS S_2 which refines S_1 which in addition describes for each pattern the required role and connector behavior. To achieve the outlined refinement of S_1, we at first transform for each pattern the related real-time behavior in form of Real-Time Statecharts into a related set of real-time HGTS rules for a separated HGTS S_2^p which also contain the elements of S_1 which relate to G_h. In addition, a special rule for activating the pattern and erasing it are added which fire non-deterministically.

For this HGTS S_2^p which only contains the pattern behavior including the non-deterministic create and destroy rules, we want then to compositionally reason that the hazard G_h is not possible. Therefore, we can use our approach for the compositional model checking of model fragments consisting of patterns and components [6] to verify that a single occurrence of the pattern will always fulfill the pattern condition.

Such a verification is possible as for the pattern occurrences holds that they behave independently of all other pattern occurrences and is sufficient to check the specific case of an HGTS S_2^{pi} with only one instance. The correctness of S_2^{pi} can thus be proven in isolation using a real-time model checker which employs an equivalent real-time automaton M_2^{pi} and the to G_h equivalent property ϕ_h, as we have to consider no structural changes. For this model containing only a single pattern instances we can prove that for all reachable states of M_2^{pi} the condition ϕ_h is excluded:

$$\nexists s \in \mathsf{REACH}(M_2^{pi}) : s \models \phi_h. \tag{3}$$

This result can then be transferred to S_2^{pi} and G_h, as both are equivalent:

$$\nexists G \in \mathsf{REACH}(S_2^{pi}) : G \models G_h.$$

As S_2^{pi} is extended by S_2^p only by a create and destroy rule, we have for S_2^p that G_h is excluded if any element of G_p is present (and thus pattern instances are covered by S_2^{pi}). Thus we can conclude that in any case $P_{h \wedge p} = G_h \cup iso(G_p)$ is excluded:

$$\nexists G \in \mathsf{REACH}(S_2^p) : G \models P_{h \wedge p}.$$

By constructing S_2 as $S_1 \| S_2^p$, we have $S_2 \precsim S_2^p$ as parallel composition implies simulation. We thus can conclude:

$$\nexists G \in \mathsf{REACH}(S_2) : G \models P_{h \wedge p}. \tag{4}$$

As parallel composition implies simulation we also have $S_2 \precsim S_1$, and thus we transfer the following fact from S_1:

$$\not\exists G' \in \text{REACH}(S_2) : G' \models P_{h \wedge \neg p}. \qquad (5)$$

These two conditions can be combined to exclude the hazard G_h due to the following counter argument: Assuming it $\exists G \in \text{REACH}(S_2) : G \models G_h$. Due to condition 5 we can then conclude for every occurrence of G_h that we also have the pattern p. This is, however, in contradiction to condition 4 which exclude $h \wedge p$ and thus no such $G \in \text{REACH}(S_2)$ can exist. Thus we must have:

$$\not\exists G \in \text{REACH}(S_2) : G \models G_h.$$

6.4   Component Behavior

We still have to refine the component instances as outlined in Section 4.4. This component realization has to preserve the proven properties of the earlier refinement steps and check locally that their processing fulfills the role constraints and excludes local conflicts between the constraints of the roles. This 4th step is required to exclude that the made guarantees are contradicting. E.g., a shuttle should not promise to brake in one pattern while it promised to not brake in another one at the same time.

We therefore refine the component behavior by adding the internal synchronization which results in a HGTS S_3 which refines S_2 in such a manner that the instantiation rules are possibly refined, the connector behavior is still present, the pattern roles are refined, and the component internal synchronization is added. Due to $S_3 \precsim S_2$ we then have:

$$\not\exists G \in \text{REACH}(S_3) : G \models G_h. \qquad (6)$$

6.5   Compositional Reasoning Scheme

The full compositional reasoning scheme has 4 steps which at first include simulation relations which are guaranteed by the chosen construction steps. Then, we have derived properties which follow from the condition 2 and 3 due to the present simulation relation and construction steps. The two remaining not derived conditions 2 and 3 remain to be proven in order to derive the required result that the hazard is excluded. This can be accomplished automatically by verifying condition 2 using our approach for invariant checking and by checking condition 3 employing our compositional real-time model checking approach.

To exclude deadlocks, which might indicate inconsistent timing constraints in form of time stopping deadlocks, it is sufficient to check independently the coordination patterns, the component behavior, and the proper refinement relation between the pattern roles and component ports (cf. [6]).

7   Related Work

No approach which combines the automatic verification of safety conditions for arbitrarily large structures or potentially infinite structures with real-time behavior like the presented approach exists. However, several approaches exist with address compositional model checking or the verification of dynamically changing structures.

7.1   Compositional Verification

The state explosion problem, which leads to scalability problems for larger systems even when no time is considered (cf. [24]), limited the applicability of model checking for complex software systems. A number of modular and compositional verification approaches have therefore been proposed. One particular compositional approach is the assume/guarantee paradigm [25]. Model checking techniques that permit compositional verification following the assume/guarantee paradigm have been developed [26, p. 185ff]. Our approach employed in Section 6.3 and 6.4 also follows the assume/guarantee paradigm, but supports time and take advantage of information available in form of pattern role protocols to derive the required additional assumed and guaranteed properties automatically rather than manually as in [26].

7.2   Verifying Dynamic Structural Adaptation

A number of approaches exist which address only finite cases for systems with dynamic changing structure. DynAlloy [27] extends Alloy [28] such that state changes can also be modeled and operational invariants for small systems can be checked. A transformation of models into a model-checker specific input has been successfully applied to verify service-oriented systems with structural changes [29]. Instead of transforming a system to a model checker's input format, Rensink performs the model checking directly on the GTS [30]. Real-Time Maude [31] supports the simulation of a single behavior of the system as well as model checking of the complete state space, if it is finite, based on rewriting logics. As all above approaches require an initial graph and a not too large finite state space, they are not appropriate for the outlined complex, networked mechatronic systems.

The automatic verification of a certain minimal sub-model of a system with dynamically changing structures and the manual generalization of this result to all possible models is proposed in [32]. We in contrast support in Section 6.1 and 6.2 a fully-automatic procedure for verifying whether only safe sub-models can be reached at run-time and then employ model checking to check that these sub-models are safe.

Only one approach exists that explicitly addresses the verification of infinite state systems with changing structures. In [33], a GTS is approximated by a finite Petri graph which consists of a graph and a Petri net that can be analyzed with existing standard tools. The approach is not appropriate, as an initial graph is required and no deletion of nodes is permitted.

8 Conclusion and Future Work

The RailCab project shows that properties such as real-time coordination via unreliable wireless networks and dynamic structural adaptation can be expected for the next generation of networked mechatronic systems which are in fact systems of systems requires and that new approaches to modeling and verification are required. The ongoing development of the MECHATRONIC UML approach addresses these challenges by exploiting observed domain restrictions, refining the UML 2.0 component and pattern model, adding support for structural adaptation, and combining a number of verification techniques into an overall scheme for the compositional verification of crucial safety properties.

A more seamless tool support for all the outlined modeling and verification steps in the Fujaba Real-Time Tool Suite[4] and the application of the approach in related domains such as automotive systems is planned future work.

References

1. Bradley, D., Seward, D., Dawson, D., Burge, S.: Mechatronics. Stanley Thornes (2000)
2. Giese, H., Burmester, S., Schäfer, W., Oberschelp, O.: Modular Design and Verification of Component-Based Mechatronic Systems with Online-Reconfiguration. In: Proc. of 12th ACM SIGSOFT Foundations of Software Engineering 2004 (FSE 2004), Newport Beach, USA, ACM Press (2004) 179–188
3. Sztipanovits, J., Karsai, G., Bapty, T.: Self-adaptive software for signal processing. Commun. ACM 41 (1998) 66–73
4. Musliner, D.J., Goldman, R.P., Pelican, M.J., Krebsbach, K.D.: Self-Adaptive Software for Hard Real-Time Environments. IEEE Inteligent Systems 14 (1999)
5. Oreizy, P., Gorlick, M.M., Taylor, R.N., Heimbigner, D., Johnson, G., Medvidovic, N., Quilici, A., Rosenblum, D.S., Wolf, A.L.: An Architecture-Based Approach to Self-Adaptive Software. IEEE Intelligent Systems 14 (1999) 54–62
6. Giese, H., Tichy, M., Burmester, S., Schäfer, W., Flake, S.: Towards the Compositional Verification of Real-Time UML Designs. In: Proc. of the 9th European software engineering conference held jointly with 11th ACM SIGSOFT international symposium on Foundations of software engineering (ESEC/FSE-11), ACM Press (2003) 38–47
7. Becker, B., Beyer, D., Giese, H., Klein, F., Schilling, D.: Symbolic Invariant Verification for Systems with Dynamic Structural Adaptation. In: Proc. of the 28th International Conference on Software Engineering (ICSE), Shanghai, China, ACM Press (2006)
8. Giese, H., Schilling, D.: Towards the Automatic Verification of Inductive Invariants for Infinite State UML Models. Technical Report tr-ri-04-252, Computer Science, University of Paderborn, Germany (2004)
9. Hestermeyer, T., Oberschelp, O., Giese, H.: Structured Information Processing For Self-optimizing Mechatronic Systems. In Araujo, H., Vieira, A., Braz, J., Encarnacao, B., Carvalho, M., eds.: Proc. of 1st International Conference on Informatics in Control, Automation and Robotics (ICINCO 2004), Setubal, Portugal, INSTICC Press (2004) 230–237

---

[4] http://wwwcs.upb.de/cs/fujaba/projects/realtime/index.html

10. Burmester, S., Giese, H., Oberschelp, O.: Hybrid UML Components for the Design of Complex Self-optimizing Mechatronic Systems. In Braz, J., Araújo, H., Vieira, A., Encarnacao, B., eds.: Informatics in Control, Automation and Robotics I. Springer (2006)

11. Giese, H.: A Formal Calculus for the Compositional Pattern-Based Design of Correct Real-Time Systems. Technical Report tr-ri-03-240, Computer Science, University of Paderborn, Germany (2003)

12. Giese, H., Tichy, M., Schilling, D.: Compositional Hazard Analysis of UML Components and Deployment Models. In: Proc. of the 23rd International Conference on Computer Safety, Reliability and Security (SAFECOMP), Potsdam, Germany. LNCS 3219, Springer (2004)

13. Tichy, M., Schilling, D., Giese, H.: Design of Self-Managing Dependable Systems with UML and Fault Tolerance Patterns. In: Proc. of the Workshop on Self-Managed Systems 2004, FSE 2004 Workshop, Newport Beach, USA. (2004)

14. Köhler, H., Nickel, U., Niere, J., Zündorf, A.: Integrating UML Diagrams for Production Control Systems. In: Proc. of the 22nd International Conference on Software Engineering (ICSE), Limerick, Ireland, ACM Press (2000) 241–251

15. Klein, F., Giese, H.: Separation of concerns for mechatronic multi-agent systems through dynamic communities. In Choren, R., Garcia, A., Lucena, C., Romanovsky, A., eds.: Software Engineering for Multi-Agent Systems III: Research Issues and Practical Applications. LNCS 3390. Springer (2005) 272–289

16. Burmester, S., Giese, H., Gambuzza, A., Oberschelp, O.: Partitioning and Modular Code Synthesis for Reconfigurable Mechatronic Software Components. In Bobeanu, C., ed.: Proc. of European Simulation and Modelling Conference (ESMc'2004), Paris, France, EOROSIS Publications (2004) 66–73

17. Burmester, S., Giese, H., Schäfer, W.: Model-driven architecture for hard real-time systems: From platform independent models to code. In: Proc. of the European Conference on Model Driven Architecture - Foundations and Applications (ECMDA-FA'05), Nürnberg, Germany. LNCS 3748, Springer (2005)

18. Burmester, S., Giese, H., Tichy, M.: Model-driven development of reconfigurable mechatronic systems with mechatronic UML. In: Model Driven Architecture: Foundations and Applications. LNCS 3599, Springer (2005) 47–61

19. Giese, H., Burmester, S.: Real-Time Statechart Semantics. Technical Report tr-ri-03-239, Computer Science, University of Paderborn, Germany (2003)

20. Larsen, K., Pettersson, P., Yi, W.: UPPAAL in a Nutshell. Springer International Journal of Software Tools for Technology 1 (1997)

21. Henzinger, T.A., Manna, Z., Pnueli, A.: What Good Are Digital Clocks? In: 9th International Colloquium on Automata, Languages, and Programming (ICALP '92). LNCS 623, Springer (1992) 545–558

22. Flake, S., Mueller, W.: An OCL Extension for Real-Time Constraints. In: Object Modeling with the OCL: The Rationale behind the Object Constraint Language. LNCS 2263. Springer (2002) 150–171

23. Rozenberg, G., ed.: Handbook of Graph Grammars and Computing by Graph Transformation: Foundations. Volume 1. World Scientific Pub Co (1997)

24. Chan, W., Anderson, R.J., Beame, P., Burns, S., Modugno, F., Notkin, D., Reese, J.D.: Model Checking Large Software Specifications. IEEE Transactions on Software Engineering 24 (1998) 498–520

25. Misra, J., Chandy, M.: Proofs of networks of processes. IEEE Transactions on Software Engineering 7 (1981) 417–426

26. Clarke, E.M., Grumberg, O., Peled, D.: Model Checking. MIT Press (2000)

27. Frias, M.F., Galeotti, J.P., Pombo, C.L., Aguirre, N.: DynAlloy: Upgrading Alloy with actions. In: Proc. ICSE, ACM Press (2005) 442–451
28. Jackson, D.: Alloy: A lightweight object modelling notation. ACM Trans. Software Engineering and Methodology 11 (2002) 256–290
29. Baresi, L., Heckel, R., Thöne, S., Varró, D.: Modeling and validation of service-oriented architectures: Application vs. style. In: Proc. ESEC/FSE, ACM Press (2003) 68–77
30. Rensink, A.: Towards model checking graph grammars. In: Proc. AVoCS, University of Southampton (2003) 150–160
31. Ölveczky, P., Meseguer, J.: Specification and analysis of real-time systems using Real-Time Maude. In: Proc. FASE. LNCS 2984, Springer (2004) 354–358
32. Caporuscio, M., Inverardi, P., Pelliccione, P.: Formal analysis of architectural patterns. In: Proc. EWSA. LNCS 3047, Springer (2004) 10–24
33. Baldan, P., Corradini, A., König, B.: A static analysis technique for graph transformation systems. In: Proc. CONCUR. LNCS 2154, Springer (2001) 381–395

Architectural Design, Behavior Modeling and Run-Time Verification of Network Embedded Systems

Man-Tak Shing[1] and Doron Drusinsky[1,2]

[1] Department of Computer Science, Naval Postgraduate School
Monterey, CA 93943-5118, USA
{shing, ddrusin}@nps.edu
[2] Time Rover Inc.
Cupertino, CA 95014, USA
dorond@time-rover.com
http://www.time-rover.com

Abstract. There is an increasing need for today's autonomous systems to collaborate in real-time over wireless networks. These systems need to interact closely with other autonomous systems and function under tight timing and control constraints. This paper concerns with the modeling and quality assurance of the timing behavior of such network embedded systems. It builds upon our previous work on run-time model checking of temporal correctness properties and automatic white-box testing using run-time assertion checking. This paper presents an architecture for the network embedded systems, a lightweight formal method that is based on formal statechart assertions for the design and development of networked embedded systems, and a process of using run-time monitoring and verification, in tandem with modeling and simulation, to study the timing requirements of complex systems early in the design process.

Keywords: Network Embedded System, Lightweight Formal Method, Architecture Design, Run-Time Verification, Statechart Assertions.

1   Introduction

With the recent advance in Internet and wireless technology, there is a new demand for high performance and intelligent automobiles, aircraft and autonomous robots to collaborate in real-time over wireless networks. These systems need to interact closely with other embedded systems and function under tight timing and control constraints. This paper addresses the need to verify the timing properties of real-time, reactive distributed systems. It presents a testing methodology that builds upon our work on run-time model checking of temporal correctness properties and automatic white-box testing using run-time assertion checking [4]. Run-time Execution Monitoring of formal specification assertions (REM) is a class of methods for tracking the temporal behavior, often in the

F. Kordon and J. Sztipanovits (Eds.): Monterey Workshop 2005, LNCS 4322, pp. 281–303, 2007.

form of formal specification assertions, of an underlying application. REM methods range from simple print-statement logging methods to run-time tracking of complex formal requirements (e.g., written in temporal logic or as statechart assertions) for verification purposes. NASA used REM for the verification of flight code for the Deep Impact project [10]. In [8], we showed that the use of run-time monitoring and verification of temporal assertions, in tandem with rapid prototyping, helps debug the requirements and identify errors earlier in the design process. Recently, REM has been adopted by the U.S. Ballistic Missile Defense System project as the primary verification method for the new BMDS battle manager because of its ability to scale, and its support for temporal assertions that include real-time and time series constraints [2].

The rest of the paper is organized as follows. Section 2 provides an overview of the StateRover statechart assertion formalism. Section 3 presents an architecture that supports high-level specification of network level objectives and policies and the enforcement of these policies by direct re-configuration of the states of individual network elements. We will illustrate the proposed architecture with an example from the automatic highway platoon system. Section 4 describes the use of run-time monitoring and verification, in tandem with modeling and simulation, to study the timing requirements of complex systems early in the design process. Section 5 presents a discussion on the approach and Section 6 draws some conclusions.

2   The Statechart Assertions

Harel Statecharts [15] are commonly used in the design analysis phase of an object oriented UML based design methodology to specify the dynamic behavior of complex reactive systems. In [5] [6], Drusinsky presented a new formalism that combines UML-based prototyping, UML-based formal specifications, run-time monitoring, and execution-based model checking. The new formalism is supported by StateRover, a commercially available tool from the Time Rover Inc. StateRover provides support for design entry, code generation, and visual debug animation for UML statecharts combined with flowcharts. The new formalism and tool allow system designers to embed deterministic and non-deterministic statechart assertions in statechart designs and execute the assertions in tandem with their primary UML statechart to provide run-time monitoring and run-time recovery from assertion failures.

2.1   A Statechart Example

Figure 1 shows the top-level statechart of a leader election (*LE*) module, which is one of the many leader election modules connected by a unidirectional ring network. The top-level statechart consists of three states, the Initializing state and two composite states named *Electing_Leader* and *Found_Leader*, together with a set of state variables declared in the associated local variable declaration box shown in Figure 1. Each *LE* module uses the *Own_Id* variable to store its unique integer identity and uses the *Leader_Id* variable to remember the identity

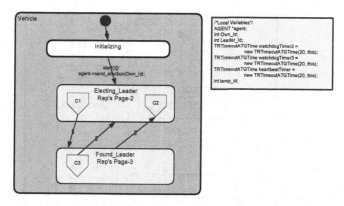

Fig. 1. Top-level page of the *LE* statechart

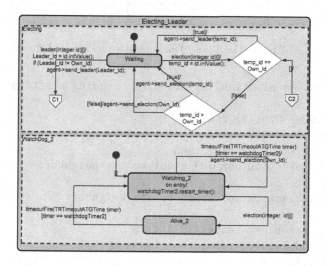

Fig. 2. The Electing_Leader statechart of the *LE* module

of the current leader, which is the largest identity value among the identities of all the active *LE* modules in the network. In addition, it has three timers and an agent object. The timers are instances of a built-in StateRover timer class, and the agent object serves as a proxy for all network communications.

The *LE* statechart starts at the Initializing state waiting for the arrival of the *start()* event from the environment. Upon receiving the *start()* event, it uses the *send_election()* method of its agent object to send an *election()* message to its neighbor in the network and then enters the *Electing_Leader* composite state shown in Figure 2. The *Electing_Leader* composite state consists of two concurrent threads, *Electing* and *Watchdog_2*. The statechart in the *Electing* thread models the logic of the following simple leader election algorithm.

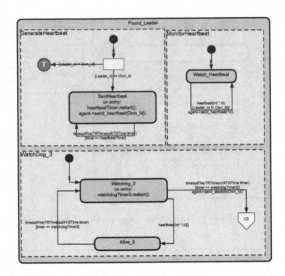

Fig. 3. The Found_Leader statechart of the *LE* module

```
if (event == election(id)) then // on-going election
{
  if (id == Own_Id) then
    send leader(Own_Id} event to its neighbor;
  else if (id < Own_Id) then
    send election(Own_Id) event to its neighbor;
  else
    send election(id) event to its neighbor;
}
else if (event == leader(id)) then
{ // found leader, terminate election
  Leader_Id = id;
  if (Leader_Id != Own_Id) then
    send leader(id) event to its neighbor;
  reset the watchdogTimer_2 timer;.
  transition to the Found_Leader state via the page connector C1;
}
```

The statechart in the *Watchdog_2* thread makes sure that the *LE* statechart receives at least one *election()* message every 60-second cycle while it is participating in an on-going election. If the *LE* statechart receives the event *timeoutFire(timer)* with *timer == watchdog2Timer* while it is in the *Watching_2* state, it will initiate another round of leader election by sending an *election(Own_Id)* message to its neighbor because it has not received any *election()* message within the last cycle.

The leader election algorithm terminates when the *LE* statechart receives a *leader(id)* message, and will transition from the *Electing_Leader* state to the

Found_Leader state via the page connector *C*1. Note that the correctness of the algorithm relies on a reliable and fully trusted network of cooperating *LE* modules.

Figure 3 shows the statechart of the *Found_Leader* composite state. It consists of three concurrent threads. While in the *Found_Leader* state, the leader uses the statechart in the *GenerateHeartBeat* thread to send out a *heartbeat(Own_Id)* message once every 60 seconds, and each *LE* statechart expects to receive at least one *heartbeat()* message from the leader via its neighbor in every 60-second cycle. If the *LE* statechart receives the event *timeoutFire(timer)* with *timer == watchdog3Timer* while it is in the *Watching_3* state, it will initiate another round of leader election by sending an *election(Own_Id)* message to its neighbor and transitioning to the *Electing_Leader* state because it has not received any *heartbeat()* message within the last cycle. Other *LE* modules will also enter the *Electing_Leader* state via the page connector *C*2 when they receive the *election()* messages from their neighbors in the network while they are in the *Found_Leader* state.

2.2   Statechart Assertions

Studies have suggested that the process of specifying requirements formally enables developers to gain a deeper understanding of the system being specified, and to uncover requirements flaws, inconsistencies, ambiguities and incompletenesses [11]. The StateRover uses deterministic and non-deterministic statecharts for the formal specification of temporal correctness properties (i.e. properties about the correct ordering, sequencing, and timing of events and responses). Figure 4 contains three statechart assertions for the following natural language requirements:

Assertion 1. Leader_Id must be greater than or equal to Own_Id whenever the LE statechart enters the Found_Leader state.

Assertion 2. At least one heartbeat occurs every 60 seconds while LE is in the Found_Leader state.

Assertion 3. There should not be 3 or more rounds of leader election within a 5-minute interval.

Assertion 1 is an example of a correctness-property assertion that ensures "the leader election algorithm correctly selects the active *LE* module with the largest identity value as the leader". Assertion 2 is an example of a timing constraint assertion that ensures "the *LE* module receives at least one heartbeat every 60 seconds while it is in the *Found_Leader* state". Assertion 3 is an example of a temporal constraint assertion to ensure the stability of the networked system.

Figures 5-6 show the combined *LE* statecharts with embedded statechart assertions, where the Assertion1 and Assertion3 statecharts now become sub-statecharts of the top-level *LE* statechart, and the Assertion2 statechart becomes a sub-statechart of the *Found_Leader* state. Sub-statecharts represent whole statecharts defined elsewhere, i.e., in a different statechart file. Using sub-statecharts facilitates reuse: the assertion statecharts are drawn once but can be reused many times in many other statecharts. A statechart with an embedded substatechart is called a *primary* statechart. StateRover provides a way to map the events

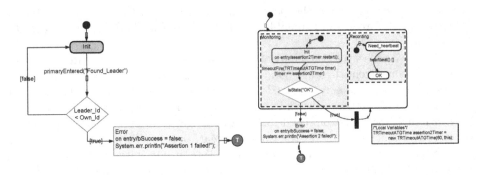

(a) Assertion1 Statechart   (b) Assertion2 Statechart

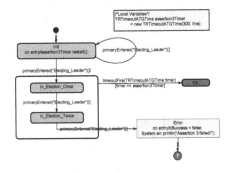

(c) Assertion3 Statechart

Fig. 4. Assertion statecharts

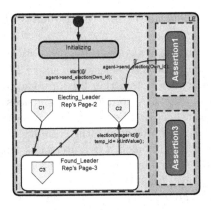

Fig. 5. The top-level page of the *LE* statechart with embedded assertion sub-statecharts

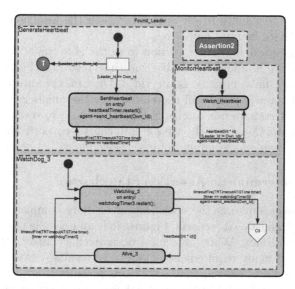

Fig. 6. The Found_Leader statechart with embedded Assertion2

between the primary statechart and its sub-statecharts. The StateRover's code generator generates code that automatically passes down events from the primary statechart to the sub-statecharts.

Figures 4a and 4b are examples of deterministic statechart assertion. (Non-deterministic assertions are discussed in Section 2.3.) Every time the *Found_Leader* state of the primary (i.e., *LE*) statechart is entered, the *Assertion2* state is entered, and the sub-statechart becomes active, starting its computation in the initial states (*Init* and *Need_heartbeat* in Figure 4b). The sub-statechart remains active until either assertion2Timer fires its *timeout* event and the *Recording* thread is not in the *OK* state, or the *LE* statechart exits the *Found_Leader* state. Once the *LE* statechart leaves the *Found_Leader* state, it is no longer in the *Assertion2* state and the assertion sub-statechart will not be executing at all. The next time the *LE* statechart enters the *Assertion2* state, the assertion sub-statechart starts its computation from its initial states all over again.

The statecharts in Figure 4 are formal specifications that assert about the primary *LE* statechart because they each make a statement about the correctness of the primary statechart. They do so using a built-in Boolean variable named *bSuccess*, and a corresponding method called *isSuccess()*, both auto-generated by the StateRover's code generator. Whenever the assertion detects a violation of the requirement it sets *bSuccess* = false, as in Figure 4b when assertion2Timer fires its *timeout* event and the *Recording* thread is not in the *OK* state. The method *isSuccess()* returns the value of *bSuccess* mainly for the purpose of JUnit testing and automatic white-box testing described in Section 2.5 and Section 2.6. Because statechart assertions are usually used to flag errors, the *isSuccess()*, which monitors the *bSuccess* variable, is set to true by default. It is the assertion developers' responsibility to set it to false when the assertion fails, as done in the Error activity box in Figure 4b.

In addition, an unlabeled transition from the *Assertion1* state to the *Electing_Leader* state is added to enable run-time recovery (Figure 5). Whenever the Assertion 1 fails, because *Leader_Id < Own_Id*, the sub-statechart reaches the terminal state (T) and will therefore cause the unlabeled transition out of the *Assertion1* state to fire, forcing the *LE* statechart to transition to the *Electing_Leader* state. Consequently, the *LE* statechart recovers from the specification failure by starting another round of leader election.

2.3   Non-deterministic Assertion Statecharts

The StateRover supports the specification of more complex requirements using non-deterministic statecharts. Figures 4c is an example of non-deterministic statechart assertions. While deterministic statechart assertions suffice for the specification of many requirements, theoretical results [7] show that non-deterministic statecharts are exponentially more succinct than deterministic Harel Statecharts. As indicated in Figure 4c, there is an apparent next-state conflict when event *primaryEntered("Electing_Leader")* is sensed while the statechart is in the *Init* state. The vanilla StateRover code generator (described in the next section) generates an error message for such a statechart. It is however a legal *non-deterministic* statechart. Non-deterministic statecharts use a special StateRover code generator that creates a plurality of *state-configuration* objects, one per possible computation in the assertion statechart. Non-deterministic statechart assertions use an *existential* definition of the *isSuccess()* method, where if there exists at least one state-configuration that detects an error (assigns *bSuccess*=false) then *isSuccess()* for the entire non-deterministic assertion returns false. Likewise, terminal state behavior is existential; if at least one state-configuration is in a terminal state then the non-deterministic statechart assertion wrapper considers itself to be in a terminal state. The StateRover also has a power-user priority mechanism to change or limit the existential default definitions of *isSuccess()* and the terminal state. This mechanism is described in details in [6].

2.4   The StateRover Code Generator

The primary StateRover rapid prototyping tool is its code generator. The StateRover's code generator generates a class per statechart model (i.e. per statechart file) in either Java or C++ language, a convenient level of encapsulation for a controller statechart that lives within a heterogeneous system of Java or C++ objects created by various tools or perhaps hand-coded. The class can then be dynamically instantiated according to the needs of the system.

In our example, we have four statechart diagram files, with the *LE* statechart in the first file and the *Assertion1*, *Assertion2* and *Assertion3* sub-statecharts in the second, third and the fourth files. The StateRover's code generator automatically connects the four statecharts objects resulting in an executable *LE* module. The controller class consists of a set of event handlers (one per transition event), the central event dispatcher *execTReventDispatcher*, and the source code for local variable declarations and methods supplied by the users via the dialog boxes of StateRover's statechart editor. In addition, the code generator also generates a Java interface, named LEIF, to allow the test drivers or other systems from the external environment to interact with the *LE* module.

Statechart orthogonality is implemented by the vanilla code generator using a fixed schedule created during code generation. For example, in Figure 3, three orthogonal *timeoutFire()* transitions, two in the *WatchDog_3* thread and one in the *GenerateHeartbeat* thread, will be realized as three if blocks within the *timeoutFire()* event handler. The order of these if blocks induces a fixed firing schedule for corresponding transitions. Besides the vanilla code generator, the StateRover has a concurrent code generator that generates multi-threaded Java code for statecharts with Harel-concurrence.

2.5   Testing of Generated Code

The generated code is designed to work with the JUnit Test Framework [1] [18]. Use Case scenarios used by the system designers to identify user needs and system requirements are hand-coded as JUnit test cases and exercised against the generated statechart code. Figure 7 illustrates the StateRover's JUnit based testing architecture. Tests, which consist of sequences of events and timing information, are either hand coded or auto-generated by the white-box test generator.

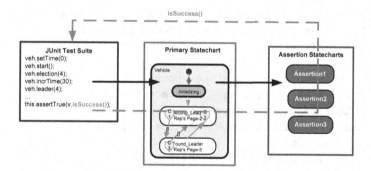

Fig. 7. JUnit based simulation and testing architecture

For example, the following hand-code test case describes a scenario in which the *LE* statechart successfully participates in two rounds of leader election within an interval of 180 seconds.

```
import junit.framework.*;
public class TestLE1 extends TestCase {
  private LE veh = null;
  private AGENT t = null;
```

```
public TestLE1(String name) {
  super(name);
}

protected void setUp() throws Exception {
  super.setUp();
  t = new AGENT();
  veh = new LE(3, -1, t); // Own_Id == 3,
                          // Leader_Id == -1
}

protected void tearDown() throws Exception {
  veh = null;
  super.tearDown();
}

// Test Scenario:
public void testExecTReventDiapatcher() {
  // first round of leader election
  veh.start();
  veh.election(4);
  veh.incrTime(30); // advance clock by 30 sec
  veh.leader(4); // found leader with id == 4

  // veh should now be in the Found_Leader state
  this.assertTrue(veh.isState("Found_Leader"));
  veh.incrTime(120); // advance clock by 120 sec

  // veh should initiate the second round of leader
  // election since it has not received any
  // heartbeat() for more than 60 sec
  this.assertTrue(veh.isState("Electing_Leader"));
  veh.election(1);
  veh.incrTime(15); // advance clock by 15 sec
  veh.election(3);
  veh.incrTime(15); // advance clock by 15 sec
  veh.leader(3); // found leader with id == 3

  // veh should be in the Found_Leader state
  this.assertTrue(veh.isState("Found_Leader"));

  // the testcase should return bSuccess == true
  this.assertTrue(veh.isSuccess());
  }
}
```

A test exercises the primary statechart model, which then automatically exercises embedded assertions. The assertion feeds back a Boolean success value, *isSuccess()*, to the JUnit based test, which then announces fail or success accordingly.

It is important to validate the correctness of the assertions early in the software development process. By keeping each statechart assertion in a separate diagram file, we can generate code and test each statechart assertion independent of the prototype design. For example, a developer might expect the following scenario to cause the Assertion2 statechart to fail, since the heartbeats do not arrive regularly; the inter-arrival time between the second and the third heartbeat is more than 60 seconds.

```
public class TestAssertion2 extends TestCase {
  private Assertion2 assert2 = null;
  ...
  protected void setUp() throws Exception {
    super.setUp();
    assert2 = new Assertion2();
  }
  ...
  // Test Scenario:
  public void testExecTReventDiapatcher() {
    assert2.heartbeat(4); // receive first heartbeat
    assert2.incrTime(61); // advance clock by 61 sec
    assert2.heartbeat(4); // receive second heartbeat
    assert2.incrTime(117); // advance clock by 117 sec
    assert2.heartbeat(4); // receive third heartbeat
    assert2.incrTime(10); // advance clock by 10 sec
    assert2.heartbeat(4); // receive third heartbeat
    // the testcase should return bSuccess == false
    this.assertFalse(assert2.isSuccess());
  }
}
```

The developer of the assertion was surprised by the assertion's success for this scenario. After a closer examination of the natural language assertion and the Assertion2 statechart, the developer decided that the error was caused by an incorrect interpretation of the natural language requirement "at least one heartbeat occurs every 60 seconds". Hence, he reformulated the natural language requirement and the Assertion2 statechart as follows:

Assertion 2 (revised). The inter-arrival time between two consecutive heartbeats cannot exceed 60 seconds.

When the extended primary statechart of Figure 6 (with the revised Assertion2 of Figure 8) is executed using a scenario similar to TestAssertion2, the revised Assertion2 statechart will detect an error in the primary statechart as it is performing REM of the primary. Automatic test generation discussed in Section 2.6

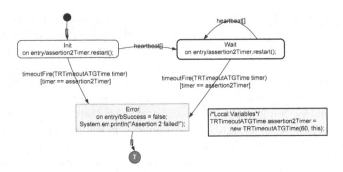

Fig. 8. Revised Assertion2 statechart

is a technique for automatically discovering violating scenarios such as TestAssertion2. This example highlights the subtleties in creating correct formal assertions and the value of testing executable formal assertions via JUnit-based simulations.

2.6   Automatic, Intelligent, White-Box Test Generation

The StateRover's White-Box Test Generator (WBTG) is an automatic code generator for a JUnit TestCase class. This TestCase, however, does not capture a single, human created, scenario as JUnit TestCase objects usually do. Rather, it contains a loop that creates a plurality of tests for a Statechart Under Test (SUT). We denote this WBTG generated TestCase the *WBTestCase*. The auto-generated WBTestCase is usable verbatim within a broader test suite that replaces the one shown in Figure 7, which may include both WBTestCase and the manually created tests. Automatically generated tests are used in three ways:

1. To search for severe programming errors, of the kind that induces a JUnit error status, such as *NullPointerException*.
2. To identify tests that violate temporal assertions. Such failed assertion are captured by a JUnit *assertFalse()* (versus the *assertTrue()*) statement using the *isSuccess()* feedback loop depicted in Figure 7.[1]
3. To identify input sequences that lead the SUT to particular states of interest.

The StateRover generated *WBTestCase* creates sequences of events and conditions for the SUT. The WBTestCase is intelligent in the following regard: it creates only sequences which "matter" to either the SUT or to some assertion statechart. For example, in Figure 1, upon startup, the SUT has one option only: to observe the *start* event. The WBTestCase therefore generates this event. Consequently, the SUT moves to the *Electing_Leader* state shown in Figure 2. There, the SUT expects a *timeout* event, an *election* event, or a *leader* event; so the WBTestCase generates one of those using one of the two algorithms the user

---

[1] To help statechart designers pinpoint specific errors, each failed test run is reported with an identification number. The causes of failure for a specific run can be investigated in detail by running the automatic white box tester in single test/run mode. Such mechanism helps developers to efficiently eliminate errors in their design.

selects: the *stochastic* algorithm or the *deterministic* algorithm described below. Hence, in general, the StateRover generated WBTestCase repeatedly observes all events that potentially affect the SUT when it is in a given state configuration, selects one of those events and fires the SUT using this event. The WBTestCase auto-generates three artifacts:

1. Events, as described above.
2. Time advance increments, for the correct generation of timeoutFire events.
3. External data objects of the type that the statechart prototype refers to.

This process describes the model-based aspect of the StateRovers WBTG. However, the StateRovers WBTG actually observes all entities, namely, the SUT and all embedded assertions. It collects all possible events from all those entities, thus creating a hybrid model-based and specification-based WBTG. For a SUT with a loop, there is an infinite number of input sequences of unbounded lengths. The StateRovers WBTG addresses these issues in the following manner:

1. The StateRover's user specifies the maximal number of test sequences the WBTestCase is allowed to generate, denoted as the *WB test-budget*.
2. The StateRover's user specifies the maximal length of any test sequence generated by the WBTestCase.

The WBTG uses two primary methods, a stochastic method and a deterministic method, for test generation. For each of three artifacts of concern, namely, the set of possible events, the set of objects the object factory can generate, and simulation time increments, the stochastic method rolls the dice and makes a selection accordingly, while the deterministic method attempts to systematically cover all possible sequences by enumerating these artifacts and traversing new sequences one by one. In addition, the StateRovers WBTG can also be configured to use NASAs Java Pathfinder (JPF) [16]. JPF uses a customized Java Virtual Machine to detect the presence of concurrency errors such as deadlock under varying firing schedules of concurrent transitions and actions. Moreover, JPF can be viewed as a sophisticated hybrid of the deterministic and stochastic methods. JPF makes sure to not revisit system states more than once by recording the state space being visited. The drawbacks of using JPF are: (1) JPF tends to run out of memory for complex systems, (2) JPF wastes resources by model-checking the assertions and the methods of the actions and activities, and (3) JPF does not work well with frameworks like JUnit and Spring.

3 Adaptive Network Architecture

Any good architecture for the networked embedded systems must be adaptive and easily reconfigurable at runtime to cope with the changing environment and to accommodate changing mission needs. In particular, we must move away from today's box-centric network architecture where the decision-making logic of the control plane is spread out over the routers and switches in support of the simple best effort distributed protocol. It is very difficult, if not impossible, to

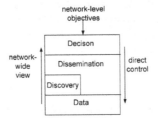

Fig. 9. The 4D architecture (after [13])

retrofit this box-centric architecture to support the more sophisticated network objectives like traffic engineering, survivability, security, and policy management, which require the increasing run-time use of reflection (systems that utilize their own models), self-adaptation, and self-optimization to satisfy the mission needs.

In [13], Greenberg et al proposed a novel clean slate 4D architecture that abstracts the network management into four components – the data, discovery, dissemination and decision planes (Figure 9). The decision plane replaces today's management plane. It consists of multiple servers (called decision elements) that make all decisions driving the network-wide control based on the real-time network-wide view coming from the discovery plane. The discovery plane is responsible for maintaining and updating information about the physical entities making up the network and synthesizes the information into a network-wide view for the decision elements. The data plane handles individual packets based on the output (e.g. forwarding table, packet filters, link scheduling weights, etc.) from the decision plane. The data plane may also collect data on behalf of the discovery plane. The dissemination plane decouples the decision plane from the discovery and data planes. It provides the option to move management information from the decision plane to the data plane and state information from the discovery plane to the decision plane using separate communication paths to avoid the need to establish routing protocols before they can be used.

3.1   Network Architecture for the Automatic Highway Platoon System

In this section, we will illustrate the 4D architecture with an example from the automated highway system, where each vehicle is equipped with vehicle-to-vehicle and vehicle-to-roadside Intelligent Transportation System (ITS) wireless communication, radars for measuring the inter-vehicle distances, sensors for measuring the vehicle's lateral position relative to the lane center, electronically controlled steering, throttle and brake actuators, and the computers for processing data from the sensors and generating commands to the actuators. In addition, the roadway is instrumented with magnetic markers buried along the centerline of each lane at four feet spacing. The magnetic markers enable the vehicle to detect its lateral position, and by alternating the polarities of the magnetic markers, they can also transmit roadway characteristics such as upcoming road geometry information, milepost, entrances and exits information to the vehicle [14]. The main objectives of the automated highway system are to reduce traffic congestions, enhance safety, and reduce human stress. These goals can be achieved using the Adapted Cruise Control technology [27], which uses sensors to maintain a small but safe inter-vehicle distance between cars while they traveling at high speed in the formation of a platoon [26]. These platoons are coordinated using a leader-follower architecture that centralizes the coordination on the leader [25].

In a centralized platoon, the task of communication to coordinate the vehicle platoon formation is only executed by the leader vehicle. To maintain the platoon formation, the leader (head vehicle) is the only entity that can give order (e.g. velocity, inter-vehicle distance, time and location for lane change, etc.) to its followers, while the followers can only apply the requested changes as well as submit requests for leaving the platoon to the leader. The leader vehicle also has to communicate with other platoons (which can be defaulted to a single vehicle) to coordinate platoon merging as well as safe lane changes, and to communicate with the roadside ITS for real-time traffic information and rules of engagements. Finally, if the leader itself has to leave the platoon, then it must issue order for the followers to select a new leader and hand over the command to the new leader before leaving the platoon.

To support the complex communication requirements of the platoon leader, we propose to apply the 4D architecture to the design of the automated highway system communication network. Figure 10 shows the UML-RT model of the high-level architecture of a vehicle for the automated highway system. UML-RT [24] is an extension of the original UML based on the concepts in the ROOM language [23], and forms the basis for the new features in UML 2.0 for modeling large-scale software systems.

The UML-RT model shown in Figure 10 consists of a set of Vehicle capsules. Each Vehicle capsule consists of a Planning capsule, a Coordination capsule, a Vehicle Control capsule, a Comms capsule and a set of sensor capsules. The Comms capsule, which represents the wireless communication subsystem of the vehicle, is made up of a Decision Element capsule, a Dissemination Element capsule, a Discovery Element capsule and one or more Data Element capsules (as indicated by the multi-object icon). Each Decision Element capsule has two ports to communicate with the Planning capsule and the Dissemination Element module. Each Dissemination Element capsule has multiple ports for communication with its associated Data Element capsules and uses single ports to communicate with the Decision Element capsule and the Discovery Element capsule, as well as forwarding management information from the Decision Element capsule of the platoon leader to the Data Element capsule of the followers via the wireless network in the Environment capsule.

Each vehicle's Decision Element can be in one of the following 3 states – *active, voting* or *inactive*. The Decision Elements will be in the voting state when they are in the process of electing a platoon leader. Once selected, the decision element of the platoon leader becomes active and is responsible for notifying the

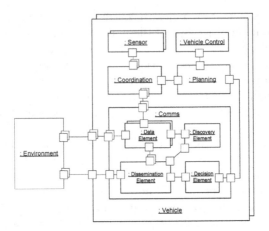

Fig. 10. The high-level architecture of a platoon vehicle

rest of the platoon about the election result. It will create the routing tables for inter-platoon, intra-platoon, as well as vehicle-to-roadside communications, and disseminate the intra-platoon routing table to the followers. The Decision Elements of the other platoon members will become inactive and turn over the control of its Dissemination, Discovery and Data Elements to the newly elected leader.

With the help of the real-time network-view from the discovery plane, the active Decision Element can quickly adapt to changes in the network environment while still maintaining the overall network objective. For example, when communication degrades, the Decision Element can make decision, in real-time, as to which messages should be sent first (via which data paths), which messages should be delayed, or even not be sent at all.

4   Modeling, Simulation and Run-Time Verification

The analysis and design of complex safety-critical networked embedded systems pose many challenges. Feasible timing and safety requirements for these systems are difficult to formulate, understand, and meet without extensive prototyping. Traditional timing analysis techniques are not effective in evaluating time-series temporal behaviors (e.g. the maximum duration between consecutive missed deadlines must be greater than 5 seconds). This kind of requirements can only be evaluated through execution of the real-time systems or their prototypes. Modeling and simulation holds the key to the rapid construction and evaluation of prototypes early in the development process.

4.1   The OMNeT++ Model

OMNeT++, which stands for *Objective Modular Network Testbed in C++*, is an object-oriented discrete event simulator primarily designed for the simulation of communication protocols, communication networks and traffic models, and multi-processors and distributed systems models [20].

Figure 11 shows a simple OMNeT++ model of a platoon system with three vehicles communicating with one another via the 4D architecture. OMNeT++ provides three principal constructs (*modules*, *gates* and *connections*) for modeling the structures of a target system. An OMNeT++ simulation model consists of a set of modules communicating with each other via the sending and receiving of messages. Modules can be nested hierarchically. The atomic modules are called simple modules; their code are written in C++ and executed as co-routines on top of the OMNeT++ simulation kernel. *Gates* are the input and output interfaces of the modules. Messages are sent out through output gates of the sending module and arrive through input gates of the receiving module. Input and output gates are linked together via connections. *Connections* represent the communication channels and can be assigned properties such as propagation delay, bit error rate and data rate. Message can contain arbitrarily complex data structures and can be sent either directly to their destination via a connection or through a series of connections (called route).

4.2 Integrating StateRover Startchart Designs with OMNeT++ Models

Figure 12a shows an object model of the Decision Element Capsule package, which is made up of a Decision Element class and the statechart classes generated from one or more statechart files. Figure 12b shows an instance of the Decision

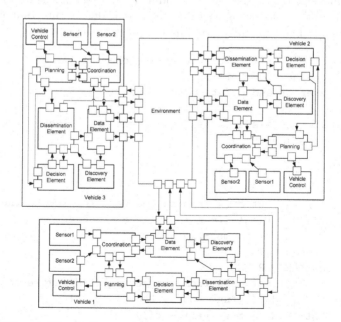

Fig. 11. The OMNeT++ model of an automated highway system

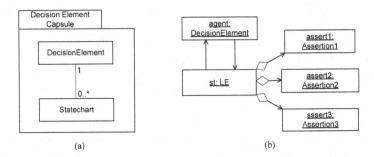

Fig. 12. The object model of the Decision Element Capsule package

Element Capsule package, which contains an instance of the Decision Element class together with an instance of the *LE* statechart for leader election.

Here, the Decision Element class extends the OMNeT++ cSimpleModule class and serves as the proxy (in place of the AGENT class) to handle as all network communications for the *statechart* object.

OMNeT++ uses messages to represent events. Each event is represented by an instance of the cMessage class or one its subclasses. Messages are sent from one module to another – this means that the place where the "event will occur" is the message's destination module, and the model time when the event occurs is the arrival time of the message. Events like "timeout expired" are implemented by the module sending a message to itself. OMNeT++ cSimpleModule class provides a virtual member function, handleMessage(), which will be called for every message that arrives at the module. In our example shown in Figure 12b, we will insert the following code into the handleMessage function of the Decision Element module to handle incoming messages to the module:

```
void DecisionElement::handleMessage(cMessage *msg) {
  if (msg->hasBitError()) {
  // log error and update error count
  }
  else if (msg->isSelfMessage()) // it is a timeout message
    processTimer(msg);
  else {
    switch (msg->kind()) {
      case ELECTION_MSG:
        // extract data from the message and invoke the
        // election() function of the st object
        st->election(msg->getValue());
        break;
      case LEADER_MSG:
        // extract data from the message and invoke the
        // leader() function of the st object
        st->leader(msg->getValue());
        break;
```

```
case HEARTBEAT_MSG:
  // extract data from the message and invoke the
  // heartbeat() function of the st object
  st->heartbeat(msg->getValue());
  break;
default: // unrecognized message kind
  // log error and output error message
  break;
}
}
}
```

In addition, the Decision Element module provides three functions, *send_ election(int id)*, *send_leader(int id)* and *send_heartbeat(int id)* for the *LE* module to send messages to the other *LE* modules in the network. When invoked by the *LE* object, these functions will create an instance of the cMessage class with an integer value set to *id* and the messageKind set to the appropriate kind, and then send the message via the "to_dissemination" output gate of the Decision Element module.

5 Discussions

5.1 Related Works

With the popularity of UML, Harel statecharts have become the tool of choice for most engineers to design complex reactive systems. While statecharts can effectively specify what a system *should do* (positive information), they tend to be less effective for the specification of safety requirements (i.e., negative information about what a system *must not do*). Hence, researchers have attempted to augment statechart specifications with other formalisms like process algebra [21], symbolic timing diagrams [19] and temporal logic [12], and demonstrated formal proofs for certain properties of the Statechart design. In the past, Temporal Logic [22] and Metric Temporal [3] have been the two primary languages used by REM tools. Some notable temporal-logic based tools are the Temporal Rover and DBRover [4] and NASA's PaX [17]. The major drawback of these approaches is that the assertions are expressed in textual form, which are hard to create and understand. The engineers need to work with two separate languages and formalisms, with assertions written in temporal logic and system designs in statecharts, The lack of a unified formalism requires users to work with two models, one for verification of the assertions and one for specification of the design, with no guarantee that the correctness of one implies the correctness of the other.

StateRover statecharts provide a coherent uniform formalism for both system designs and requirements assertions. It is easier for system designers to create and understand statechart assertions than text-based temporal assertions because statechart assertions are visual, intuitive, and resemble statechart design models. For example, statechart assertions are event driven just like statechart models, while temporal logic is purely propositional. Moreover, statechart assertions are Turing equivalent and are therefore significantly more expressive than temporal logic. While many commercial tools (e.g. Statemate, Rhapsody, Rational Rose RealTime) provide the capability to generate target code from statechart designs, StateRover supports the specification of and code generation for non-deterministic statecharts, which is essential for the specification and REM of more complex requirements.

Modeling and simulation plays a vital part in the development of network systems. All prominent simulation tools (e.g., OPNET, OMNeT++, Ptolemy) provide a rich set of reusable models to simulate various communication protocols, network devices and links. The availability of these reusable models provide cost-effective means to study the temporal and performance requirements of complex networked systems via run-time monitoring and modeling and simulation early in the development process. Most of these simulation tools support system models that are made up of agents (i.e. black boxes) communicating via message passing. This paper presents an architecture that wraps the StateRover generated code inside these black boxes (called modules) in the OMNeT++ models. Similar architecture can be developed for the StateRover generated code to work with OPNET and Ptolemy as well.

5.2   Reuse of Statechart Assertions

Reuse is one important reason for separating assertions from the statechart model. Java interfaces are a convenient tool for separating components. The StateRover uses two interfaces for primary-statechart/assertion-statechart separation: ITRPrimary is the interface for the primary statechart whereas ITRAssertion is the interface for the assertion statechart. The interfaces are extendible (being in source code form). This allows a primary to pass down custom information to the assertion without the assertion "knowing" who the primary is, and vise versa.

Event mapping is the simple mapping of event names from the primary statechart name space to the assertion name space. While the Assertion2 statechart uses the primary's event name (*heartbeat* in Figure 4b), it could be written with a generic event name such as P. A particular instance of this assertion inside the LE primary would then map *heartbeat* to P using the StateRover tool. The StateRover supports name mapping of assertion events to the primary statechart event space and will generate code to implement such mapping.

In [9], we present a process for the development and evaluation of statechart assertions early in the development process. The ability to test the statechart assertions independent of the prototype design ensures that system designers truly understand the required system behavior without being tainted by any pre-conceived solutions. With the help of StateRover's code generator, we can create a library of executable assertion patterns consisting of generic statechart assertions and the accompanying scenario-based test cases. The use of pre-tested generic statechart assertions will lessen the development time and improve the quality of the statechart assertions in rapid prototyping.

6   Conclusions

This paper brings together several technologies (statechart assertion formalism, run-time monitoring, discrete event simulations, JUNIT based test methodology) to support the behavior modeling and run-time verification of complex networked system temporal requirements. The novelty of the proposed approach include: (1) writing formal specifications using statechart assertions, (2) JUnit-based simulation and validation of statechart design and assertions, (3) automatic, JUnit-based, white-box testing of statechart prototypes augmented with statechart assertions, and (4) the use of discrete event simulation in tandem with run-time verification for networked system prototypes. In addition, this paper presents a clean-slate 4D architecture to support the complex communication requirements of complex networked systems. To demonstrate the code design described in Section 4.2, we have implemented a simple OMNeT++ model consisting of 4 instances of the Decision Element capsule connected in a unidirectional ring. Our next step is to develop a prototype for the highway automated system shown in Figure 11, and test the timing behavior of the design with the different platoon maneuver scenarios.

The StateRover Eclipse plugin is currently under development. This plugin will enable the development as UML statechart models and diagrams under the Eclipse IDE like any C++ or Java file. The StateRover will include support for system-level UML modeling and specification. For the system-level modeling view it will support component diagrams whereas the system-level verification view will support a formal specification language based on message sequence charts. The StateRover will include code generation and REM for both types of diagrams.

Acknowledgments. The research reported in this article was funded in part by a grant from the U.S. Missile Defense Agency. The views and conclusions contained herein are those of the authors and should not be interpreted as necessarily representing the official policies or endorsements, either expressed or implied, of the U.S. Government. The U.S. Government is authorized to reproduce and distribute reprints for Government purposes notwithstanding any copyright annotations thereon.

References

1. Beck, K., Gamma, E.: Test infected: Programmers love writing tests. Java Report. **3(7)** (1998) 37–50
2. Caffall, D., Cook, T., Drusinsky, D., Michael, J.B., Shing, M., Sklavounos, N.: Formal Specification and Run-time Monitoring within the Ballistic Missile Defense Project. Tech. Report NPS-CS-05-007. Naval Postgraduate School, Monterey, California (June 2005)

3. Chang, E., Pnueli, A., Manna, Z.: Compositional Verification of Real-Time Systems. Proc. 9th IEEE Symp. On Logic In Computer Science. (1994) 458–465
4. Drusinsky, D.: The Temporal Rover and ATG Rover. Lecture Notes in Computer Science, Vol. 1885 (Proc. Spin2000 Workshop), Springer-Verlag, Berlin (2000) 323–329
5. Drusinsky, D.: Semantics and Runtime Monitoring of TLCharts: Statechart Automata with Temporal Logic Conditioned Transitions. Proc. 4th Runtime Verification Workshop (RV'04), Invited paper (2004)
6. Drusinsky, D.: Modeling and Verification Using UML Statecharts A Working Guide to Reactive System Design, Runtime Monitoring and Execution-based Model Checking. ISBN 0-7506-7949-2. Elsevier (2006)
7. Drusinsky, D., Harel, D.: On the power of bounded concurrency I: Finite Automata. J. ACM. **41(3)** (1994) 517–539
8. Drusinsky, D., Shing, M.: Verification of Timing Properties in Rapid System Prototyping. Proc. 14th IEEE International Workshop in Rapid Systems Prototyping. San Diego, California (June 9-11, 2003) 47–53
9. Drusinsky, D., Shing, M., Demir, K.: Creation and Validation of Embedded Assertion Statecharts. Proc. 17th IEEE International Workshop in Rapid Systems Prototyping. Chania, Greece (June 14-16, 2006) 17–23
10. Drusinsky, D., Watney, G.: Applying run-time monitoring to the Deep-Impact Fault Protection Engine. Proc. 28th NASA Goddard Software Engineering Workshop (Dec. 2003) 127–133
11. Easterbrook, S., Lutz, R., Covington, R., Kely, J., Ampo, Y., Hamilton, D.: Experiences using lightweight formal methods for requirements modeling. IEEE Trans. Software Engineering. **24(1)** (Jan 1998) 4–11
12. Graw, G., Herrmann, P., Krumm, H.: Verification of UML-Based Real-Time System Design by Means of cTLA. Proc. 3rd IEEE International Symposium on Object-Oriented Real-Time Distributed Computing (ISORC 2000) (15-17 March 2000) 86–95
13. Greenberg, A., Hjalmtysson, G., Maltz, D., Myers, A., Rexford, J., Xie, G., Yan, H., Zhang, H.: A Clean Slate 4D Approach to Network Control and Management. ACM SIGCOMM Computer Communication Review. **35(5)** (2005) 41–54
14. Guldner, J., Patwardhan, S., Tan, H.S., Zhang, W.B.: Coding of Magnetic Markers for Demonstration of Automated Highway Systems. Preprints of the Transportation Research Board Annual Meeting, Washington, DC (1997)
15. Harel, D.: A Visual Formalism for Complex Systems. Science of Computer Programming. **8** (1987) 231–274
16. Havelund, K., Pressburger, T.: Model Checking Java Programs Using Java PathFinder. International Journal on Software Tools for Technology Transfer. **2(4)** (April 2000)
17. Havelund, K., Rosu, G.: An Overview of the Runtime Verification Tool Java PathExplorer. Formal Methods in System Design. **24(2)** (March 2004) 189–215
18. JUnit.org, http://www.junit.org/
19. Lüth, L., Niehaus, J., Peikenkamp, T.: HW/SW Co-synthesis using Statecharts and Symbolic Timing Diagrams. Proc. 9th International Workshop on Rapid System Prototyping. (3-5 June 1998) 212–217
20. OMNeT++ Discrete Event Simulation System. http://www.omnetpp.org/
21. Park, M.H., Bang, K.S., Choi, J.Y., Kang, I.: Equivalence Checking of Two Statechart Specifications. Proc. 11the International Workshop on Rapid System Prototyping (21-23 June 2000) 46–51

22. Pnueli, A.: The Temporal Logic of Programs. Proc.18th IEEE Symp. on Foundations of Computer Science (1977) 46–57
23. Selic, B., Gullekson, G. and Ward, P.: Real-Time Object Oriented modeling. John Wiley & Sons (1994)
24. Selic, B., Rumbaugh, J.: Using UML for Modeling Complex Real-Time Systems. Unpublished white paper, Rational Software (Apr. 4, 1998) http://www.rational.com/media/whitepapers/umlrt.pdf
25. Tsugawa, S., Kato, S., Tokuda, K., Matsui, T., Fujii, H.: A cooperative driving system with automated vehicles and intervehicle communications in demo 2000. Proc. IEEE Intelligent Transportation Systems Conference (2001) 918–923
26. Tan, H.S., Rajamani, R., Zhang, W.B.: Demonstration of an Automated Highway Platoon System. Proc. American Control Conference. Philadelphia, Pennsylvania (June 1998) 1823–1827.
27. Xu, Q., Hedrick K., Sengupta R., VanderWerf J.: Effects of vehicle-vehicle/roadside-vehicle communication on adaptive cruise controlled highway systems. Proc. 56th IEEE Vehicular Technology Conference. **2** (2002) 1249-1253

Approaches for Inheritance
in the TMO Programming Scheme

K.H. (Kane) Kim[1], Moon-Cheol Kim[1], and Moon-Hae Kim[2]

[1] DREAM Lab., EECS Dept., University of California, Irvine, CA, USA
{khkim,mckim}@uci.edu
[2] CSE Dept., Konkuk University, Seoul, Korea
mhkim@konkuk.ac.kr

Abstract. Inheritance in real-time object-oriented programming is a young subject for research, let alone for practice. Issues in inheritance design are discussed in the context of TMO (*Time-Triggered Message-Triggered Object*) scheme for real-time distributed object programming. The TMO scheme guides programmers to incorporate timing specifications in natural, modular, and easily analyzable forms. The scheme thus makes it relatively easy to practice inheritance design. Some TMO structuring rules and styles that enable efficient design of inheritance are presented. A GUI-based approach for TMO-framework programming with exploitation of inheritance is also discussed.

Keywords: object-oriented, real time, distributed computing, inheritance, TMO, time-triggered, message-triggered, timing specification, global time.

1 Introduction

When the object-oriented (OO) programming approach emerged, *inheritance* was touted as one of several most significant, new features of the approach. Since then, inheritance has been exploited vigorously in software developments involving layered software structuring [1,2,3,4,5].

Since the incorporation of the OO approach in real-time (RT) programming is a subject of relatively young and immature research efforts, both research and practice of inheritance in RT OO programming are in states of infancy. Among the most ambitious RT OO programming approaches in terms of the *level of abstraction* at which programmers are allowed to exercise their logics is the TMO (*Time-Triggered Message-Triggered Object*) programming and specification scheme [6,7,8,9]. The TMO scheme is not only a RT OO programming approach but also a RT distributed computing (DC) component scheme. TMO combines the complexity management benefits of the OO structuring paradigm with the ability to explicitly specify temporal constraints in terms of *global time* [10] in natural forms. The expressive power of TMO is strong such that all conceivable DC applications, including both non-RT and RT applications, can be structured in the form of TMO networks. In this paper, we are discussing in what forms inheritance can be exploited in TMO programming.

F. Kordon and J. Sztipanovits (Eds.): Monterey Workshop 2005, LNCS 4322, pp. 304–316, 2007.

There is a question regarding how widely inheritance will be used in RT DC programming. Limited experiences have indicated that inheritance has been used considerably in development of middleware and APIs (application programming interfaces) supporting RT DC programming. However, it appears that use of inheritance in actual development of RT DC application programs has not been as appealing and compelling. When a RT computing object is designed, it needs to be validated for its timely service capabilities. Such an object class may be inherited in developing another similar object but then the latter derived object must go through the validation process again. Unless the validation of the derived object becomes considerably simpler due to the inheritance of an already validated object class, the benefit of using inheritance over copying the object class and extending it may be marginal. Future research and experiments will enable a more concrete statement on this.

Currently the TMO programming is facilitated by the same basic language tools used for non-RT application programming in OO styles, i.e., C++ compilation systems such as Visual Studio for C++, GNU C++ Compiler, etc. There is no fundamental obstacle in facilitating TMO programming in other basic OO programming languages such as Java or C#. However, a TMO program requires a new execution engine which is typically a combination of hardware, commercial OS kernel, and middleware specifically built to support TMOs. The core of this engine is the middleware and one particular version built by us in UCI is the *TMO Support Middleware* (TMOSM) [8,9,11]. A friendly programming interface wrapping the execution support services of TMOSM has also been developed and named the *TMO Support Library* (TMOSL) [7,8,9]. It consists of a number of C++ classes and approximates a programming language directly supporting TMO as a basic building block.

Therefore, the TMO programmer uses a C++ editing and compilation system along with TMOSL in programming TMO-structured programs. No new compilers are involved. A TMO program consists of the main function (main()) plus TMOs which are logically networked. Some times I/O device drivers supplied by commercial vendors require *callback functions* to be supplied by application programmers. In TMO-structured RT DC application programs, such callback functions are not inside any TMO. They typically perform simple things such as picking data from certain buffer areas and then call TMOs.

The TMO programming scheme and supporting tools have been used in a broad range of basic research and application prototyping projects in a number of research organizations and also used in an undergraduate course on RT DC programming at UCI for some years.[1] TMO facilitates a highly abstract programming style without compromising the degree of control over timing precisions of important actions.

Although TMOSL has been designed to make the TMO programmer feel like using a close approximation of a new language, there are occasions where programmers make mistakes which could be detected quickly if a new language processing system were available. In certain parts of a TMOSL-based TMO

---

[1] http://dream.eng.uci.edu/eecs123/learn.htm

program, several parameter-preparation statements followed by an API function call are used whereas the same effects could be created by use of one keyword in a new TMO programming language. Inheritance handling can involve such parts and thus could become somewhat more complicated than what it could be in an environment where a new language is available. Certain structuring rules and styles must also be observed to facilitate efficient design of inheritance. Those rules and styles will be discussed in Sect. 2 and Sect. 3. A GUI-based approach for TMO-framework programming with exploitation of inheritance is discussed in Sect. 4.

2   An Overview of the TMO Programming Scheme

TMO is a natural, syntactically minor, and semantically powerful extension of conventional object structure. As depicted in Fig. 1, the basic TMO structure consists of four parts:

1. **ODS-sec** (*Object-data-store section*). This section contains the data-container variables shared among methods of a TMO. Variables are grouped into *ODS segments* (ODSSs) which are the units that can be locked for exclusive use by a TMO method in execution. Access rights of TMO methods for ODSSs are explicitly specified and the execution engine analyzes them to exploit maximal concurrency.

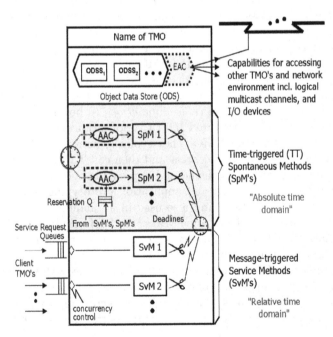

Fig. 1. Basic TMO structure (adapted from [6])

2. **EAC-sec** (*Environment access capability section*). Contained here are "gate objects" providing efficient call-paths to remote TMO methods, logical multicast channels called *Real-time Multicast and Memory Replication Channels* (RMMCs) [9], and I/O device interfaces.
3. **SpM-sec** (*Spontaneous method section*). These are time-triggered methods whose executions are initiated during specified time-windows.
4. **SvM-sec** (*Service method section*). These provide service methods which can be called by other TMOs.

Major features are summarized below.

Use of a global time base. All time references in TMOs are *global time* references which are valid regardless of the locations of the platforms on which TMOS run. That is, a global time base established by the TMO execution engine should provide information on the current time such that it can be referenced from anywhere within the distributed computing (DC) systems with well understood error bounds. A global time base is an abstract entity which is layered on and *approximated* by local clocks in DC nodes with the known error bound [10]. To keep the approximation errors within a target bound, distributed clocks are synchronized periodically among themselves and/or to a common source such as the global positioning system (GPS).

Distributed computing component. The TMO is a distributed computing component and thus TMOs distributed over multiple nodes may interact via remote method calls. To maximize the concurrency in execution of client methods in one node and server methods in the same node or different nodes, client methods are allowed to make non-blocking service requests to service methods [8]. In addition, TMOs can interact by exchange of messages over RMMCs [8,9].

Clear separation between two types of methods. The TMO may contain two types of methods, time triggered (TT) methods (spontaneous methods or SpMs), which are clearly separated from the conventional service methods (SvMs). The SpM executions are triggered when the RT clock reaches time values determined at the design time. On the contrary, SvM executions are triggered by calls from clients that are transmitted by the execution engine in the form of service request messages. Moreover, actions to be taken at real times, which can be determined at the design time, can appear only in SpMs.

Triggering times for SpMs must be fully specified as constants during the design time. Those RT constants as well as related guaranteed completion times (GCTs) of the SpM appear in the first clause of a SpM specification called the *Autonomous Activation Condition* (AAC) section. An example of an AAC is:

```
for t = from 10:00am to 10:50am every 30min
    start-during (t,t+5min) finish-by t+10min
```

which has the same effect as

```
start-during (10:00am,10:05am) finish-by 10:10am,
start-during (10:30am,10:35am) finish-by 10:40am
```

Basic concurrency constraint (BCC). This rule prevents potential conflicts between SpMs and SvMs and reduces the designer's efforts in guaranteeing timely service capabilities of TMOs. Basically, activation of a SvM triggered by a message from an external client is allowed only when potentially conflicting SpM executions are not active. A SvM is allowed to execute only when an execution time-window big enough for the SvM exists and does not overlap with the execution time-window of any SpM that accesses an ODSS needed by the SvM. However, the BCC does not stand in the way of either concurrent SpM executions or concurrent SvM executions.

Guaranteed completion time (GCT) of the server (i.e., a SvM of a server TMO) and the result return deadline imposed by the client. The TMO incorporates deadlines in the most general form. Basically, for method completions of a TMO, the designer guarantees and advertises execution time-windows bounded by start times and completion times. In addition, deadlines can be specified in the client's calls for service methods for the return of the service results.

As mentioned in the introduction, the *TMO Support Middleware* (TMOSM) is a TMO execution support middleware model which can be easily adapted to most commercial OS kernel platforms. Prototype versions of TMOSM currently exist for Windows XP, Windows CE and Linux 2.6. The *TMO Support Library* (TMOSL) is a friendly programming interface wrapping the execution support services of TMOSM [8], [http://dream.eng.uci.edu/eecs123/learn.htm]. It consists of a number of C++ classes which are selectively inherited and/or instantiated in building TMOs.

3   Inheriting a Whole TMO

In TMOSL-based programming a TMO is designed by writing a TMO class first and then adding an instantiation statement. Therefore, in principle, once a TMO class is implemented, it can be inherited in developing another similar application TMO. However, since a TMO contains features unique in RT programming, certain structuring rules and styles must be followed in order to avoid undesirable effects. Such rules and styles are discussed in this section.

3.1   The Roles of TMO Constructors in TMOSL-Based Programming

Parts of a TMO are associated with timing specifications. The specified timing requirements must be honored by the TMO execution engine. Timing specifications of SpMs and SvMs in a TMO must be passed onto the execution engine before the specified *execution-time-windows* for the SpMs and SvMs arrive. Therefore, in TMOSL-based programming the constructor of a TMO must contain steps for passing the timing specifications of SpMs and SvMs to the execution engine. Such steps are basically calls for API functions:

```
RegisterSpM ((PFSpMBody) SpM1, &SpM1_spec);
RegisterSvM ((PFSvMBody) SvM7, &SvM7_spec);
```

Here **PFSpMBody** is the function pointer type for the SpM, and **PFSvMBody** is the function pointer type for the SvM. **SpM1** is the function name of the SpM in the TMO and **SvM7** is the function name of the SvM in the TMO. **SpM1_spec** and **SvM7_spec** are the data structures containing the timing specifications and other attributes for **SpM1** and **SvM7**, respectively.

Therefore, these API functions also pass onto the execution engine the pointers to the codes of the relevant SpMs and SvMs. The constructor then contains a step for registering the entire TMO via an API function call, **RegisterTMO(&TMO_spec)**. Among other things, one effect of this step is to let the execution engine know that earlier registered SpMs and SvMs belong to the TMO just registered with a unique global name.

To give some further details, **SpM1_spec** contains the timing specifications in the form of AACs, e.g., "for t = from 10am to 10:50am every 30min start-during (t, t+5min) finish-by t+10min". In addition, it contains the list of the IDs of ODSSs (i.e., object data member groups) which **SpM1** accesses along with access modes (i.e., read-only or read-write). This kind of ODSS access right specification is included in **SvM7_spec** as well. The execution engine can analyze these ODSS access right specifications to determine ways to exploit concurrency maximally during the execution of the TMO.

As an example, Fig. 2 shows a simple TMO class, **TMO_Send_Class**, which contains just one SpM, **Sender_SpM**, and two data members which are ODSSs, **RMMC_1g** and **m_MIC**. **RMMC_1g** is an object serving as a gate for accessing the logical multicast channel **RMMC_1**. Through **RMMC_1g** a TMO method (SpM or SvM) can multicast a message and pickup a message multicast by other TMOs. **m_MIC** is an object serving as a microphone device driver interface.

Figure 3 provides the constructor of the TMO. The constructor of **TMO_Send_Class** contains a step for initializing a microphone device, a step for registering **Sender_SpM**, and a step for registering the host TMO, **TMO_Send**. The second step is carried out by the local function **Sender_SpM_register_detail()**. In that function an AAC is created and

```
class TMO_Send_Class : public CTMOBase
{
private:
    int Sender_SpM(); // SpM function body
       int Sender_SpM_register_detail(); // SpM registration function
    RMMCGateClass RMMC_1g;    // RMMC gate
    Mic_Wrapper_Class m_MIC;  // Wrapper object for audio-in device
public:
    TMO_Send_Class();  // Default constructor
    TMO_Send_Class(TCHAR *, tms);  // TMO constructor
};
```

Fig. 2. An example of a TMO

```
void  TMO_Send_Class::Sender_SpM_register_detail () {
    // Initialize data members for Sender_SpM execution
    . . .
```
```
    /* Specify time-window for SpM  - (1) Parameters for AAC */
    MicroSec from = (MicroSec) WARMUP_DELAY_SECS * 1000 * 1000;
    MicroSec until = (MicroSec) SYSTEM_LIFE_HOURS * 60 * 60 * 1000 * 1000;
    MicroSec every = (MicroSec) SENDER_SPM_PERIOD * 1000;
    MicroSec est = 0;
    MicroSec lst = est + LASTEST_SPM_START_TIME * 1000;
    MicroSec by = SENDER_SPM_DEADLINE * 1000;
```
```
    /* Specify time-window for SpM  - (2) Instantiation of AAC object */
    AAC aac1 ( NULL, // NULL for a permanent AAC
              tm4_DCS_age (from), tm4_DCS_age (until), every, est, lst, by);
```
```
    /* SpM registration */
    SpM_RegistParam SpM_spec;
    // Insert AAC into SpM_spec
    SpM_spec.build_regist_info_AAC (aac1);
    // Insert RMMC gate as ODSS into SpM_spec
    SpM_spec.build_regist_info_ODSS (RMMC_1g.GetId(), RW);
    // Insert device wrapper as ODSS into SpM_spec
    SpM_spec.build_regist_info_ODSS (m_MIC.GetId(), RW);
    if (RegisterSpM ((PFSpMBody) Sender_SpM, & SpM_spec) == FAIL)
        TMOSLprintf (_T("Failed to register Sender_SpM method\n"));
}


/** Contructor */
TMO_Send_Class::TMO_Send_Class (TCHAR* TMO_name, tms& start_time)
  : RMMC_1 (_T("RMMC_1")) {
    m_MIC.OpenMic (); // Initialize the WaveIn device
    Sender_SpM_register_detail () ; // Register Sender_SpM
```
```
    // Register TMO
    TMO_RegistParam    TMO_Send_spec;
    _tcscpy (TMO_Send_spec.global_name, TMO_name);
    TMO_Send_spec.start_time = start_time;
    RegisterTMO (&TMO_Send_spec);
}
```

Fig. 3. An example of a TMO constructor

then inserted into SpM_spec. One gate for RMMC_1, RMMC_1g, is inserted into SpM_spec as an ODSS along with the access mode descriptor, RW (i.e., read-write). Similarly, a microphone device driver interface, m_MIC, is inserted into SpM_spec as an ODSS along with the access mode descriptor, RW (i.e., read-write). Thereafter, Sender_SpM is registered to the execution engine and that is, SpM_spec is passed onto the execution engine. When the execution engine performs an execution of Sender_SpM, it locks the two ODSSs, i.e., the RMMC_1g and m_MIC, for exclusive use by the SpM execution. The locks are released when the SpM execution (one execution, not all executions periodically occurring between "from" and "until") is over.

In the case of a data structures containing registration parameters for a SvM, e.g., SvM7_spec, the timing specification contained there consists of:

1. *Guaranteed execution time bound* (GETB),
2. *Pipeline degree* which is the maximum number of concurrent executions allowed for the SvM,
3. *Maximum invocation rate* (MIR) and *basic period*, which are associated with the meanings that the maximum number of invocations of the SvM in every interval of the length equal to the basic period is MIR.

Registration parameters for a SvM also include ODSS access right specifications and a character string serving as the name of the SvM that can be called by client objects. When a TMO contains multiple SvMs, the names (character strings) of those SvMs that can be called by clients must be distinct. However, a SvM in one TMO and another SvM in a different TMO may have the same name that can be called by clients.

As shown in Fig. 3, the parameters for TMO registration include a globally unique character string serving as the globally recognized name of the TMO and the start time of the TMO.

3.2   Structuring Rules and Styles Enabling Efficient Design of Inheritance of Parts of a TMO in TMOSL-Based Programming

The unique aspects in inheriting a TMO produced with C++ TMOSL are mostly related to the timing specifications a great majority of which are contained in the constructor.

In the case of a SvM, there is no problem in inheriting the entire timing specification. GETB, pipeline degree, MIR, and base period can be inherited in most cases. A proper style is to write a function SvM_register_detail() similar to Sender_SpM_register_detail() in Fig. 3.

In the case of a SpM, some parts of the timing specifications are expressed in terms of global time instants unlike in a SvM of which the timing parameters are in terms of durations. The "from" and "until" fields in an AAC are usually global time instants. In general, all appearances of global time instants in a TMO should be checked carefully to see if they can be inherited without any modification. Therefore, the cases of inheriting the timing parameters of a SpM class without any modification occur relatively infrequently. This means that a function SpM_register_detail() that is different from SpM_register_detail() in the parent TMO class needs to be provided more often than not. In the parent TMO class, the SpM_register_detail() function should be called from a custom constructor which is not a default constructor. Otherwise, double registrations of the SpM may occur during the instantiation of the derived TMO class.

There are two other types of areas within a TMO where global time instants may appear. One type of area is where a service request (i.e., call) is made to a SvM in another TMO. In the case of a blocking service request, a deadline for result return is specified. This deadline specification usually takes an expression of duration and in such cases, it rarely presents a problem during the design of inheritance. On the other hand, it is also possible to use a constant expression of global time instants although it is done rarely. Such cases require careful checking during the design of inheritance. Therefore, specifying deadlines for result return in terms of durations is a preferred style.

The other type of area is where a message transmission and receiving over an RMMC is executed. A message-sender specifies an *official release time* (ORT) [8,9], which is the time at which the message should become accessible through subscriber RMMC-gates to consumer methods in receiving TMOs. A message-receiver may specify a *timeout* value. These timing expressions often involve global time instants. They thus need to be checked during the design of their inheritance.

3.3 Access Qualifiers

A SvM in a TMO is always invoked via a service request from a client TMO which takes the form of a message transmitted from the node hosting the client TMO to the node hosting the called SvM and TMO. Even if both the server TMO and the client TMO reside on the same node, a service request takes the same form of a message which is processed partly by the network message handling part of the TMO execution engine. Therefore, there is no reason to declare a SvM as a public function member of a TMO. A SvM invocation, i.e., a service request to a SvM, should be done through TMOSL APIs such as OnewaySR(), BlockingSR(), etc.

To facilitate TMO inheritance, it is the most appropriate to declare access-qualifications of SpMs, SvMs, ODSSs, and RMMC gates as "protected" in C++ TMOSL-based TMO programming. By declaring them as protected members of a TMO class, any direct access to ODSSs, including RMMC-gates, and any direct invocation of SpMs or SvMs from outside the owner TMO, which are all design / coding errors, can be detected by the compiler. At the same time, protected members of a base class can be inherited in a derived class and accessed directly from member functions of the derived class. Therefore, such an arrangement enables TMO inheritance. For further details of these aspects, consider the following example.

This example application consists of two TMO classes, CBaseTMO (Fig. 4) and CDerivedTMO (Fig. 5). CDerivedTMO class inherits components of CBaseTMO as their names imply. One ODSS class, CODSS, is used in this example. This ODSS class has one data member, count.

CBaseTMO has two SpMs, SpM1() and SpM2(). There are two constructors for this TMO class, one default constructor to support TMO class inheritance and the other for registration to the TMO execution engine. Note that all members except constructors are declared as protected members. Thus, any direct invocation of SpMs or direct access to ODSSs from the outside of the TMO class is disabled while proper inheritance of the SpMs and ODSSs is facilitated.

A TMO class, CDerivedTMO, inherits components of CBaseTMO. Because data members and function members of CBaseTMO are declared as protected members, all those can be accessed from the constructors of CDerivedTMO. CDerivedTMO has two new function members, SpM1_register_detail() and SpM2_register_detail(), which override the function members of CBaseTMO

```
class   CBaseTMO : public CTMOBase {
protected:
    CODSSClass ODSS1;
    int SpM1 ();
    int SpM1_register_detail ();   // registration function
    int SpM2 ();
    int SpM2_register_detail ();   // registration function
public:
    CBaseTMO () {};                // for inheritance
    CBaseTMO (TCHAR *,  tms);
};
```

Fig. 4. A base TMO class

```
class   CDerivedTMO : public CBaseTMO {
protected:
    int SpM1_register_detail ();   // registration function
    int SpM2_register_detail ();   // registration function
public:
    CDerivedTMO () {};             // for inheritance
    CDerivedTMO (TCHAR *, tms);
};
```

Fig. 5. A derived TMO class

that have the same names. The two new function members are called from the
constructor, CDerivedTMO(TCHAR *, tms). The two functions are thus executed
during an instantiation of CDerivedTMO and their effects are the registrations of
SpM1 and SpM2 of the newly instantiated TMO to the execution engine.

4   Inheritance Support in ViSTMO

ViSTMO (*Visual Studio* for TMO) is a visual design and programming tool
for developing application TMOs [12]. ViSTMO provides a *graphics-based design editor* that supports interactive design of application TMO frameworks
and provides user-friendly GUIs (graphic user interfaces). It also has a *code-
framework generator* that generates code-frameworks based on the information
provided by a TMO programmer via the graphics-based design editor. By primarily filling the empty fields in dialog boxes, programmers can produce designs
of application TMO networks that are complete except for function bodies of
member functions. Once code-frameworks are generated, programmers can then
manually insert function bodies to complete the programming. Experiences have
indicated a great potential of ViSTMO in enabling significant improvement of
the productivity of TMO programmers.

ViSTMO has recently been enhanced to support the practice of the inheritance
programming styles discussed in this paper. When a user creates a new TMO

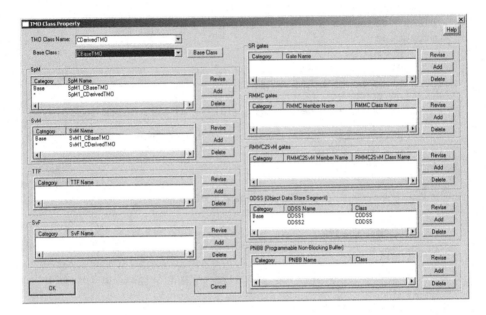

Fig. 6. ViSTMO support for inheritance

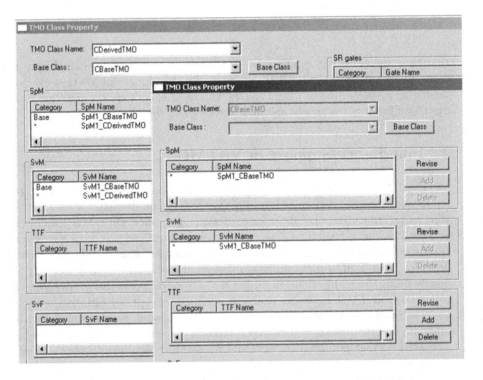

Fig. 7. A base class and a derived class displayed in ViSTMO

class, ViSTMO provides an opportunity for inheriting a base class as shown in Fig. 6 which is a snapshot of ViSTMO in action. A user can select any existing TMO class as its base class from the "Base Class" combo box. When a base class, CBaseTMO in this example, is selected, all members of the selected base class are displayed in the same window. These base class members are denoted as being in the "Base" category and cannot be edited from this window. Those marked "*" in the category field, e.g., SpM1_CDerivedTMO, are members of a newly created class.

In addition, clicking the "Base Class" button right next to the "Base Class" combo box results in a display of the information of the selected base class in a separate window (or dialog box) as shown in Fig 7. A user can back-track the class hierarchy of a class by recursively following the base classes until the display reaches a class without a base class, which means its base class is CT-MOBase that is in TMOSL and serves as a default base class for all TMO classes.

For each SpM and SvM listed, clicking the associated "Revise" button results in opening of a window displaying various registration parameters. A new SpM or SvM can be added by opening a new window via clicking the "Add" button in the relevant section and then filling various registration parameter fields in the newly open window.

TMO inheritance can thus be designed almost completely in ViSTMO without necessitating intermittent generation and manual editing of code-frameworks.

5   Conclusion

Exploiting inheritance in RT OO DC programming is largely an immature art. The TMO programming and specification scheme makes it relatively easy to practice inheritance design. It is largely because the TMO scheme guides programmers to incorporate timing specifications in natural, modular, and easily analyzable forms. Some structuring guidelines and styles that enable efficient and easily analyzable design of inheritance have been presented in this paper. An approach incorporated into a GUI-based tool for TMO-framework programming in order to support inheritance design has also been presented. It is hoped that future research produces better understanding of how useful inheritance is in a broad range of RT DC programming situations.

Acknowledgments

The research reported here is supported in part by the NSF under Grant Numbers 03-26606 (ITR), and 05-24050 (CNS). No part of this paper represents the views and opinions of the sponsors mentioned above.

References

1. Harel, D., Kupferman, O.: On object systems and behavioral inheritance. IEEE Transactions on Software Engineering **28**(9) (September 2002) 889–903
2. Hofmann, H.D., Stynes, J.: Implementation reuse and inheritance in distributed component systems. In: Proceedings of the 22nd Annual International Computer Software and Applications Conference (COMPSAC '98), IEEE Computer Society Press (August 1998) 496–501
3. Johnsen, E.B., Owe, O.: Inheritance in the presence of asynchronous method calls. In: Proceedings of the 38th Annual Hawaii International Conference on System Sciences - 2005 (HICSS'05), IEEE Computer Society Press (January 2005) 282c
4. Philippi, S.: Modeling and inheritance of behaviour in object-oriented systems. In: Proceedings of the 5th International Conference on Information Visualisation, IEEE Computer Society Press (July 2001) 342–347
5. Taivalsaari, A.: On the notion of inheritance. ACM Computing Surveys **28**(3) (1996) 438–479
6. Kim, K.H.: Object structures for real-time systems and simulators. IEEE Computer **30**(9) (August 1997) 62–70
7. Kim, K.H.: APIs for real-time distributed object programming. IEEE Computer **33**(6) (June 2000) 72–80
8. Kim, K.H.: Real-time object-oriented distributed software engineering and the tmo scheme. International Journal of Software Engineering and Knowledge Engineering **9**(2) (1999) 251–276
9. Kim, K.H., Li, Y., Liu, S., Kim, M.H., Kim, D.H.: RMMC programming model and support execution engine in the TMO programming scheme. In: Proceedings of the 8th IEEE International Symposium on Object-Oriented Real-Time Distributed Computing (ISORC 2005), IEEE Computer Society Press (May 2005) 34–43
10. Kopetz, H.: Real-Time Systems: Design Principles for Distributed Embedded Applications. Kluwer Academic Publishers (1997)
11. Jenks, S.F., Kim, K.H., Henrich, E., Li, Y., Zheng, L., Kim, M.H., Lee, K.H., Seol, D.M., Youn, H.Y.: A linux-based implementation of a middleware model supporting time-triggered message-triggered objects. In: Proceedings of the 8th IEEE International Symposium on Object-Oriented Real-Time Distributed Computing (ISORC 2005), IEEE Computer Society Press (May 2005) 350–358
12. Kim, K.H., Kang, S.J.: A GUI approach to programming of TMO frames and design of real-time distributed computing software. In: Proceedings of the 6th International Symposium on Autonomous Decentralized Systems (ISADS 2003), IEEE Computer Society Press (April 2003) 53–60

Author Index

Lecture Notes in Computer Science

For information about Vols. 1–4302

please contact your bookseller or Springer

Vol. 4349: B. Cook, A. Podelski (Eds.), Verification, Model Checking, and Abstract Interpretation. XI, 395 pages. 2007.

Vol. 4348: S.T. Taft, R.A. Duff, R.L. Brukardt, E. Ploedereder, P. Leroy (Eds.), Ada 2005 Reference Manual. XXII, 765 pages. 2006.

Vol. 4347: J. Lopez (Ed.), Critical Information Infrastructures Security. X, 286 pages. 2006.

Vol. 4346: L. Brim, B. Haverkort, M. Leucker, J. van de Pol (Eds.), Formal Methods: Applications and Technology. X, 363 pages. 2007.

Vol. 4345: N. Maglaveras, I. Chouvarda, V. Koutkias, R. Brause (Eds.), Biological and Medical Data Analysis. XIII, 496 pages. 2006. (Sublibrary LNBI).

Vol. 4344: V. Gruhn, F. Oquendo (Eds.), Software Architecture. X, 245 pages. 2006.

Vol. 4342: H. de Swart, E. Orłowska, G. Schmidt, M. Roubens (Eds.), Theory and Applications of Relational Structures as Knowledge Instruments II. X, 373 pages. 2006. (Sublibrary LNAI).

Vol. 4341: P.Q. Nguyen (Ed.), Progress in Cryptology - VIETCRYPT 2006. XI, 385 pages. 2006.

Vol. 4340: R. Prodan, T. Fahringer, Grid Computing. XXIII, 317 pages. 2007.

Vol. 4339: E. Ayguadé, G. Baumgartner, J. Ramanujam, P. Sadayappan (Eds.), Languages and Compilers for Parallel Computing. XI, 476 pages. 2006.

Vol. 4338: P. Kalra, S. Peleg (Eds.), Computer Vision, Graphics and Image Processing. XV, 965 pages. 2006.

Vol. 4337: S. Arun-Kumar, N. Garg (Eds.), FSTTCS 2006: Foundations of Software Technology and Theoretical Computer Science. XIII, 430 pages. 2006.

Vol. 4335: S.A. Brueckner, S. Hassas, M. Jelasity, D. Yamins (Eds.), Engineering Self-Organising Systems. XII, 212 pages. 2007. (Sublibrary LNAI).

Vol. 4334: B. Beckert, R. Hähnle, P.H. Schmitt (Eds.), Verification of Object-Oriented Software. XXIX, 658 pages. 2007. (Sublibrary LNAI).

Vol. 4333: U. Reimer, D. Karagiannis (Eds.), Practical Aspects of Knowledge Management. XII, 338 pages. 2006. (Sublibrary LNAI).

Vol. 4332: A. Bagchi, V. Atluri (Eds.), Information Systems Security. XV, 382 pages. 2006.

Vol. 4331: G. Min, B. Di Martino, L.T. Yang, M. Guo, G. Ruenger (Eds.), Frontiers of High Performance Computing and Networking – ISPA 2006 Workshops. XXXVII, 1141 pages. 2006.

Vol. 4330: M. Guo, L.T. Yang, B. Di Martino, H.P. Zima, J. Dongarra, F. Tang (Eds.), Parallel and Distributed Processing and Applications. XVIII, 953 pages. 2006.

Vol. 4329: R. Barua, T. Lange (Eds.), Progress in Cryptology - INDOCRYPT 2006. X, 454 pages. 2006.

Vol. 4328: D. Penkler, M. Reitenspiess, F. Tam (Eds.), Service Availability. X, 289 pages. 2006.

Vol. 4327: M. Baldoni, U. Endriss (Eds.), Declarative Agent Languages and Technologies IV. VIII, 257 pages. 2006. (Sublibrary LNAI).

Vol. 4326: S. Göbel, R. Malkewitz, I. Iurgel (Eds.), Technologies for Interactive Digital Storytelling and Entertainment. X, 384 pages. 2006.

Vol. 4325: J. Cao, I. Stojmenovic, X. Jia, S.K. Das (Eds.), Mobile Ad-hoc and Sensor Networks. XIX, 887 pages. 2006.

Vol. 4323: G. Doherty, A. Blandford (Eds.), Interactive Systems. XI, 269 pages. 2007.

Vol. 4322: F. Kordon, J. Sztipanovits (Eds.), Reliable Systems on Unreliable Networked Platforms. XIV, 317 pages. 2007.

Vol. 4320: R. Gotzhein, R. Reed (Eds.), System Analysis and Modeling: Language Profiles. X, 229 pages. 2006.

Vol. 4319: L.-W. Chang, W.-N. Lie (Eds.), Advances in Image and Video Technology. XXVI, 1347 pages. 2006.

Vol. 4318: H. Lipmaa, M. Yung, D. Lin (Eds.), Information Security and Cryptology. XI, 305 pages. 2006.

Vol. 4317: S.K. Madria, K.T. Claypool, R. Kannan, P. Uppuluri, M.M. Gore (Eds.), Distributed Computing and Internet Technology. XIX, 466 pages. 2006.

Vol. 4316: M.M. Dalkilic, S. Kim, J. Yang (Eds.), Data Mining and Bioinformatics. VIII, 197 pages. 2006. (Sublibrary LNBI).

Vol. 4314: C. Freksa, M. Kohlhase, K. Schill (Eds.), KI 2006: Advances in Artificial Intelligence. XII, 458 pages. 2007. (Sublibrary LNAI).

Vol. 4313: T. Margaria, B. Steffen (Eds.), Leveraging Applications of Formal Methods. IX, 197 pages. 2006.

Vol. 4312: S. Sugimoto, J. Hunter, A. Rauber, A. Morishima (Eds.), Digital Libraries: Achievements, Challenges and Opportunities. XVIII, 571 pages. 2006.

Vol. 4311: K. Cho, P. Jacquet (Eds.), Technologies for Advanced Heterogeneous Networks II. XI, 253 pages. 2006.

Vol. 4310: T. Boyanov, S. Dimova, K. Georgiev, G. Nikolov (Eds.), Numerical Methods and Applications. XIII, 715 pages. 2007.

Vol. 4309: P. Inverardi, M. Jazayeri (Eds.), Software Engineering Education in the Modern Age. VIII, 207 pages. 2006.

Vol. 4308: S. Chaudhuri, S.R. Das, H.S. Paul, S. Tirthapura (Eds.), Distributed Computing and Networking. XIX, 608 pages. 2006.

Vol. 4307: P. Ning, S. Qing, N. Li (Eds.), Information and Communications Security. XIV, 558 pages. 2006.

Vol. 4306: Y. Avrithis, Y. Kompatsiaris, S. Staab, N.E. O'Connor (Eds.), Semantic Multimedia. XII, 241 pages. 2006.

Vol. 4305: A.A. Shvartsman (Ed.), Principles of Distributed Systems. XIII, 441 pages. 2006.

Vol. 4304: A. Sattar, B.-H. Kang (Eds.), AI 2006: Advances in Artificial Intelligence. XXVII, 1303 pages. 2006. (Sublibrary LNAI).

Vol. 4303: A. Hoffmann, B.-H. Kang, D. Richards, S. Tsumoto (Eds.), Advances in Knowledge Acquisition and Management. XI, 259 pages. 2006. (Sublibrary LNAI).